CRISTINA

Princess Cristina Belgiojoso,
oil by Henri Lehmann, 1843

CRISTINA

Portraits of a Princess

BETH ARCHER BROMBERT

The University of Chicago Press
Chicago and London

The University of Chicago Press, Chicago 60637
The University of Chicago Press, Ltd., London

90 89 88 87 86 85 84 83   1 2 3 4 5

Library of Congress Cataloging in Publication Data

Brombert, Beth Archer.
  Cristina, portraits of a princess.

  Originally published: 1st ed. New York: Knopf,
1977.
  Bibliography: p. 385.
  Includes index.
  1. Belgiojoso, Cristina, 1808–1871. 2. Italy—
Princes and princesses—Biography. 3. Revolutionists—
Italy—Biography. 4. Romanticism—France. 5. Italy—
History—1849–1870. I. Title.
[DG551.8.B3B76   1983]   945'.08'0924 [B] 82-17537
ISBN 0-226-07551-6 (pbk.)

For Victor, Lauren, and Marc

Contents

Illustrations

(following page 212)

Acknowledgments

THE MANY PEOPLE who helped me in the preparation of this book are more gratefully remembered than these few words can express.

I should like to thank: Marchesa Ludovica Niccolini di Camugliano, great-granddaughter of Princess Belgiojoso; Marchesa Vittoria Valperga di Masino, widow of the Princess's great-grandson; and Marchese Annibale Brivio-Sforza, great-grandnephew of Prince Belgiojoso, for generously providing the portraits, family papers, and recollections that enrich this work. I am especially grateful to Marchesa Valperga for inviting me to the castle of Masino and allowing me to examine the Princess's correspondence and most personal possessions; and to Marchese Brivio-Sforza and his family for receiving me so warmly at Villa Belgiojoso in Merate, where Cristina and Emilio Belgiojoso lived as newlyweds.

My thanks also to Marchese Gianfranco Litta and Conte Franco Arese, for their cordial reception and gracious assistance; the Rockefeller Foundation's Study and Conference Center at Bellagio, and the Camargo Foundation at Cassis, for making my work there so agreeable and so profitable, with special thanks to Mr. William Olsen, Director, and Mr. Robert Celli, Administrator, and their staff at Villa Serbelloni, for kindnesses too numerous to list here; Professor Yvonne Knibiehler, whose discovery and generous offer of unpublished letters made possible the writing of chapter 5; Doctors Gilbert H. Glaser and Leon Strebel for the medical counsel, bibliography, and fascinating insights they provided; Professors Hermann Weygand, Victor Lange, Steven Scher, and Mrs. Hana Demetz for their very kind assistance with the Heine chapter; Roger Pierrot, Conservateur-en-chef of the Bibliothèque Nationale in Paris, and Simone Balayé, Conservateur chargé d'expositions, for making accessible to me all the services of this superb library; Professor Arnaldo Pizzorusso, Dr. Carlo Weiss, and Mr. Aldo Caputo, for their efficient help with documents and illustrations; Signora Maria Colnago, for information about Locate di Triulzi and its former inhabitants; Harold C. Schonberg, for unknowingly inspiring this work, and Raymond Lewenthal for encouraging it; Joseph Frank, for his excellent suggestions, which helped me over a difficult hurdle; Robert Gottlieb, Martha Kaplan, Becky Mlynarczyk, and Sally Rogers for making this a book; Victor, for more than can ever be calculated; and Lauren and Marc for their interest and salutary humor.

B.A.B.
Princeton, 1976

CRISTINA

Who Was She?

IN THE PARIS OF THE 1830's the name Cristina Belgiojoso (pronounced *Beljoyozo*) made hearts quicken and tongues wag. An Italian, an exile, noble by birth, her meteoric success in a city surfeited with shooting stars would have been unusual for a man; for a woman it was unique. Many startling figures swept across the Romantic horizon; most of them faded quickly. Cristina Trivulzio, Princess Belgiojoso, though deliberately obscured in later years, was so exceptional, yet so representative of her time, that to re-create her is to recapture the extraordinary period in which she lived.

For the men of her day, and above all the leading artists who frequented her brilliant salon—Balzac, Heine, Musset, Liszt—she was an obsession, a cult. They wrote about her—to her, and to each other—as they wrote of no other woman. The winter starkness of her beauty—gleaming black hair framing a perfect oval of phantasmal whiteness, huge black eyes, a willowy body as delicate as her long, tapered fingers—stunned everyone who saw her. Women, often as effusively as men, spoke of her captivating appearance, her dramatic taste for white gowns and jet beads, the strange eloquence of her silent immobility, like a dancer's, when she listened to music. Marie d'Agoult, jealous of Liszt's interest in her and envious of her position, paid her grudging homage in letters and memoirs by speaking of her frequently and bitterly. One remark is significant: "Never did any woman equal Princess Belgiojoso in her exercise of the art of *effect*."

Years later, Henry James, who never met her but knew of her as a friend of William Wetmore Story's in Rome, was impressed by this same quality: "Her striking name was in the air when we were very young. . . . Nothing is more curious than the apparent mixture in her of the love of the thing in itself and the love of all . . . the eccentricities and superfluities of the thing; a mixture which may represent little more than the fact that she was romantic . . . that the romantic appearance at least . . . was forced upon her."

Romantic she was indeed; her own contemporaries saw in her many of the dominant characteristics of Romantic taste and temper. Her fragile figure and spellbinding eyes earned her the epithet of Romantic Muse. Deathly pale, chronically ill, but free-spirited, she refused to yield to social or political coercion, thus condemning herself to solitude and persecution—the natural condition of a Romantic hero. She was such a perfect exemplar of the Romantic ideal that she returned to the pages of the literature from which she seemed to have emerged, and reappeared as the model for new heroines. Balzac portrayed her so often that he assumed Stendhal had done the same, and said so in his review of *The Charterhouse of Parma*. Heine and Musset, both desperately in love with her, found in her a source of inspiration that flowed through many of their works. And yet, she was rarely recognized by their biographers or critics, despite all the clues in their writing and all the evidence in their correspondence. Few ever looked beyond George Sand in Musset's case, or Mathilde in Heine's; as for Balzac, his heroines were naturally ascribed to his known mistresses. Similarly overlooked is Liszt's decades-long attachment to her, eclipsed in the public eye by his overdocumented liaison with Marie d'Agoult. And most surprising is Lafayette at seventy-four, palpitating like a schoolboy over what his children resentfully called his *engouement,* his infatuation for Cristina.

Born in 1808, she grew up in the bitter aftermath of Waterloo. At sixteen she married a dashing libertine prince, from whom she separated four years later rather than submit to the humiliation of his infidelities, just as she left Italy, then under Austrian rule, rather than bend to imperial tyranny. Her defiant stance, her energetic commitment to Italy's liberation, quickly captured the interest of Parisians, always avid for new celebrities. Not yet twenty-three, her revenues sequestered, almost destitute though she had inherited one of Italy's great fortunes, she arrived in Paris at the right time with the right attributes. For a spirit like hers, forceful and complex, the dramatic events of her disastrous marriage and flight from Italy were a blessing in disguise. The disillusionment, the oppression, the diseases that might have crushed her had she stayed in Milan, became instead the galvanizing forces of an extraordinary personality. Paris was a haven of freedom and a hearth of new ideas. Such a woman and such a city were admirably matched. Against the backdrop of a brand-new constitutional monarchy, with Lafayette for a leading man and revolutionary ideas for a scenario, she was ideally cast in the role of frail heroine with a will of iron—the new Romantic woman. All she had to do was walk out on stage, and she did—with éclat.

The salon she opened, as soon as her revenues were released, became a dazzling prism of Parisian cultural society under the citizen-king, Louis-Philippe. The concerts performed there entered musical history; the people who gathered there made political and literary history. Her own passionate interests—a united Italy under a constitutional monarch, with a free press, education for women and the lower classes, and the right of nationals to travel freely; a revitalization of the early spirit of the Church; Saint-Simonian and Fourierist ideas—reflect and often reveal the terrible tensions of post-Waterloo Europe, a world rechained in arch-reaction after the exuberant quarter-century of Napoleon. Instantly identified with the Italian cause, she became the protectress of other exiles, subsidizing them, recommending them, introducing them to French society.

As noteworthy as her representation of the spirit of national independence is her characterization of feminine independence. In a changing world that made room for token emancipation—women wrote and published, often under their own names; educated salonnières were considered the intellectual equals of the men they received—she was in a way more startling than George Sand in her determination to live as she pleased. Society was shocked by Sand's sexual candor, but her publicized love affairs were merely an extension of a known phenomenon: women had always had lovers. To live with them openly was no more than an affirmation of a woman's right to love, while at the same time a confirmation of her traditional role of consort or concubine. Sand's behavior was not aberrant; it was at worst a modification of established mores, whereas Cristina, a beautiful woman who steadfastly rejected the most eligible suitors, assumed the greater independence of living *without* men. Because her behavior could not be explained by passion, because the use she made of her fortune, the choice of her friends, the pursuit of her interests was not determined by husband or lover, she was a threat to masculine domination, an offense to masculine vanity.

Feminism had come to be equated with a woman's freedom to *choose* among men, not to reject them. This was little more than an assertion of femininity in a sexual context: to be mistress, wife, or mother with the man of her choice. Even a Mme du Barry still remained a function of Louis XV. The paradox of Cristina's manless feminism was stressed by her intrusion into masculine activities. It had become acceptable for women to write novels—about love; the heart was a woman's domain. Cristina wrote on politics, history, theology, philosophy. This was not a woman, but a monster; at best, a sacred monster. Victor Cousin, a bachelor philosopher who did not feel threatened by her, epitomized her as "femina sexu, genio vir." Unlike Cousin, most men were incapable of admiring a masculine spirit in the body of a desirable woman. Perhaps for that reason they preferred to dismiss her rather than understand her.

Her impact on those who admired her, and even on those who did not, has fortunately been recorded. For half a century her image was effaced or distorted. She became an embarrassment to her family, an irritation to her compatriots. But a wealth of material, some of it ignored, some of it misread, documents her celebrity during the most exciting decades of the nineteenth century. Her complex personality baffled her devotees, her successes as journalist, social reformer, political activist, historian, exasperated her enemies. For ten years she was a thorn in Metternich's diplomatic side; for nine years Musset refused to believe he could not seduce her. The one man her name was linked with, François Mignet, was a sober historian so lackluster he was rumored to be impotent. It was also rumored that Cristina and George Sand had been lovers, and that Mignet destroyed all traces of their relationship. Certainly there is something mysterious about the fact that not a scrap of firsthand evidence remains to prove they even knew each other, though they surely did. However, Cristina's recently discovered correspondence with Mignet reveals many other unknown facets of the woman, as does a fresh reading of familiar texts—letters, poems, novels—by famous artists of her time. It is through these multiple mirrors of her contemporaries' view of her, and her own view of herself, that this study proposes to capture her intriguing personality. For, by hearing Balzac speak of Liszt, Liszt of Heine, Heine of Musset, all of them of "la belle princesse," and she of herself, one relives the turmoil of her life and the turbulence of her time.

Thanks largely to her contact with France, some of her fascination can be resurrected today. Her French friends were considerably kinder in her lifetime and left a more flattering view of her than her Italian compatriots. An adopted daughter of France, writing in French, living her most dynamic years in Paris, she proved the adage: everyone has two homelands, Paris and his own. Her salon of the 1830's was remembered in most French studies of salon life under Louis-Philippe; her beauty, her originality, were recalled in numerous memoirs of the period. In the 1840's her translation into French of Vico's *Scienza nova,* preceded by a one-hundred-page essay; her four-volume study of the development of Catholic dogma; her pamphlet on Austrian repression in Lombardy; her articles on the Italian revolutions of 1848, all reverberated in newspaper columns and private correspondence. Her role in Italian politics, the newspapers she published and wrote for—even the New York *Daily Tribune* carried her articles—made her a national heroine during Italy's first attempt at independence. In 1849 her gifted direction of all hospital services in Rome under the French siege earned her the admiration of three noted Americans: Margaret Fuller, who worked under her; William

Wetmore Story, who left his glowing impressions in his diary and in *Roba di Roma;* and Henry James, whose vivid sketch in *William Wetmore Story and His Friends* reveals the interest she generated. She led a battalion of volunteers from Naples to Milan, was almost killed by an assassin's dagger in Turkey, crossed uncharted deserts and mountains on horseback during a year's journey to the Holy Land, and wrote voluminously. When she died in 1871, she was a serene grandmother and the proud citizen of a united Italy she had helped to create.

WHY THEN WAS SHE FORGOTTEN? Why, if she was a Risorgimento heroine in 1848, was she dismissed in 1924 by an Italian historian of the Risorgimento as "impulsive, avid of violent sensations and romantic contrasts, craving notoriety and theatrical appearances to impress the Parisian public for whom she posed incessantly"?[1] Doubtless because a woman of such independence, and such talent in fields considered the private reserve of men, was abhorrent to a masculine world. The only way to cope with such a creature was to malign her and eventually dispose of her as sick, abnormal, fraudulent, unspeakable. Her health was an easy target: she was epileptic. How could she evaluate the confused character of Federico Confalonieri, imprisoned in the fortress of Spielberg by Austria during the purges of 1821, when she herself was unstable? "She less than anybody," wrote Alessandro Luzio, "had the right to censure the victim of Spielberg, since Cristina Trivulzio's entire life was a fabric of incoherency and eccentricity, in part excusable because of the terrible malady she had in common with Confalonieri—epilepsy!" As to her writing, too good to be denigrated as feminine dabbling, that too could be minimized by questioning its authenticity. "We cannot determine how much is to be ascribed to her in the newspapers she directed and the works she published, or how much should rather be claimed by her collaborators, since in women writers, as has been cleverly said, *le style c'est l'homme.*"[2]

In France women had at least been nominal leaders of society; the most cultivated circles since the eighteenth century had assembled in what were known as *salons de femmes.* In Italy, great and powerful ladies of the Renaissance, like Isabella d'Este, had evidently been forgotten, for in the twentieth century Cristina was reproached with not being a *"brava italiana* who should have devoted herself to the normal activities, the tranquil interests of domestic life." Nor was she herself immune to this view of woman's predestined role, for in the midst of her most rebellious act against society—her decision to leave her husband—she wrote, "The vocation of us women is to be good wives and mothers.

Whoever opposes this calling falsifies natural inclinations and sooner or later repents." Bradamante, her glorious epithet in 1848, belonged between the pages of Ariosto's epic. In real life, such a heroine was an irksome reminder of masculine hypocrisy, a threat to the status quo of society and established rule, and to many of her countrymen an embarrassing reprimand for their inability to organize efficiently.

Even Cavour, loudly praised by Cristina for his selfless devotion to their common cause and grateful for her support, was not above malicious gossip about her. His damning imprint on her image has been left for historians to snigger over. When she asked him to arrange for the release of an impounded shipment of tombeky (an analgesic leaf she smoked for relief of her neuralgias), he wrote his Director General of the Interior: "Princess Belgiojoso is reclaiming a package of tombeky destined to procure her the inebriation that her senses can no longer offer. The princess, no longer able to find anyone who will intoxicate her with caresses, spends her life smoking lord knows what oriental narcotic, to which she adds heavy doses of opium. To deprive her of such pastimes in her aging days would be a cruelty of which our customs officials' hearts, however pitiless, would be incapable. Would you, therefore, have her poison returned to her, while making her pay the heaviest tax possible." This letter, published in a widely read work on Cavour,[3] is probably the origin of a remark made to me by an eminent historian when learning of my project: *"Ah, quella putana! Ed era drogata in più!"* (Oh, that whore! And a drug addict besides!).

Cristina was not lucky. She was judged more harshly than many women who earned their disrepute. Marie d'Agoult's escapade with Liszt, her abandonment of husband and children, her forays into journalism, into Italian affairs, were condoned and even praised. Cristina's participation in the political events of her own country, her books and articles based on firsthand knowledge of those events, were decried as personal ambition. George Sand's affair with Musset became a Romantic idyll; Cristina's refusal to become his mistress earned her the reputation of a heartless flirt. Whatever she did, whatever she was, whatever she had, was held against her. Her beauty was a menace to the men she refused to gratify; her wealth was a threat to Austria; her poverty while her estate was sequestered was called a pose; her scholarship was attributed to others; her political acumen was discounted as unrealistic. Heine, her faithful paladin, defended her in print by making her detractors sound barbarous: "Princess Belgiojoso, that beauty who longs for truth, can also be wronged with impunity. Anybody is at liberty to fling mud at a Raphael Madonna: she will not fight back."[4]

Because she was seen and heard, she was vulnerable. Unlike most women of her time and her country, she published her opinions. She was sent by Mazzini to secure arms and ships from France and to serve as intermediary with the French government. Her salon, her newspapers, were the hub of current politics. That her opinions were sensible and often foresighted did not make them more palatable. How dare this *woman* question the appointment of an illustrious poet to the ministry of education? What she was questioning was the need for such a ministry at all in the provisional government, at a time when students were on the battlefield. Was it not more urgent, she argued, to organize a quartermaster corps for the efficient distribution of supplies?

Equally irritating was that this woman saw, long before her male compatriots, the need to utilize the press as an organ of propaganda. It was her idea to launch publications, modeled after English and French reviews, that would diffuse abroad a true picture of the Italian situation, and assemble for domestic use social and economic information related to every state in Italy. Her awareness of social inequities was still another cause for derision. How ridiculous, this princess who embraced socialist ideas!

The shrewdness of Austrian policy toward Italian patriots was initially responsible for her defamation. The purpose of this strategy was to undermine the image of any public figure suspected of sedition. If such an individual could be vilified on moral or physical grounds, true or not, his effectiveness would be neutralized. The emperor was well served in this operation by his chief of police in Milan, Baron Carlo Giusto Torresani, whose persecution of the liberal upper classes exceeded his orders. Perhaps because his title had come with rank, not birth, he became particularly vindictive toward Cristina when she dared go over his head to request a passport. That she obtained it from the governor of Lombardy, an Austrian aristocrat free of Torresani's paranoia, whereas he rigorously denied such requests, was more than his pride could bear. He became her implacable enemy, sending spies after her, determined to force her humiliated return to Milan. His spies were only too eager to earn their wages; it was too lucrative an occupation to lose. When information was lacking, they invented it. Ignorant, amoral, their sole concern was money. Anyone who had it was fair game, especially a woman—young, rich, beautiful, and independent.

Torresani's feelings of lèse-police chief were transmitted to Vienna as lèse-majesté, which implied treason. Austria's anxiety over the plots of Lombard aristocrats, and especially those like Cristina who had managed to outwit imperial officials, assumed such proportions that it is not surprising to see Metternich and the emperor himself speculating on the domestic affairs of the princess and her family. Their wealth was of interest to Austria and Italy alike. Austria feared the support that the aristocracy was capable of offering Carbonaro revolutionaries, if one can

call Italians trying to rid themselves of foreign occupiers "revolutionaries." Emigrés and conspirators also vituperated against the aristocracy,
whose wealth was constantly exaggerated, because they did not give
enough. And the poor, in that feudal society, resented not only that the
rich were rich, but that they led a movement which should have toppled
the upper classes along with Austria. Memories of the French Revolution
were still very fresh in the 1820's. The estateless third estate did not
really believe in such miracles for Italy, but it had happened in France.

A personage as notable as Princess Belgiojoso was caught in the
crossfire of all these camps and became the scapegoat for those who
managed to conspire quietly at home. Had her marriage been successful,
she too might have remained in the background, never incurring the ire
that pursued her or provoking the scandal that distorted her. The hostility she engendered should not be viewed as a just measure of the woman,
but rather of her milieu. A woman of her rank, if she had intelligence
and charm, organized a salon to encourage the men around her; she did
not meet with heads of state herself. Women like Mme du Châtelet or
Mme de Staël were unknown to the spies who compiled their reports in
rudimentary spelling with elementary ideas, nor were they remembered
by the compatriots who inveighed against Cristina. Furthermore, they
were French. Who judged Italian women by such standards? An Italian
princess who left her husband, traveled alone, met with revolutionaries
and republicans, could only be a Messalina.

Happily, there were people who judged her by more enlightened
criteria. Through their views, she emerges as a remarkably modern
woman, convinced of her rights, secure in her dignity, capable of utilizing her own talents, independent of mind and body. Her awesome beauty
and captivating charm excited the Romantic imagination, which often
recoiled on discovering her unbending will but left an ample record of
her passage. Hidden between the lines of poems, letters, novels, are a
series of eloquent portraits long overlooked or misinterpreted. The writings of such eminent figures as Heine, Balzac, Musset—presumably
glossed to exhaustion—present unsuspected mirrors that reflect different
aspects of Cristina's image. Their letters, together with those of Liszt,
Lafayette, and others, betray a singular attachment to her. Their repeti-
tive use of the word "cult" serves as a common denominator of their
devotion to her. Her own letters and publications, rarely mentioned, even
more rarely quoted, disclose a personality that is intricate yet surprisingly
candid, generous and at the same time reticent, appealing but difficult to
love.

She certainly made excellent material for the historical novels,
romans à clef, and fictional biographies that were constructed around
her. Memoirs written fifty years after the events recorded, rumors passed

from generation to generation, sensational details out of context or undocumented, all created a figure so grotesque even her descendants were afraid to examine the archives in their possession. An example of this distorting process is a book published in 1906 by a popular writer and pasticheur, Marcel Boulenger, that claimed to contain the memoirs of a Marquis de Floranges. These so-called *Souvenirs* provided decades of later writers with details of Cristina's fifth-floor apartment, presumably littered with esoteric volumes in Hebrew and Latin, stilettos, skulls, and a sign on her door reading "LA PRINCESSE MALHEUREUSE." In fact, they were a hoax concocted with ingredients from Théophile Gautier's satiric portrait of her in *La Croix de Berny,* which appeared in the 1840's. Those of Gautier's readers who recognized Cristina were vastly amused and understood it was a satire. Boulenger's readers, less astute, launched the tradition of a macabre conspirator-bluestocking, an image too beguiling to rectify. Boulenger never confessed this prank* but in 1926 published an article defending Cristina's treatment of Musset after she had been tarred and feathered by a Musset biographer. Here is the "Marquis de Floranges's" much-borrowed description of Cristina's theatrical garret:

> It was the misery of a lyric poet. A miniature placed on an easel displayed the ascetic face of the princess. . . . But she had, it seemed to me, gotten even thinner, if that was possible. Farther on, a skull, gaping and desiccated, rested on an open book whose characters I was able to verify as Hebrew, yes Hebrew! Farther still lay a guitar with broken strings, paints, a palette; a very sharp stiletto was placed in full display on a table, and everywhere sheets of paper . . . blackened with Cristina's handwriting. . . . For Princess Belgiojoso was indeed writing books, big, heavy books; not content with conspiring, being beautiful, knowing how to play the guitar and wield a dagger, paint fans, and let all of Paris know that Austria was persecuting her, she also read Hebrew and composed books, and what books!

It is hard to understand how those "memoirs" were ever taken seriously enough to be quoted, yet their authority lingers on. In 1971 a biography of Cristina that appeared in England cites the "marquis" as an accredited historical figure, and from his testimony the author deduces Cristina's general behavior.

---

* He did feel obliged to recant another he had perpetrated. After publishing an "undiscovered" tale by Perrault, he made a public retraction when it was reprinted in Perrault's complete works. The inauthenticity of the *Souvenirs du Marquis de Floranges* is documented in *La Bibliographie des auteurs modernes de langue française:* "This work is a complete fiction from the pen of Marcel Boulenger."[5] Even the call number of the work in the Bibliothèque Nationale is that of a fictional title.

The Marquis de Floranges, in his *Souvenirs,* relates how in an
outer suburb of Milan he was almost knocked down by a donkey
that had strayed into his path: "A youth in rags was astride its back.
'You idiot!' I cried . . . I was so angry I gave him a blow. He almost
fell off the beast and as he struggled to keep his seat I saw him
full face . . . I stood amazed as I recognized the vagabond to be the
Princess Belgiojoso. I seized the false mendicant and pulled her toward
me. 'Cristina!' I exclaimed. She struggled furiously . . . stabbed me
first in the shoulder then in my side."

Dressed in this fashion, Cristina went around the slums of Milan
stirring up the poor against the Austrians and inciting them to prepare for the day when they might stage a mass struggle and evict the
foreigners.[6]

The author's notion of Cristina's patriotic activities is as fanciful as
Boulenger's portrayal of "la princesse malheureuse." And in 1975 the
March issue of *ZEITmagazin* carried an article about Cristina by Rudolf
Leonhardt, editor of *Die Zeit,* who unmistakably repeated Boulenger's
fantasies with a few embellishments of his own (Chopin is at the piano
in her salon while the skull sits draped in white silk by her bed). Happily, Boulenger's "marquis" has now been unmasked and after seventy
years of high living has finally relinquished his disfiguring hold on
Cristina.

SINCE LETTERS are the only direct contact we have with people we have
not known, I have taken great care to translate* faithfully and quote
accurately throughout. Even today, with all our devices for conserving
voices and images, there is little more authentic, more characteristic of an
individual than his intimate correspondence. No diary, no ex post facto
memoirs, can reveal the spontaneous wit, the immediate impressions,
reactions, emotions, of hastily scrawled letters. To have read Cristina's
letters, seen her strong vertical script, the crossings-out, the curious habit
of placing afterthoughts, or lines too few for another sheet, across the
long side of the first or last page, was to discover the living creature who
penned them. Hers was not the careful penmanship of a self-conscious,
constructed individual, but rather the artless expression of a natural,
expansive personality. At the risk of overquoting, I have indulged my
own taste as a reader of biography. Nothing is more exasperating than a
biographer's paraphrases when one wants to read for oneself what the
subject said. All of my conjectures, all of my conclusions, have therefore

* All translations—letters, documents, literary texts—are my own.

been based on a personal reading of Cristina's letters and those of her correspondents. Secondary sources are not always reliable, since the lines left out are often more important than the ones selected. For this reason I have quoted at considerable length, not wishing to deny the reader the pleasure of examining these documents himself. So much depends on a word, a tone, a willful or inadvertent ambiguity. It was rightly said, *le style c'est tout*. And style is something Cristina and her friends possessed in abundance.

Part One

THE
MODEL

1

ℐleeping ℬeauty

I T ALL BEGAN like a fairy tale. "Princess Christine* possessed all the gifts that one attributes to the child whose cradle was surrounded by good fairies."[1] Born into the ancient Lombard family of Trivulzio, she had been given unusual beauty, a voice as rich in speech as in song, sharp intelligence. Equally talented at the easel or the keyboard, naturally elegant, courageous, and idealistic, Cristina, her contemporaries concurred, had the rarer gift of charm. Her biting wit and stubborn integrity were mitigated by generosity, compassion, and the love of laughter. But like the princess of the tale, she had been cursed by the wicked fairy. Sickness and misfortune were to deny her the happiness her many gifts should have assured. A tragic Sleeping Beauty, she was to remain dormant even though, and perhaps because, Prince Charming embraced her.

Born in Milan the morning of June 28, 1808, she was baptized with twelve names, of which Cristina was the second.† Her father, Gerolamo—descended from the fearsome Gian Giacomo Trivulzio, marshal of France and governor of Milan under Louis XII—was a distinguished figure at the court of Napoleon's viceroy. Until the end of the Napoleonic interlude, Gerolamo abandoned his hereditary title of marquis for that of Comte de l'Empire, bestowed on him by Napoleon. This turned out to be a costly choice, for it placed the family in ill favor when Austria returned to power. In 1812 Gerolamo suddenly died in the full vigor of his thirty-two years, leaving Cristina his only heir to the Trivulzio palace, vast estates, and one of the greatest fortunes in Lombardy.

Her mother, Vittoria, widowed at twenty, was an opulent beauty of

* Cristina's French friends always gallicized her name, as she did herself when writing in French.

† Her names included Maria, Cristina, Beatrice, Teresa, Barbara, Leopolda, Clotilde, Melchiora, Camilla, Giulia, Margherita, Laura.

great musical talent who sightread the music of young Bellini, too timid
to play his own compositions at her keyboard. After "a brief year of
widowhood," as Cristina later called it, Vittoria married another young
marquis, Alessandro Visconti d'Aragona, eminent member of the Milanese aristocracy. An admirer of Rousseau and new ideas, a passionate
dilettante of botany and landscaping, he was a close friend of such major
cultural figures as Alessandro Manzoni, Silvio Pellico, and Federico
Confalonieri. Through a new review, *Il Conciliatore*, they hoped to re-
vitalize the stilted thinking that centuries of imperial occupation had
imposed on the region. Visconti participated in the construction of the
first steamboat to navigate the Po, and aligned himself with the political
activists who saw Austrian dominion as the death of Lombardy. His
interest in the diffusion of science and the reform of elementary education was enough to label him a subversive in official records. When in
1821 the conspiracy led by Confalonieri was betrayed, Visconti was arrested, though he had played no active role in it. Held for two years, he
was finally released for lack of evidence because his quick-witted wife
had burned all incriminating papers before the police searched their
house. He returned an aged and broken man, unable to recapture the
verve he had lost in prison.

Four children were born of this marriage, giving Cristina a brother
and three sisters close enough in age to have grown up together. But a
shadow had fallen over them. Still a young girl herself, she wrote, "What
saddens me . . . is that in this family so dear to me and so deserving of
contentment and tranquillity, there is not a person whose face radiates
serenity of the soul. Not even these dear children, still in purest innocence, not even they are immune to sad concerns, anxiety, and anguish."
The harsh repressions of the 1820's, when most of their friends had
relatives in prison or under investigation, the alternating depressions and
agitations of her stepfather, the brutality of Austria's reinstated tyranny,
all left their mark on an insecure, sensitive adolescent.

Except for a few letters, the only extant document regarding Cristina's childhood is her reply to a phrenologist, written in 1842, when the
pseudo-science of the skull's topography was in great vogue. She found
his analysis of her as strong-willed, vain, self-possessed, and gregarious
completely mistaken. "I was a morose child, serious, introverted, quiet. I
do not know where I got the even and cheerful disposition I enjoy now;
the circumstances of my environment were not at all conducive to that
end. . . . I was so timid I often burst into tears in my mother's sitting
room because I thought someone was looking at me. . . . I was often
punished because I preferred old dresses to new ones which I put on
backward rather than look in a mirror."

Her education was probably like that of any girl of her background:

French, English, Latin, music, painting, literature. But the grim events of her early years gave her a sense of history and politics, even if her formal training in those areas was rudimentary. Her stepfather's scientific interests may have been communicated to her, for she became extremely knowledgeable in medicine, economics, and agronomy. Her mother's musicianship, and the many soirées at home with Rossini and Bellini, surely enhanced her training in piano and voice. Ernesta Bisi, esteemed portraitist of an entire generation of Lombard nobility, did much more than teach Cristina the graphic arts. Bisi, long committed to the Carbonaro movement, may well have been Cristina's first political mentor. She was certainly Cristina's first, and for many years closest, confidante. Their correspondence provides an intimate view of Cristina's adolescence and marriage. In Bisi, Cristina found the special affection and understanding so often characteristic of teacher-pupil relationships. It may well have been this one that formed Cristina's reverence for friendship throughout her life.

When Liszt went to Milan in 1838, Cristina asked him to visit Bisi:

> There is in Milan a person who is for me a second mother and older sister, all in one. Ever since I lost my mother, she alone awakens in me some of the emotions that had been reserved for her. This kind and lovable woman is named Mme Ernesta Bisi; she is an artist, wife of a painter of great merit, mother of seven daughters, and lives in my mother's house, palazzo Visconti. . . . Go to her in my name and tell her that I am sending her through you a half-hour of enchantment. . . . Look for a small piano in the corner of her little salon; open it and play whatever your fingers like. . . . Tell her that you know I love her; then turn on your heel, and goodbye.

Until her death in 1859 she remained Cristina's second mother and older sister.

At fifteen Cristina's eyes fell on a young prince, eight years her elder, whose reputation for gallantry was as established as his Carbonaro affiliation. By any standards but those of a Trivulzio—a princely family founded in the twelfth century—Belgiojoso was a worthy name. (Cristina's aunt had preferred spinsterhood to contamination of her Trivulzio blood. When her confessor tried to humble her, telling her that in the end we are all worms, she retorted, "A worm yes, but a Trivulzio!") The Belgiojosos, a Lombard family even older than the Trivulzios, were princes of the Holy Roman Empire. Two of their palaces are still to be seen in Milan: one, a majestic edifice constructed at the beginning of the nineteenth century, which became the viceroy's residence under Napoleon and is now the Gallery of Modern Art; the other, the elegant baroque façade that dominates piazza Belgiojoso, one of Stendhal's familiar haunts.

An hour from Milan, in the village of Merate, still inhabited by Belgiojoso descendants, is a summer villa of regal proportions and vistas.

This particular Belgiojoso, Prince Emilio Barbiano di Belgiojoso d'Este, was admired by many but approved of by few. He had a tall athletic body, a fine head of blond hair, even features, seductive eyes, and an engaging smile. His charm, his grace, his gorgeous tenor voice made him welcome everywhere. It was a voice so unusually beautiful that Rossini tried desperately to persuade Emilio to sing in the opera house. He would not have been the first Italian nobleman to do so: Count di Candia, known throughout Europe under the name of Mario, was then delighting opera audiences. Emilio, though a confirmed partisan of Lombardy's liberation, remained as much a tourist in politics as in music. His only genuine commitment was to the pursuit of pleasure. Irresistible to women, pleasing to men, he had critics but no enemies. One of his closest friends and a fellow roué, Edmond d'Alton-Shée, left a delightful portrait of him.[2] "As though all his advantages of name, body and personality were not enough, generous fate gave him a captivating voice. All these qualities were in the service of Byronic intemperance, an insatiable desire for sensual pleasure; he understood life to be a succession of raptures and carried them to excess. Born to seduce, he pursued his career without scruples or remorse." Emilio's robust health continued to withstand his excesses long after his fortune (and d'Alton-Shée's stamina) gave out.

Fifteen-year-old Cristina was hardly the dish for a man of Byronic appetites (who had also savored of Byron's last mistress, Countess Guiccioli). However, the young heiress had the means to subsidize his entertainments; her dowry alone came to four hundred thousand Austrian lire, not counting sumptuous revenues. She would never distract him from his voluptuous *madaminas,* but her dark eyes and dimpled chin were not without charm. A portrait of her, painted at the time of her marriage by Ernesta Bisi, shows a round-cheeked childish face with heavy eyebrows and great black eyes soft with innocent reveries. D'Alton-Shée evidently learned from Emilio that her eyes were not what attracted him: "His paternal inheritance ran the risk of being sapped when the convenience of a marriage interrupted the course of his pleasures."[3] But not for long.

More perplexing, at first glance, is Cristina's attraction to him. His notorious reputation was no mystery to her; his escapades and squandering were the talk of Milan. One might expect this shy, troubled girl, twice deprived of a father, to seek the secure affections of a more temperate man. She was four when her father died, and thirteen when her stepfather's imprisonment left him a pitiful facsimile of his earlier self. Neither of them represented a fatherly figure. Her father had been barely past thirty at his death, and her stepfather in his early thirties at the time of his arrest. Twice then, Cristina had been robbed of the love not of an aging patriarch, but of a man in the prime of his life. Her mother's exuberant youth may also have been a factor. Casting off her widow's veil for a bridal veil at twenty-one, she offered Cristina a new father who—after his collapse had left Vittoria widowed again, so to speak—was then in turn supplanted by a dashing Sicilian. Count di Sant'Antonio, an accomplished flute player, skilled in all the arts of the salon, introduced his compatriot Bellini into the Visconti household and himself into Vittoria's boudoir. The presence of Countess di Sant'Antonio in the Visconti salon seems to have concealed nothing from Cristina, who never missed a chance to denigrate the count in her letters to Ernesta Bisi. This sensual aura over her family life surely affected the imagination of a melancholy adolescent.

She saw Emilio as precisely the kind of man to restore the love she had lost and to reveal to her its greater mysteries: the love her mother had shared with the missing fathers, the love other girls whispered about, the loves for which Emilio was notorious. It took no great effort to super-impose a seasoned twenty-four-year-old Emilio on the fading image of her thirty-year-old fathers. Despite warnings, gossip, and general dis-approval, Cristina became Princess Belgiojoso on September 24, 1824, three months after her sixteenth birthday. According to d'Alton-Shée's interpretation, "the beautiful heiress, rejecting a host of suitors, set her heart on the only one who ignored her. . . . She saw the monster and engaged her pride to tame it."

It is more likely that she responded to the powerful attraction that can still be sensed from Emilio's portraits. This man alone could make her feel loved, desired, beautiful, for not until long after did she even surmise her charm. She was a mature woman of thirty-four when she wrote: "It is only very recently that I suspect I might be beautiful; in my early youth I believed I was not, but merely pleasant looking; in my childhood I thought I was positively ugly, and I still think I was." That she was not without romantic imagination appears from a charming letter to Ernesta Bisi, written a month after her fifteenth birthday. Visiting Verona, she went to see Juliet's tomb.

> That marble tombstone, sacred and precious to every sensitive soul, lies in a miserable courtyard in the custody of a decrepit old hag with a terrorizing appearance. In years past it was in its proper place, that is, in a garden that served then as a cemetery for the monks of that monastery. To see that tomb, the hollow where the body of that victim of love, and of hate, rested . . . one's spirit is seized by a shudder, I would almost call it pleasant. Since not even an atom is lost or annihilated, since everything that was created is, and will always

be, Juliet is still in that garden. She is only earth now. But that earth
that I trod was the resting place of a tender and passionate soul, that
earth was a body, was animated, was . . . Juliet.

Cristina's style in Italian is remarkably personal and, though highly liter-
ate, is free of the academic syntax or expressions one would expect (and
that persist today in alumni of higher institutions). Already then, the
word was at her command. As to her sensibility, it is all the more remarkable in that she claimed, "Until my marriage I never read novels other
than Miss Edgeworth's."

She seems to have reached adolescence convinced of being unloved,
unattractive, unhappy. These are sentiments quite natural to most adolescents, but she may have had better reason than others. Envious perhaps of
her mother's flamboyant beauty and vitality, however much she loved
her, a fragile single child in a second family, however much she willed
herself part of it, bereft of a father's affection, subjected to a stepfather's
neurosis, conscious of an outsider's intrusion in her mother's attentions,
her life was not exactly filled with cheer and security. Her only remarks
about her childhood suggest that the robust health and gaiety one might
expect of five children in a wealthy family were generally lacking.

If, in addition, she was already afflicted with epilepsy, her melancholy is all the more comprehensible. To be subject to convulsions and
any of the concomitant disorders—fainting, nausea, headache, visceral
pain, fever, thoracic discomfort intense enough to be misdiagnosed as
pleurisy or inflammation of the lungs—is to grow up with the tragic
awareness that one is less than others, a disappointment to one's family,
an outcast. Curiously enough, there is no trace of resentment in her
personal writings about either her health or her family. And yet, she was
not unaware of her dispiriting existence and the depressive personality
that resulted from it. In her early letters to Bisi, she never complained
about being sick, but her comments about the excellence of her appetite
and her well-being at the time of writing indicate the exception to the
rule. One does not point out the pinkness of one's cheeks unless one is
usually pale. When she became seriously ill after her marriage, her
letters to Bisi reveal that her patient endurance was born of chronic
debility.

In her response to the phrenologist, quoted earlier, she recalled that
"immediately after the birth of my brother, I was given to him [*je lui fus
donnée*] to amuse him, and my hours of recreation were spent, without a
murmur from me, in pulling his little carriage and other diversions of the
same kind." It may be that she was thought too delicate for any other
kind of recreation. Not only did she never resent that half-brother,
Alberto, or her three half-sisters, she later assumed the role of surrogate

mother, remaining attached to them all her life, especially to Alberto. The very closeness of that attachment suggests her need to assert herself once she emerged from the gray cocoon of her childhood. She who had understandably felt secondary in the new family was able to requite that dreary past by arranging marriages for her sisters, inviting the four of them to travel abroad with her, providing for them the pleasures of Paris once she settled there. Through their eyes she could see herself as strong, capable, amusing, surrounded by attractive people who admired her. Nor was it merely a matter of compensation. She genuinely wanted their love, generously gave of her own. How much her clouded childhood contributed to her exalted notion of family life is hard to assess. Certainly, it contributed to her intense need for friends and admirers, who may have provided a better facsimile of family affection than could lovers. A lover, like the man she married and the young men who had been her fathers, could abandon her, leaving her wounded in her deepest emotions. Friendship did not expose her to the same risk of loss.

Emilio was clearly the moving force behind her metamorphosis from a shy, introverted child to the self-assertive, convivial young woman seen by the phrenologist years later. To have captured an exciting man like Emilio was to prove, to herself at least, that the pale sickly pupa could become as vivid a butterfly as any other. He may also have served as an escape from whatever chafed her at home. Once married, she would become the mistress of her fortune and her future. And Emilio, debonair, hedonistic, sensual, would reveal the gaiety and passion she hoped were in her.

The revelation never occurred, and for substantial reasons. Emilio was neither father nor husband. Love for him was a commodity to be squandered as frivolously as money at the gaming table. Writing ten years later to d'Alton-Shée of his current successes, he candidly expressed his view of women: "I still prefer my old ones, with all their inconveniences, to the romantic and sentimental kind, and above all to the monotonous possession of a mistress, though I have always had three of them. . . ." A wife surely had no place in such a universe. For Cristina it had been a marriage of impulse, for Emilio a marriage of convenience. Had there been any real love between them, this adolescent bride might have discovered what she yearned to know. As it was, her extreme youth and precarious health and Emilio's miscast role in her life revealed little more than her own frustrated desires.

Among the warnings Cristina received before her marriage was one that turned out to be tragically prophetic. It arrived the morning of her wedding day in the form of an elegantly rhymed libel of eight stanzas written by Count Ferdinando Crivelli, distinguished member of Milanese aristocracy. His attempt to enlighten her was noble but useless. Crivelli knew the bridegroom well enough to foresee the future that awaited the headstrong bride united to a Don Giovanni (the resemblance is evoked by the paraphrase of da Ponte's libretto in lines five and six of the first stanza), and told her so in surprisingly indelicate language.

STANZE EPITALAMICHE PER LE FAUSTISSIME NOZZE STABILITE
FRA DONNA CRISTINA DEI MARCHESI TRIVULZIO CON IL
PRINCIPE EMILIO BELGIOJOSO

E sarà dunque ver, Cristina bella?
Un pezzo Principesco hai tu voluto?
Ma incanagliar ti fà maligna Stella:
Che poi che teco alquanto avrà goduto,
Lussureggiando andrà con Questa e Quella,
E invano ti udirem gridare ajuto:
Ma come indietro più non si ritorna,
Render solo potrai corna per corna.

. . . .

Sangue Belgiojoso, non ti conosco!
Sì chiaro un giorno, or ti se' reso fosco.

Prence? Di Prence un fantasma, un'ombra
Sol veggio in te: d'ogni elevata idea
E fù sempre, e sarà tua mente sgombra:
Oziar ne' Caffé, nella Platea,
Puttaneggiar, tutta tua vita adombra,
Fuggendo i Studi ond'alto Cuor si bea:
Prence di nome e Birrichin di fatto,
Poiché Donna ama il peggio, il colpo hai fatto!

Tempo verrà, né fia lontano molto,
Che tu, Cristina, morderai le dita,
E teco ti dorrai del pensier stolto
Per cui ti fosti a simil Prence unita,
Nobil, ricca, gentil, d'amabil volto,
Qual non avrebbe la tua man gradita?
E quanto grave più sarà tuo affanno,
Tanto più spesso udir dovrai, tuo danno.

. . . .

(Il ché tutto si avverrà)[4]

NUPTUAL STANZAS FOR THE MOST PROPITIOUS MARRIAGE
DECIDED BETWEEN DONNA CRISTINA DEI MARCHESI*
TRIVULZIO AND PRINCE EMILIO BELGIOJOSO

Can it thus be true, lovely Cristina?
A princely morsel is what you wanted?
But how he debases you, oh bitter fate!
For when he has taken his pleasure with you,
He will go off wantonly with this woman and that,
And in vain will we hear you cry for help:
But since there is no turning back,
All that remains is for you to render horn for horn.

. . . .

Belgiojoso blood, I do not recognize you!
Once you were limpid, now you have become muddy.

Prince? Of a prince only a phantom, a shadow
Do I see in you: of any lofty thought
Your mind always was and will be void:
Idling in the cafe, in the theater,
Whoring, shades in your entire existence,
Fleeing the studies that beatify a higher spirit:
Prince in name and scoundrel in fact,
Since woman is drawn to the worst, you have brought it off!

The time will come, and not far off,
When you, Cristina, will bite your knuckles,
And will repent the foolish notion
For which you joined yourself to such a prince,
Noble, rich, well-bred, fair of face,
Who would not have desired your hand?
And the deeper your grief
The more often will you hear: your mistake.

. . . .

(All of which will be confirmed)

It took less than two years for Cristina to discover how right Crivelli
had been. How strange that the poem was not instantly crumpled and

---

* Since a daughter, or second son, cannot inherit a title, such offspring of a marchese
are known as "dei marchesi."

thrown away, given the day of its receipt. Did she keep it to prove them all wrong? Or did she hold on to it over the years as a bitter memento of her own error? It was as though the wicked fairy had accomplished her curse. Through his habit of *"lussureggiando con questa e quella,"* Emilio infected his adolescent bride with a disease that was to lead her on a *via crucis* for the next forty years.

In an exhaustive three-volume biography by Aldobrandino Malvezzi, this horrendous occurrence was euphemized in a single ambiguous sentence: "After two years of marriage, a new and very sad factor appeared in Cristina di Belgiojoso which perhaps contributed to determining her future attitude toward her husband—that is, an alarming aggravation of her already unstable health."[5] At the beginning of her marriage her health seems to have been very stable, for she wrote to Ernesta Bisi, a few months after the wedding, that she had gained weight and her cheeks were flushed with health: *"Insomma, per parlare chiaramente, io sto bene"* (In short, to speak clearly, I am just fine). But Malvezzi does not speak clearly, for after reading over a thousand pages of otherwise admirable scholarship, we learn nothing about Cristina's state of health, which is, after all, a major factor in any individual. In Cristina's case, to know merely that she was often sick and underwent frequent cures is to ignore the most essential reasons for much of her behavior.

UNTIL VERY RECENTLY, Cristina's entire medical history was tactfully shrouded by her biographers. And yet her own letters are so candid, so descriptive, there is no way of denying the epilepsy to which she refers unequivocally over the years. For centuries so misunderstood that one shuddered at its mention, epilepsy has only recently begun to lose its sinister connotations. That kings, generals, and writers suffered from it did not efface the stigma attached to it by ignorance and superstition. In Cristina's case, every effort was made to bury this fact as though it were a disgrace, or to allude to it so passingly as to diminish its importance. Without documents to date the onset of the symptoms, it is nevertheless evident from her letters that in 1829 her condition was already chronic: "I am up, I go out, but my health prevents me from doing what I would do if I were really well. Still, I consider myself fortunate and endure with patience a few reminders of the old maladies [*gli antichi malanni*]. For us chronic patients [*malati cronici*] a pain or two is not a torment, since that is our habitual state." It may well be that the diagnosis of epilepsy was not made in her childhood or adolescence, since little was understood about the disorder before the middle of the nineteenth century. Even today, an eminent specialist in the field points out that the visceral manifestations of epilepsy are so dominant that they are often misdiagnosed as symptoms of gastro-intestinal or cardio-respiratory diseases, rather than originating from an epileptic seizure; ". . . in addition," he says, "the common association of these symptoms with a picture of bizarre behavior or mental activity may lead to a diagnosis of a psychiatric disorder."[6]

Surely epilepsy, with its stigmatic associations,* was the last diagnosis that doctors would have made in the case of a young girl of such noble background. They spoke of weak lungs, intestinal malfunction, vague nervous disorders, as it appears from certain early letters. Yet she must have known the truth by 1829. It was not until 1841, when a gifted doctor (and amateur hellenist) named Paolo Maspero became her physician,† that she was successfully treated and enjoyed long periods of remission. That epilepsy was seen, as late as 1936, as a derogation of Cristina's image is apparent from Malvezzi's treatment of the subject. He never mentions the disease, except in a note to the second volume containing a medical opinion of his day, which attributes to a form of hysteria the very symptoms that point to epilepsy: ". . . she presents the manifestations of a pithiatic** type in the relation between the nervous attacks and certain periods, the association of such attacks with emotional factors, and finally, the constant and certain foreseeability of the attack."[7]

The *epileptic aura* is precisely what makes the attacks foreseeable, and in Cristina's case, the region of the aura was the epigastrium, called "the chest" by her biographers, weak lungs being more romantic than epilepsy. Her own letters are much more clinical. In one of them, to her brother, she described an attack in such detail as to satisfy any diagnostician.

> I was again stricken by one of my old epileptic attacks, from which Maspero liberated me so many years ago and which we thought to be gone forever. However, this new attack did not occur completely unforeseen by me, since for perhaps more than a year, I felt from time to time the so-called epileptic aura, which always preceded my attacks. . . . The very morning of this last attack, I had had three auras of excessive force; after the third, I fell asleep and woke up surrounded by my maids. Only then did I learn that one of them had found me lying on the ground with my head under the table, completely unconscious. I only know what I was told, since I . . . re-

---

* Epileptics were commonly thought to be possessed by the devil.

† In 1858 Maspero published *Della epilessia e del suo miglior modo di curarla*. Very few doctors were even qualified in the field at the time, let alone specialized in it. His translation of the *Odyssey*, dedicated to Cristina, had appeared in 1845.

** *Pithiatisme* was a term created by Babinski in 1902 to designate disturbances caused and cured by suggestion.

tained no memory of it whatever. However, I immediately remembered the three precursory auras and understood what had happened.
A few hours later Maspero arrived and found me fully recovered. . . .
The attack must have been light since neither my tongue nor lips
were bitten. . . .

On the basis of such precise documentation as her correspondence
with Maspero[8] and others, it has been possible to determine that Cristina
suffered from psychomotor-temporal lobe epilepsy,* of which Flaubert
was another distinguished victim. In any biographical study the health of
the subject is interesting, but here it is particularly significant since so
much of Cristina's uncommon behavior was attributed to ambition, affectation, mental instability, and sexual frigidity. Recent research in epilepsy,
and specifically temporal lobe epilepsy, has uncovered previously unsuspected relationships between the disease and personality. Excessive manifestations of courage and productive energy, common to such epileptics,
have been recognized as compensatory aspects of the disorder, which in
turn appears to have an inhibiting effect on sexuality. This is not to say
that Cristina's activities and interests were determined by her illness, but
that certain natural attributes were intensified by it. Many epileptics devote
themselves to idealized causes, such as extreme religious preoccupations.
Cristina's inordinate participation in the Italian nationalist movement is
more reasonably explained by the compensatory motivation of her malady, and her unhappy marriage, than by arrogance or publicity-seeking.
Few men and fewer women have devoted themselves so productively to a
great cause, and when one considers how much of her life was spent in
pain and debility, she is rather to be admired than maligned for her
intrusion into masculine affairs. The febrile activity of her periods of
remission is yet another trait common to epileptics. And the nature of her
interests is related not only to epilepsy, but to chronic invalidism: care of
the sick, social reform, theology. Which is, again, not to say that one
need be epileptic to be a social reformer or a religious historian. However, the converse has been found often enough to be more than coincidental. Had she enjoyed good health, or suffered from a different
malady, she might have been content to paint, or conduct a salon, or
remain peripheral to the nationalist movement. The point is that Cristina
had the compelling drive common to epileptics of her type which led her
to develop those of her talents that could set her apart from the norm,
and compensate for the normalcy she lacked.

The question of her sexuality, more difficult to analyze than any other
aspect of her personality, has been raised by everyone who ever knew her
or wrote about her. Police spies and paparazzi of her time gossiped about

---

* Thanks to Dr. Gilbert H. Glaser, Professor of Neurology, Yale School of Medicine.

her in syllogistic conclusions drawn from her husband's debauchery. Others, stung or mystified by her rejection, dismissed her as frigid, coquettish, prudish, and even lesbian. Here again, epilepsy may explain much that was attributed to mistaken causes. To the surprise of most researchers, recent investigations have revealed that the nature and placement of the lesion causing psychomotor-temporal epilepsy produces a significant and permanent diminution of sexual activity, contrary to other forms of epilepsy in which there are no permanent sexual effects.

> This lack is not the simple fact of impotence or frigidity in the accomplishment of the normal sexual act. It testifies on the contrary to a profound indifference to everything that has to do with sexual behavior. . . . In fact, what must be stressed is the absence of fantasies or erotic dreams as well as inhibition, which makes the interrogation of patients on so delicate a subject very easy. The absence of a sexual life generally leaves them indifferent. If they are troubled, it is always for very particular reasons: feelings of guilt toward the partner, anxiety over the consequences on marriage. . . . In short, one is in the presence of a veritable weakening of impulse, a deficiency of the sexual instinct, without any relation to genital malformations or glandular disorders.[9]

The effects of her illness were aggravated by still other circumstances. Given her extreme youth and constitutional disinclination, it is easy to conjecture that she was a less exhilarating partner than Emilio was accustomed to. A patient, tender husband might have aroused in her an emotional, if not an erotic, desire for love. The inveterate voluptuary she married could only be expected to seek his pleasures elsewhere, which would have happened sooner or later in any case. This alone surely caused great stress in her, for not only had Emilio not given her the pleasure, the love, the normality she hoped for, he confirmed her inadequacy by openly gallivanting around Milan. And as if that were not enough to disturb the delicate balance of an epileptic's health, Emilio's infidelities were exacerbated by the contagion of his philandering. Discovering that his wanton choice of bedmates had infected her with syphilis, Cristina's pride collapsed with her health.

Since epileptic seizures are often precipitated by emotional upsets it is not surprising that she entered into the period of ill health mentioned by Malvezzi. It is even possible that "the alarming aggravation" he spoke of was caused by syphilitic meningitis, which usually appears within two years of the onset of syphilis, and is commonly associated with headaches and convulsions. Such symptoms could easily be ascribed to epilepsy, or to any nervous disorder, since syphilis was as little understood as epilepsy at that time. That syphilis seems nonetheless to have been recognized, or at least suspected, is evident from the treatment she received then, and again three years later—mercury and sea-water baths, the classic therapy for syphilis until Ehrlich's Salvarsan. A letter of April 1829 informs Bisi of this: "My health is fairly unsteady. But on top of that is added the so-called tic douleureux* in the face which extends all the way to the chest, being my weakest part. This misfortune is highly painful. All of it attributable to the same old cause, the doctors repeat, for which applications of mercury have again been prescribed before going on to the baths. I will do the first in Naples, the second in Ischia, and will begin the cure next month."

Forty years later, still suffering the effects of syphilis, she makes patently clear in her correspondence with Maspero that she continued to be treated for the disease since she was taking the then-famous Pollini powders. What does remain in doubt is the cause of her seizures, an open question with her doctor as late as 1842: "I find that your reasoning regarding my syncopes is excellent," she writes Maspero, "but, if you will forgive me, I remain in my opinion as to their origin. . . . If I could explain all the observations that go through my mind I might succeed in persuading you that the uterus also figures in this affliction, if not as the principal agent, then at least as the secondary one. . . . Do not believe that I underestimate your counsel . . . but I feel almost invincibly condemned by a cause less noble than the brain to recurrences of these syncopes." Maspero's arguments that her epileptic seizures were independent of a venereal infection apparently did not convince her. She believed that syphilis had affected her nervous system, which in fact was the case, but it does not seem to have been the origin of her seizures. While it is possible for syphilitic meningitis to produce an epileptogenic lesion in the brain—a fact unknown at the time—her own letters suggest that she was already subject to a nervous disorder before she contracted syphilis, although the second disease severely aggravated the first. For the rest of her life, she endured excruciating neuralgias, often so severe that she was unable to lay her head on a pillow. The catalogue of her suffering and the medications prescribed—all documented in her correspondence with Maspero and others—is staggering. Aconite, strychnine, belladonna, quinine, opium, and datura stramonium (these last two believed by the uninformed to have been taken for nonmedicinal reasons) were administered to her over the years, often providing more discomfort than relief. Belladonna, an anticonvulsant, prescribed in large doses in 1842, left her unable to read because her pupils were so overdilated. Opium, which she

---

* Tic douleureux [facial neuralgia] and intercostal neuralgia, more common in women than in men, are frequent concomitants of syphilis. "Tabes dorsales [a form of tertiary syphilis] is an occasional cause of paroxysmal attacks within the [facial] area." "[Intercostal neuralgia] may be due to inflammation of spinal dorsal roots especially in syphilis."[10]

took under medical supervision and used with great discretion,* earned her the reputation, via Cavour, of being an addict. Tombeky, a tobacco-like leaf she discovered in Turkey and smoked in a narghileh (and that Cavour mistook for just another narcotic) finally relieved her neuralgias more effectively than any Western medication. Her suffering was ultimately a boon to others, for her acquired knowledge of diseases and pharmacology enabled her to help those around her, as well as herself, when doctors were unavailable.

IN 1826 CRISTINA began her long odyssey of cures. Instead of finding in Emilio a haven of compassion, not to mention contrition, she discovered that he had found distraction from his ailing wife in the arms of a lady well known to Milanese society, Paola Ruga, the very lady who distracted the bored Cristina while both were taking the waters at Recoaro! "I am somewhat less unhappy than the other imbibers," she wrote Ernesta Bisi, "having found lodgings in the same house as Signora Ruga, which affords me some company, but there are still boring hours, very boring indeed." By 1828 she recognized the debacle. She had evidently tried to dance to her husband's tune, participating in the life of Milan's jeunesse dorée before her health broke down. Expressing his disappointment over Cristina's way of life, an acquaintance remarked: "La Belgiojoso is the victim of her husband who, along with his qualities of character, has all the vices of Milanese nobility, their only occupations being flirting, feasting, theater, music and gambling. I still hope Cristinetta Belgiojoso will turn out well."[11] This was not a life for Cristina—although Emilio was perfectly satisfied with it and was fair enough to offer the same privileges to his wife, who had been paying off his debts—nor was this Cristina's idea of marriage. Perhaps she even forgave him for not fulfilling her dream, holding her deficient health responsible. Certainly, her letters have none of the bitterness one might expect. However, a Trivulzio's pride and an adolescent's idealism could not tolerate the hypocrisy of such a union.

In the fall of 1828 she confronted Emilio with an ultimatum—he must give up his mistress. Contrary to the legend that has her appearing

* In 1856 she wrote to Victor Cousin, "Let me give you a piece of medical advice. If you suffer from any other malady but apoplexy, do not fear opium for it is the elixir vitae of nervous sufferers like us. And do not forget that morphine is none other than opium purified of its . . . aptitude to make blood rush to the head. Morphine works directly on the nervous plexus without activating or impeding blood circulation. But remember too that if you always take the same dose, whether opium or morphine, it is absolutely as though you took nothing at all" (Unpublished letter, Bibliothèque Victor Cousin, folio 397, Correspondance générale, vol. III).

at La Scala in widow's black for her dead marriage, she abruptly left for
her mother's country estate. Milan was the last place in the world she
wanted to be or be seen in. Neither frivolity nor conspiracy prompted her
to begin her travels. Medical care and distance from Milan's gossip led
her to the baths of Lucca and Ischia, and to the milder climate of Genoa.
In a long letter to Ernesta Bisi, written before her departure, she examines her entire situation, and reveals her strength of character as well as
her decency.

Borgo Vico
14 November 1828

Cara Ernesta! . . . My husband has not accepted the offer of reconciliation, or rather the condition I stipulated for such a reconciliation.
He proposed a hundred other solutions, all of which were intended to
keep me in his house and allow him to continue his relations with la
Ruga. These two things I declared mutually incompatible; however,
since my husband seemed truly unhappy over the total dissolution of
our marriage and begged me not to request the formalities of church
and law court, giving me at the same time his solemn word of honor
that my freedom would not be jeopardized by such a concession, I
was unable to maintain an obstinate refusal and accepted his promise
of a total separation but without legal intervention. I found nothing
better to reconcile the protection of my dignity with what my heart
asked. My husband was more than kind toward me, I would even
say affectionate; he did not stop offering me his friendship and asked
me to write to him. If I believed I owed it to my decorum and to my
title of wife not to ratify his relations with la Ruga, I nonetheless felt
I should not eliminate all possibility for a future though remote
reunion. Perhaps I was too weak, but I do not regret that weakness.
I am also of two minds, since the total dissolution of marital bonds is
compatible neither with our divine nor our human laws. Having
further arranged to pay my husband's debts, bit by bit, and without
a promissory note, I would always be able—should my husband try to
use his rights to force me into something disagreeable to me—to stop
payment for his debts and have my freedom granted. I will probably
leave for Genoa the first of December; I have already requested a
passport and have taken the necessary steps. I shall not go to Milan,
and will thus not see you for a long time. . . . Consider, my dear,
my absence from Milan may be a long one, perhaps longer than all
of you and even I imagine; a goodbye before I leave you for who
knows how long would be very precious to me!

November 1828 marked the Rubicon of her life. The decision to
separate, to leave Milan, family, friends, property, and to request a passport—this last, banal as it would seem, became a knot of Gordian pro-

portions—determined most of her later activities and misfortunes. Much of her future behavior can be explained by the intense deceptions she suffered between the ages of sixteen and twenty. Her marriage had been a disaster, and all the more so for one who, still fresh from its wounds, could write: "The vocation of us women . . . is to be good wives and good mothers of families. Whoever opposes this calling distorts the ways of nature and sooner or later regrets it. Vittoria [sister of her correspondent] should choose an honest man who will establish her . . . at the head of her own family, and who will charge her with the only duty which befits a woman, that of scattering flowers on the exhausting, difficult life of her companion." Far more serious than her wounded pride were her shattered illusions. Not only had her health been broken; not only had she not discovered love, physical or emotional, with Emilio; it was as though a part of her had been amputated by this dreadful experience. Her capacity for sharing love with a man had been nipped in the bud. The plant lived on, but without ever really flowering. Ten years later, she had a child with another man but, as will be seen, she did not discover with him the passionate love that might have healed the physical and psychological wounds which never ceased to inhibit her. She remained as aloof from desire as she became desirous of attention. Fearful of submitting to love, she nonetheless needed to know that she could inspire it.

Her decision to separate formally, though not legally, while maintaining amicable relations with Emilio for another decade, paying his debts, keeping an apartment for him in her Paris house, indicates a recognition of her own responsibility for their empty marriage. Considering how he had wronged her, her docility would otherwise be incomprehensible. She evidently realized that she had married him with as little love as he had for her; he was as much her means to self-discovery as she was his to self-indulgence. Had she loved him, faced with his infidelity at the outset of their marriage, she might have raged, threatened, tried to arouse his jealousy, or simply held fast in the knowledge that he was hers in the eyes of God and the law. She would not have left him, certainly not at that time or in that society; a husband's peccadilloes were as commonly tolerated as open separation was rare. The heart of the matter was not that he was unfaithful, but that the whole marriage was pointless; there was nothing to salvage. Had it been merely her wounded pride that motivated the separation, she would surely have expressed deeper resentment. Her long letter to Bisi of 1828, partially quoted above, expresses less outrage than an even-tempered examination of Emilio's attitude and her own position. In this light, Emilio almost appears to be less of a scoundrel than he actually was. A few years later, in France, cut off from her family and her fortune, she still maintained the same gentle tone when responding to Emilio's blissfully ignorant offer to purchase for her some jewels that had come up for sale: "I thought about the proposition you made regarding the jewels [the price was 40,000 lire], and though it might have suited me, I am too short at the moment to allow myself such luxuries as jewels. . . . I thank you for the interest you take in my health. It is passable. It may perhaps be true that physical well-being can often replace moral well-being. I experienced both at the same time; but both of them disappeared at the same moment, and therefore I cannot judge which of the two better compensates for the absence of the other. Adieu Emilio, live happily, and remember that my greatest consolation is to be useful to you. Your affectionate, Cristina." With a body as sick and a morale as crushed as hers were then, she had neither the energy nor the taste for recriminations. More than anything she needed dignified repose and distraction.

The combined effects of her marital and physical misfortunes flung her into all the makeshift compensations she could find. Seconded by her natural inclinations, she was led to a political apostolate that replaced father and husband; a commitment to social progress to rectify human injustice; an exalted practice of friendship to substitute for intimate relationships. Her later reputation as a tease, an *allumeuse,* as she was called by the biographers of the men she rejected, has to be understood in this context. The only one to have scratched the surface of her overchronicled flirtations was a minor writer, Benjamin Crémieux, who, in a light-hearted book with a frivolous title—*Une conspiratrice en 1830, ou le souper sans la Belgiojoso*—grouped her long-dead contemporaries around a dinner table and placed in Stendhal's mouth this sensitive appraisal: "Just as non-believers do not discourage their friends from going to mass, so la Belgiojoso delights in being surrounded by adorers who look at her believing in miracles. She does not yield to them, or as little as possible, but she takes the greatest care to fan their flame so as to warm herself when her heart is too cold."[12] What her rejected French suitors never understood was something Italianists like Stendhal and Crémieux did: the vivacity and directness of Italian women are an invitation to social, but not necessarily sexual intercourse.

2

Passport to Patriotism

ITALY IN 1828 was a mythical entity whose only unity lay in its configuration. Within the boot was a jigsaw of provinces each belonging to a different master, most of whom were not even remotely Italian. By blood, marriage, or alliance they were tied to Austria, so that in effect the whole of Italy was under Austrian domination. Italians—that is, native-born residents of each state, duchy, or kingdom—were obliged to present passports when traveling from one state to another, and in some cases from one city to another within the same state (for example from Milan to Venice, although both were Austrian provinces). Thus when Cristina decided to leave Milan, ruled by Francis I in Vienna, and go to Genoa, ruled by Charles-Felix in Piedmont, she had to apply for a passport since she was in fact going to a foreign state. This routine application turned out to be Pandora's box, containing not only the confusion that reigned over Italy, but the troubled events of Cristina's future.

To understand the magnitude of this imbroglio one has to look back a few years to the French invasions of 1786 and 1801. Napoleon, leading his revolutionary armies across the Alps, founded the first kingdom of Italy. His new geography erased the ancient boundaries drawn by foreign invaders who had carved the peninsula into feudal states. And what the foreigners had not taken, the Church continued to hold in its Papal States. Under Napoleon, Italy was an independent kingdom attached to the French Empire, with its own constitution, its own ministries (war, foreign affairs, education, and so on), its own legislative and judiciary bodies, and its own capital. The new kingdom bestowed a new consciousness of nationhood on a dismembered people, something the French were historically qualified to impart. Napoleon, himself of noble Tuscan origin and not just a Corsican upstart, was eager to sharpen the edge of Italian nationalism as a weapon against the Austrian eagle. When Milan

became the capital of his short-lived kingdom it also became the foun-
tainhead of modern ideas and, inevitably, of political discord.

Stendhal, an eyewitness, traced the history of those first years in *The
Charterhouse of Parma,* as accurate as any textbook and far more enjoyable. "The departure of the last Austrian regiment marked the fall of old
ideas: to expose one's life became fashionable . . . it was necessary to
love one's country and to seek heroic actions."[1] The miracle of French
bravery had awakened a people forced into somnolence by the Spanish
conquest of 1535 and kept anesthetized for over two centuries by the
Austrian heirs of Charles V. To assure this torpor Austria carefully kept
Lombards out of the imperial army: a conquered people are best held in
check by the conqueror's army.

In the first of her three histories of this period,* Cristina pointed out
that initially Italians were distrustful of French promises; they accepted
the doctrines of 1789 merely as philosophical and juridical abstractions.
Such ideas were beyond the people of Italy and dangerous to its social
health. But the first taste of freedom, which lasted only until the French
defeat at Cassano in 1799, had created an appetite. To all but Napoleon-
haters—and there were many among Italian aristocrats—the thirteen
months of Austrian reoccupation were unbearable. When Napoleon returned to Milan on June 2, 1800, twelve days before his triumph at
Marengo, whoever was young in age or thought, whoever wished to
explore new ideas and expose the superstitions inculcated by an ignorant
clergy, recognized that to become French meant more than to cease being
Austrian. For fifteen years Milan blossomed under Napoleon's viceroy,
Eugène de Beauharnais.† All that was trampled at Waterloo. The Allies,** on restoring Lombardy and the Veneto to Austria, unleashed a
more ferocious tyranny than Lombardy had ever known. Austria was determined to extinguish the last flicker of nationhood that had been kindled
in Milan.

In all three studies devoted to the history of modern Italy, Cristina
tried to analyze the events and resulting behavior of her compatriots with
the insights of a psychologist. She was only a child during the Napoleonic period, but she grew up among those who had lived it and herself
experienced its aftermath. It thus seems appropriate to sketch this era
from her own views, many of which were firsthand. The immediacy of
the events described is enhanced by her statement of the first book's
purpose: "Each day carries off one of the men who took part in the

---

* Published anonymously, as were all her books until 1850.

† On marrying Josephine, Napoleon adopted her son Eugène and daughter Hortense,
later queen of Holland and mother of Louis-Napoleon, future emperor of France.

** The Allies, so called in their joint fight against Napoleon, were England, Royalist
France, Austria, and the Holy See.

dreadful scenes of those years. Most of those witnesses carry with them the secrets they possess and to which history is entitled. This is why, casting aside any personal considerations [for her own safety] I hasten to gather together my memories and those of my contemporaries so as to prepare this material for future historians of Italy."[2] She was thirty-eight when she published this work, old enough to evaluate the preceding three decades of her country's agony under Austria.

Not all Lombards saw Austria as the enemy. There were the "pure pro-Austrians," whose only concern was to erase the memory of Napoleon. There were "mixed pro-Austrians," for whom Austria's peacekeeping mission in Europe seemed the best safeguard of Italy's interests. And there was the "Italian" party, composed of would-be liberal aristocrats, so jealous of their privileges they became unwilling allies of the Austrians. These willy-nilly pro-Austrians had one common hatred, the French, and one common fear, the people. "The plebe was a cage of wild beasts ready to devour them if its yoke was even slightly lightened."[3] They abhorred the French doctrine that education of the people is the sacrosanct duty of the cultivated classes, viewed the propagation of scientific studies as certain to incur the wrath of God, and scorned the acquisition of titles and honors by those not born to them.

On June 12, 1814, all the internecine squabbling came to an end. A proclamation informed the "people of Lombardy, the states of Mantua, Brescia, Bergamo and Cremona, [that] a happy fate awaits you; your provinces have been definitively reintegrated into the Austrian empire. You will remain united and protected under the scepter of the very august emperor and king Francis I, adored brother of his subjects, desired sovereign of the states that have the honor of belonging to him." By the end of the summer Austria had abolished every ministry, every independent governing body, and placed all power in the hands of the regency. In August 1815, with the creation of the Lombardo-Venetian kingdom, under the emperor's brother as viceroy, a few thought that independence might be in sight. It was, however, merely an Austrian tactic to lull them. Laws promulgated from 1815 on encouraged denunciation, even by doctors, of any manner of crime. "The spirit of the eighteenth century disappeared, and the clergy returned as powerful as under the Spanish domination."[4]

After 1815, Lombards suffered as never before "the intolerable weight of the chains" placed on them. Still impassioned fifty years after those events, Cristina wrote of that bitter time, "Civil and political liberties are so great a good that it sufficed to have glimpsed them in the future and merely hoped for them, for it to become impossible to forget or renounce them. Of such liberties Italians had experienced only the hope. Only the right to speak of them had been thus far granted, so that when the Austrian and Bourbon rulers proscribed the magic word and revealed themselves as the incurable tyrants they are, were, and always will be, Italians felt, perhaps for the first time, the intolerable weight of their chains, cursed them, and readied themselves for the noblest sacrifices in order to break them."[5] It was then that Federico Confalonieri, one of the leaders of the Italian party, transferred to Austria the hatred he had earlier harbored against France.

The year of Napoleon's exile to St. Helena, Italy was once again dismembered. The House of Savoy became master of Piedmont, Genoa, and Sardinia*—this last providing it with the name of Kingdom of Sardinia. Lombardy and Venice were reduced to provinces of the Austrian empire. Parma and Piacenza became a duchy for the emperor's daughter, who "betrayed her husband when he was betrayed by fortune and the Allies."† Modena and Reggio (Emilia) were ruled by an Este duke who was half Austrian. Tuscany was restored to its duke, nephew of the Austrian emperor. And Rome, no longer a French *département*, was once again "the fief of Saint Peter's successors who had nothing saintly about them." Naples, having barbarously assassinated the Napoleonic king, Murat, after his attempt to regain his throne, "offered its bloodied hands to the royal couple Ferdinand and Caroline, a couple truly worthy of that lurid homage." Like the rest, they were also Bourbons, related to the emperor and maintained on the throne by Austrian troops. "Italy once again descended into its sepulcher."[6]

Piedmont, guardian of Italy's natural borders on the north, ruled by the only Italian dynasty on the peninsula, and with the best army on Italian soil, was determined to remain Italian. Victor Emmanuel I, alas, was not the man to carry the torch of nationalism. "His head was in the eighteenth century and his heart was with Austria"; he was furthermore married to an Austrian princess.[7] The liberals of Piedmont, hoping to extend their banner to all of Italy and realizing that civil liberties had to be introduced into the kingdom, sought a constitution. On assuming the crown restored by the Allies, Victor Emmanuel had promised never to grant such reforms. His liberal subjects, determined to sacrifice neither royalty to liberty, nor liberty to royalty, were forced to wait for better times while their king restored all the rituals of court and church that accompanied absolute monarchy. The year 1821 saw the liberation of Greece from four hundred years of Ottoman rule, the institution of a constitutional monarchy in Piedmont, and the renewal of hope in northern Italy. Preferring to abdicate rather than submit to pressure for re-

---

* After Waterloo, England decided that Sardinia should be joined to the crown of Piedmont as a safeguard against any future French invasion.

† Napoleon had married Marie-Louise after divorcing Josephine, in the hope of producing a legitimate royal heir to his empire.

forms, Victor Emmanuel had yielded the throne to his brother, Charles-Felix, then in Modena. In the absence of the new king, his nephew Charles-Albert, of the Carignano branch of Savoy, was appointed regent. On the day of his appointment, March 2, 1821, he granted the constitution so long desired. It was an illusory victory, for Charles-Felix, a despot of the same temper as his brother, had three hundred thousand Austrian bayonets at his disposal only too ready to squelch any claims from his liberal subjects. Instead of assuming the leadership of a united liberal movement which had placed its faith in him, Charles-Albert weakly yielded the throne to his uncle and rescinded the constitution, thus sealing the fate of Italy for another generation.

Austria in the meantime had been cleaning her Lombard house with fearsome thoroughness. In 1820 the *Conciliatore* was suppressed and Silvio Pellico,* the noted dramatist who had been its prime mover in collaboration with Confalonieri and Porro, was arrested as a Carbonaro. The governor of Lombardy declared the Carbonari dangerous to the state and threatened dire punishment if citizens did not denounce people and facts relating to it. The secret society of Carbonari† (which numbered Byron among its distinguished members), dedicated to constitutional government and the expulsion of foreign rulers, had gained an important foothold in Naples under Murat's protection. (Though himself a foreigner, Murat had upheld civil liberties and had been as inimical to Austria and to the temporal power of the Vatican as the Carbonari.) In 1820 they succeeded in obtaining a constitution from Murat's Bourbon successor, Ferdinand. With fifty thousand Austrian troops dispatched to him, Ferdinand soon regained control and set out to destroy the society. The constitution granted by Charles-Albert a few months later was to have been the springboard for an insurrection organized by the Carbonari of Lombardy and Piedmont, who counted on Charles-Albert to lead his army to Milan and integrate Lombardy into the Kingdom of Sardinia. The conspiracy was betrayed by an agent provocateur in Milan, and Austria began a veritable purge. The Federazione was decapitated; Confalonieri and its other leaders were sentenced to Austria's most dreaded prison, Spielberg. The remaining Carbonari, now scattered throughout Europe like errant knights, tried to keep the faith alive. Austria would one day be evicted, but in the meanwhile she kept Lombardy under her imperial heel by considering any innovation—gas lamps, steam navigation—potentially seditious. The Church, her stanchest ally, also sought to

---

* Later to write *Le Mie Prigioni,* the account of his incarcerations in Austrian prisons from 1820 on. The book, published in 1832, became famous throughout the world.

† La Carboneria took its symbolic name from *carbone,* coal, which ignites into a brilliant flame. The Lombard Carbonari called their organization La Federazione, which was headed by Confalonieri.

stamp out every ember of nationalism. Any notion of a united Italy, however embryonic, was an inevitable threat to the secular hold of the Church. The divisive effect of foreign domination was thus the Vatican's surest weapon against a federation of Lombardy and Piedmont. No movement for Italian independence could survive under multiple sovereignty.

A YEAR BEFORE Cristina decided to leave Milan, her stepfather had requested a passport for the south of France in the hope that a change of climate might alleviate his depressed condition. The request went all the way to the emperor. For Francis I considered it his imperial duty to protect the moral health of his subjects, and especially of such noble deviationists as former friends of Confalonieri. Any departure was thought to be unsalutary, but a trip to France, the Babylon of seditious ideas, was pernicious. Not only was the request denied; the governor of Lombardy was instructed not to grant a passport for *any* destination to Visconti or his wife, whose relationship with Count Sant'Antonio had whispered its way to Vienna. Evidently no one in that family was morally dependable, not even young Cristina, who had married a gambling, wenching Carbonaro.

The emperor was zealously aided by his chief of police in Milan, Torresani (as relentless as Hugo's Javert in *Les Misérables*), who kept subjects in check by denying them any freedom of movement. In her *History of Lombardy,* Cristina depicts this form of persecution through reconstructed dialogues between Torresani and his supplicants. To someone requesting a passport to France for the pleasure of travel, she has Torresani reply: "You will not take it amiss, sir, that since your proposed trip has no better justification, I deny the passport." And to someone claiming business in France, he says: "I do not see that your business there is so important or your presence so indispensable. You can send a power of attorney." Cristina knew very well that nothing was to be gained from approaching Torresani, and consequently made her request directly to the governor, Count Strassoldo. Perhaps to avoid suspicion, both Belgiojosos applied, although they had separated and had no intention of leaving Milan together. On November 28, 1828, Strassoldo's office routinely issued the passports, which also granted the princess permission to travel without her husband.

On December 1, Cristina left for Genoa from her mother's country estate, Affori, without even stopping in Milan for goodbyes. She was making a clean break with the past four years and with everything related to that shattering marriage. A few days later, gossip was rife in le Tout-Milan over the reasons for her sudden departure. Had she delayed it by so much as a week, she might not have been able to leave. Fortunately, Torresani did not learn of her passport or her departure until she was outside Lombardy's borders. Police reports, received ten days later in Vienna, suggested that she and her mother, both enamored of Sant'Antonio, had planned a tryst in Naples. The reactionary society of Milan, possibly encouraged by an offended relative who had planned a match between Cristina and her own son,* conjectured that Cristina's relationship with Bisi and with Emilio's Carbonaro friends had led her to some political adventure. Torresani, furious that she had gone over his head and yearning to punish her, unleashed the spies whose grotesque reports were to crisscross Europe for years to come.

As yet unaware of the consequences of her act or of the companions prepared for her, Cristina became resigned to her lonely future within the first months of her new independence: "I am destined to live alone, isolated from my family," she wrote to a friend. She was only twenty, but she knew with prophetic certainty that this was no passing melancholy. The wounds Emilio had inflicted on her were incurable. He had destroyed her belief in her own capacity for happiness. Her girlish idealism had been mocked by a cynical society and by a husband for whom pleasure was the only criterion in life. Years later, she said: "I can detach myself from the past because I suffered in it as I hope never again to suffer." A few days after her arrival in Genoa, she wrote a letter of profound disillusionment to the son of a family retainer, about to be ordained: "To live in the midst of the world and remain unlike it is harder than anyone can believe who has not experienced it. But I have seen the world, I have more than seen it. Alas, I was not just a simple spectator. . . . We are not made for truth and falsehood at the same time. Bit by bit, we tire of the coldness we discover in what we once found ardent and glowing."[8]

On her arrival in Genoa, the third of December, she was warmly greeted by the city's society, many of them originally from Milan or related to Milanese families. One of her hostesses and a great Italian patriot, Marchese Teresa Doria, providentially introduced her to a notary, Barnaba Borlasca, who became Cristina's general factotum. Two years later he proved his ingenuity and devotion when her safety was at stake. In Genoa, Cristina felt free; she was not bothered by malicious gossip, there was nothing to remind her of the past. Her health was poor,

---

* Giorgio Trivulzio, Cristina's cousin. The story was still around in 1838 when Liszt was in Milan, for he wrote her: "I know you were happily deprived of conjugality with the elongated marquis."

the treatments ineffective, but her morale had improved. "Being no longer surrounded by people whose judgment of me was as unjust as it was unfavorable, whose minds were completely and wholly inclined to find malicious interpretations of whatever I did, contributes in no small way to making me lose that haughty reserve which was displeasing in the past," she wrote Bisi. Always objective, even about herself, she recognized that her sorry situation was one to inspire an unfavorable first impression. Where in Milan she saw herself judged irrevocably—"A woman separated from her husband probably does not deserve a place in the memory of such irreproachable people as the Manzonis,"* she told Bisi in bitter explanation of their silence—in Genoa, she felt that any initial prejudice against her was alterable. "Since I recognize the reasons for this perhaps unjustifiable but understandable prejudice, I can . . . undertake with courage and good humor to dispel it. So far, I think I have succeeded among people I know and this happy success encourages me."[9] She surely aroused more sympathy than aversion. Even the governor of Genoa, Count Venanson, in an official report, blamed her husband, "libertine to the last degree, [for] the state of health which afflicts her," and for his impression that she had little time left to live.

It is therefore doubtful that she engaged in any political activity in Genoa, for as late as March, four months after her arrival, she told Bisi that she was capable of no more than curling up in an armchair. Nonetheless, it was from this period that the first accusations against her were formulated. Her limited acquaintance with Bianca Milesi Moyon—a well-known Milanese liberal and former pupil of Bisi, eighteen years Cristina's senior—was enough to make her suspect. And the concocted testimony of an agent provocateur, who passed himself off as the Marchese Doria, was incriminating. Had the police spent more time investigating genuine evidence, they would have known from Cristina's letters that Bisi's old pupil was less appealing to Cristina than their teacher had hoped. Bianca was an ostentatious Jacobin and social climber all in one. However, in the simplistic thinking of the police, Bianca was a Giardiniera (the women's division of the Carbonari)†; she and Cristina were both pupils of another subversive; ergo, Cristina was also a Giardiniera. As to the charlatan Doria, on his arrest in 1831, the newly crowned king of Piedmont, Charles-Albert, recorded in French: "After a two-month pursuit, the swindler, Marquis Doria, has finally been arrested; a police spy who had himself accepted as a Carbonaro, he played both sides and

---

* Twelve years later, Alessandro Manzoni, author of the classic novel *I Promessi sposi*, offended her even more deeply by denying her entrance to his house, where his mother lay dying. He was punished for his bigotry by his children, who disgraced and neglected him.

† Two distinguished Giardiniere in Milan were Teresa Confalonieri and Mathilde Dembowski, Stendhal's great love.

did all the harm he could."[10] It was nevertheless spurious testimony of this kind that swelled Torresani's files and later substantiated proceedings in absentia against Cristina.

The year she traveled the length of Italy, 1829, was a year of great agitation among Italian liberals in all regions. The insurrection of 1831 was already fomenting and everywhere conspiracy was in the air. If foreigners then touring or residing in Italy noted this in their diaries, the police, with spies all over the peninsula, were equally well informed. Cristina most probably did not become a Giardiniera until her stay in Rome, but her contact with the notorious liberals and patriots who filled the ranks of Genoa's titled society was enough to place her under suspicion.

From the end of April to the end of May, Cristina discovered Rome. "The city, its inhabitants, resemble no others. In Rome one is not half-cultured; here local history is universal history," she reported enthusiastically to Bisi. Her health, still poor, did not prevent her from enjoying the first world capital and political center of her experience. She was presented to Hortense de Beauharnais, former queen of Holland, whose salon was the very heart of conspiracy. The ex-queen, who assumed the title Duchesse de Saint-Leu, was pleased to welcome the daughter of her brother's old friends. Since Hortense's two sons were the only Bonaparte heirs, all Bourbon-haters centered their hopes on these two young men. Her salon became the general headquarters of Carbonaro activity as well as a sanctuary of Bonaparte memorabilia.

It was there that Cristina met the young Prince Louis-Napoleon, like her, twenty years old at the time. Twenty years later he was to cause her the last great deception of her life. It seems a curious destiny that every man she entrusted to fulfill her political dreams proved as disappointing as the man who betrayed her sentimental dreams. One after the other—Charles-Albert, Mazzini, Louis-Philippe, and finally Louis-Napoleon—they all failed to support Italy's liberation, or to achieve it. Italy's cause had become so much her own that their failure to accomplish her mission became a personal offense. It was in Rome, with Louis-Napoleon, that the cycle of her political life began, at a time when the future of Italy and the Bonapartes lay ahead. It was there that it ended two decades later when Mazzini's provisional government fell to French troops sent by Louis-Napoleon, newly elected president of the young French Republic.

Writing bitterly after that defeat, she sketched a portrait of this man who had betrayed his own past as well as her hopes. "Is it not the former prisoner of Ham . . . who still agrees to leave political prisoners in the fortress of Belle-Isle? Is it not he, who on every occasion refuses pardon or even hope of betterment to unfortunate captives? He has forgotten everything: his prison, his suffering, his ennui, his despair. I spent at that time a few hours in the sad room where he was confined, and remember only too well everything he said to me there. It was in Italy that I got to know this illustrious personage. He was with his mother, Mme la duchesse de Saint-Leu, whose graciousness everyone lauded but could not exaggerate. Very young at the time, Prince Louis already spoke of the duties that his name imposed on him. An ordinary life, he said, was not his fate, he had the obligation of maintaining the glory of his name, Bonaparte. Since nothing in his abilities justified such pretensions, I was considerably annoyed by these tedious repetitions; by not showing it, I hoped to reciprocate the attentions that [his mother] showered on me. So that when the wild escapades of Strasbourg and Boulogne circulated around the world* I was among the few who were not surprised, but did not boast of my former relations with the pretender."

Cristina's Roman stay in 1829 was well spent. Her political initiation did much to raise her spirits; her mind was stimulated by the people around her; their approval encouraged her self-assurance. By the time she reached Florence, on her return north after a long and apparently successful cure in Naples, she was confident about her ability to live alone in the world. Replying to the newly ordained priest, son of her mother's overseer at Affori, she says she will not go there or to Como during the summer: "Insofar as it depends on me, I shall keep myself at a respectful distance from Milan." In a later letter to the same correspondent, discussing moral and religious bigotry, she says about herself: "Falsehoods have never contaminated my lips, which entitles me in my view to state loudly and freely my way of thinking; it may well be erroneous, but in this case and at this moment I believe it to be just. Do not think me arrogant for speaking well of myself. I know how little I am worth, I know which and how many are my faults and do not try to conceal them, but at the same time, I do not believe in hiding the little good I find in myself."[11]

Florence, reputed in 1830 to be the gayest of cities, especially by its foreign diplomats, found Cristina enchanting. Balls and amateur theatricals—in which she performed Shakespeare and Sheridan with the English colony—brightened her evenings. It was at one of those balls that Edmond d'Alton-Shée first saw her: "Amid the most elegant and most beautiful women I was struck by the apparition of a strange beauty. Her red and black gown was simple and unusual; fine black hair, naturally waved and unadorned, the broad forehead of a young Faust, heavily drawn brows, the large wide-spaced eyes of an ancient statue, a mysterious

---

* Louis-Napoleon twice attempted to seize the throne of France and was imprisoned in the fortress of Ham following his aborted coup at Boulogne.

expression—all this gave the upper part of her face a quality of severity and seriousness. While the perfection of the nose, the delightful smile and the appeal of a dimpled chin revealed feminine grace in all its charm. . . . She was barely twenty and seemed to be living for the second time. I asked her name: Princess Belgiojoso. Seeing her surrounded by Lord Normanby, comte de la Rochefoucauld, and other notables, I gave up the idea of being presented to her."[12]

A short while earlier, on arriving in Milan, d'Alton-Shée had informed the French consul that he wanted to meet Prince Belgiojoso, to whom he had a letter of introduction. "Young man," the consul exclaimed, "beware of making so dangerous an acquaintance; the prince is a don Juan"[13]—which sent him running to the Belgiojoso palace the very next morning. Ten years younger than Emilio, d'Alton-Shée was understandably drawn to the notorious roué. Long after he stopped carousing with Emilio, d'Alton-Shée remained his friend, which did not prevent a close friendship with Cristina as well. His memoirs, published forty years after his meeting with the Belgiojosos, at the end of a long career in diplomacy and government, convey his exuberant first impressions of them and their era.

Aside from the appeal of its social life, Florence was a safe asylum for exiles from other Italian states. The Duke of Tuscany, secure in his power, could afford to be hospitable to refugees and spies alike. Since everyone conspired freely in Florence, it was only natural that other states should send their spies to uncover the plots being hatched against them. The "center of disorder," in the lexicon of secret reports, was the bookshop and lending library of Pietro Vieusseux, a cultivated gentleman whose hospitality provided a meeting place for expatriates, conspirators, and the intellectual elite of the day. Writers, socialites, liberals came there more often to meet and read than to conspire, but in the eyes of secret agents, even the most innocent were guilty by association. Cristina's most subversive activity was probably her occasional visit to the Gabinetto Vieusseux. She did, however, see Napoleon-Louis, Hortense's older son, who had settled in Florence when declared persona non grata in the Papal States for his Carbonaro affiliations. When he died prematurely in 1831, Louis-Napoleon became the sole Bonaparte heir. This was Italy's great loss, for Louis-Napoleon's eyes, unlike his older brother's, were glued to the throne of France; Italy's future could be sacrificed to his own.

In March 1830, Cristina had her lapsed passport renewed by the Austrian ambassador to Florence, one of the pillars of Florentine society and one of Cristina's new friends. Another was Lord Normanby, a long-time resident of the city because of his differences with Parliament. With her passport validated for France and Switzerland, she arrived in Geneva in early May to establish political contacts for her exiled friends in Florence, and to seek medical care. One of the distinguished physicians of Geneva—a city highly respected for its medical facilities—was Dr. Jacob d'Espine, a friend of Lord Normanby and his neighbor in Carqueiranne, where they both had properties. The mild climate of this southern French village near Hyères, made it an ideal winter residence.

If Rome served as her initiation into Italian politics, and Florence as her novitiate, it was in Geneva that she acquired her first Weltanschauung. In Geneva, it was said, one could feel the pulse of Europe. When Cristina arrived, much of Europe's finest blood was throbbing there in exile. From France, Italy, Spain, Poland, Germany, and England, post-Waterloo outcasts, Bourbon-haters, modern thinkers who were later to forge the destiny of Europe, all assembled there. Suffering their anguish and sharing their hopes was the economist-historian Sismondi, around whom they gathered much as the liberals in Paris gathered around Lafayette.

Hoping to see her family again, Cristina left Geneva for Lugano, a short journey from Milan and an even shorter one from the family's villas near Como. At the end of July, in Bern, she applied to the Austrian envoy for an extension of the passport renewed in Florence so that she could spend the winter in Carqueiranne. She submitted a statement from Dr. d'Espine certifying her need for a warm climate. The envoy, finding nothing irregular about the request, not only extended the passport, but did so without limit of time or destination. On the Italian side, her mother requested a passport from Torresani for herself, her children, Ernesta Bisi and three of her daughters, and for the young priest with whom Cristina had been corresponding. Shortly after their festive reunion took place, remarkably unhindered by Torresani, Cristina wrote Bisi a nostalgic letter telling her that she planned to see her mother again in Genoa, and revealing her pitiable maturity.

> Your wonderful visit left me lonelier than I was before. How quickly one loses the habit of living alone. Despite a long novitiate of solitude, I cannot hide from myself that my life is a failure. I try to make good use of it, but fear I cannot fill it. Do not believe, however, that I have repented the momentous step that closed the doors of Milan to me. My situation today is the consequence of that first fatal and irremediable step which deprived me of every benefit and confronted me with an alternative of evils of which my present situation is the lesser. Surrounded by your large family . . . you do not know what it is to live with someone who does not appreciate you, or to be removed from every loving tie. . . . You said you found me improved, but in what? I have lost the freshness of ideas and feel-

ings . . . and what have I gained in return? Perhaps a bit of experience, but acquired at a heavy price.

This is one of the rare occasions on which Christina indulged in self-pity.
Her brief reunion with her family and friends had understandably made
her isolation seem greater once she waved goodbye, and her future
seemed as uprooted and as melancholic as her present. Just as she was
beginning to despair of any meaning to her life, fate provided some
distraction. Marchesa Visconti's passport application had stated the true
purpose of her trip—to see her daughter. In retrospect, this honesty
appears foolish, for it offered Torresani a fresh start in his persecutions
of Cristina. However, Vittoria Visconti was no scatterbrain. If she made
no attempt to conceal the purpose of her trip, it was because she knew
that her daughter's documents and her own motive were above suspicion.

Torresani also knew there was nothing irregular about Cristina's absence from Milan, but he took advantage of the appointment of a new
governor, Count Hartig, to revive an old grudge. In his letter to Hartig,
regarding Marchesa Visconti's request, Torresani recognizes that there is
no reason to deny the passport but does not see why the entire clan
should be allowed to accompany her to Lugano. He then comments on
Cristina's stay abroad in terms that would arouse the suspicions of the
most lenient Austrian official. Why should she be in Lugano, whose "only
distinction is that of a meeting place for exiles of all nations and a
breeding ground for revolutionary machinations"? For this reason he
claims to be anxious about her presence there, uncertain furthermore that
she is "legally outside the Austrian state, since she did not obtain her
passport through [his] office."[14]

This insinuation, willfully slanderous, was the most damning of all,
since to be illegally absent from the state was a crime tantamount to
treason. In his report to Hartig's recently deceased predecessor, Torresani
had acknowledged Cristina's intention to remain abroad because of ill
health, and to go to Lugano. There was no mention of illegality then.
But Strassoldo was dead; Torresani could safely assume Hartig would
not bother checking into a routine passport case. By questioning the
legality of Cristina's passport, Torresani hoped to secure all power in
Milan for himself. How could he assure the surveillance of Austrian
subjects if passports were issued indiscriminately outside his jurisdiction?

For the next eighteen years, despite the intervention of Austria's ambassador to France, of Metternich himself, of imperial amnesties, of
medical certificates, Torresani persisted in maintaining that Cristina was
illegally outside the Austrian state, which allowed him to defame her
morally and politically. She was perhaps his favorite victim, but he was

similarly hostile to much of the Lombard aristocracy, which he considered so decadent as to be seditious out of vanity or cupidity. Fortunately, Hartig and his superiors, true aristocrats themselves, had a more deferential view of their Lombard peers.

The society Cristina frequented in Lugano provided Torresani with unhoped-for ammunition. The first week of September 1830 saw the peaceable ratification of a new constitution in the canton of Ticino, which guaranteed freedom of the press and assembly, enlarged the number of representatives to the Council, and provided for the election of a president. Hardly a nightmare of revolutionary excesses, especially in a confederation that had long ago instituted democratic processes. But the Swiss canton of Ticino, Italian in language and customs, bordered on the Austrian province of Lombardy; and Lugano, its major city, was on a lake that lay half within the borders of Lombardy. Any reforms enacted in Lugano, within shouting distance of Lombard ears, were too close for comfort. When Cristina gave a ball in honor of the new Council, it was viewed as a public affront to the Austrian viceroy. Letters were hastily dispatched by Austria's spies in Lugano to Milan and Vienna, as though the empire depended on Cristina's ball. One of these dispatches, written from Lugano three days later, reveals the tone and optic of their writers: "The many silly things [le tante sciocchezze] that Prince Belgiojoso's wife has always done and continues to do abroad during her travels now warrant some consideration, quite apart from the salutary principle for any government of preventing the rich from squandering their money in foreign countries. Princess Belgiojoso is a madcap [una pazzarella] who would do better to stay home in Milan instead of running around abroad making herself ridiculous, compromising herself perhaps, and compromising others."[15]

For a princess, and above all an Austrian subject, to be friendly with such notorious liberals as Giacomo Luvini, the new Council President, implied a threat to the empire. Hartig himself, otherwise conciliatory and gentlemanly, felt that this time the princess had gone too far. She was openly manifesting her solidarity with Austria's enemies, and at a time when Austria began to feel the hot breath of liberalism on its neck. France's July revolution was barely three months old and quivers of hope were felt throughout Italy. On Lombardy's northwestern borders Charles-Felix, an autocrat of the old school for whom the Napoleonic occupation was a nightmare to be forgotten, and a stanch Austrian ally, was dying. Rumors were about that the monarchic liberals of Piedmont looked to Charles-Albert once again—still unforgiven by his uncle for his rashness in 1821, yet nonetheless heir apparent—as an enlightened monarch who might finally grant the constitution that had been withdrawn nearly a decade before. Austria felt it was therefore time to shorten the reins and return this extravagant filly of a princess to the security of Milan.

The provincial delegate of Como, Fermo Terzi, by chance on legation business in Lugano, was instructed to advise the princess that her passport had lapsed and that she was to return to Milan within the week. When Terzi called on her and announced his business, she at once presented her up-to-date passport. He retreated so quickly he never mentioned the order to return. The dishonesty of the allegation was of little importance. *L'Affaire Belgiojoso,* as it was known in official files, proved the necessity for extreme measures. For without the careless validation of her passport she would now be sitting at home in Milan under Torresani's watchful eyes, instead of flaunting her contempt for Austria.

Terzi admitted in his subsequent report to Hartig that he had found it useless to tell her to return to Milan. She was nonetheless considered contumacious: she had implicitly disobeyed a formal order. For Torresani this was a victory. He was now free to construct his scenario: not only was she illegally absent, she refused to return when ordered to, thus revealing herself an enemy of the state who had left in the first place to conspire against it. If he alone authorized passports, such things would never happen. Hartig, less touchy in his official pride, informed Metternich, with a cavalier ten-day delay, that not having obtained her return to Milan he did "not regret to see her elsewhere than amid our refugees." For Cristina, not at all reassured by her triumph over Terzi, had precipitously left Lugano for Genoa two days after his visit. With remarkable intuition, she informed Ernesta Bisi the very day of Terzi's visit, October 22, that her situation was precarious. Telling her that she could no longer extend a previously discussed loan, she added: "I cannot explain, but in a short while I fear you will know why I am reduced to such very tight circumstances." If one can extrapolate from the various events, it would seem that her intention to spend the winter in Carqueiranne was part of her plan to expatriate to France. This would have required financial arrangements before her departure, which explains Cristina's projected meeting with her mother in Genoa, announced earlier to Bisi. All her foresight could not tell her how little time she had.

Metternich did not take Terzi's fiasco, or Cristina's arrival in Genoa, as casually as Hartig. In subsequent documents, Hartig's tolerant adjective "extravagant" was replaced with Metternich's "indecent" and "scandalous." From the moment he received Hartig's report, orders began to fly. To the Austrian legations in Florence and Bern orders were sent never to renew the passport of a subject except for his re-entry to the Austrian states. To the legation in Turin, instructions were sent requesting Charles-Felix's Ministry of Foreign Affairs not to grant the princess a

visa to leave Piedmont's borders, and to keep her under surveillance
"with the discretion due her rank." At the same time Hartig sent an
order to the consuls of other Italian states in Genoa to deny her a visa for
anywhere but Milan, since her passport had lapsed. Untrue, of course.
The trap was laid. She could not leave Genoa without a visa and no
consulate would issue her one.

Cristina decided to wait for her mother in Genoa, confident that she
would obtain a visa when she was ready to leave for France. Two weeks
later, on November 13, a major police operation rounded up a large
group of political undesirables, including Mazzini, in an attempt to break
a Carbonaro network. This event, following so soon after Terzi's visit,
caused Cristina to hasten her departure. On November 15, unable to
imagine the web spun for her, she applied for a visa to Nice (until 1860
part of the Sardinian kingdom), leaving her passport with the Genoese
police. Even today, no one short of a criminal under threat of extradition
would suspect that an independent state might confiscate the passport of
a foreigner. The Genoese police, however, were so notoriously corrupt
that Charles-Albert, on acceding to the throne, revamped the entire force,
knowing that it had even been in the pay of the French consul against
him. Orders were so explicit that once Cristina's passport was confiscated
it was handed over to the Austrian consul, who in turn sent unequivocal
directives to the governor of Genoa. Count Venanson, so solicitous during her first stay in Genoa, was now obliged to give orders that no post
horses be rented to her and that guards be placed at her door. But he was
first of all a gentleman. Preferring not to have to stop her, or worse still
arrest her, he had her notified of the measures taken.

Still hoping to outwit Austria, and doubtless to gain time until her
mother's arrival, Cristina informed Venanson's emissaries that if her
Austrian passport was not valid enough to insure her freedom of movement, she had another whose validity could not be questioned—a Swiss
passport from the canton of Ticino, to which she was entitled by ancient
right of the Trivulzios. Venanson, though sympathetic, could not let her
embarrass him in the function of his duties. Ordering the border guards
in Nice not to let her pass, he warned her that she would be arrested at
the frontier if she attempted to cross it. Not only was she trapped in
Genoa, she was told that if Austria managed to lay hold of her she might
be sent to a convent. Given the alternatives, no risk seemed too great.

On November 17 she was at home discussing her situation with her
notary, Barnaba Borlasca. Without advising her servants and with only
the clothes on her back, she and Borlasca left the house by way of an
unguarded exit. They were nonetheless followed a moment later, as we
learn from Borlasca's letter written to Cristina a few days later. "Even
now, if I think of that accursed man with the umbrella . . . I have

palpitations!" He escorted her to Bianca Moyon's house, notified her servants that she had gone to the country for a few days, as she often did, and had a bag packed for her with the necessities of a short stay. The cash she had in her desk he brought to Bianca, who changed it for gold. That night, in a coach he had hired, Cristina left for Nice with her maid and a lawyer friend of Borlasca's. At noon on the nineteenth she reached the Piedmont bank of the Var, where a relative of Borlasca's met her. While he concocted plans with yet another member of Borlasca's mafia of liberal lawyers—Daideri, by name, owner of property on the French side—Cristina rested in a sordid inn. At nightfall, cautiously avoiding the bridge guarded at either end, Daideri waded across the river with Cristina on his back.

It was an escape worthy of Dumas and in itself fabulous enough to make a heroine of her without the fake memoirs of Boulenger's "marquis de Floranges." Perhaps it was this picaresque adventure that led Parisian writers to romanticize her life. Though not recounted by her early biographers,* it surely circulated among her friends and doubtless inspired the young journalists who fabricated serials for a living. What they later held against her was that her private life was so pale, which may account for the caricatures of Théophile Gautier and other disappointed hotbloods.

Borlasca's letters contain the inventory of the scant possessions he managed to send with friends: two shawls, five winter dresses, a pearl necklace, a few other jewels, a case of music, two trunks of clothing. Cristina's servants were prevented by the police from leaving Genoa in order to punish the mistress who had slipped through their fingers. Much harder to transmit than personal effects was money. After deducting the expenses of her stay in Genoa and her trip to Nice, Borlasca had only 4,000 lire left to send her. He reported to her the exact terms of Austria's injunction against her departure for France: with her "exalted brain," and her "great pecuniary means," she could "facilitate relations between the government's enemies." She knew that Austria would not leave her escape unpunished. For the moment, news traveled slowly. It took ten days for her flight to be discovered in Genoa. It would take five months before the punishment was proclaimed.

CRISTINA ARRIVED in Carqueiranne with her salvaged possessions, no longer a house guest in need of a warm climate, but a refugee in need of

---

* These details, first published by Malvezzi in 1936, were gathered from Borlasca's letters and the deposition of the maid, interrogated on her return to Italy.

a home. Dr. d'Espine, a fervent Methodist who divided his energies between medicine and the propagation of the faith, was a generous host and a compassionate friend. She could not have found a friendlier haven. Waiting to meet Cristina was another house guest, the distinguished historian Augustin Thierry, then considered one of the giants of the generation born under the Directoire. This man, called by Chateaubriand "The Homer of History," became for Cristina the "cher frère" of a twenty-five-year friendship. At twenty-nine locomotor ataxia crippled his body. Four years later progressive blindness condemned him to total infirmity. He never saw the beautiful young woman who befriended him during their stay under Dr. d'Espine's roof, but was immediately captivated by her intelligence, her wit, her sincerity. When they met in November 1830 he was thirty-five and she twenty-two, both already marked by the suffering that made them old beyond their years, and susceptible to a fraternal tenderness that awoke at once. Their chance encounter as guests of the same host was to affect Cristina's private destiny as much as her future vocation. The summer following his meeting with Cristina, Thierry went to a spa where a cultivated thirty-year-old spinster happened to be staying. An admirer of his works, she asked to meet him. Julie de Quérangel had spent her youth caring for an aged father. Her notion of contentment was to devote the rest of her life to this blind paralytic. Cristina, who became a sister to both of them, served as a witness of their twelve-year happiness together. When Julie died, Cristina assumed the responsibility of caring for him.

Thierry's six-volume history of the Norman conquest of England had established him, in 1825, at the center of a new approach to history. Using history's own materials—literature, official documents, social customs—he wanted to narrate rather than define, and thereby free history of the philosophical abstractions that the eighteenth century had imposed on it. He rejected Vico's method because it treated all national histories as though created in the image of Roman history. But it was nonetheless Vico who had led him to discover that the anonymous masses were more responsible for the destiny of nations than the traditionally celebrated gods or heroes. "The essential object of this history," he wrote in *La Conquête d'Angleterre*, "is to envisage the destiny of peoples and not just the destiny of a few famous men, to present the adventures of societal life and not those of the individual."[16] To do this, he used the optic of the sociologist and the techniques of the novelist. His true masters were not historians but Chateaubriand and Walter Scott, who had written literature as history, just as he would write history as literature. His attempt to give historical life to the unsung people of the past never lost its focus on the present, "for every new era gives to history new points of view and a characteristic form." As a writer, his influence was felt by all the Romantics; as a historian, he left an indelible mark, despite later differences, on Mignet, Michelet, Carlyle, and Renan (who had been his reader as well as his disciple). Thierry's influence on Cristina was truly formative. Through her contact with him and his acolytes, she was led to translate and explicate Vico, to attempt a fresh perspective of the heresies and countermeasures that formulated much of early Catholic dogma, and to examine her own national history from certain of Thierry's viewpoints.

The impact of Thierry's conviction that history is determined by the opposition of peoples to foreign subjugation or internal oppression is felt in her 1846 study of Lombard history, which tried to rouse Lombards from their apathy by showing them how Austria had subverted their will. And her articles on the 1848 rebellion in Milan, which seemed indeed to support Thierry's view, demonstrated that a people once aroused could rout an occupier's army. Certainly, the revolution of 1830, described by Michelet as "a revolution without heroes, without proper names [in which] society did everything," exemplified Thierry's argument. Those three days of July, without an army or a police force and without violence, promised to fulfill the ideals of 1789. This "revolution of historians," as it came to be known, succeeded largely because a newspaper, *Le National,* directed by Thierry's friends François Mignet, Adolphe Thiers, and Armand Carrel (his former secretary), had galvanized public opinion. Thierry's own experience as secretary to Saint-Simon had contributed to his interest in social evolution, which he in turn communicated to Cristina.

It was in this heady climate of new political institutions and social reforms that Cristina and Thierry talked under the winter sun of Provence. His idea that nationhood emerged from reaction to foreign occupation excited her imagination. If three days in Paris could rid France of Bourbon rule, then surely Lombardy could expel the Austrian tyrant. The new citizen-king Louis-Philippe, surrounded by such seasoned fighters for independence as Lafayette, would have to support Italy's cause against Austria—arch-symbol of autocracy and oppression.

Cristina, in that miraculous new year of 1830, encouraged by France's revolution and safe within her borders, could already envisage Charles-Albert on the throne of a federated kingdom, a constitutional king like Louis-Philippe or William IV of England. Filled with such ideas as Thierry's prediction of a federated Europe—"a time will come," he said, "when all the peoples of Europe will feel the need to settle problems of general interest before descending to national interests"—she, and many others, believed that an organized action by Italy would be sustained by

France. Her own disoriented existence suddenly had a purpose. "If I can be of some use to our cause," she wrote Bisi, "I shall never regret the life I have accepted, a hazardous, agitated, unfeminine life."

From Carqueiranne, she went to Marseille, where she spent the next few months in close contact with Italian exiles who had set up insurrectionary committees there and in Lyon. In early February, she engaged a refugee lawyer, recommended by her family, to serve as her secretary, as the function was called. Pietro Bolognini, then thirty-three, was descended from an old Emilian family. A Carbonaro at twenty-three, he had been arrested during the repressions of 1821, escaped from prison, and fled to France under the name of Bianchi, which remained his nom de guerre. When Cristina hired him, he was a member of the committee in Marseille and well placed to serve as her go-between. As a lawyer he was also capable of handling her financial affairs, thus serving as chaperone, attorney, and notary. In Genoa, Borlasca had served in this function, as had a retired army captain, Giovanni Beltrami, in Lugano, hired by Marchesa Visconti. In a period when the well-born handled no money and a lady made no direct contact with creditors or conspirators, such a factotum was both a necessity and a convention. Nonetheless, Torresani's spies reported Bianchi to be her lover—as they had Beltrami before him—and the real motive for her extended absence from Milan. There is not a scrap of evidence from her correspondence that Bianchi was any more than a trusted retainer, although he later turned that trust to his personal advantage.

JUST AS SHE was organizing her life for action, uprisings in Modena, ruled by the Austrian house of Este, and in Bologna, part of the Papal States, created a surge of excitement among the refugees who had flocked to southern France. Less than three weeks later, on February 22, an invasion force bound for Savoy began its march from Lyon, intent on substituting Charles-Albert for his reactionary uncle and liberating Lombardy under his banner. To their amazement, Louis-Philippe ordered the expedition stopped before it crossed the French border into Savoy, in pious respect for the principle of nonintervention promulgated some months before by his Foreign Minister, Sébastiani. This marked the death of the Carbonaro movement and the birth of Mazzini's Giovine d'Italia, an organization of young republicans completely divorced from the monarchic ideas and the leaders of 1821. For Cristina, this aborted insurrection was more than the first defeat of a budding activist. It was the beginning of serious charges by Torresani, no longer founded on her litigated passport, but on her contribution of 35,000 Austrian lire, officially magnified to the colossal sum of 60,000 francs (then equal to $16,500 and $34,000, respectively). To her previous contumacy was now added sedition, and a trial in absentia was opened in 1833.

Belief in France's support of this expedition was not just the pipe dream of an extravagant princess and her hotheaded friends. Lafayette himself contributed 5,000 francs, having gained the assurance of Laffitte, then Prime Minister, that it was in France's interest to have compatible states on her borders. France could not overtly aid such an expedition but she would not permit Austria to interfere, and would herself intervene with arms if necessary. The Minister of Justice, Dupont de l'Eure, had publicly stated: "Tell the Italians to act, all of France will rise up to succor them if need be." And even more striking, though less public, an agreement was signed by Lafayette and the Italian general La Cecilia, dated February 18, 1831, that Savoy would be annexed to France and Corsica would go to Piedmont after Charles-Albert's accession to the throne. Lafayette's authority to sign such a document may seem questionable; however, as commander of the National Guard it would have been within his power to overthrow Louis-Philippe and install a republic. Laffitte's cabinet fell just as the expedition set out. His conservative successor, Casimir Périer, took very seriously Metternich's threat that Austria would risk war rather than tolerate any revolutionary movement in Italy. And Louis-Philippe groaned, "If I cannot free myself of Lafayette's tutelage I will always remain a king *in partibus.*" This explains why Lafayette was relieved of his post as soon as the conservatives newly in power were able to vote a reform of the National Guard.

On March 15, Périer was installed as Prime Minister with Sébastiani retained as Minister of Foreign Affairs. France was tired of revolutions and wanted peace in Europe at any cost, including Italy's freedom. "French blood belongs only to France," Périer announced in his inaugural address. Lafayette, at once alarmed by the implication of this remark, asked if France had not declared, in view of the policy of nonintervention, that she would never consent to Austria's entry into the Italian provinces then in rebellion. Sébastiani's awkward reply made the situation clear: "France does not consent to Austria's intervention in Italy's affairs but does not oppose it." Ten days later *Le National* vehemently protested France's inertia.

> The Bolognese now know what to expect of the men in charge of France's destiny. . . . A government that does not want to commit suicide must never, under any circumstances, retreat from the principles that created it. The role of powerful mediator which the interests and dignity of France imposed on her cabinet, which could have been fulfilled without the expense of a cent or a soldier, was handed over to Austria.

General Zucchi, leader of the Provisional Government's Armies of the United Provinces of Emilia and Romagna, was unable to hold out alone against Austria's massive attack. Retreating to Ancona, he chartered a boat and made for Athens with 104 unarmed comrades. An Austrian warship commandeered the boat, threatening to sink it if all aboard did not surrender, and took Zucchi and his officers to Venice, an Austrian province. France stood by in flagrant violation of her own policy, to the unbelieving horror of her deputies.

In the bitterness and confusion that followed, Cristina had no choice but to return to Carqueiranne and try to formulate plans for her future. Perhaps urged by Dr. d'Espine, she considered settling in Geneva and even began negotiating for a property there. France had disappointed her, why remain there? On March 16, before news of the Périer cabinet had even reached her, she wrote to one of the leaders of the Savoy expedition: "I don't know where to turn. . . . Let us at least remember that we owe no gratitude to France and that she has helped us only when our ruin threatened her own. There is talk of a new government which would perhaps be worse than this one, except for the Minister of Foreign Affairs in place of whom anyone at all would still be preferable to Sébastiani." General Zucchi's capture provided her with a direction: Paris. France just then was not where she wanted to live, but only in Paris could reliable information be had, only there could help be obtained.

Imprisoned with Zucchi were friends of Cristina's, among them Count Terenzio Mamiani. Before leaving Ancona they had obtained French passports from the consulate, thus placing them, at least technically, under French protection. In Venice, Austria was free to hang them or imprison them for life in the dreaded Spielberg. Inflamed by the iniquity of this act and encouraged by Thierry, Cristina undertook the mission of liberating them. In the palm-shaded sunlight of Carqueiranne, with a blind paralytic as her guide, Cristina began her fateful odyssey. Her departure from Milan in 1828 had left the door ajar. On April 19, Torresani bolted the gates of Milan to her: if she did not return to Austrian states within three months, she would be faced with civil death and the confiscation of all her properties. Her family could not protect her, her rank provided no security. To be tried as a traitor was hardly an alternative.

WHILE IN MARSEILLE she had been able to receive money from Italy. In Carqueiranne, as Dr. d'Espine's guest after the debacle, she had not needed much. But in Paris, a princess seeking help for her country needed more than a cause and a title. She arrived at the end of March with a few hundred francs, a few personal effects, and Bianchi as her sole retinue. All she had of practical value was a letter of introduction from Thierry to François Mignet, recently appointed Director of Archives of the Ministry of Foreign Affairs, who had achieved great celebrity for his contribution to the July revolution.

March 26, 1831

I count on you to acquit my debt of gratitude toward a woman who has showered me with friendship in my exile, and to whom you can render important services. Mme la princesse Belgiojoso, Milanese, voluntary émigrée, has contributed her fortune and her activities to the Italian revolution. The dangers that today threaten the cause to which she has totally committed herself have determined her to come to Paris to see if she can be helpful to her compatriot refugees and if all hope of support on our part is decidedly lost. Placed as you are in the world of politics and close to the Ministry of Foreign Affairs, you would be able to help her and direct her, give her precise information on things and people, and place her in contact with persons whose counsel or protection she may judge necessary. In short, my dear friend, you will exercise for her the talent of divination: it is the only name I can give it. By that glance so steady and so wise with which you pierce the shadows of the most muddled political future, you will tell her what your forecasts are for the destiny of her country's freedom, so that she will be reassured if such is the case. For she despairs, grows bitter, accuses, and it is us she accuses with an intensity I understand, but which pains me. I do not speak to you of her charm and her wit; you will judge for yourself, and after talking with her it will no longer be for my sake that you wish to render her all the good offices in your power.

Mignet's response to Cristina exceeded Thierry's hopes; he fell in love with her. He at once introduced her to Lafayette, whose already inflamed sentiments made him eager to help. On April 12, Lafayette wrote Cristina a long letter confirming Zucchi's capture and assuring her of his support. A French courier had already left to protect Zucchi "from Austrian vengeance"; the Prime Minister had agreed to see him the next day "on behalf of our unfortunate brothers." And on April 13, in a highly emotional debate in the Chamber of Deputies, Lafayette stated sharply: "Must it be said once more that Monsieur le Ministre [Sébastiani] is understood to have declared to Austria that we will not consent to her intervention in the insurgent regions of Italy? That certainly meant something quite different from the interpretation given to it today!"[17] *Le National,* expressing all the accumulated outrage over this incident, published a scathing editorial two days later. In it, the French government was "loudly condemned" for not having sent its own vessels cruising near Rome to protect the insurgents, as they were instructed to protect the Pope and the cardinals in the event of Zucchi's victory. "Why, when Austria intervened in spite of France, did the ministers born under the July revolution not save some of their solicitude for those less powerful unfortunates?" At stake here was more than geopolitics; it was the very principle that had been fought for in 1789—the rights of man—and that the July revolution had determined to ratify forever. "Those men, the elite of the free cities of the Italian insurrection, were barbarously thrown into the hold of an Imperial Navy warship. . . . All of civilized Europe will refuse to believe that in the nineteenth century an assault could have been committed which violates both the rights of men and the laws that govern empires."

To understand Cristina's instantaneous celebrity in Paris it has been necessary to recall the events that preceded and accompanied her arrival. *Le National* and other leading papers published daily reports of Austria's iniquitous invasion; it was headline news for weeks. *Le National*, which had been instrumental in seating the present government, was in a singular position to influence public opinion. And it was *Le National*'s former editor, Mignet, who introduced Cristina to Paris. This striking young woman, herself now a victim of Austrian injustice, became as much a symbol of France's shame as of Italy's plight. The liberal Bavarian newspaper, *Die Augsburger Allgemeine Zeitung,* printed in large capitals for all of Europe to read: "The French . . . after priding themselves on inexhaustible resources and their principle of non-intervention, are obliged to admit that they have neither the army nor the courage to oppose an Austrian invasion in Italy." Hardly surprising that all the leading politicians in the new government, and all the important salons, were eager to receive her hospitably. It is comforting to acquit one's moral guilt through symbolic gestures.

Lafayette, fired by his sympathies for Cristina's cause and her personal misfortunes, used all his diplomatic skill to enlist Sébastiani's intercession with Metternich. Cristina seems to have charmed Sébastiani as well, for despite Lafayette's fiery oratory in the Chamber and Cristina's recent harangue before a closed session, Sébastiani wrote a very importunate letter to Metternich on May 8. "I dare hope you will allow her to remain in France," he said in closing, "without being exposed to the loss of her fortune through the confiscation of her property or the privation of her revenues through their sequestration. I attach great importance to this request, which I earnestly beg you to grant and which I hope to obtain from you as a personal favor."

On May 17, Metternich informed his ambassador in Paris, Count Antoine Apponyi, of Sébastiani's "very singular approach" by sending him Sébastiani's letter along with his own dispatch, and an appended "true history of the Princess Belgiojoso" since 1829 culminating in her participation in the recent Savoy expedition. "Once in Marseille, she surrounded herself with the large mob of Italian refugees who were spinning plots there against Italy's tranquillity. Mme de Belgiojoso became the heart of these intrigues and at the time of the invasion project of these refugees, foiled by the wise sternness of the French government, this Lady provided 60,000 francs for the expedition and, despite the failure of this enterprise, is known from reliable sources to be not at all discouraged." Far from exempting her from the punitive measures taken against her, Apponyi was instructed to "point out again in a fatherly way, the harm this senseless conduct does to these individuals themselves,* for they do none to the State which, in no way regretting the absence of a few madcaps, should be satisfied to see them far from their homes where their presence can cause greater harm than in a country where a few more factious characters do not matter." She was nevertheless summoned to return. It was the duty of His Majesty's paternalistic government to protect "an illustrious name from a criminal or shameful act," to which she would certainly be led by "her principles, her inexcusable behavior, and the class of people she has frequented and continues to frequent in Paris." Prince Belgiojoso was also recalled from the canton of Ticino, where "he cultivates his nullity and his democratic opinions." Sébastiani was quite willing to retreat from this hornets' nest once Apponyi showed him the documents; he had made his *grand geste.* It would take greater ingenuity than Sébastiani's for Cristina to be reprieved, and a new emperor before she was amnestied.

In the meantime, she settled into a modest apartment on the fifth floor of number 7, rue Neuve-St. Honoré (now rue Vignon), in sight of the Madeleine. Barely able to feed herself, lacking a servant to help with the simple chores that were utterly unfamiliar to her, she was a very humble princess. With the exalted drive characteristic of epileptics, she refused to borrow money, even from Lafayette, determined to endure every privation rather than submit to Austria's persecution. Her sympathizers were astounded by this young woman whose physical condition and upbringing were hardly suited to such hardships. Others found it ridiculous and called it posturing. Bianchi, who had other means of subsistence besides his secretaryship, was managing well enough to bring her gifts of food from time to time. But he had to resort to ruses to make her accept them, pretending that some friend had caught the fish or game he brought.

---

* Earlier in the letter Metternich had stated that her stepfather, Marchese Visconti, and her husband, along with a few others, were also illegally absent.

Whatever else she lacked, she was not lacking in company or invitations. Thierry's letter to Mignet had opened many doors in Paris, and Lafayette's interest provided her with his daily attentions. Only the ultra-faubourg Saint-Germain, then in mourning over its deposed king Charles X, looked askance at this impoverished princess whose credentials were unimpeachable, but whose friends were its enemies.

3

Paris c'est la France, la France c'est le monde

THE REVOLUTION OF 1830 turned Paris into the capital of the modern world. The court of the Sun King moved not to the Tuileries but to the Faubourg Saint-Honoré, where bankers now patronized the arts and bourgeois salons radiated new ideas. A constitutional monarchy incorporated the ideals of 1789, the press was free, the Chamber of Deputies guaranteed the rights of self-determination to other states with its new edict of nonintervention, pride of a bloodless victory swelled every heart. "The people, drunk with clemency, raised up the vanquished who in their turn, mute with admiration, forgave them their defeat."[1] For a brief moment, the irresistible beauty of justice conquered partisan hatred. Legitimist Bourbonites sulked in the Faubourg Saint-Germain, but on the Right Bank nobleman and commoner, shopkeeper and banker, embraced in the fraternal euphoria of a new era.

America's 1776, France's 1789, Greece's 1821, all resounded in Lafayette's constitution. The "Hero of Two Worlds" embodied the dynamism of Byron, the reason of Voltaire, the idealism of Rousseau. By 1832 the hero was considered an old nuisance; by 1834 he was no longer around to harass Louis-Philippe and his ministers. But for those who did not find in the citizen-king the fulfillment of their dreams, Lafayette's memory was kept alive in the salons, if no longer in the Chamber. To French dreamers were added the tens of thousands proscripted in Italy, Portugal, Spain, Germany, Hungary, Poland, Russia—liberal noblemen, idealistic warriors, censored writers—for whom France was a paradise after the tyrannies they had left, and who came to find the torch lit by Napoleon. It was they who fanned the flame after it went out in France, for each group was fired by its national mission which was brought to the new Parisian salons in the search for converts to the faith.

The graceful frivolities of the ancien régime were replaced by polemical discussions. An eyewitness to both societies lamented that "evenings at which political exiles were present necessarily centered around public affairs, and that was not amusing. If in that salon there were statesmen, it was even sadder. Those who participated in the government were so attacked by the newspapers and the Chamber of Deputies that they could not conceal their distress. The July monarchy was thus fatal to the amusements of the few [Restoration] salons that remained open."[2] Political agitation ran so high there were quarrels even at balls.

As idealism began to falter, materialism gained a foothold. "The only passion that remained was for money, to procure the material pleasures that take the upper hand when the spirit declines."[3] A disgruntled youth, denied the promised glories, sank deeper and deeper into melancholy and turned its thoughts to Gothic romances, Renaissance heroes, Napoleonic battles. Happiness was in another time, another place. The future seemed to have died with Napoleon.

The generation born around 1810, torn between political consciousness and the lack of opportunity for action, lapsed into hedonism after the Polish insurrection was quashed. Edmond d'Alton-Shée, close friend and coeval of Musset, and Emilio Belgiojoso's younger confidant, relates this moment in his memoirs: "My story, but for a few exceptions, is that of the leisure class of my generation. How many fell from their enthusiasm, their devotion to public work! A few, older, hostile to a retrograde king, became republicans in the cause of the people, socialists in the hope of a solution to misery. The others, descended from the heights of collective sentiment, rushed with an irresistible impulse into pleasure and sought in its unbridled pursuit the fulfillment of noble aspirations. One was in a hurry to live, heedless of ruin or death. Poets, composers, artists came to support our tendencies with an entire literature in our image, amusing, impassioned, evanescent, wafting like the smoke of their beloved cigars, inflaming the imagination like the alcohol they abused."[4] Polish counts, Italian princes, Spanish grandees deprived of their freedom but not their fortunes joined the ranks of this derailed youth that had retreated from the forum or the battlefield to the Café de Paris. The jeunesse dorée supplied the wine, the artists the entertainment. Hugo, Lamartine, Heine, Musset offered poetry of sensuality and irony; Balzac, Dumas, and Sue brought heroes of infinite vitality and occasional melodrama; Hoffmann added fantasy more real than reality. Rossini contributed his subtle laughter that concealed tears; Bellini, tears of stifled heroism; and Pasta, Malibran, Mario, Rubini, Nourrit sang their golden spell. Rachel, Marie Dorval, Lemaître rekindled the tragic embers left by

Talma. Paganini, Liszt, Thalberg, Chopin provided magical sounds never heard before. There was no energy left for action. The senses reeled from one orgy to another. A new world was born.

The revolution of 1830 proved to be politically sterile, but it did generate a literary revolution that was immensely fertile. The academies were the only remaining link with tradition; each writer now created his own language, his own grammar, his own prosody. The revolution of 1830 was as much a revolution of mores as of literature. Arsène Houssaye —man of letters, director of the Comédie Française, Inspector-General of Works of Art—whose life spanned the near-century from 1815 to 1899, was a scintillating chronicler of his time. In his *Confessions d'un demi-siècle,* a compendium of fact and gossip about the great and small of his time, he traces the evolution of this epoch:

> Since reason never advances without money, the bourgeoisie was a greater threat to the nobility than the people, and the nobility would have been suffocated if it had not replenished its empty coffers with the riches of the nouveaux-riches, whose daughters provided the means to polish their tarnished escutcheons. And so in the absence of powdered wigs, a new style of long hair appeared, symbolic of a disheveled soul; the measured step of the minuet was replaced by the dizzying waltz. *L'homme fatal* was born, endowed with a power of imagination greater than the noble sword, whose fiery eyes and tormented passions found a new heroine in the spectral figure arisen from Gothic crypts, floating in marble whiteness, her black hair framing the mysterious dark eyes that reflected an inner devouring flame.

Needless to add, Cristina was the heroine he had in mind, as Musset was the hero—both of them major figures in his memoirs.

At this same time a new institution came into being, the salon of the "femme politique." Each was dominated by a statesman: at the comtesse de Castellane's, Molé; at the princesse de Lieven's, Guizot; at Mme Récamier's, Chateaubriand. Since many of the statesmen were writers as well, it was natural that the elect went beyond politicians to philosophers, historians, artists of every calling. In daily contact with one another, since each salon had its day of the week, the groups exchanged ideas and gossip more efficiently than we with our telephones. They talked, laughed, and commiserated together, judged plays, read books, and dressed for each other. And all this was presided over by some muse. Even Rachel, coarse in speech, boorish in manner, but divine on stage, held a salon on Thursday evenings, when she worked out new roles for a largely masculine audience composed of legendary names like the ducs de

Noailles, de Fitz-James, de Richelieu, de Guise, along with other un-titled but equally famous ones.

THE ADVENT OF THIS NEW WOMAN had been encouraged by two prophets, Charles Fourier and the comte de Saint-Simon. Though close in thought, they were very different in temper and orientation. Saint-Simon, a grand seigneur, was dominated by ideas of authority and hier-archy; Fourier, a man of the people, was committed to the need for emancipation. Born in 1772, Fourier had already established his theories by 1808. Saint-Simon, twelve years older, died twelve years before Fourier (in 1825), leaving disciples to interweave their ideas for another decade. Each contributed greatly to awakening a feminist consciousness in women and men alike. Christianity had released women from the bonds of slavery placed on them by the Romans, but they were still condemned to an inferior social rank and were excluded from all civil and political func-tions. Saint-Simonism, basically conservative, proclaimed the emancipa-tion of women while upholding matrimony. But the wife must be equal to the husband and associated with him in the state, the family, and the exercise of the Christian cult. "If until now," declared Bazard, one of Saint-Simon's principal disciples, "humanity was represented by a single masculine individual, in the future the social individual will be repre-sented by man *and* woman."

Fourier, even more revolutionary than Saint-Simon, by dint of a plebeian background, proposed an entirely new concept of society. He discovered the attraction of passions, analogous to Newton's theory of the attraction of matter. All passions have to find their place in the human system, as do heavenly bodies in the astral system. A social system that op-poses the free development of the passions falsifies the necessary relation-ship between them, since all passions, good or bad, are legitimate and unalterable because of their divine origin. In contrast, society, a creation of man and like him perishable, can be altered. In Fourier's harmonious society—grouped into phalansteries of four hundred families, or 1,620 individuals,* instead of cities or states—humanity would live in an associa-tion of work, capital, and talent. Ideally, this was similar to Saint-Simon's notion of "To each according to his capacity, to each capacity according to its production"—but with the added incentive of free choice. Work

---

* Selected according to a musical translation of his theory of numbers: the seven whole and five half tones of the octave produce a complete series of 810 assonant chords. All the instinctive harmonies can thus be found in 810 people of each sex, which equals 1,620. Since the twelve passions (sight, taste, smell, touch, hearing, love, friendship, family senti-ment, ambition, intrigue, variability, union) can be notated musically, the "musical scores" of any two individuals can be compared. If the chords prove harmonious, a harmonious marriage results.

should be a matter of option and preference, however numerous the preferences. For duty comes from man, attraction from God. And in this harmony of passions and options, "we will not," says Fourier, "commit as we did in the past the stupidity of excluding women from medicine or teaching, reducing them to the needle and the soup pot. We will know that nature distributes to both sexes, in equal portions, aptitudes for sciences and the arts." Out of this equality between the sexes arises the greatest impulse for productivity: love. The free enterprise of love creates a chain of love, work, pleasure (*volupté* is the term he uses). "The one who has had the greatest pleasure in life, has yielded to the most immoderate passions, will be the wisest, the saintliest, the greatest."

This proclamation (which one would be mistaken to construe as orgiastic) naturally had a limited audience, yet Fourier's utopian harmonies resounded across continents. There were phalansteries as far flung as Texas. In Paris, Fourierism provided a buttress for Romantic fancies and took its place alongside Saint-Simonism and the religious revival led by Lamennais. Each group had its disciples and its publication; all had adepts in the feminine salons and among artists. Saint-Simonians, true followers or fellow travelers, met in a salon on the rue Taitbout in a fashionable new quarter whose residents soon included George Sand and Chopin, Caroline Jaubert, Thiers, Mignet. The Fourierists, under Considérant, pored over issues of *La Démocratie pacifique,* to which many of the most celebrated writers in Paris contributed. Cristina herself was an ardent supporter; she bought shares in the paper when it was founded and solicited articles for it among her friends, one of whom was Balzac. Lamennais's democratic Catholic movement was preached in *L'Avenir* and from the pulpits of his disciples, Lacordaire and Coeur. In all of this, women were hailed, not for the fruit of their womb but for their gifts of mind and spirit; they were the promise of a better future.

Fourier's 1808 prophecy—"the extension of women's privileges is the general principle of all social progress. . . . Women once liberated will surpass men in all the functions of body and spirit that are not the attributes of physical force"—was being fulfilled in the emergence of George Sand and the resuscitation of Mme Roland. By 1805, Stendhal had already read Mme Roland's memoirs, published five years before. This Girondist heroine, whom Stendhal called "la divine Madame Roland," told her husband she loved another but sacrificed her love to conjugal fidelity. (Today, she is best remembered for her last words at the guillotine, "Oh Liberty, what crimes are committed in thy name!") In 1832, George Sand's Lélia, a heroine for once not a sex object but a sensual subject, opened Sainte-Beuve's eyes to what he termed "the singular moral and literary movement that has appeared in France among women." In 1835 he wrote the first of no less than five studies of Mme

Roland, whose courage in her private and political life was awe-inspiring. By then another, unrelated Roland, Pauline by name, had taken a lover to have a child and thus discredit once and for all what she called "the monstrous inequality that made the glory of one the dishonor of the other." Feminist reviews were flourishing: *Le Journal des Femmes, La Femme libre, La Femme nouvelle.*

Today's women's movement seems less revolutionary if one looks back a hundred and forty years.

Not since the time of the troubadours had women been so venerated, so admired. The term "cult" became a near-cliché in artistic vocabulary. It might be argued that such a concept does not imply partnership in love; but at least it does not imply possession, which is a great improvement over the eighteenth century, when women were little more than erotic instruments. While pressing for recognition, which their male supporters rushed to offer, the feminists' tone remained even, their manners gracious. And there were impressive numbers of them writing, speaking, performing, even loving, in public.

Marie d'Agoult's elopement with Liszt must be viewed in this context. A few years before, she might have been threatened with destitution by her family and ostracism by society. In the 1830's she was enacting the current claim: the right to love. Hortense Allart, herself a liberated woman who wrote and loved as she chose, said of the duchesse de Berry* in 1836: "She was heroic; she became pregnant. So what? Does one question the private affairs of heroes? . . . She was a daring woman, a complete woman: a heroine and a mother." It was the first time that the old argument had been clamorously disproved; a woman did not have to choose between heroism and motherhood any more than a man between heroism (or anything else) and fatherhood. Women were now proclaiming their own emancipation.

Compared with the mooning male of that generation, the woman of 1830 was an Amazon, a Bradamante, a Valkyrie. The young men of the day had contracted *le mal de René* but lacked Chateaubriand's robust constitution. Alongside "this society of mites," as Chateaubriand wrote contemptuously in his *Mémoires d'Outre-Tombe*, "we [in 1815] were giants." If the young men of 1830 retained any taste for revolution they had lost the energy for it. Everything about this Romantic generation, the incarnation of immobility, was distasteful to him, from their king, the

---

* Widowed by her husband's assassination in 1820, she was forced into exile with her father-in-law, Charles X, after the July Revolution. In 1832 she returned to France to foment a rebellion against Louis-Philippe in favor of her twelve-year-old son. Captured when the rebellion was defeated, she gave birth to a daughter in prison. It was this pregnancy that aroused hilarity: a pregnant warrior! Her secret marriage to an Italian count legitimized the child, but ended her aspirations to the regency.

standard-bearer of his nation's mediocrity, to their "infertile civilization that can produce nothing." All they could do was suffer, like their earlier fictional models Obermann and Adolphe. Obermann's corrupted Cartesian formula, that *"I feel . . .* makes for the certainty of my being, and also for its torment," stands as a motto for the young Romantics. Adolphe suffers from "a perpetual analyzing that corrupts all sentiments." Stendhal, reacting against such self-indulgent cerebration, ridiculed these "Parisian eunuchs" who degraded the memory of Bonaparte with their *"manie discutante,"* their *"maladie de trop raisonner."* Lucien Leuwen's father expresses Stendhal's sentiments when he says, *"Mille fois heureux qui déraisonne par amour dans ce siècle où l'on ne déraisonne que par impuissance et médiocrité"* (a thousand times happier is he who raves out of love in this century in which one only raves out of impotence and mediocrity). Balzac is even more vituperative. For him constitutional monarchy turned out to be worse than the Restoration. While the latter demonstrated the physical and moral decline of a worn-out aristocracy—a generation of "ambulating coffins" (as he called them in *La Cousine Bette*)—the bourgeois regime was responsible for "a tidal wave of mediocrities" (*Le Curé de Village*). Many of Balzac's characters —Victor d'Aiglemont, Lucien de Rubempré, Raphael de Valentin, Calyste du Guénic—are cruelly drawn specimens of this degenerate race, which should have been the flower of French manhood in 1830. Louis-Philippe flattered the bourgeoisie, as Louis XVIII had flattered the Third Estate, by imitating its crassness and encouraging its materialism, whereas the bourgeoisie, as Mme Ancelot judiciously observed, "wanted to raise itself, not have another lower himself to its level."

What Balzac later termed "the great female emancipation of 1830" took place in a transfusion of vitality from defeated Napoleonic youths to a new generation of educated, forceful, dissatisfied women. The duchesse d'Abrantès, Balzac's friend and one-time mistress, claimed in 1831 that "a woman possesses a hardy soul, a courageous heart, patriotic and civic obligations," adding that if it can be achieved through the power of will, she can do anything a man can do. Unlike her male contemporary, the woman of 1830 looked to dynamic figures of the eighteenth century, real or fictional, for models. Mme Roland and Charlotte Corday had been living proof of how strong the weaker sex could be. Already under Louis XIV, women like Mme de La Fayette, Mme de Sévigné, Mlle de Scudéry had established their fame as writers. The progress made by women to extend their education was reflected in Molière's satires of *"la femme savante"* and her bourgeois imitators, *"les précieuses ridicules."* Under Louis XV, a golden age of intellectual women flourished, women who were furthermore their own masters. Balzac, in one of his more astute comments about Cristina, noted that "with respect to the Liszts and the

Mignets and all her caprices, she is of the age of Louis XV." Whatever Balzac's intent, this is in fact high praise if one considers the women of that age. Mme du Deffand's correspondence with Walpole and Voltaire reveals her keen judgment and crisp "masculine" style; Mme de Châtelet, a mathematician and physicist who propagated Newton's ideas in France, also found the energy to live two decades with Voltaire and with her own husband; Mme d'Epinay patronized Rousseau and left incisive memoirs; Mlle de Lespinasse conducted the Encyclopedists' salon as a participant, not just a hostess. Rousseau's *La Nouvelle Héloise,* of 1761, synthesized in Julie d'Etanges these *femmes philosophes,* whose prodigious offspring was Mme de Staël. Her *Corinne* marked the proclamation of feminine independence. "My independent existence," says the heroine, "pleased me so much that I twice broke the bonds which the need to love had made me contract." Mme Récamier offers an interesting example of this same spirit. When Chateaubriand's wife died, Mme Récamier preferred to continue receiving him when and how she liked rather than legitimize their decades-old union.

Corinne recognized that the exercise of ambition was virtually impossible for a woman. Condemned to a passive role in society, all her energy flowed into love, the only passion granted her. Nurtured on Byron and Scott, she dreamed of deploying her thwarted vitality in a love shared with an exceptional man. Marie d'Agoult is a prime example of the Romantic woman whose *vague à l'âme* found a focus in a man of genius. That she was inferior to her role and unfit to be Liszt's companion is irrelevant; she broke the chains society had placed on her and lived for a time the ideal of Stendhal's heroines. Mathilde de la Mole, in *Le Rouge et le Noir,* asks where a sensitive young girl can find powerful sensations outside of love. And she does find them, not in a member of her own decrepit class, but in the son of a woodcutter bursting with Bonapartist vitality. Feminine heroism (the concern was necessarily that of the educated upper classes) can only express itself in an *amour déclassé,* a love affair with a social inferior—a commoner, a bandit, a revolutionary, in Marie d'Agoult's case a commoner *and* a musician—or a married man. Here too Cristina adheres to the pattern: her only known liaison was with Mignet, a commoner, the son of a locksmith, whose social and intellectual ascendance was a Napoleonic phenomenon. In fact, all of Cristina's close friendships express the modernity of her tastes and views. Liszt, like Mignet, was a post-Revolution creation; in the eighteenth century he would have been a glorified servant, music-maker to some lordly patron, like the Trivulzios or the Belgiojosos. And so with Heine, a republican, the natural enemy of aristocrats of Cristina's lineage.

Stendhal set out to create women who are not the passive victims of men and circumstances. They are the very opposite of the princesse de

Clèves or Mme de Mortsauf, who would sooner yield their life than their virtue. Stendhal's heroines are full-blooded women, modern women, whose virtue lies precisely in giving rather than withholding. As Richard Bolster points out, Armance is the only Stendhalian heroine to preserve her virginity, and that only because Octave is impotent.[5] Also significant, his heroines are most often young girls, and adultery is thus rarely at issue. These forceful young women, the antithesis of their male coevals, are granted the moral freedom Stendhal preached in *De l'Amour:* "There is only one way to obtain fidelity in married women, it is to grant freedom to girls and divorce to married couples." The point is not sexual freedom per se. The only way these girls can prove themselves—like ancient heroes compelled to accomplish impossible feats—is through an outrageous love. Their abandonment to passion—the only course open to them—symbolizes their freedom as individuals and confirms their "superior souls." These feminist heroines are no longer functions of a man but willful expressions of their own desires. Cristina went even further. She not only defied society by refusing to accept her husband's infidelities —a wife's complacency was an unwritten law of marriage; she defied an even deeper ethos by refusing to sacrifice her independence, her obligations, even to the men who loved her, some of whom were indeed exceptional.

Balzac's feminist sympathies were restricted by the perimeters of his greater male chauvinism, and by the more limiting circumstances provided his heroines: they are largely married women. His generosity goes only as far as his idea that a woman's freedom is justified by passion: "her only excuse for breaking conjugal bonds is the excess of her love."[6] Her participation in society is limited to her "virtue as a wife and mother," in keeping with the old adage *"L'homme fait les lois, la femme fait les moeurs."* Any woman who goes outside that function, except out of need, becomes a menace. Balzac approved of female education; only an educated woman could appreciate his books. She should study and even write, he said, on condition that she burn her writings.[7] As to women with impulses other than passion, single women whose energies have not been ravaged by love, married women who have not succumbed, they represent "the feminine peril," they are destroyers of men. One can readily see in this context how ambivalent Balzac necessarily felt toward Cristina. He could not help admiring her, but she was a veritable compendium of everything he feared: she wrote, she thought, she acted, she did not love. Stendhal's epitaph for himself (VISSE, SCRISSE, AMÒ [he lived, he wrote, he loved]), slightly modified, admirably fits her: VISSE, SCRISSE, NON AMÒ.

Balzac was nevertheless very sensitive to the yearnings of superior women, even if their field was narrowed. He understood the oppressive atmosphere of the provinces, the inadequacy of most husbands as lovers or companions, the joys and sorrows of motherhood, the tortures of illicit love. However, in his novels, it was most often to foreign women, or actresses, that Balzac granted the freedom to love. When it came to a respectable Frenchwoman his rules were strict: she stayed home, gave up her lover, died if need be. If she did transgress the laws of society it was because she had been traumatized by a clumsy husband, which justified her action. This was an aspect of Cristina that intrigued Balzac. Her Italian nationality was perhaps even more significant than her miserable marriage. Balzac seems to have reserved a special place for his *italiennes;* most are in his philosophical novels, which sets them apart as exceptional women.

Stendhal, like his younger contemporaries, had always looked beyond the borders of France for his dream woman. Mme de Rênal and Mathilde are all the more remarkable because they are French. In contrast to the artificial Frenchwoman of the Restoration (fast changing after *Le Rouge et le Noir* appeared in 1830), the Italian woman was seen by Stendhal and Balzac as generous of heart, independent of spirit, authentic of character. This raises a curious paradox, for Italian men were far more vain and conservative than the French, and traditionally kept their women on a much shorter leash. How then did the Italian woman, in a far more reactionary society, manage to develop her "superiority"? The question was never raised, but in any case those oppressive Moslem attitudes never applied to upper-class women and particularly not to those of northern Italy. It had been demonstrated by Mme de Staël and others that in warm climates, specifically in lands that fell under Rome, women were historically oppressed, whereas cooler northern climates were more favorable to them, even allowing them equal rights on the battlefield and in the assembly among the Gauls and the ancient Germans. The Italian heroines of Stendhal and Balzac are all distinguished northern ladies. And Cristina was the most northern of Italians, a Lombard (in fact, the Longobards were of Germanic origin). Italian, Spanish, Slavic women invaded literature and Parisian society as paragons of the new woman, and perhaps also as substitutes for their Carbonaro compatriots, whose impotence caused the revolutionary flame to remain extinguished for close to two decades. It is from this perspective that one should view Cristina's appearance on the Parisian scene. Her instant success was related to the ideologies of the day: political, Romantic, feminist.

Certainly exoticism, spatial and temporal, was an active ingredient in the Romantic imagination. Poets gazed into the mysterious dark eyes of distant beauties; to qualify they had to appear on the ramparts of Seville, the steppes of Russia or the piazze of Italy. Few Frenchwomen could unlock a poet's aching heart. And Frenchwomen in their turn looked to the north for their dream loves: Byron, Scott, Shakespeare, Ossian,

Goethe. Napoleon's glorious career had also awakened them to action, commitment, and sacrifice for a noble ideal—with a touch of Pauline Bonaparte for zest. They would leave comfort and security to follow their hounded lovers into exile, or lacking a lover would take up any worthwhile cause. Anaïs de Bargeton, the provincial muse of Balzac's *Illusions perdues,* exemplifies those longings, and Balzac, the eternal male, intuits the secret reason:

> She palpitated, she swooned, she rhapsodized over every event, over the devotion of a Gray Sister. . . . She envied Lady Stanhope, that bluestocking of the desert; she was seized by the desire to become a Sister of Saint Camille and die of yellow fever in Barcelona while caring for the sick: that was a great, a noble destiny. . . . To many she sounded like a lunatic whose lunacy is harmless, but to some perspicacious observer, these things would surely have appeared as the debris of a magnificent love that crumbled as soon as it was built, in short, a love without a lover.*

And how indeed could such a woman find an outlet for her passions, an equilibrium between her yearnings and her possibilities? Tossed by the stormy works she read, with their escapades, their elopements, their tragic loves; transported by the sublime melancholy of Dante and Petrarch, Bellini and Chopin, all she could do was sigh in meter or in dotted notes.

"If literature is the expression of society," wrote Sainte-Beuve in 1834, "it is no less true that society is the willful expression and translation of literature." Nothing could be truer for this particular period, and even more so for the women, who composed the majority of the reading public. Stendhal confirms this with his petulant remark that "in Paris one is nothing except through women; the solitary artist can produce all the masterworks he likes, no one will tell the public they must be admired."[8] And no one knew better than Balzac how to pluck the strings of his feminine readers' hearts. A kind of osmosis occurred through the printed page. In a vast public of women eager to assert themselves, readers found their exemplars in this new species of forceful heroine. Cristina is a fine example of this mechanism. Balzac, whose heroines were among the most widely admired, used her over and over again to lend striking traits to his characters. He drew from her background of Italian aristocracy for Francesca Colonna, in *Albert Savarus* (mentioning her family, Trivulzio, by name and adding a private detail of his own, the date of

---

* It is highly probable that Balzac had Cristina in mind, for by the time he wrote this, her surrogate passions were well known, as were her empty marriage and her liaison with Mignet—truly a love without a lover. The allusion to Gray Sister is even more direct: this order was often cited to mock the stark simplicity of Cristina's dress and her generous charity toward the sick.

their meeting, to commemorate within the novel its eleventh anniversary); he gave Julie d'Aiglemont, in *La Femme de trente ans,* Cristina's personal tragedy of having been made frigid by a husband "handsome but null" (Julie, to flatter Balzac's machismo, is completely cured when she falls in love with a "superior" man); Diane de Maufrigneuse, in *Les Secrets de la princesse de Cadignan,* recalls, apart from her title, Cristina's empty marriage, and even more her political interests, her "virile" spirit: as d'Arthez (one of the characters in the novel) says of her, "That woman's greatest offense is to poach on men's preserves"; Anaïs de Bargeton suffers from Cristina's "lunacy": the substitute passions of a frustrated woman; not to mention more elaborate portraits in *La Peau de chagrin* and *Massimilla Doni,* discussed in a later chapter. Bolster, in his section on *"la femme nouvelle,"* affirms that Balzac's assumption that Cristina was Stendhal's model for the Duchess Sanseverina, and his insistence that "the character exists" after Stendhal's unconvincing denial, only reveals the importance Balzac attributed to living models in fictional invention: "It is thus not surprising that the princesse de Belgiojoso acquired a kind of immortality as the model for a figure . . . who personified an interesting feminist cause."[9]

Beaumont-Vassy, a shrewd observer of society under Louis-Philippe, remarked in his memoirs that "the habits, tastes and manners of an age are bound by the tightest bonds to the historic events that constitute it, and most often explain them better than the most conscientious analysis." Historic events had refashioned the face of Paris in 1830. Its political structure was the product of two revolutions and five regimes, its destructured society the result of the Terror and Napoleonic wars, its economy the outgrowth of those wars' necessities and the ingenuity of a new banking class. Added to this de-stabilized world, for Paris *was* the world in terms of new concepts and mores, was an influx of foreigners such as had never been seen before. Of Germans alone there were thousands (Heine's exaggerated figure was eighty thousand).* Testimony to France's official hospitality under the July monarchy is the wording of Heine's pension, awarded with Cristina's help a few years after he escaped Austria's tentacles:

> Monsieur Henri Heine is a political refugee. He was obliged to leave Germany after the revolution of 1830. A pension of 4,800 francs was granted him at a time when refugees from various countries almost naturally became pensionaries of France. . . . This help was given to an eminent poet, a political exile, who has always shared France's ideas and who has suffered for her cause.[10]

---

* It was more probably twenty or thirty thousand, but still a sizeable number for a city whose population was then just under 775,000.

After the revolution of 1848, Heine's pension was reduced to 800 francs, although he was not in lesser need.

Of all the foreign nationals, Italians occupied a privileged position. Italophilia was raging throughout Europe, and the highest temperature was recorded in Paris. Barely three years after Beethoven's death, Rossini had all but obliterated his memory. Rossini was probably the best known, most played, and highest paid composer who ever lived. No concert could take place without an overture, aria, duet, quartet, or at least a piano transcription, from one of his operas. Musicians of every kind, pupils or professionals, grabbed up his scores as they were published. Every young lady *comme il faut* had her repertory of Rossini arias. On March 9, 1831, Rossini's genius was sanctified as Italy's genius by Paganini's sublime concert. With all due respect to Newton and Einstein, this event can go down as the revelation of yet another natural force, another new dimension. Paganini's playing was in its way a breaking of the sound barrier. Singers, pianists, string players, all were inspired to go beyond the established capacities of their instruments and reach for new sounds, unexplored textures. July 1833 saw Bellini's arrival in Paris. His *Puritani,* premiered six months later, marked an apogee of lyric drama, exalted melody, and vocal style whose marvels of legato and coloratura have never been surpassed. Bel canto moved from the opera house into every area of composition. Chopin was the greatest exponent of the style in nonvocal music; Liszt exploited it to near parodistic excess. Fortunately for impecunious Italian exiles everybody wanted to know Italian; many of them in fact survived by giving language lessons. Musical Italomania had reached epidemic proportions. Berlioz was among the few to remain immune. Considering Italian music of the day vulgar, he tried to promote a festival of German music—with little success it should be added. Even a cultivated aristocrat, the poet Terenzio Mamiani, found German music "full of pompous doctrine and over-elaborate counterpoint."[11] If this is how Mamiani felt, little wonder that Paris's latter-day music buffs preferred roulades to fugues.

CRISTINA SAILED INTO PARIS on the wave of this frenzy. Her unusual beauty, her titles, her frozen assets, her heroic stance against husband and emperor, her mission to liberate Italian prisoners held by Austria, all titillated the imagination. Rossini was an old friend, Bellini her protégé; by 1833 her salon was the center of Italian thought and art. Her apartment, furnished in the Italian style with Renaissance furniture and paintings, was an innovation in Paris, where gilded bergères and pastel silks had reigned for decades. The dark wood and sober fabrics led to grotesque exaggerations on the part of those who had never been her guests. Gautier's funereal images were repeated by dozens of others, including Marie d'Agoult, who had heard about the brown velvet and inlaid ebony in the salon, the embossed leather in the study, the flowered organdy in the bedroom, but had never laid eyes on them. To the readers of tabloids and society supplements Cristina Belgiojoso was surely more intriguing than Jacqueline Onassis or Elizabeth Taylor today, for they had not even seen a likeness of her. All they knew was that on the streets of Paris—described by Mamiani as "those enormously long streets divided in half by a filthy rivulet that did not add to their beauty or grace"—rode a fairy-tale princess, quite unlike run-of-the-mill French nobility, a fabulous character such as exists only between the covers of a book. It was not so much Cristina's eccentricities as the eccentric imagination of the time that projected her into a characterization far beyond her own reality.

From her first entry into Parisian society, possibly at one of Lafayette's receptions, she captivated her audience. Every Tuesday evening at eight o'clock a motley crowd of generals, politicians, veterans, and refugees arrived on foot and climbed the stairs to Lafayette's apartment on the rue d'Anjou. According to Beaumont-Vassy, one entered first into an austere dining room "testifying to republican taste," then into the salon where were gathered mostly family, young girls and ladies "whose gowns and haircombs held the eye. Among them was an Italian of a strange and remarkable beauty. . . . It was Princess Belgiojoso." If her own salon later became one of the most interesting in Paris, it was because "original in her beauty, original in her tastes, the princess was a unique figure in the midst of Parisian society." Beaumont-Vassy does not exaggerate the importance of her salon, for even in the historical section of the *Nouveau Petit Larousse* she is described as "an Italian patriot long exiled in France, where her salon was a meeting place for prominent men," with no mention of her political activities or published writings. By all contemporary reports, her salon was singularly attractive because it was not limited to any one group, nor did it suffer from the hypertrophied snobbism of aristocratic salons that closed their doors to low-born artists and writers, whom the duchesse de Dino called, after an unwelcome visit from Balzac, *"tous ces publicistes, gens de lettres, faiseurs d'articles que je crains horriblement."* Cristina received diplomats and poets, historians and novelists, musicians and conspirators, without regard to wealth, rank, or even success. It is to her credit that she supported Liszt long before he became an idol, and Heine before he had been translated into French. She was as devoted to Jules Mohl, then an obscure orientalist of German origin, as to Adolphe Thiers, a minister in Louis-Philippe's government. Her ideas were young, her tastes eclectic, her curiosity limitless, which is doubtless why her world was considered bizarre if not downright scandalous. Une princesse de Bohème! Until Lent there were concerts on Saturday followed by improvised balls in the dining room, where the piano was moved for the occasion. Cristina loved to dance, particularly the waltz. After Ash Wednesday more sober music was played. Wednesdays were reserved for intimate gatherings with close friends.

The English and Austrian embassies were the sites of lavish entertainments where people came to look, not talk. Lord and Lady Granville celebrated Victoria's favorite pink and white by offering nosegays and boutonnieres of roses and lily of the valley to the guests. As early as September 1831, Cristina had already made an impact on Lady Granville, who informed her sister, "Yesterday I saw at Mme Bourke's Princess Belgiojoso, slim, *distinguée*, pale, eyes big as saucers, very slender hands, grand and gracious manners, extremely intelligent, *de l'esprit comme un démon.*" At the Austrian embassy, Count and Countess Antoine Apponyi offered springtime déjeuners-dansants beginning at two-thirty so that the pastel flowers and diaphanous gowns could be admired in sunlight. The count distinguished himself in the diplomatic corps by wearing a handsome moustache above his decorations—facial hair was generally reserved for the military—and by knowing how to please his retrograde government and France's liberal one without betraying his own principles. A case in point is his affable social relationship with Cristina, despite his obligation to keep this rebellious subject under surveillance. Metternich never doubted his ambassador's loyalty; Cristina never doubted his sympathy.

The ambassador's cousin, Count Rodolphe Apponyi, posted to Paris in 1826 at the age of twenty-three, spent the next quarter-century there consolidating his conservatism and perfecting his nasty tongue, which he wagged in three volumes of memoirs. No one escaped, not even Lafayette: "He had the heart of a weak woman and the petty vanities that are often its apanage. It is shameful that such a man can halt the progress of government." In December 1830 Rodolphe Apponyi's ultra sympathies were outraged by the changing scene: "There are no longer any magnificent carriages on the streets of Paris; one goes on foot or in a cab for fear of shocking the people." He was, as one might expect, constantly shocked by Cristina and her entourage. In 1836 Cristina's mother tried to persuade her to sell her Lombard properties to someone in their inner circle (Count Sant'Antonio, Vittoria's lover). The stratagem was intended to circumvent Austria's continued threat of confiscation if Cristina did not return within a stated period, repeatedly prolonged with the ambassador's help. To this Rodolphe Apponyi, less tolerant than his cousin, objected: "The princess would thus become completely independent and could remain in Paris with all those young and old *barbouil-*

leurs de papier [scribblers] who pour sentiment into their novels at 25 sous the page."[12] He was scandalized by Cristina's frequent visitor, Musset, who reeked of cigars and talked about his past affair with George Sand in front of Countess Apponyi (the ambassadress); and by Balzac's absurd clothing and ignorance of social propriety. "Is it any wonder," he summarized, "that Princess Belgiojoso, surrounded as she is by young men so poorly bred, should assume their behavior and take the airs of a superior woman while not observing the rules of decorum and manners."[13] From the number and length of his entries about her it is evident that he saw quite a lot of her, and in her own salon. It is not evident why he was willing to expose himself to such contamination. One of his choicer paragraphs, reflecting the imperial blend of slander and paternalism, deserves quotation:

> Princess Belgiojoso, aside from her pretension of being a second Sappho or Corinne, takes pleasure in looking like a specter; she has a ghostly pallor, wears turbans and haircombs of unusual style, gowns so excessively décolleté and singularly vaporous, with such bizarre draping, that one imagines a dagger hidden in their folds. . . . I was so astounded by all the extravagance that surrounded me [Musset had his feet on the table, Liszt wore a black velvet shirt without a tie, Mignet casually surveyed the scene] that I could hardly start a conversation. The princess, who delights in surrounding herself with the most extravagant young men on the one hand, and on the other with distinguished scholars, is a bizarre mixture of absurdities and rhapsodic erudition, which inspires admiration alternating with pity.[14]

There can be no doubt about the phenomenal pallor of Cristina's complexion. Many, like Heine, found it gorgeous; others spoke of blue-green tints that made her look positively spectral at night. Mme Ancelot, her great admirer, tells the story of her own husband, who when asked if he found Cristina pretty, replied: "The princess? She must have been very beautiful when she was alive!" Marie d'Agoult, anything but an admirer, described her as "Pale, thin, bony, eyes aflame, she played on spectral or phantasmal effects."[15] By the time Théophile Gautier wrote his celebrated caricature of her, her beauty had been fixed on canvas by Henri Lehmann and others, her book on Catholic dogma had appeared, and her prominence was so firmly established that Gautier's "marquise romantique" was quickly recognized by a rather large audience. The text appears in an over-written letter-novel jointly authored by Delphine Girardin, Jules Sandeau, Méry, and Gautier. Each assumed a character and wrote letters to the others in a series of mystified identities. Gautier flattered himself, in the role of Edgar de Meilhan, as having had to flee the "marquise's" attentions—doubtless referring to Cristina's reputation as Musset's temptress. Gautier never saw the apartment he described, yet he served as an eyewitness of its décor for a host of biographical dabblers, including Marie d'Agoult, who did Gautier and Cristina the injustice of quoting only the most denigrating lines. Gautier's portrait warrants extensive quotation since it incorporates most of the opinions held about Cristina and some of her satirizable traits.

> You have doubtless met somewhere that famous bluestocking known as *la marquise romantique*. She is beautiful; the painters say so. In fact, they are not wrong, for she is beautiful in the manner of an old painting. Though young, she seems to be covered with a yellow varnish and walks as though surrounded by a frame. . . . Her apartment is a veritable series of catafalques and seems to have been done by a funeral parlor decorator. The salon is hung in purple damask, the bedroom in black velvet, the furniture is ebony or old oak; crucifixes, holy water basins, in-folio bibles, skulls, daggers, stud this amiable interior. . . . The evocation of a catacomb is intended to highlight the waxen cheeks and bister eyes of the dwelling's mistress: she does not inhabit it, she haunts it.
>
> Do not believe, after this funereal beginning, that your friend has fallen prey to some ghoul or demon or vampire; the marquise is, after all, a rather beautiful woman; she has regular, though somewhat Jewish features, which prompts her to wear a turban more often and earlier than need be; she would be merely pale, if instead of white she wore red; she has lovely aristocratic hands, a bit too thin, a bit too delicate, overladen with bizarre rings, and her foot is no larger than her shoe, rare indeed!—for women, in the field of footgear, have proved false the geometric axiom: the content must be smaller than the container. She is even, to a point, a woman of good company, and very well placed in society. . . . I had the misfortune of charming her . . . for this unhung canvas did not please me at all. . . . I got a whiff of literature underneath and looked at her hem to see if some blue tinge did not alter the whiteness of her stockings. . . . I loathe women who take baths in blue ink. Alas, it was worse than an avowed woman of letters. . . . The marquise contemplates didactic novels, social poetry, humanitarian treatises, and on her tables and chairs one sees solemn tomes dog-eared at the dullest spots. . . .[16]

Gautier, never more than a social acquaintance, had seen Cristina— and assuredly Lehmann's portrait, the sensation of the 1844 salon— closely enough to be able to blend fact with fantasy. Her hands were incredibly delicate, her feet minute—Heine spoke of her "mandarin foot"—and her nose arched and long, in a manner more often called aristocratic than Jewish on a noble face (Louis XIV was also said to have a Jewish nose). As for the skulls and daggers, Bibles and crucifixes,

Gautier was poking fun at her interests in theology and politics. Though belabored, it was fairly amusing the first time around. But everyone who followed him—Apponyi, d'Agoult, Houssaye, and into the twentieth century—scavenged so relentlessly that all humor was lost. It is clear where Boulenger's "Marquis de Floranges" got his details, though no one was ever struck by the near plagiarism. Marie d'Agoult varied at least one detail, the bedroom, making it all white, "the catafalque of a virgin."

The background to Gautier's caricature offers an interesting piece of social history. Gautier was an acolyte of Emile de Girardin, the first newspaper tycoon and Delphine's husband, the bastard son of a nobleman whose name he usurped; Delphine's literary talents were less respected than her husband's power allowed her to believe. They naturally divided the Parisian scene into two groups: their sycophants, whom they extolled, and their rivals, whom they execrated. Cristina was one of the latter. To begin with, Delphine, the self-styled Tenth Muse, shared her divinity very biliously with Cristina, hailed as the Romantic Muse. In addition, Cristina's intimate circle—particularly Mignet and Thiers, who despised Girardin for having killed their colleague Armand Carrel in a duel in 1836—viewed Girardin's aristocratic pretensions and journalistic practices with open contempt.

The final antagonism occurred in 1843, when an Academy of Women, patterned after the French Academy, was founded by an eminent social figure, Jules de Castellane, with the help of his friend, Mme Ancelot. Castellane's magnificent mansion on the rue du Faubourg Saint-Honoré was famous for its theatricals and for what was known as its incomparable sanctum of "causeuses transcendantes" (transcendent female conversationalists). The forty women of the proposed academy, like the forty "immortals" of the Académie Française, were to wear black robes embroidered with green palms, presided over, it was hoped, by George Sand. Delphine, a member of snobbish coteries before her misalliance with an illegitimate publicist, saw the academy as an ideal vehicle for reintegrating herself into this society that now snubbed her. "In vain," writes the chronicler of this short-lived institution, "did writers and artists ceaselessly shower her with excessive praise and daily proclaim her a woman of genius, in the hope of thus obtaining a piece of a column or a scrap of advertising in her husband's newspapers. . . . No one was fooled by this flattery."[17] If she headed this academy she could reconquer all those pen-wielding ladies of high society, who would be kept out by serious professionals like George Sand or Virginie Ancelot. Delphine informed Mme Ancelot and Castellane that she would consider the presidency, never offered her, of a select academy purified of those awful bourgeoises who wrote for a living. The slur was aimed at George

Sand, who had never been eager to accept the presidency and was even less eager to enter this lioness's den. With George too reluctant and Delphine too willing, a compromise was sought in Mme Reybaud, then an esteemed novelist; she too withdrew demurely. Mme Ancelot then proposed Princess Belgiojoso, who, though not French, the chronicler relates, "was a woman of great patrician allure, intimate friend of George Sand,* and would certainly have been an outstanding president."

Faced with the candidacy of so eminent a rival, Delphine finally understood she was not wanted and later vented her fury against the academy in three articles in *Le Vicomte de Launay.* Her vengeance against her rival was taken more surreptitiously, as the same chronicler tells us: "Mme de Girardin, not daring to reveal her personal spite, had Mme de Belgiojoso attacked by friends in the literary world with the most incredible virulence. Thus, in *La Croix de Berny* she slipped a horrible portrait of the Italian princess into a passage signed by Théophile Gautier, a portrait that furthermore guaranteed this rather boring volume an enormous *succès de scandale.*" The same writer also struck out at another member of Delphine's circle, Countess Merlin, whose fortune is revealed to have come from slave trading. To please Delphine, the writer says, Mme Merlin "transformed Princess Belgiojoso," in her *Lionnes de Paris,* "into a demonic and criminal adventuress. This indecent novel also had a passing vogue in fashionable society, always avid for such defaming flatteries." Cristina, evidently not one to hold personal grudges though unyielding in political ones, drew an exquisite portrait of Mme Merlin in her memoirs. Recalling Victoria's coronation at Westminster Abbey, Cristina withholds the countess's age and merely places her in the setting of "that memorable contest in which she had as competitors the youthful beauties of three united kingdoms. . . . these young ladies had to yield to the dean of beauties whose well established charms seemed to be consolidated with time . . . every man turned to Countess Merlin as though attracted by a bottle of vintage wine, generous and vermilion . . . placed amid an assortment of insipid syrups."

Needless to say, long before these polemics began Cristina declined the presidential "immortality" of the Academy of Women. Whether Delphine's work or Gautier's, the portrait of "la marquise romantique" gives one an idea of France's sharpest weapon, the provocation of laughter

* The greatest mystery yet unsolved in Cristina's life is her relationship with George Sand. It was assumed by her contemporaries that they were friends and mutual admirers. Georges Lubin, mystified by the absence of a single letter among the thousands he has classified, assured me he found no more proof than I of any relationship whatever between the two women, except for an exchange between Sand and Cristina's brother-in-law, Count Charles d'Aragon.

through ad hominem ridicule. Fourier justly remarked: "Laughter is fatal
in France; it denies one the ability and desire to go to the heart of
things."

Cristina easily survived this mockery. If anything, it only added to her
celebrity. She had graver concerns; these were lilliputian barbs. Happily
there were other women, less competitive, who were generous in their
judgments and their sentiments. Mme Récamier, Cristina's first patroness
in Paris, remained a close friend until she died in the cholera epidemic of
1849. This Aphrodite of the Directoire was over fifty when they first met
but she was still beautiful, graceful, sparkling. Her long liaison with
Chateaubriand had been made official by his daily visits to l'Abbaye-aux-
Bois, where they held court together. Volumes have been written on
those afternoons when Chateaubriand confided his *Mémoires d'Outre-
Tombe* to an elect circle. None has ever quoted Cristina's delightful account enlivened by her less than reverential attitude, where others had
been worshipful supplicants. Her *Souvenirs dans l'exil*—a collection of
letters sent from Greece and Turkey to Caroline Jaubert, who had become
her closest friend in Paris—depict that salon, which recaptured eighteenth-
century elegance and serenity. At the same time they reveal her own style
and wit. Because the work was published as a supplement to *Le National*
and is a great rarity (to my knowledge only one copy exists at the
Bibliothèque Nationale), this passage is quoted extensively.

> Mme Récamier transported into our century a few traditions from that
> society, and it is her memory above all that fills for me the salons of
> Mmes de Choiseul, d'Epinay, and du Deffand, with an indefinable
> breath of freshness and consolation. Even the furnishings of Mme
> Récamier's salon—the heavy draperies that only allowed pale rays of
> daylight to enter, the somewhat outmoded scent of carnations, the
> parquet always gleaming without any of the soft rugs that one finds
> today in the least sumptuous of hotels, the regularity with which
> twelve chairs and six armchairs were aligned along the wall and
> around the foyer, the ceremonial of those reunions—carried me back
> to the salons of the Marais, where one read and judged books and
> rarely felt the rebound of outside events. . . .
>
> Ensconced in a large armchair at the side of the fireplace, dressed
> with the most exquisite elegance in chiffon and lace, Mme Récamier
> looked in the half-light of her salon like an airy white cloud from
> which issued not thunder or lightning, but the sweetest voice and the
> purest speech. Opposite her, comfortably settled in his armchair,
> his cane between his legs, hands on pommel, chin on hands, was M. de
> Chateaubriand, the veritable idol of the temple in which Mme
> Récamier wished only to serve as priestess. M. de Chateaubriand in-
> timidated me in a singular way, and all the more in that I felt he was
> not well disposed toward me. You know, chère amie, my ineptitude

for compliments. I do not have the habit of exclaiming: oh, how beautiful! how I love it! . . . If I have decided to tell an author that I enjoy his work I tell him simply and baldly as though speaking of a third party. . . . And if the person who received my praise begs me to spare him, well then, I do. . . . M. de Chateaubriand was not accustomed to such discretion and could do without it. There was still another grievance. Never had I expressed the desire to attend those famous readings of his *Mémoires d'Outre-Tombe.* . . . One day, Mme Récamier carried her graciousness so far as to ask slyly what I thought of public readings. It was a door she opened to help me escape from the dungeon where the rays of M. de Chateaubriand's benevolence would never reach me. But I, who only saw the prospect of a séance to which I would have to bring my contingent of compliments, hastened to stammer that *they bored me to death.* I can still hear Mme Récamier's stifled sigh and see the half-smiling half-despairing expression on her face which seemed to say: "I have done what I can; there is no hope of refining such a nature; I give up."

For many years I dragged out my existence in M. de Chateaubriand's disgrace until one fine day, on entering Mme Récamier's salon, turning to make my usual pitiful bow which never received more in return than a slight lowering of the head . . . what did I see? René's forehead brightened; his whole face broke into a smile . . . and it was to me that this luminous smile was addressed as well as a little gesture, inviting me to sit beside him. What had I done? or said? There are problems in this world that have never been solved and this is one of them. What is certain is that from then on M. de Chateaubriand honored me with a predilection all the more flattering in that it was late in coming. . . .

Did I ever tell you how surprised I was, newly arrived at the time from across the Alps, by the ceremonious manners that Mme Récamier and M. de Chateaubriand always maintained toward each other? . . . Mme Récamier first opened her salon at four o'clock; from three to four she received no one but M. de Chateaubriand. Since I spent the summer in the environs of Paris and was only in town for brief moments regulated by the railroad clock, Mme Récamier, kind and generous as always, made an exception for me and admitted me to the sanctuary at that special hour. I made many people jealous by saying that I went to l'Abbaye from three to four. And I was often asked how this mysterious hour was spent. I did not reply, for I was not displeased to appear initiated into some great secret which the vulgar could not penetrate. . . . If I kept my silence perhaps one day I would read that for fifteen years Mme Récamier and M. de Chateaubriand conspired for one hour a day in favor of the elder branch* or that it was Mme Récamier who wrote his books and used

---

* The elder branch of Bourbons had been deposed by the July Revolution: Louis-Philippe descended from Louis XIV's younger brother, the duc d'Orléans.

that hour to keep him abreast of what he was supposed to have written. . . . What indeed did they do between three and four? They drank tea!!!

What I found remarkable is not that two friends drank tea together beside the fire each day for ten or fifteen years, for I might be capable of that, but at the end of fifteen days I would drink my tea out of habit, almost without noticing and certainly without bothering. Such was not the case of these two illustrious friends. To see them one would think they were having tea together for the first time in their lives and needed to study each other to find the unison for that important act. . . . "Would you like some tea, Monsieur de Chateaubriand?" (He had been saying yes for the past ten years.) "After you, Madame." "And shall I add some milk?" "Just a few drops." "May I offer you a second cup?" And so on for half an hour.

I observed this and admired it with sadness. I even envied this fortunate disposition, which belongs almost exclusively to the French, and even more so to the French of the last century, of never eliminating any of society's adornments of convention and etiquette. Thanks to this precaution the most insignificant acts, the most trivial and ordinary things acquire and conserve in the form itself something of the charm that comes from newness. On the other hand, people like me brutally grasp everything with both hands, turn it in all directions, analyze every feeling, wanting to know the intensity and above all the sincerity of each; we fear exaggeration and affectation; and yet, does not reality benefit from being veiled? . . . Seeing pathetic truth all naked we make a sour face, shrug our shoulders, turn our backs and say "Pooh, what a trifle!"

Place me one hour a day for a month before a tea table in the company of anyone you like. The first day I will behave and sound like Mme Récamier. The second I will offer my companion tea with a gesture but without a word. By the end of the week we will each take our cup without bothering about the other. And at the end of the month, unless one of us is seized with a violent passion for this Chinese beverage, we may well . . . forget to meet and love one another. Nothing in this world has an intrinsic value; each thing is related to another, like the link of a long chain whose ends are lost in infinity. He who sees in each little link no more than a valueless little circle and casts it aside remains alone, lost in a vast nothingness. Blessed was Mme Récamier, who scorned nothing that could add charm to her life and to herself.[18]

Cristina had learned a precious lesson from Mme Récamier's example but she was hard put to follow it. Perhaps life was kinder to Mme Récamier; the few winds of adversity to touch her had been mild enough merely to sway her supple nature. Cristina was hit with gale force; her unbending ideals and peremptory character resisted mightily at the heavy price of loneliness. She was not content to serve as priestess to an idol's cult; less blessed than Mme Récamier, she never found her idol although more than one proposed himself. If she had any cult, other than the liberation of her country, it was friendship. She never forgot the tender attentions she first received from Mme Récamier and twenty years later her gratitude was still fresh: "I must say in praise of Parisian society that I was welcomed on equal footing without hesitation. Mme Récamier, the duchesse de Broglie, M. de Lafayette patronized me with enthusiasm." Their unpublished correspondence, a series of fond letters between a young woman and her older friend, shows the easy but respectful cordiality they shared, the informality of Cristina's frequent visits, her eagerness to be of service as, for example, when Mme Récamier planned a trip to a spa Cristina knew well. Over the years, Cristina had been in a privileged position to view, with her particular sensitivity, the decline of the remarkable couple. Though long forgotten, her letter-memoirs rhapsodized those two aged lovers, whose devotion survived old age and painful infirmity. Chateaubriand's memory stopped like a broken clock before the July Revolution. "He had, so to speak, anticipated eternity by losing all awareness of time and space. His heart alone guided him each day to the side of the one he had loved and continued to love." Mme Récamier, by then nearly blind, used every ruse to keep him from discovering her affliction and to hide her own lapses of memory. She passed the word around their little circle never to discuss politics after the Restoration or tell anecdotes set after 1815. "Such abnegation and devotion, do they not offer the key to the passionate and lasting sentiments of which Mme Récamier was the object?" Cristina's almost envious appreciation of their relationship reflects her deep nostalgia for a lasting love, a faithful companion, neither of which she had when she wrote those words in 1849.

When Chateaubriand died on July 4, 1848, Cristina was still mourning her young secretary, Gaetano Stelzi, who had died a fortnight earlier. Where Chateaubriand had been to Mme Récamier a friend and lover combined, Cristina had found only fractions of each in Stelzi and Mignet; in July 1848 she was without either. Mignet remained a friend long after he ceased being a lover, but in many important things he could not provide the sympathy or help she needed, and circumstances kept them apart much of the time. Stelzi had been an unfailing supporter for three of her most active years as a political journalist and, though not her lover, had offered and received something more intimate than friendship since he was part of her household. Cristina's letter of condolence to Mme Récamier (never before published) is a moving document of the compassion and the grief shared by these two women.

Locate, July 14, 1848

Chère Dame,

Permit me to intrude on your thoughts at this painful moment. You have lost the one who for so many years filled your life, and alas, there is no consolation to offer those who have felt dry up in them every source of joy. You will become resigned, chère Dame, if it has not already happened; but what is this resignation so highly praised? If it is not indifference, it is the patient wait for that which one cannot hasten.

I will not tell you, ma chère Dame, that your pain will abate— even should you have before you long years and new emotions, you could still not bear today the thought of forgetting in the future. The pain caused by the loss of people we love finds solace only in faith, and in the hope inspired by faith that we will find them again elsewhere. This faith you have, ma chère Dame, and with it eternal separation becomes no more than a brief absence.

Death has left me too, Madame, alone, alone with my daughter. The young man who, full of wisdom, purity and delicacy, had become attached to me and to my fate to the point of not wishing to reserve the option of leaving me when age would have made me tiresome, and when for his long service he would have had the right to rest and to an independent life; he, whose advice was always sound, whose affection was always disinterested, whose sentiments were pure and noble, whose heart was faithful and sincere, died suddenly in my arms after having accustomed me to the happiness of his company which I shall never find again. It is thus weeping that I imagine your tears.

A Dieu, ma chère Dame, let me hope that on my next trip to Paris I shall find you in fairly good health.

Your devoted friend,
Christine Trivulce[19]

When she returned to Paris in September of that year she saw Mme Récamier for the last time. The events of the next months were to cut her off from l'Abbaye-aux-Bois forever: Mme Récamier died in May, while Cristina was in Rome, about to embark on another odyssey. Paris in that fall of 1848 was just beginning to settle after the revolution in February. Cristina arrived, a supplicant as she had been seventeen years earlier, seeking help for her martyred Lombardy, which had just lost its brief independence. There were few who understood, even fewer who acted. Among her close friends only Caroline Jaubert never disappointed her, since politics was an avoidable subject between them.

Mme Jaubert, born Caroline d'Alton-Shée, was five years older than Cristina. Her younger brother Edmond, although Emilio Belgiojoso's comrade in debauchery, remained very close to his sister and to Cristina as well. Caroline was twelve and Edmond five, when their father died in 1815. Three years later, Caroline was asked by her mother, concerned for the future of her orphaned children, what she thought of Maxime Jaubert, then thirty-seven and a distinguished lawyer. Finding him no worse a match than any other, Caroline agreed to marry him, telling him he would replace her father. Maxime may have thought that touching at the time of their engagement, but after the wedding he preferred not to be reminded. Having no qualms over imaginary incest, he boldly exercised his rights; nine months later a daughter was born. "Let this not happen to you again, Monsieur," Caroline warned, threatening to leave him. "I can no longer say I am your daughter, but know that from now on I am your widow!"[20] Maxime evidently accepted this arrangement, for he continued to live with his "widow" for many years.

Her minute proportions and enormous charm made her an outstanding figure in society. Musset, who met her through Cristina, called her "godmother" and shared with her "a nameless sentiment," deeper than friendship but less than love. His letters to her during his crises over Cristina reveal a great deal about this pampered poet who could not take no for an answer. Through Cristina, with whom she often spent weeks at a time at La Jonchère and later Port-Marly, Caroline also came to know Heine. Both poets poured out their woes to her about their hopeless love for Cristina. Caroline had the gift of friendship. She knew how to accept the confidences of mutual friends without ever betraying them. Except for Ernesta Bisi, she was Cristina's closest friend and in many ways even closer than Bisi, for in Paris she and Cristina were in almost daily contact, frequented the same people, attended the same concerts, laughed over the same jokes. Caroline was a witness to Cristina's turbulent relationship with Mignet in the 1830's, as revealed by their correspondence. When Cristina went into exile in 1849, the journal-letters she sent from the Near East so fascinated Caroline that she insisted on having them published. Thanks to her, we have *Souvenirs dans l'exil,* whose impressions of people and places, reminiscences, and moving accounts of Rome besieged, offer a singular view of Cristina's wit and style. Far from Paris and the people she enjoyed, she often remembered episodes of that earlier life. It is this firsthand source that provides the anecdotes about her friends cited in this work. Caroline's own memoirs, published long after Cristina's death, were often quoted by biographers of Musset and Heine, but many of the anecdotes came originally from Cristina's memoirs of 1850. Through all the difficulties and wanderings of Cristina's life, Caroline remained for her a solid link with the city that had become her second home, and in many ways her first.

4

Birth of a Bluestocking

CRISTINA'S VOCATION as political propagandist was determined at the very beginning of her contact with Paris. Her first frenetic weeks there placed her in a position that far exceeded any ambition she might have had, a position that few men and fewer women ever enjoyed. Instead of cowing her, the decree of April 19, 1831, threatening her with civil death, seems to have catalyzed her energies and strengthened her resolve for independence at any cost. In view of her generous contribution to the Savoy expedition, and her open association with insurrectionary exiles in southern France, the penalty was hardly a surprise. Yet her friends and new acquaintances in Paris were shocked. The wording of the decree, signed by Torresani, left only one course of action open to her: obedience. She was ordered to return to imperial states within three months "under pain of civil death and confiscation of all properties, presently declared under rigorous sequester."[1] Giacomo Luvini, president of the canton of Ticino, who had befriended her in Lugano when she feted the new constitution and his election, was incredulous to learn that she had taken no measures to safeguard her future. He urged her to return to Milan:

> I thought that during the months of your sojourn in France, warned as you were of the possibility of a summons to return, you had arranged your affairs by selling your estate to some Frenchman, which would have regularized things in Milan. With utter amazement, I have just been informed that you did not think of your own affairs. Now, dearest Cristina, it is time to pay serious attention to this, because you must not expose yourself to the risk of finding yourself, if not in need, then in restricted conditions which would incommode you, especially since you would find yourself deprived of the pleasure of helping the unfortunate who have always found in you protection and relief from their misery.

Convinced that her return to Milan would cause her no personal harm, Luvini urged her to settle her affairs there and then come to Lugano, "where you will be welcomed with transports of joy by everyone." To reinforce his argument, he added that Emilio, then in Lugano, had told him that her mother was very upset and ill. Would she not at least go to Genoa, where her mother could meet her? Luvini, evidently attuned to her personality and aware of her reckless unconcern for herself, understood that the only possible tactic was to reach her through others: her mother, the unfortunate she had helped. If she went to Genoa, her mother might be able to persuade her to return to Milan on sentimental grounds, or together they could make some arrangements to protect her fortune. But Cristina had already learned that Genoa was no haven. Only six months earlier, in November, the Genoese police had delivered her passport to the Austrian legation; this time they might well deliver her, since according to the decree and the letter of Austrian law, she was "illegally absent," thus in criminal contempt and extraditable.

Lafayette, who had instantly assumed the role of her protector, had obtained no results from Sébastiani's appeal to Metternich. Since diplomatic channels were ineffective, Baron Poerio, a Neapolitan lawyer then in exile in Paris, took counsel with a colleague in Milan and advised Cristina to appeal directly to Austria before the three-month time limit elapsed. Throughout May and June, and for the next seven years, Cristina's attitude vis-à-vis Austria was one of temporizing: she had every intention of returning to Milan but for the moment, for reasons of health, she could not. A dispatch to Metternich from Apponyi demonstrates her strategy and carries enough compassion to have made it convincing: "The princess has for some time been in great pecuniary embarrassment and in a very pitiful state of health, which has obliged her to consult the famous physician, Monsieur Dupuytren. She would like to return to Milan now but, on the one hand, her ill health seems to impede this, and on the other, she has expressed the fear that by reappearing in Milan she might be locked in a convent, which, she says, would cause her death." Ironically, the Austrian ambassador proved to be her most effective ally. The advice offered by Poerio's colleague, Marocco, to submit her case to Austria in an act of contrition, was rejected by Cristina in a letter that eloquently demonstrates the maturity of this twenty-three-year-old, not at all the foolhardy aristocrat playing at revolutionary, but a dignified individual fully cognizant of a perilous situation.

Dear Poerio,

I have read Marocco's reply and read it with all the attention you could wish from me. The careful consideration that I imposed on myself as a duty has only confirmed my first opinion. I consider

humiliating and useless the supplication Marocco proposes I address
to the Austrian government. I find it humiliating because it would
seem that after having tasted the bitter bread of poverty, I found it
too bitter, more bitter than I thought, more bitter than submission to
a government I abhor and whose legality I do not recognize.

I find it useless because I could ask that the sequester be lifted,
at least regarding the collection of my revenues to provide for the
pressing needs of my life, but as Marocco said himself, it seems unlikely to him that I could obtain this. . . . What would I therefore
achieve through the humiliation to which I would have subjected
myself? No, dear Poerio, try as I may to question my reasoning, and
to silence my feelings, my reason shows me no other way than the
one my feelings indicate. . . .[2]

Instead of humbling herself, she sent Metternich a letter protesting the
injustice of the action against her, and pointed out that the validation of
her passport in Florence and Bern, by Austrian officials, made her absence
from imperial states perfectly legal.

Her stubborn pride seemed unrealistic and ridiculous to many whose
view was strictly material, not least among them her own compatriots in
exile who would no longer benefit from her generosity, and who were the
first to accuse her of having sold herself to Austria when her revenues
were restored. This is perhaps the price of philanthropy: the donor is
almost always despised by the beneficiary for having superior means. To
others who could not conceive of an impecunious princess, her self-
imposed austerity looked like an affectation. Princesses, they reasoned,
are not like you and me, they have rich families and rich connections to
help them. There were nonetheless a few who understood her stance and
respected it: Odilon Barrot, abhorred by the legitimists for his role in
dethroning Charles X; General Fabvier, hero of the 1821 Greek insurrection and the 1823 constitutional war in Spain; François Corcelles, Carbonaro, republican, and close friend of Lafayette; General Lamarque,
pacifier of the royalist rebellion in Vendée led by the duchesse de Berry;
and of course Mignet and Lafayette. These were among the names cited
by Cristina in a letter to her mother describing a reception she gave on
April 25 for some forty Italian and French acquaintances she had made
during her first month in Paris. This letter, intercepted by the Milan
police as was all her mail, should have sufficed to declare her an enemy
of the state. Nonetheless, Metternich was unwilling to have her become a
cause célèbre, however much he wanted to discipline her. To persecute a
Trivulzio-Belgiojoso was to call attention to the repressive methods of
his emperor. Francis I could not be dissuaded by his own chancellor from
pursuing his brutal policies within the empire. They had become a source

of embarrassment to Metternich, who was more concerned with Austrian hegemony in Europe than with the suppression of every potentially dissident subject. For this reason, Metternich was particularly irritated by "L'Affaire Belgiojoso"; Cristina made it difficult for him to exercise his own principles of moderation.

Most important of all her new friends in the spring of 1831 was Lafayette. "The Hero of Two Worlds" was then seventy-four. His white hair masked by a brown wig, his skin unwrinkled, his back straight with military carriage, he was as young in heart as in mind and principle. Only his walk betrayed his age; a fracture of the leg in 1809 had left him with a limp and the need for a cane. He was still the same ardent liberal who, as vice-president of the National Assembly, had promulgated the Declaration of the Rights of Man forty-two years before. For all of liberal Europe, he had remained the symbol of these rights, still being sought by those who had lost them after Waterloo. Heine, one of the disfranchised, said of him in 1831, "Lafayette has raised himself a column preferable to the one in the Place Vendôme [Napoleon's] with a pedestal more solid than if it were marble or metal. Where can one find marble as pure as the heart of old Lafayette, metal as firm as his constancy?"

It was this youthful septuagenarian who developed an affection for the young princess that soon went beyond paternal solicitude. Always responsive to lovely ladies—although as virtuous in his habits as a seminarian, drinking only water and eating sparingly—he seems to have found in Cristina the final excitement of his adventurous life. It is doubtful that he ever transgressed the decorum imposed by their age difference, but his vast correspondence with her—he wrote to her almost daily until his death in 1834—reveals the place she quickly acquired in his life. In his first letter to her, of April 12, he told her:

> It is only too true, Princess, that General Zucchi was taken by an enemy frigate; a French courier has left to protect him from Austrian vengeance. The Prime Minister [Périer] has given me an appointment for tomorrow morning; I shall also see Sébastiani [Foreign Minister] in the morning on behalf of our Italian brothers. It was discussed today in the Chamber of Deputies and will be again tomorrow. But these are feeble measures compared with those to which we were entitled. . . .
>
> It is through a sad circumstance for your country that I have just had the honor of being presented to you. I am doubly distressed by it, as an ally of Italian patriotism and as a French citizen. But nothing can prevent me from feeling the personal advantage of this day, since I received an expression of your kindness and was myself able to offer you my homage.

Less than a month later, on May 7, he wrote: "You will consider me very presumptuous in my claims to your friendship,* but I will tell you with the liberty justified by the accident of my having been born fifty years before you, that it has become a necessity for my heart and is at least deserved by the friendship you inspired in me. Until Monday, my very dear Princess, Lafayette." Personal remarks of this kind were always preceded by detailed news of behind-the-scenes politics. Lafayette's power was soon to be eclipsed by Louis-Philippe's growing conservatism, but his influence remained considerable for the rest of that year. His aphoristic definition of the July monarchy as "A popular throne surrounded by republican institutions," would soon be parodied as "A doctrinaire throne surrounded by republican dismissals." (*Destitutions,* the French term for dismissal from public office, allows for a play on words.)

Throughout the spring of 1831, concerned with the release of General Zucchi and the other prisoners taken at Ancona, Cristina was too immersed in Italian affairs to be occupied with her own. Her rapid ascension to Parisian celebrity, her close contact with men of influence, attracted crowds of Italian exiles, who swarmed around her with requests for help: a job, money, news of an imprisoned relative, a recommendation, an introduction. Such attention would have turned the head of a more seasoned public figure. What her position of apparent influence—which was not insignificant since Lafayette and a wide circle of political dignitaries were at her disposal—did for her was far more beneficial for her morale than for her vanity; she became convinced of her ability to manage, without husband, family, or even fortune. If Malvezzi, forty years ago, recognized her state of mind in 1831 as "an exaltation that could be called sickly and that prodded her to busy herself ostentatiously, to want to surpass herself"—unaware as he was of the effects of epilepsy on the personality—it is evident today that her "magnificent crisis of pride" was a striking manifestation of her disorder. Her pathological need to outdo herself, to prove that she was not only as capable as others, but even stronger than most (epileptic soldiers are known to engage in feats of extraordinary heroism) was intensified by the insecurities of her childhood and the humiliations of her marriage. Her stubborn refusal to humble herself before the emperor, to borrow money even with Lafayette as guarantor; her frenetic activity on behalf of others; her ready acceptance of penury at the risk of her health—all appear as revenge against Emilio and her malady. She would not only suffice unto herself, whatever the hardships, she would suffice unto others, make herself the

---

* *Amitié* can have a more intimate connotation than "friendship"; here, it serves as a decorous circumlocution.

instrument of their salvation, their happiness. Every cause but her own was now hers, and the cause of Italy became the culmination of them all.

It WAS THEN that the bluestocking was born, the woman of ideals and ideas, too serious for frivolous pastimes, too disillusioned for passing flirtations. She was young; she was beautiful; she loved to dance, to laugh; she knew how to enhance her striking appearance with the right gown, the right hairstyle; she could ride with the best of horsemen and parry sallies with the sharpest of wits. But under it all she was far removed from girlhood, she had become a woman prematurely aged, determined in her principles, fearful of emotional risks. She would risk her health and her possessions, lavish her time and her affection, but her heart and her body were locked in the grip of distrust and disease. It was no longer a Prince Charming she sought to awaken her, but rather an antidote to his poisoned kiss administered by a wise doctor. Three such "doctors" dominated this decade of her life: Thierry, Mignet, Lafayette, each of them old—in suffering, temperament, or years. They healed her wounds, molded her thinking, and set the pattern of her future life. In a matter of months, each one laid claim to her forsaken affections, each one fashioned a part of the woman who would soon be using her mind in place of her beauty to establish her peace with the world, and her place in it.

Of the three, Lafayette may have exercised the greatest influence during her first year in Paris. He opened the doors, not only of Parisian salons and political circles, but of her personality, escorting her through the corridors of self-discovery: her usefulness to others, her capacity for generating interest in her ideas, her talent for rhetoric. Through him she learned of events before they reached the press, learned who and what were behind them, who had power and how it was used. It was a privileged apprenticeship to the ablest of masters. In Marseille and Lyon the winter before, she had been involved with conspirators and insurrectionists, but had herself been little more than a paying spectator. Under Lafayette's tutelage, she was behind the scenes, swaying opinion, arguing the fate of prisoners and exiles with ministers and diplomats—not in anterooms as an anonymous supplicant, but in their own salons as an equal and often, in rank and prestige, as a superior. And she was a diligent student, for according to a spy's report of November 1831, "she hardly ever goes to the theater, but regularly attends sessions of the Chamber of Deputies."

Her rapidly achieved prominence is demonstrated by a dithyramb,

dated May 4, 1831, from the pen of the Swiss poet Charles Didier. He
sent her a thirty-stanza ode, which reads in part:

> *En souffrant avec vous l'exilé se console*
> *Et son amour confond dans une même idole*
> *Vous et la liberté.**

How she and liberty became fused into a single idol is explained in an
earlier stanza, which lauds her personal sacrifices for freedom:

> *Un coeur noble se plaît aux nobles sacrifices,*
> *Et vous avez brisé la coupe des délices*
> *Pour le pain de l'exil.†*

Didier doubtless heard about her in Geneva during her stay in his
native city, for his covering letter states that the verses "were inspired by
you and composed in part in your salon. . . . I knew you, Madame,
long before being known by you." Didier's view of Cristina was shared
by many others with, and without, his poetic imagination. She had indeed
become one with the idea of Italy's liberation. She was object and symbol,
the reality and its representation. Herself a victim of Italy's oppressor,
she was the ideal emblem for Italy's suffering, hope, and beauty. The
importance of this factor cannot be stressed too much, for it explains her
overexposure to the public, which led to the inevitable distortion of her
own reality. From adulation to ridicule—such is often the fate of idolized
figures.

The ridicule began with her impoverishment. Strange as it seems,
Cristina received no support from her family during those first months in
Paris. A letter from Borlasca, her notary in Genoa, confirms this situation
with considerable emphasis: "I remain dumfounded at the thought that
you could be reduced to earning your living with your own hands; is it
possible? And your mother who is rich permits this?" To justify in his
own bewildered eyes the unexplained behavior of Marchesa Visconti,
Borlasca asks if perhaps "an act of generous pride" made Cristina reject
any subvention, "even that which would have come from maternal
hands?" In which case, and with all due respect, he feels that she has
gone too far. All that remained of her account in Genoa was 4,101.14

---

* Suffering with you the exile is consoled
  And his love blends into a single idol
      You and liberty.
† A noble heart delights in noble sacrifices,
  And you have shattered the cup of pleasures
      For the bread of exile.

lire, which he was enclosing in a draft. In May 1831 that was the extent of her resources, and there was little likelihood of a change in her situation since all her assets had been frozen by the decree of April 19. It is more likely that Cristina's mother was unable to get money safely out of Milan than that Cristina proudly refused her help. Unless Cristina, aware of the danger to her family resulting from her pending threat of civil death, had written—for the police to read—that she would not accept their help and could manage on her own. Certainly, the Viscontis were under surveillance and any discovered attempt to send Cristina money could have implicated them as accessories to a plot. Visconti's two-year detention for suspected conspiracy in 1821 did not make him a trustworthy subject. A second offense, even on a false allegation, would be far more serious, and could be used to force Cristina's return to Milan in exchange for his acquittal.

Much wiser indeed to hold out in Paris without money than to find herself a virtual prisoner in Milan with her fortune intact. "When one has no money," she said in her *Souvenirs dans l'exil,* recalling this period, "one must work to earn some." It was then that her career in journalism began. Alexandre Buchon, editor of *Le Constitutionnel,* a liberal paper under the Restoration that had lost favor with post-1830 liberals, hired her to write on Italian politics and to translate articles from the English press. It cannot have amounted to much of an income, but it assured her subsistence and introduced her to the world of journalism, from type faces to intrigues. Lafayette, solicitous over her health and position, was not at all enchanted by this commercial arrangement, preferring that she borrow money and live according to her rank. Three revolutions had still not shaken his eighteenth-century aristocracy. Yet he congratulated her with paternal pride: "You can imagine with what interest I read the articles on Italian politics in *Le Constitutionnel,* as well as the translations from English papers. I look for my dear and industrious girl in them [the articles were naturally anonymous], which will restore *Le Constitutionnel* to first rank among my newspapers." The articles were extremely well informed, Cristina having access to sources unavailable to other correspondents, such as freshly arrived refugees and Lafayette's inside information. The newspaper quickly became the leading organ of Italian news and soon attracted the ire of Italian authorities, not least the Vatican Secretary of State, who protested to the French ambassador that papal policy was being attacked in the French press.

Buchon then suggested that Cristina do a series of portraits of the newly elected deputies, to appear as an album of lithographs, printed by the firm belonging to Lafayette's son-in-law, Comte de Lasteyrie. This time, Buchon wanted Cristina's name to appear, and spread the news that the artist was "une princesse ruinée." (This was doubtless the origin of

Boulenger's name plate for her door, "LA PRINCESSE MALHEUREUSE.")
To this, Lafayette responded with the moral disapproval of a parent and,
more interesting still, with the tenderness of a lover. Little has been
written about Lafayette's friendship with Cristina, but even less about his
deeper attachment to her or her apparent reciprocity. Lafayette's daily
climb to her fifth-floor apartment becomes more understandable in the
light of his letters to her.* There is no need to speculate; his candor is
astonishing.

On July 10, writing from his country estate Lagrange, where she had
spent a week the month before and hurt herself in a riding accident,
Lafayette took great pains to spell out the emotional bonds that entitled
him to question her new activities. Apart from his disapproval of some of
them, he thinks she is overextending herself for she has also decided to
give private lessons in drawing and painting (later distorted as fans she
painted and peddled in the streets).

> If emotions were calculable, my dear Christine, I would not be certain
> that your affection, which makes me so happy, is a good bargain for
> you. So long as I live I think it is; for it is pleasant to be loved as I
> love you and appreciated as you are by me. But the difference between
> our ages is such that by attaching yourself to your old friend, you are
> preparing for yourself great unhappiness. I could also tell myself
> that by giving myself over as I did, and could not have prevented my-
> self from doing, nor did I in any way try, to the feeling that you in-
> spire in me, I recognize the need to be the first object of your
> tenderness. This is possible, I hope, for a woman who does not love
> her husband, is separated from him and has no children, since in that
> case a father is not without a fair chance of occupying first place; but
> when a woman is young, charming, admired, another sentiment, which
> the greatest filiality cannot equal, may sooner or later take hold of her
> heart, and you know that far from knowing your horoscope, I do
> not even know your biography. Nonetheless, I do not regret having
> abandoned myself, with all the ardor of a young man, the tenacity of
> an old man, and the confidence of my character, to that passionate
> affection which will have so much influence on the rest of my life.
> The reciprocity of your promise to me commits you considerably, for
> mine is a very loving heart and you have readily seen what you
> mean to it.

For Cristina this was a totally satisfying, and totally safe, commitment. His ardor was youthful, but he was nonetheless past seventy. For
Lafayette this was an immersion in the fountain of youth. One can feel
his pulse race and his heart skip a beat as he slipped into a sober letter of

* Published by Malvezzi in his biography, but apparently unknown to later writers.

May 14, recounting his efforts on her behalf, a very personal remark: "It is thus not until tomorrow, *ma chère et généreuse amie,* that I will know your fate. I know that mine is to be very tenderly attached to you for the rest of my life."

Her injured knee and a new cure of sea-water baths prevented her from returning to Lagrange, where he could have talked with her about her projects. Apprehensive that they would tax her health and lead to more embarrassment than profit, he wrote at length on July 10 and again on the following day. This, he says, is not his opinion alone, even if others, specifically Bianchi, do not dare tell her so. Lessons and portraits produce barely enough to live on, were she not a princess, but are more than her delicate health can tolerate. Furthermore, she would find it distasteful to discover that her "past situation and present poverty entered into the arrangements" made with her. "Will the necessary delicacy be properly observed by people who exploit your affairs in the interest of their vanity, their loquacity, their amusement? The Buchon enterprise and the use made of the dear artist [*la chère artiste*] had already reached me through Corcelles and others." She would be engaged for a pittance by people whose only interest was to boast about their generosity toward a destitute princess and to twitter over the idea of being taught to draw by a Trivulzio-Belgiojoso. To become the object of such gossip was demeaning, in his view. His second letter was even more specific in warning her against Buchon:

> Without wishing to speak ill of your associates, there is one, doubtless a capable fellow, whom I have seen involved in many an enterprise, exploiting in some of them his relationship with a Greek prince and fantasizing about the prince's sister, in others telling everybody about his intimacies with this one and that, and it has already come back to me from that source that all you had left was 1,000 francs reduced to 600, that happily he let you earn 200 francs for articles in *Le Constitutionnel,* and other gossip incommodious for you. I fear, *chère amie,* that without any ill intentions on his part, his protectorate of the ruined princess is somewhat in the service of a speculation for profit, and very much a speculation of vanity.

Two days later, her testy reply made him ask her pardon. But how could she have reproached him for pointing out the unpleasantness of poverty instead of encouraging her to endure it with patience and courage? "I beg you to believe me when I assure you on my honor that far from blaming I admire, I love that determination to seek out resources in your own work and in the employment of your charming talent. It is only about the accessories that I allowed myself to make observations, dictated by the exaltation of my tenderness for you." One can imagine the rush of irked feminist pride that made her object to his solicitude, and all the more irksome coming from the man who claimed to be "very surprised if there is a heart in the world that appreciates you and understands you better than I." He, then, better than anyone should foster her efforts, however demeaning to her title or name, to support herself. Honest work is never undignified.

Six days later, on July 17, peace having been made, he was still agonizing over the episode and complaining about "the unhappiness that your letter caused me and the long torment of your silence"—two days had elapsed between his second letter of warning and his apology to her reply, hardly a long silence. "Let us mutually forget our irritabilities; the rashness of mine was an error of tenderness, of solicitude, of abandon for you." Grateful that in her annoyance she did not deprive him of news that her knee was better, he breathed easily again. Every one of his letters of that period carries anxious remarks about her knee, her cure, the doctors she should consult, his eagerness to make appointments for her with the best of them. "Your letter, while easing my heart and mind, makes me garrulous; my sad anxiety was great, much greater than I dare admit even to you. But did you not assure me that none of my daughters could love me more than you do, and the word *daughter* that ended your letter, was that not a renewed assurance?"

His letters, always bearing greetings from his family and expressions of their concern for Cristina's health, give no inkling of the prickliness caused by her sudden eruption in his and their life. A widower since 1807, after thirty-four years of marriage to a woman he had deeply loved and admired, he was surrounded by a bevy of daughters and grandchildren, to whom he was completely devoted. A true patriarch, he presided over the combined families of his son and his two daughters, who in turn lovingly shielded him from the loneliness of old age. They received for him at his apartment on the rue d'Anjou; they stayed with him when he went to Lagrange. Stendhal claimed that Lafayette was fond of pinching pretty girls, but there seems never to have been any rival to the attention he lavished on his family. Until Cristina. Were it not for his letters to her, one would know nothing of the passion that exploded in the heart of this ascetic septuagenarian who had devoted his life to political ideals and paternal attachments. And were it not for her *Souvenirs dans l'exil,* one would not know how threatened his family seems to have felt on discovering that this foreign exile was invading the family circle. For nowhere in the many biographies of Lafayette consulted is there even the mention of her name, although the first to cover his personal life*—

---

* Written as a series of letter-memoirs at the request of Isaiah Townsend, it was first published in 1834 in the New York *Evening Star,* and in the original French two years later.

written immediately after his death by his doctor and close friend, Jules Cloquet, and cited by all subsequent writers—speaks of her in a way that should have aroused curiosity, since no other female friend is so distinguished in this account.[3]

> A lady, as remarkable for her beauty as she was eminent for the charms of her mind and the qualities of her heart, Princess Christine de Belgiojoso (née Trivulzi), offered Lafayette the most assiduous attentions when his condition permitted him to receive her [during the last weeks of his life]. Lafayette had, so to speak, adopted her as one of his children: he had for her that kind of pure attachment which superior qualities of the soul always inspire in people who know how to respond to them and appreciate them. I often found that excellent lady at his bedside: her intelligence, as solid as it was varied, the pleasure of her conversation, charmed his boredom, made him forget for a few moments his suffering. Lafayette often spoke to me about the rare merit of this lady, of the nobility of her character, and her beneficence toward her unfortunate compatriots.

Cloquet's admiration for her is easy to understand in the light of Lafayette's statement, quoted earlier, that he felt "pity or contempt for those who allowed themselves to be oppressed without resisting, and horror for their oppressors." What is hard to understand is that in this detailed account of Lafayette's last days, which mentions only his family, his valet, and his attending physician, Cloquet's remarks about Cristina should have gone unnoticed. Particularly noteworthy is that Cloquet records only one final message from Lafayette to anyone:

> Two days before his death, when all outside visits were prohibited, Lafayette said to his grandson, M. Jules de Lasteyrie: "You will tell *cette bonne princesse* de Belgiojoso how touched and grateful I am for her visits, and how much I suffer to be deprived of them." Since the general's death [this chapter was written six months afterward], the princess continues to see the family of her illustrious friend in intimacy, and mingles her painful memories with theirs.

At one in the morning of May 20, 1834, seeing that Lafayette's labored breathing of the past forty-eight hours would soon cause suffocation, Cloquet summoned the family and a few intimate friends. Cristina, if not already in the house, lived only a few doors away on the same street. At four-twenty, tenderly glancing at the faces surrounding his bed, he died clutching Cloquet's hand. Once again, Cristina lost a father; this one, she later said, "the best of fathers for me."

Her own account of that relationship is succinctly told in four paragraphs of her *Souvenirs dans l'exil,* along with an admirable evaluation of Lafayette as a historical figure. Beginning with those first weeks in April and May 1831, when she did all her own housework while awaiting money from Borlasca, she tells of Lafayette's almost daily visits on his return home from the Chamber of Deputies. Crossing the river and the Place de la Concorde to her apartment near the Madeleine, he began his trek up the five flights, announcing himself with the tapping of his cane. Since his arrival generally coincided with dinner time, she ushered him into her kitchen, where "as clumsy or as capable one as the other in the culinary arts, we held counsel on the manner of preparing the food at hand, which resulted in delightful discussions, great bursts of laughter, and not much to eat. Marquis de Lafayette's exquisite courtesy would not allow him to tolerate any effort on my part in his presence. A struggle of politeness ensued during which we ended up by fighting over the handle of the pan and a place at the stove. Protesting over his lack of obedience, I complained of the inconvenience of having as scullion the hero of two worlds."

Commenting wryly that this was the title that had been bestowed on him at the time, but that since his death considerable effort had gone into diminishing his reputation, she reflects on his place in history, which would be attributed with more rigorous judgment than during his own time, but perhaps with greater fairness.

> It will be recognized, I am convinced, that his political errors were caused by too high an opinion of mankind and men; he judged the latter by his own conduct. One can understand the error he committed in attributing to others the probity, the rectitude, and the sincerity that were only in him.

She was especially bitter about her own compatriots who withheld any public expression of sympathy when Lafayette died. The radicals, who felt he had outlived his usefulness, reproached him for not having led a revolt against Louis-Philippe that would have resulted in a republic certain to come to Italy's rescue—as though Lafayette alone were master of France's destiny and responsible for Italy's. Others who had benefited from his generous help were afraid to stand alone in honoring him. Had not Mazzini complained that Lafayette's only contribution to the Italian cause had been "words"? Cristina finally convinced a few friends to send a formal letter of condolence to the family—a month after his death! It was signed in the name of Italy by Emilio Belgiojoso, General Pepe, Mamiani, Gioberti, and Tommaseo. Once it was made public, those who had refused their tribute to Lafayette now resented that only titled signers spoke for them.

Recalling her frequent invitations to Lagrange, where she could study him in the leisurely atmosphere of his country estate, she evokes the historical quality of the place, the conservation not only of his own glorious past in the accumulated mementos, but of his ancestors and a whole world gone by. His family, as much as he, maintained the customs and manners of ancien régime aristocracy, "which made all the more pungent the discussions whose liberal tone was always set by him." In that populous world of children and grandchildren of which he was the soul, Cristina was made to feel at first like an intruder. "Those who belonged to him by blood ties did not share what they called his *infatuation* for me. I responded with docility, understanding up to a point the jealousy whose object was the affection of this eminent man. With time, this state of hostility vanished, and later our relations became friendly."

The intensity of her feelings for him is revealed, despite her great reticence, by her use of the word "father" and the implication that she has always kept his letters near her.

> . . . I won M. de Lafayette's complete tenderness and he became
> for me the best of fathers. If numerous occupations prevented him
> from seeing me for a day, he never failed to write. Those letters were
> enchanting; I have kept them all, and have managed to save them from
> various shipwrecks.

LONG BEFORE LAFAYETTE'S DEATH, Cristina had regained possession of her revenues, although her estate remained technically under sequester until the general political amnesty of 1838. She was again living like a princess, her salon was in full swing, another man became important in her life, but she never betrayed the "filiality" toward Lafayette that he had feared would be displaced by "another sentiment." Certainly, between 1831 and 1838 Cristina developed a very special sentiment for François Mignet, with whom she had an intimate and frequently agitated relationship. He was not an unattractive man, but seemingly charmless and no one's idea of a lover. Taken for granted as her ever-present cavalier, although they never lived openly together, his privileged status never deterred other men from seeking her love. His name never linked with other women, a confirmed bachelor in his habits and manners, Mignet was easily dismissed as a rival by the warmer blooded males who pursued Cristina. His only display of real temperament seems to have been an occasional crisis of jealousy. A southerner by birth, he was very northern in his fair coloring and phlegmatic nature. Judging from contemporary accounts and from his own correspondence, he was not the man to have swept Cristina, or any woman, off her feet. Yet he seems to have been the only man who succeeded where others failed, as will be seen.

Cristina's "various shipwrecks" began at the end of 1838 with the birth of her daughter. After a year of apparent secrecy—there is not even a record of the child's birth in the municipal archives of Versailles, where she was born—Cristina made it known that she had had a daughter named Marie, who may have been generally accepted as the prince's. Emilio had lived under her Parisian roof often enough—in fact, he was staying at the rue d'Anjou when Marie was born—so that such an assumption was not unthinkable. However, as will be seen from Emilio's own testimony, such was not the case. Hoping to establish Marie's legitimacy where it would matter most—in Lombardy, the site of her future inheritance if she could be proved the legal heiress to her parents' fortunes—Cristina returned to Italy in July 1840 for the first time since her dramatic departure ten years before.

In keeping with tradition, when Ferdinand was crowned emperor in Milan, in September 1838, a general amnesty was declared. Cristina was finally cleared of the charges that had been pending for eight years, and the sequester was officially lifted. Emilio, similarly amnestied though for lesser charges, had returned to Milan to participate in the celebrations. Count Hübner, in his memoirs of that year, *Une année de ma vie,* recorded Emilio's presence there: "Milan was in a state of festivity and the salon of Prince Metternich, who had accompanied the court, was the meeting-place of Lombard aristocracy. Alongside la Pasta, with Rossini at the piano, one heard Prince Belgiojoso, who, like so many others, had returned from exile. He was a tenor *di primo castello.* 'What a voice!' exclaimed Princess Metternich. 'And what a loss for music,' answered Belgiojoso, 'if your husband had had me hanged!' "[4]

Instead of taking up residence in Milan, where Emilio regularly disported his charms and talents when not doing so in Vienna, Paris, Geneva, or Lugano, she settled in Locate—some ten kilometers to the south, on the plain of Lombardy that rolls away from the Po—the ancient estate of the Trivulzios. A feudal castle of characteristic Lombard brick rose above fields and filthy hovels. A later baroque addition of stucco created an imposing carriage entrance leading into a handsome court frescoed with family emblems. Here, in the midst of squalid peasants and poorly administered lands, a good hour's drive from the comforts and pleasures of Milan, Cristina set out her lares. Her only companion was her daughter's English governess, Mrs. Parker; her only distraction, the vast library stacked to the ceiling with tomes of early Italian history. Seven years of Mignet's influence now bore fruits.

Where Lafayette had led her through the maelstrom of current politics, Mignet led her to the serenity of past events. It was he who tried to teach her the value of sober reflection and rational opinions. His example of elegant journalism, readable scholarship, and analytical thinking was not lost on her even if her volatile nature and partisan views were often at odds with him. He cultivated her taste for history, taught her the pleasure and discipline of research, refined her thinking and her style. She could never have endured the solitude of Locate, nor opted for such a life, without his influence. Her contacts with his historian friends, with the political and religious thinkers of the day, led her to occupy her idle loneliness with ponderous activities. The enormous enterprise of examining the origins of Catholic dogma, and of writing a hundred-page preface to her translation of Vico's *Scienza nova,* was conducted under his tutelage.

Her first interest in the early Church Fathers was for her own edification. Later, she used it to demonstrate the development of Christian thinking to an audience like herself, enlightened but untrained in theology. After little more than her first year in Locate, she had advanced far enough to send Mignet the introduction and first chapters, indicating that she had begun reading and taking notes much earlier. The introduction begins with an apology: "This book will be neither a history nor a treatise, for it lacks order and development in the arrangement of material, as well as depth in the exposition and examination of doctrine." (She had begun the work as mere notes on her readings, with no thought of producing a book until urged by her friends to do so.) This initial statement of humility, doubtless intended to shield her from accusations of historical presumption, is followed by a more solemn one of piety, intended to ward off any suspicions of heretical thinking. "I will have expressed my thoughts poorly if each word of this book does not express total submission to the decrees of the Catholic church. I believed even before I knew, but on reading the history and establishment of our religion, I abandoned blind faith to receive from knowledge a faith no less complete." Her reason had rebelled against certain orthodox views; her research led her to discover that, despite universal misconception, the Church had never passed judgment on those matters. Dogma, she explains, is not truth, but merely an expression of truth. As such, it was— and still is, she implies—open to interpretation.

The book—*Essai sur la formation du dogme catholique*—turned into a vast undertaking of four volumes, the first part appearing in August 1842, the second eight months later. If there is any single theme running through this rambling work, written with verve and directness, it is that of free will. From the very outset, beginning with Philo, the dogma of the Fall is questioned. Adam named everything but himself because the mind can perceive everything outside but not itself, thus proving that the universe must have existed on two separate levels. The mind could only communicate with the material world through the senses, and conversely, the senses could only perceive their own existence through the mind. A point of encounter between the two thus became necessary, and that point was sensuality. Since the initial union of mind and senses must have occurred through divine will, it becomes inconceivable that God's own creatures could have been punished for exercising their God-given faculty.

Turning to Origen, she finds another statement of the two natures created by God, the spiritual and the corporal. Both must be infinite, for if matter is not eternal then God's creative power is finite, since it would have had a beginning. Though both natures were of divine creation and coexisted eternally, they tired of being in perpetual adoration and withdrew in varying degrees. Church doctors rejected this theory as limiting God's power, since his creation was the impulse of his will, not the degree of his power. Upon which Cristina sardonically remarks, "Always zealous about granting God the attributes that would least satisfy human vanity, they thought it offensive to deny Him the faculty of having or satisfying a whim." In Origen's view of the two natures, she saw the possibility of a grave heresy, for if the spiritual nature could endure separation without falling, why then should the material—of equally divine creation—fall into sin?

Cristina did more than merely popularize theology. Proceeding by reason she confronted these doctrines with scripture and theological disputations, in order to arrive at a personal commentary that is often subtle and perspicacious. Her approach has the freshness of a direct encounter with the texts, uninhibited by the time-honored pontifications of Church and lay theologians. For she read those apologists herself, and not through the intermediary of their critics or interpreters. Speaking for example of Origen, not as a third-century Church Father but as one might of a contemporary philosopher, she says "Origen wrote only out of the need to communicate the discoveries of his intelligence. . . . He never speaks of himself in his works, yet after reading them one would easily believe one had lived long in the author's intimacy." The same might be said for Cristina, whose personal response to the ideas discussed makes her recondite material extremely communicable.

The central figure of her study is St. Augustine. The chapters leading up to him and going beyond him trace the heresies, each of whose eradication gave rise to a dogma. Until St. Augustine's appearance, well into the second volume, she had been sketching the history of Christianity in its attempt to define God and creation. By volume two, she had mastered her material sufficiently to indulge in occasional irony ("During the first two centuries of Cristianity, almost all the virtues were to be found on the side of Christians, and the vices on the side of pagans") and irreverent judgments ("Because of the high favor St. Augustine always enjoyed, his astuteness passed for profundity"). By re-creating Augustine's doubts and inner turmoil through skillful use of indirect discourse, she achieved a psychological portrait of the man before she presented her view of his doctrines: "The exaggeration with which he paints the blackness of his soul . . . cannot move the serious reader very deeply." His early interest in literature and philosophy placed him in the first rank among Christian philosophers; however, "these beautiful doctrines underwent fatal changes. One might say he had forgotten the uplifting sources from which he took his early ideas." His greatest shortcoming in her eyes is his inability to adore God, as Origen did. Augustine "loved God more than anything else, but what he understood was God's power, not His goodness." And she asks if Luther and Calvin could have dealt their terrible blows to the Church without Augustine's forceful battle against Pelagianism or his conception of God as a vengeful master. For it was in Augustine's writings that "that frightful doctrine [predestination] took its principal dogma."

According to her presentation, all the injustices of later Church practices stemmed from Augustinian inspiration, as concretized in the fifteen precepts attributed to him after his death by the Marseille priests—for example, (8) God does not want the salvation of all men but only of a small number of predestined ones; (9) the Lord was not crucified for the redemption of all; (13) there are men who were not created by God for eternal life but only to serve as ornaments for this world and for the use of other men. In her iconoclastic summary of St. Augustine, one feels the deep indignation of a defender of the Catholic Church, and primarily of its crucial doctrine of God's infinite mercy.

> More curious than deep, more cold than grave, even more argumentative than convinced, more indefatigable than strong, St. Augustine needed movement as much as disciples. He did not know how to speak to equals, and his language always exuded humility, disputation, or authority, but never unconstraint or affection. . . . Inaccessible to shameful passions, he acquired a reputation for tenderness which he did not deserve; incapable of fatigue . . . his heart passed, though wrongly, for energetic and ardent.[5]

One can easily imagine that such remarks did not go by without causing a hue and a cry. The most insolent, which appeared in *La Revue des Deux Mondes*,[6] aimed directly at the author on the assumption that there would be enough shrapnel to destroy the book. "It is in conversation that women accomplish most of their thinking. Thus, they cannot create, since writing requires solitude. The writer of *Essai sur la formation du dogme catholique* is, however, an exception to this natural order, but the faults of the book can be attributed to the general lacunae of women. . . . Metaphysics and theology should have been the substance of the work, instead it is biography that dominates." Scandalized by her treatment of St. Augustine, he sermonizes: "We do not know if Mme de Belgiojoso decided in advance to find a victim among the Church Fathers, but the choice was unfortunate; there are colossi against whom no one, not even a woman, is allowed to raise a hand." Obligated, however, by the rules of gallantry, he offers a patronizing pat at the end of his review: "One finds in the *Essai* neither ardors of faith nor flashes of understanding; believers will be scandalized, philosophers will be dissatisfied. Nonetheless, the book has its merits. It is remarkable that a woman took the trouble to read, or glance at, so many historical documents, and to analyze them. The style of the biographies and summaries which compose the book has an accuracy, elegance, and at times precision that tends to elevate it to the seriousness of history."

Although the book was published anonymously, its author's name had become an open secret. Another reviewer, in *Le Journal des Débats*,[7] made no mention of name or sex, but offered every possible clue in his encomium. "On reading these pages, written in the most eloquent, most concise and masterful style, and with irreproachable precision, one would not suspect that we owe them the honors of hospitality. But elite intelligences have a common homeland, and the author belongs to France for the perfection with which he writes the language, and for the noble use he makes of a great name and great leisure." While respecting the author's desire for anonymity, he adds "the name it hides is known to refugees and poor people; from now on, it will also be recognized by literati." And this reviewer admires precisely what the other reproached: "The form the author gave his work has a particular attraction, that of biography. . . . Great ideas always inspire more interest when they are represented by great men." But he warns that the author's "serene independence of mind and sureness of analysis may not be easily absolved."

Another notable characteristic of the book is what it reveals about Cristina. Her interest in the early African church ("I would say that Africa was the spirit of Christianity, Greece the word, and Rome the action"), characterized by its mysticism and its emphasis on redemption, suggests a wounded sensibility in search of compassion and forgiveness. When she voices her admiration for the hermits and ascetics of that ancient church, one senses a desire to justify her own reclusion and ideals.

> One is seized with admiration and respect for these ascetic men, devoted to an idea, making it the study and concern of an entire life, renouncing the world, enjoying pain and privation so that their soul may become more detached from the material body, and may sink

more easily into the depths of its mysterious existence. These men were mistaken: the future rejected their hopes, and humanity their ideas.[8]

IN THE MIDST of all her recondite theological studies, Cristina found time during the late summer of 1843 to sit for a portrait by Henri Lehmann, better known today for his 1840 portraits of Marie d'Agoult and Liszt. Exhibited in the Louvre among Lehmann's entries of the Salon of 1844, the painting placed Cristina in the broad spotlight of public scrutiny. Irresistibly captivating as she looks at the spectator with her enormous black eyes, her every salient characteristic was captured by Lehmann's brush—exquisitely chiseled nose, heavy eyebrows extending almost to her temples, delicate mouth with its sensuous lower lip, dimpled chin, gleaming black hair framed by a regal braid, and long sensitive fingers ideally suited to the keyboard. Set in a neo-Renaissance cornice, the corners of which repeat the damask background, itself a repetition of her damask gown, the composition and technique of the portrait lie midway between Raphael and Ingres. The pose evokes the classic position and serenity of a Raphael Madonna, while the sculptural sheen of the skin, elegant draping, and enamel-like surface suggest Ingres's restatement of the Renaissance. Despite its graphic qualities and alluring subject, contemporary art critics were horrified by the painting. Saint-Martin, in the *Revue Indépendante,* wrote: "This woman has neither a chest nor shoulders; there would not even be room for a heart under that thin narrow surface that is supposed to represent the bust; the hands, however, are well painted. This ill-fated woman, deceased, passed on to the state of a frightening shade, is this the beautiful and charming Princess Belgiojoso?" And Pleisse, in the *Revue des Deux Mondes,* expostulated: "This portrait is at the same time a disaster and a calumny. By seeking style and character, by chasing after some doubtless unattainable ideal, M. Lehmann sacrificed the body for a shadow and outlined on his canvas this cold, immobile, dead image." Sainte-Beuve reflectively concurred that "there is indeed something strange about this portrait! It is not a portrait, said one spectator, it is an apparition!" And yet, it was that very quality of apparition, that unique pallor starkly contrasted against the shimmering ebony hair and huge coal-black eyes that sent Heine to rhapsodic heights and drove Musset to hysteria. Critics of the day were evidently less Romantic than artists.

Almost simultaneous with the preparation of the last two volumes of the *Essai* was Cristina's translation of Vico's *Scienza nova*—a seminal work for philosophical historians and juridical philosophers—which appeared in 1844. Michelet, who considered Vico his only master, had published an abridged translation in 1827. Cristina's was therefore the first complete French translation of a work that had been widely discussed since its appearance a century before. Until well into the twentieth century, Cristina's remained the only complete French translation. Her hundred-page introductory essay attempted to do for Vico's abstruse thinking what her elegant French had done for his hermetic prose. For the uninitiated reader, she traced the development of this eighteenth-century Neapolitan's ideas from his first awareness of metaphysics through the Greek philosophers, to his own personal system, which held law to be the unifying principle of human thought. Through his study of Roman law and history, he came to see Roman civilization as the connecting link between primitive expressions of justice, "poetic wisdom," and conscious philosophical systems, "occult wisdom." Vico's concept of justice as divinely generated, one and immutable like its creator, but evolving in three phases—divine, heroic, human—is an idea that surely held much appeal for Cristina at that time.

Despite her profession of total obedience to the Church, the *Essai* clearly reflects her resistance to inflexible doctrine, exemplified by her horror of predestination. The very flexibility of Vico's system, the notion of progress, of a continuous dialogue between the divine and the human, of civil—rather than theocratic or autocratic—law as the ultimate expression of divine will, all correspond to Cristina's rejection of doctrinaire thinking, as much related to Catholic dogma and Austria's despotic rule of Italy, as to her own personal condition of woman, wife, mother, and imperial subject. She was a woman trying to do a man's job for her country, she was condemned to remain the wife of a man who flaunted his contempt for marriage, she was the mother of a child whom the law would not allow her to recognize as her own, she was the subject of a tyrannical monarch. Her attempt at independence—certainly not to flout tradition but merely to escape its suffocating clutch—made her look for some philosophical justification. Basically conservative and evolutionary in her thinking, although some of her ideas and behavior seemed radical, she respected and believed in established institutions, but with an open mind and the desire for modifications. She genuinely believed in the sanctity and moral validity of the Church though she rejected the misinterpretations of its teachings and the errors of certain practices. She believed in a constitutional monarchy for Italy while advocating the overthrow of Austrian rule and admiring republican dynamism. She believed in marriage and the family so deeply she refused to participate in the travesty of her own. In the black and white world of everyday life, such contradictions are not readily acceptable.

Specialists may rightly have questioned her competence to vulgarize

Vico's complex philosophy of history in her essay, but her achievement of rendering his ideas accessible to French readers was nonetheless hailed. Her translation, together with the *Essai,* established her reputation among cognoscenti as a serious scholar. Even the curmudgeonly Sainte-Beuve recommended the *Essai* to a noted lady theologian of the time, Countess Edling, telling her that "until now the princess did not give one reason to surmise the doctor in her who has suddenly been revealed with as much seriousness as distinction."[9] Still, she antagonized less brilliant women and less productive men, who gossiped that she had been helped by her historian and theologian friends—Thierry, Mignet, l'abbé Coeur— as though men worked unaided or uninfluenced by their friends. Juliette Adam, a woman of letters herself, wrote of Cristina: "Men avenge themselves cruelly on women who are more passionate about ideas than about love. They feel robbed."[10]

Cristina's scholarship, though certainly encouraged and directed by her friends, was produced by her own efforts, in the isolation of Locate, with her own talents, instigated perhaps by the very absence of men in her private life. There was no all-absorbing passion for a lover, no day-to-day existence with a husband, to distract her from her interests or deter her from pursuing them. There was, however, one man who played a dominant role in her life.

5

Le Beau Mignet
et la Belle Princesse

THIERRY'S LETTER to Mignet of March 26, 1831, was more than an introduction of Cristina; it was a prophecy. His closing sentence (". . . after talking with her it will no longer be for my sake that you wish to render her all the good offices in your power") foretold the relationship that was to last for forty years despite major differences and serious difficulties. François Mignet was then thirty-five years old, hero of the July Revolution, celebrated journalist, respected scholar, as much appreciated for his elegant carriage and handsome face as for his rigorous mind and integrity. His blue eyes and waving blond hair earned him the epithet of "le beau Mignet," which he still carried at the age of eighty. Born in Aix in 1796, Alexis-François-Auguste Mignet grew up with three younger sisters in a city whose university and law court had made it a center of enlightenment. A bachelor all his life, his attachment to his family and native city remained constant. His father, a journeyman locksmith from Poitou, had settled in Aix, becoming a successful artisan of wrought-iron gates and balconies still to be seen today. Mignet's mother survived his father by forty-five years (there was a twenty-year difference in age). When she died at past eighty, Mignet was disconsolate. As the only son, and the first-born, Mignet's protective attitude during his mother's long widowhood may have influenced his decision to remain a bachelor. The liberal ideas he had heard discussed in his father's atelier certainly contributed to his political and intellectual orientation.

A brilliant student from his earliest classes, he was awarded a scholarship to the Imperial Lycée in Avignon. In 1814, having completed his studies there, he wanted to defend the empire that had allowed him to go beyond his father's condition of artisan. However, his responsibility for three sisters forced him to abandon his dream of a military career and settle for a teaching post in history at his former lycée. A year later, with allied troops swarming over France, he returned to Aix to enter law school, where he met Adolphe Thiers, a fellow student from Marseille. From 1815 until Thiers's death in 1877 their friendship remained fraternal. As different in appearance and character as they were similar in views and brilliance, they received their law degrees at the same time, each awarded a prize for his thesis. These two contrasting figures—Thiers was small, ugly, excitable, ambitious, and a rather successful womanizer; Mignet was tall, attractive, remote, studious, and ascetic—complemented each other in a friendship that never failed. Opportunities for such young professionals without family influence were very few under the Restoration, and Mignet soon determined to follow his natural vocation for history. A series of prize-winning essays led to the writing of *De la Féodalité, des institutions de Saint-Louis,* which was submitted to the Académie des Belles-Lettres in Paris. The prize he collected there, 750 francs, was almost enough to provide a modest living for a year. The manuscript was soon sold to a publisher for 600 francs, and a month later Mignet joined the staff of the *Courrier Français.* Within little more than a year after his arrival in Paris, he contracted to write a history of the Revolution and was invited to give a series of public lectures at the Athénée, which were to secure his fame and material independence.

The Athénée, founded in 1784, was a private institute to which members subscribed (120 francs for men, 60 for women and students) for the privilege of attending Thursday-evening lectures from December to April, and access to a well-stocked library and salons for discussion, near the Palais Royal. The high fee attracted a well-to-do audience whose political leanings were distinctly liberal. *"L'Athénée* is the only liberal literary society in France," wrote *Le Globe* in 1824. Mignet's lectures were a triumph. During his two seasons there he became a celebrity among the intelligentsia and political malcontents of Paris. Convinced of opportunities for success in Paris, Mignet urged Thiers to join him in September 1821. They shared a grim two-room apartment, in which they produced those first works that established them as historians and journalists. Lafayette, Benjamin Constant, and Talleyrand rapidly offered their protection to the "Provençal twins" (as they came to be known), who had the youth, the energy, and the talent needed to combat the retrograde institutions imposed by Louis XVIII and Charles X.

Already under the reign of Louis XVIII a major intellectual movement had started to foment. The revolutionary flood, briefly dammed by the Empire and the Restoration, began to pour over into history, art, poetry. The influence of German and English thinkers on France's eighteenth-century luminaries had broadened the study of history, and the rapid succession of regimes stimulated an interest in the interaction of past and present, awakening the need for a fresh appraisal of ideas and events, no longer based on rhetoric but on documents. Mignet's approach marked him as a forerunner of the movement, beginning with his 1822 lectures on the religious reformation of the sixteenth century, and his 1823 lectures on the revolution and restoration in England. The implicit analogies between England's past and France's present had a profound impact on his audiences, for as Mignet presented it, history had dusted itself off and become a vital part of current political thought.

When Charles X succeeded Louis XVIII, Mignet became all the more vociferous against the censorship of the press and the suppression of civil liberties. The death of his friend Jacques Manuel—a lawyer from Provence, a member of the Chamber of Deputies, and a liberal journalist—suddenly propelled a fundamentally prudent man into reckless action. The funeral procession, barred by armed police from crossing Paris and forced into taking the outer boulevards to avoid a public demonstration of sympathy for an enemy of the regime, led to a minor riot which the official press grossly exaggerated. Mignet, outraged by this exploitation "of the august dignity of a funeral" for suppressive ends, instantly wrote *Relation historique des obsèques de Monsieur Manuel,* printed in two hundred copies for private distribution. During the trial that ensued Mignet was hailed for his defense of the freedom of the press. Acquitted, he founded a newspaper with Thiers and Armand Carrel, a soldier turned journalist who had become Thierry's secretary. On January 3, 1830, *Le National* began publishing the articles that incited public opinion against Bourbon violations of revolutionary ideals, and led it toward the concept of a constitutional monarchy.

Mignet has been largely forgotten. However, from 1822 to the revolution of 1848 he was foremost in that remarkable generation of historians, more widely read than Michelet or Thiers, and considered the worthy equal of Thierry and Guizot. Even after he lost favor with the younger historians, his later works on the court of Philip II, on Mary Stuart, and Benjamin Franklin were immediately translated into English, German, and Italian. His articles, lectures, and above all his *History of the French Revolution,* laid the groundwork for a new philosophy of history, inspired by Montesquieu and eighteenth-century thinkers. The point of departure was not original but it was Mignet who spread the idea of historical determinism, although the term itself did not gain dictionary recognition until 1842. (Karl Marx was one of Mignet's more attentive readers.) "He led his public to recognize that in history as in physics, the same causes produce the same effects, making history an experimental science that determines action," wrote a recent biographer.[1]

This was an inflammatory concept, for in drawing analogies from earlier revolutions Mignet implied a rule: when monarchy becomes reactionary and autocratic—in the past a necessary development in the evolution of centralized government—it engenders a revolution. A prophetic view indeed, and to all but ultras a consoling thought in a Europe once again oppressed by the Restoration.

Through his contact with Manuel and Benjamin Constant, Mignet had become convinced of the potential influence of the journalist, a role more consistent with his reflective, unambitious nature than political office. "The task of the journalist," he said, "is of all pursuits the one that most resembles action." As early as 1822 he courageously wrote that the Holy Alliance had betrayed its peace-keeping mission by sacrificing common interests to personal ones when it declared war on Spain: "The insurrection in Greece was the cause, and the policy toward Spain the occasion." Mignet's commitment to modern ideas was stated in 1825: "Now that one finds criteria in political law, morality in man, knowledge in observation, and none of these in faith, it is impossible to find anywhere but in society the ties that link men. No longer in communion through faith, men must find communion through government." A defender of liberty to the point of distrusting popular revolutions because they degenerate into despotism, he used *Le National* to elaborate a clear program of legal action. He tried to promote a bloodless revolution that would produce a liberal monarchy, using as his model the English revolution of 1688. His continued attacks against the government finally provoked its ire. On the evening of July 26, 1830, the presses of *Le National* were smashed by the police but repaired in time for the morning edition, which carried the protest of Parisian journalists. Mignet's name was at the head of the list as author of the protest. "The due process of law has been interrupted, a regime of force has begun. The government has today lost its character of legality which commands obedience. As for us, we shall resist it; it is for France to determine how far her own resistance will go." The next three days saw the installation of a constitutional monarchy in place of a monarchy of divine right.

The Glorious Days of July, *Les Trois Glorieuses,* which introduced Lafayette's constitution and Louis-Philippe's reign as citizen-king, were as much a personal triumph for Mignet as a national victory. For Mignet, the battle was now over. Thiers, a man of action who enjoyed the political arena, at once entered the new government, soon becoming Minister of the Interior. Mignet's distaste for personal exposure was confirmed by his unsuccessful candidacy in 1831 for the Chamber of Deputies. Pressed by friends, he had presented himself as a candidate from the Var and was defeated by one vote. The July Revolution was the "Revolution of Historians." It was now to history that Mignet wanted to devote all his energies. Free to request almost any position in the cabinet, he chose to become the first Director of Archives of the Ministry of Foreign Affairs. As such, he had access to the secret records that he needed for his study of the Reformation in sixteenth-century Europe. As a Counselor of State, concomitant with his directorship, he remained in a sensitive if not a policy-making position. And his close friendship with Thiers (who until his marriage shared Mignet's official residence on the rue Neuve-des-Capucines) allowed him to exercise his judicious influence on the cabinet.

There were many, however, who did not approve of such passive participation. *Le Figaro,* in an editorial of December 3, 1830, voiced the disappointment of Mignet's former partisans: "That sublimity of intelligence which seemed to aspire to the regency of a republic or to the consolidation of a monarchy has descended to vulgar appetites. A fat sinecure satisfies that ambition which promised to be so active and voracious. The liberal of the Restoration, confined within a sumptuous residence, like the rat of the fable within a cheese, now entertains himself by nibbling a few old archives and looks with pity on debates over no less than the future of the nation." The editorialist not only mocked Mignet's abdication of responsibility toward the nation he had helped to found, but cruelly satirized certain of Mignet's shortcomings as a scholar that might otherwise have been overlooked. "The future is not doctrine. . . . No one knows better than he how to put a fact through the mill, divide and subdivide it, abstract it and reconstitute it into a general idea. He predicts the past, demonstrates the veracity of truth and the potential of the already achieved."

WHEN CRISTINA ARRIVED in Paris, Mignet's credit in the government and in society was still at its zenith, the *Figaro* editorial notwithstanding. He was a young man of great maturity, impeccable elegance, and excessive prudence. It is reported that when Thiers was correcting the proofs of a new dictionary which he had helped edit, he jotted in the margin: *"SAGE, voyez EGOISTE; EGOISTE voyez SAGE; et pour les deux, voyez MIGNET."* All verbal portraits of him reveal the same contrast between the charm of his appearance and the rigor of his nature, caricatured in the *Figaro* editorial: ". . . . an elegant hat unsmartly worn, a tie fashionably knotted on a narrow collar stiff with electoral gravity, an exquisitely cut tailcoat on a torso that moves in a straight line . . . the whole of this young personage is a combination of the Dutch uncle and the dandy."

Coveted by women inclined to matrimony, esteemed by serious men, this attractive bachelor was known to be as chaste in private as he was reserved in public. He was the favorite pupil of one of France's best fencing masters, yet his posture lacked the grace of a supple body; his blond curls and blue eyes sought to seduce no one. He was unanimously considered affable, but Stendhal found him lacking in wit, an irredeemable failing in Stendhal's eyes. Others were more generous but complained of his dogmatism: "When someone proposes an idea to him he rallies all the power of his intelligence to make it fit the systematic arrangement he has in mind. . . . Classification has its merits, as one can see by reading his *Histoire de la Révolution française,* but when he speaks in a salon one also notices the aridity of his conversation."[2] Even Sainte-Beuve, who admired him publicly in *Portraits contemporains,* and Heine, who consistently praised him as an orator in *Lutèce,* contributed to this picture of a man with all the gifts of mind and body, but charmless.[3] Yet this stolid rhetorician was at once smitten by Cristina. His reply to Thierry's letter of introduction betrays a glimmer of masculine sensibility, and his uncontrollable pedantry as well.

> My dear Thierry,
>
> I have seen Princess Belgiojoso, who is beautiful, charming, witty, and to whom I shall render all the help I can provide. I obtained the general's [Lafayette's] assurance of the government's active interest in her, should that become necessary. Until such a necessity, which would be sad indeed, for the good will she would find here is no guarantee of success elsewhere, it is important to remain quiet.
>
> This is what I advised the princess . . . in her interest so as to avoid as much as she can the attention of the Austrian government.
>
> Since everything is moving toward order within and to peace without, the government will perhaps become less persecutive and we shall achieve some compliance for our requests. The war is postponed, though not avoided, and half the task of July remains to be accomplished. Accomplished in France, it must be accomplished in Europe as well, where the counter-revolution was completely established in 1814–1815 through the restoration of the Bourbons and the treaty of Vienna. However, this second part of the Revolution, once resumed, will be slower to achieve and no harm will come from waiting.
>
> It will be achieved in as orderly, as invincible a manner as the other. We will no longer flow over Europe like a torrent and will refashion the borders of the States as we re-established our liberties, with the experience of past excesses and the moderation of definitive victory.

The contrast between "la belle princesse" and "le beau Mignet" would appear to be irreconcilable in terms of character and background. The formidable aristocrat, secure in her opinions and privileges, was as forceful as the scholar of humble origin was retiring. But in the ideological context of the July Revolution, their compatibility was stronger than their differences. On the common terrain of constitutional monarchy, a destitute princess-in-exile and an elegant plebeian ensconced in the Ministry of Foreign Affairs were barely distinguishable. In fact, Cristina's circumstances were downright niggardly compared with Mignet's. There was much hilarity in the gossip columns over the fifth-floor garret where she first received Mignet, Lafayette, and Thiers. Fifty years later, on Mignet's death, the obituary writer of Paris's leading newspaper was still smirking over those frugal meals that had turned into legendary omelettes.[4] The style of this text, with its many inaccuracies and innuendoes, reveals the image of Cristina that was projected into posterity.

FRANÇOIS-AUGUSTE-ALEXIS MIGNET 1796–1884*

Two Siamese twins from Provence had the singular faculty, for over half a century, of remaining distinct while remaining united. Both of them became journalists, both of them *Carbonari,* both of them historians. Adolphe [Thiers] marching ceaselessly, Alexis asking only to sit down. . . . Thus not comparable, Mignet never for a moment envied the political success and European fame of Monsieur Thiers. For if M. Thiers was powerful, and even all-powerful, M. Mignet was handsome, and even very handsome. Indeed, on the testimony of his contemporaries, M. Mignet was not a prince charming, but one of those adorable bourgeois of the constitutional reign of Louis-Philippe. Adorable and adored bourgeois! An Italian princess, a real princess, Mme de Belgiojoso, exiled from her country for her political opinions, made innumerable omelettes with him. . . . It was the Provençal bourgeois who broke and beat the eggs, it was the princess who held the frying pan [far more suggestive in French: *qui tenait la queue de la poêle*]. Those omelettes à deux were often shared by three, and the third fork always found them succulent. Rue du Montparnasse and later in Port-Marly, the third fork often changed name: Alfred de Musset, Victor de Laprade, the pianist Doehler, whom Heine mocked. Those names never spotted the princess's tablecloth, but one evening the dinner was disturbed by Alfred de Musset, who brandished his fork like a trident and wounded the princess's face. That fork thrust left its mark in the works of the poet; we have all read that charming piece *Sur une morte.* . . . Alfred de Musset is dead and his *Morte* no longer seeks to live in the splendid villas of Lago Maggiore, while François-Auguste-Alexis Mignet, almost octogenarian,

---

* The order of names Alexis-François-Auguste is the one given by Knibiehler, the most authoritative source on Mignet. He never signed with his first name in any correspondence, but when he initialed anything it was always "F.M." Even with his closest friend, Thiers, he signed himself "Mignet."

still passes straight-legged along the Quai Malaquais, Immortal . . .
and perpetual! *

Cristina's own account of that period, mysteriously overlooked
though it was published in 1850, leaves no doubt that her poverty, ridiculed well into the twentieth century as a pose, was perfectly genuine.

> If, at the time of my first exile, I had thought of coming to these
> lands [Turkey], I would have avoided the painful situation in which
> I found myself in France when I arrived from Italy, having managed,
> despite my extreme youth, to get into political trouble with Austria,
> whose government sequestered my properties. Under those circum-
> stances, Paris, which I had longed to know, became for me a place of
> terrors. Without support, my double quality of princess and refugee
> served precisely to give me the airs of a dramatic heroine. Rich heiress,
> brought up in the traditions of Milanese aristocracy, I knew absolutely
> nothing about the realities of life. Never had I touched money and I
> could not imagine what a five franc piece represented. On the other
> hand, I did not hesitate to classify an ancient coin according to its
> value. Ignorant of the price and commercial value of a consumer ob-
> ject, I thoroughly understood the relative value of art objects. I could
> paint, sing, play the piano, but did not know how to hem a handker-
> chief, cook a boiled egg, or even order a meal. The task of ordering
> and paying for my household had always been entrusted to a ser-
> vant. . . .
> I had jewels of considerable value; nothing simpler than to sell
> some of them. I must admit the thought never occurred to me. I
> understood nothing, but nothing, about business dealings. As a
> rigorous logician, I applied to my situation that elementary law of eco-
> nomics: when one has no money one must spend none. The conse-
> quence of this reasoning was that I thought of doing my own cooking.
> You missed something, my friend, not to have seen me in operation
> [this was a letter addressed to Caroline Jaubert]; I still laugh when I
> think about it. It did not last long it is true since it was proven to me
> by those interested in my situation that I was not in the state of
> penury I imagined. But believe me, for a few weeks, I prepared my
> modest meals with my own white hands.

Not even her closest friends, and certainly not her suitors, seem to
have understood her attachment for a man so pale beside her verve, so
self-possessed beside her spontaneity, so unadventurous beside her temerity, so reserved beside her inexhaustible affection. Always correct, most
often formal even in his voluminous correspondence with Thiers, overtly

---

* As a member of the Académie Française, he was one of the forty *Immortels;* he was
also Secrétaire perpétuel of the Académie des Sciences Morales.

affectionate only with his family, there is not a trace of madness in Mignet, except one—he was deeply in love with Cristina. Sent on a diplomatic mission to Madrid in 1833,* he begged Thiers to help shorten his stay: "I did what you wanted, I left my work and my affections. . . . See that I am authorized to return within eight to ten days." Complaining that the courier had brought no news regarding his return to Paris, he added: "He did however bring me a letter which I thank you for having sent [from Cristina transmitted by diplomatic pouch], but which did not calm my anxiety about the health that means more to me than anything in the world. . . ." Cristina's ill health at the time was the cause of his impatience to return to Paris.

Fifty-six unpublished letters from Cristina to Mignet, spanning thirty years,† reveal the insufficiencies of the man: his limited emotional and intellectual range, his inability to give generously of himself. Yet it was precisely this man—whose tepid virility made few demands on her traumatized sensuality, whose prudence and judgment reined her impulsiveness—to whom she may have offered the only intimacy of her life as a woman. It was Mignet's erudition and experience in political journalism that led her to the career which eventually filled her life. Without him she might not have learned how to utilize the periods of seclusion her ill health often imposed on her. It is not surprising that they had their worst quarrels when she was relatively well, for that was when she led her brilliant social existence. They disagreed over many crucial things: the future of Italy, Cristina's extended absences from Paris, Mignet's stubborn resistance to travel, the interest other men showed her. Their intimacy slowly eroded, but until the end of her life Cristina continued to seek his approval, solicit his advice, commiserate over his misfortunes, and communicate her deep affection for him. Everything she wrote in French was submitted to his criticism, more valuable to her than the praise of others: "I receive many compliments [for the first part of *La Formation du dogme catholique,* which she was writing in 1841] but do not believe they spoil me. I prefer your corrections to the greatest number of such compliments and consider them all to be dictated by politeness,

---

* The Foreign Ministry wanted to manifest France's support of the regent, who was defending her daughter's succession to the throne against salic law. Mignet's three-week stay was a triumph of diplomacy but aroused rumors of personal success with the queen, reported even in *Le National:* "That elegant man, that hair always well-combed, that language of the salon always so gallant—he is another Buckingham sent to another queen regent."

† For which I am deeply indebted to Yvonne Knibiehler, professor of history at the University of Aix-en-Provence. While preparing her doctoral dissertation and subsequent book, the first modern studies on Mignet (see Bibliography), she classified and copied Mignet's entire unpublished correspondence from family archives in Aix.

indulgence, or mockery." Her trust in his judgment was so great that she accepted his criticisms without discussion: "I would like to disagree with you on some of your corrections so as to prove, by yielding, the total faith I have in you."

After a twenty-year relationship, during which her peripatetic life had accustomed her to separations and silences, she could still write Mignet a letter of passionate resentment over his neglect, a letter whose tone and content are unique in her rather sizeable correspondence. She took few people for granted, having learned bitterly that her own notion of friendship was not always shared. But of Mignet, she demanded what she expected of no one else. No silence distressed her, no interest delighted her, as much as his. Whatever doubts remain as to the nature of their relationship, the following letter would seem to dispel a fair number. In view of Mignet's unyielding character, this letter reveals not only his importance to Cristina, but implies her rights over him. And for once, the circumlocutory Cristina gave full vent to her feelings.

Ciaq Maq Oglou [Turkey]
24 March 1853

Have you forsaken me enough? neglected me enough? mistreated me enough? It is not in my nature to make advances on two occasions and make a nuisance of myself; and so I decided to follow your example and behave as if I had never known you. But I cannot bear the thought that you doubtless believe I have no reproach to make you with regard to me. It is to undeceive you that I break my vow of silence. It is to tell you this: I want you to know, you who consider yourself virtually faultless, who believe you behave according to established and infallible principles, you who rest in the serenity of your conscience and would willingly offer yourself as a model to mankind, know that your behavior toward me has been unkind, ungrateful, and unfaithful. Know also that I would not change my conscience for yours, for if I have great faults, if I made great mistakes in my life, I can at least say that never was I failing when it came to friendship or to a friend. Know that for you I have always affirmed the surest and sincerest affection, that I have never let a day go by without thinking of you; that your misfortunes, the displeasures that you experienced, have afflicted me more than my own; that in all my reverses of fortune I have never forgotten you, and what is more, while you and your countrymen worked against my country I never condemned you, recognizing that political and other opinions can sometimes take precedence over personal affections.

Do you really believe that if one of these mornings you read in the newspapers the announcement of my death, your arrogant conscience would not suffer a shock? Do you believe that conscience

would not ask whether this was the opportune moment to withdraw
your friendship, and whether the pretext was adequate for doing so?
What is that pretext? That M. Thiers's misfortune made all correspondence difficult for you? Correspondence with indifferent people
I might understand, but I am convinced that you behaved differently
with them than with me. You know how they would have taken
such an excuse and you did not expose yourself to their blame. With
me it is different. You know that I will complain to no one and consequently you have no need to be considerate. Ah, Monsieur, is that
the friendship you so often promised me, and that I counted on for
the past twenty years? What? You know I am in a foreign land, in
the midst of barbarians, exposed to a thousand dangers, suffering all
the privations that are inevitable when one inhabits such lands, you
know I am exiled, alone, almost totally ruined, without friends, without help, without consolation, and you do not have the slightest desire
for news of me? I could go on like this for a whole day and would
still not say enough; I will only add that you and I were not cast in
the same mold, that whatever you do I will never forget that I loved
you, and that nothing that happens to you will ever find me cold and
indifferent. May he to whom you have sacrificed all the rest compensate you for what you have lost. My wishes for your happiness will
follow you always and everywhere.

                                                          Christine

Thiers had recently been exiled for his belated opposition to Louis-Napoleon, who was now Emperor Napoleon III. Cristina's resentment of
Mignet's friendship with Thiers is expressed here for the first and only
time in her extant correspondence. But her bitterness is not incomprehensible: Mignet seemed more concerned over Thiers's fall from grace than
over Cristina's perilous exile, and according to her, had abdicated from
personal ambition in Thiers's favor. Her accusation that their friendship
sapped the energies Mignet should have reserved for her is unfair:
Mignet's apathetic nature was responsible for his willingness to live in
Thiers's shadow, and his negligence toward her was quite deliberate, as
will be seen.

The exact nature of their relationship up to 1839 must remain conjec-
tural. Prudence certainly made them circumspect for Cristina, at least
until 1848, assumed that her correspondence was censored in Italy. She
continued to address him as "Cher Monsieur Mignet" until the summer
of 1846. But she signed "Christine" below such affectionate closings as
*votre meilleure amie, votre toute dévouée, mille et mille tendresses, toute
à vous,* which might have led censors to believe she was writing to an
elderly mentor. A striking proof of her fidelity, or her submission, to
Mignet, is the presence in his personal archives of a letter Heine wrote to

her in 1835 (see page 255), a letter so personal one can understand why she entrusted it to Mignet: what better collateral against her devotion to him?

In February 1836, after a serious quarrel, Cristina, with Mignet at her side, had a mass celebrated in the company of a few friends. The ceremony—inspired perhaps by the recent sermon of a noted prelate on the pardon of offenses—may have been the consecration of a union recognized by all their friends. Or was it merely the formal celebration of their reconciliation, the mutual pardon of offenses? Or perhaps, as Knibiehler asks, "the rupture of amorous relations sublimated in an oath of eternal affection?"[5] Whatever the purpose, their relationship for the next two years seems to have been cloudless. Cristina's guests, in Paris or in the country, took Mignet's presence for granted. Mignet himself invited their mutual friends to either of her residences, transmitting news of her health and her greetings as would a husband, for example to Victor Cousin: "I have been entrusted with the most affectionate regards of all who reside at La Jonchère" (Cristina's summer house until 1840). No one in their immediate circle could have taken Emilio's occasional sojourns at the rue d'Anjou for a conjugal reconciliation. However, for the world at large, his sporadic appearances lent an air of propriety to a marriage whose likes were common enough in a society less concerned with morals than with manners. Emilio had every reason to be a complaisant husband; his wife's generosity was a useful adjunct to his expensive tastes in women and fashion, and until 1839 she provided him with an apartment and a carriage for his stays in Paris. All the more surprising that a few months after Cristina gave birth to a daughter, Emilio should have written to d'Alton-Shée in outrage over his wife's behavior, while jubilating over his own debaucheries in Vienna. In May, he announced: "On my return to Paris I will live elsewhere than the rue d'Anjou, for the dear Princess has behaved very badly toward me, let it be said in passing. That is always the recompense for being discreet and kind. The way she has gone about it, the pleasure of having lived in her house and used the cabriolet with César, will have cost me very dearly. For the rest, so much the better, and I regret not having done this when I first arrived in Paris in 1831." And in July, contemplating a rest in Switzerland before his return to Paris, he again wrote to d'Alton-Shée, who was apparently familiar with the situation:

What a tiger, what an animal this will make of me! Here the city is very animated, the society charming, the young people gay and stylish, French wines, and lots of pretty girls. I have of necessity become a hunter of high-class women—for as to the whore type, forget it!—and despite my advanced age [he was thirty-nine] I

have had much success. I am astonished to recognize that I still prefer
our old ones, with all their inconveniences, to the romantic or sentimental type, and above all to the possession of a mistress, though I
have always kept three and one of them had the kindness to follow
me all the way here. . . .

You are right, however, to advise me not to tell her to go completely to hell [*ne pas l'envoyer entièrement faire foutre* is more
pungent than the translation can render] because of society and
scandal. But when you know all, you will understand that it is hard
for a man of bon ton like me to have any respect for a woman who
has behaved as she has. It's too bad I can't divorce and be finished
with her. All I would have to do is become a Protestant!

Two years later Emilio thought nothing of the scandal that rocked
Paris when he eloped from a ball with Countess Anne de Plaisance,
daughter of Napoleon's favorite general, Berthier, elevated to Prince de
Wagram. She left a husband, a seven-year-old daughter, and the scintillating life of Paris to live with Emilio in a magnificent villa on Lake
Como, La Pliniana. After ten years, the mysterious spring, described by
Pliny, that flows and ebbs under the villa, the midnight swims, the exquisite rooms where they entertained sumptuously had lost their charm.
Emilio had become a complacent husband, faithful at last, but inattentive
to the needs of a thirty-five-year-old beauty whose future was bleak. She
could not marry him until her own husband died, and if Emilio died first
she was a pariah rather than a desirable widow. Out of lassitude and the
need to establish an independent existence, she rented a villa directly
across the lake at Carate. One afternoon during Emilio's siesta, she
slipped out of La Pliniana as she had left the ball nearly a decade before.

Emilio's letter to d'Alton-Shée in 1852, just after his abandonment,
rounds out the picture of this man whose self-indulgence reached sublime proportions. "I am old enough to be surprised by nothing, to understand and forgive. I have suffered, for I did not expect, after twelve years
of such an intimate liaison, to be treated as I was since it would have
been easy to arrange things without causing a scandal. I have no reproaches to make myself. I forgive her the harm she has done me and
wish her long happiness. . . . I had so stupidly convinced myself this
would last all my life that now I am lost and cannot, old as I am, make
any plans or do anything as yet."[6]

UNTIL 1971,* no one writing about Cristina had ever suggested anything
equivocal regarding the birth of her daughter, Marie. Malvezzi delicately

* Knibiehler first raised the question of Marie's legitimacy in her article (see Bibliography).

implied that Marie was the product of a reconciliation between the estranged spouses. Emilio was in fact in Paris in December 1838, when Marie was born, but Cristina was in Versailles for the event as she had been for the preceding six months. Her unpublished letters to Mignet throw a great deal of light on this shaded episode. They have finally made possible a hypothesis that explains not only the question of paternity but, more important, the otherwise incoherent pattern of Cristina's life after 1838. It is too simplistic to attribute her apparent instability, her changes of residence, her variegated activities merely to ill health or a state of nerves, as her defenders have done. On the contrary, rarely does one find an individual marked by so many personal tragedies—the death of her father, the imprisonment of her stepfather, the betrayal by her husband, her contraction of syphilis from him, her own epilepsy, exile, persecution—who nonetheless retained mental equilibrium, emotional constancy, and direction of purpose in spite of her appalling health. Even when friends and fortune failed her she managed to hold the reins of her life on a course that led her to personal security and to the achievement of her goals. Her views regarding the ultimate unification of Italy under the House of Savoy reflect the same determined coherency that she applied to her private life after Marie's birth.

On December 23, 1838, Cristina gave birth to the child she named Marie and also Gerolama, in memory of her father. (There is no record of the birth in the municipal archives of Versailles; it was either removed or listed under assumed names.) For months before and after her delivery, Cristina lived in seclusion in her summer house suffering, in addition to the discomforts of pregnancy, from a recurrence of epileptic seizures—understandably provoked by the emotional upheaval of her joyless condition. A letter from Confalonieri, written two days before Marie's birth to a friend in Italy, informs us that Emilio was in Paris: "La Belgiojoso is not well at all and she has wanted to come to Paris for some time but is not moveable. Emilio will leave before the end of the year." No mention of an expected heir—a choice piece of news after all—merely the reference to Cristina's poor health. Neither Confalonieri nor any of their circle had seen Cristina in months. Since no correspondence of the period, not even spies' reports, mentions her pregnancy, one can only assume it was unknown.

Two brief notes to Mignet of that period indicate he was one of the very few to penetrate her claustration. Thanking him for a gift he had sent her, she wrote: "Certainly your little vases please me enormously and decorate my cell, which has much need of decoration. . . . You would have me regain a taste for the fineries of society, but I must shield myself for you use charming means. I envy your freedom of movement and am somewhat resentful of the Académie, to which you give more of yourself than to others. As for me, I limp along while awaiting you." A short while later, she asks for news of his health and gives an account of her own: "I give battle to my seizures though with little success up to now; the combat exhausts me almost as much as defeat and I fear that by giving in to my somewhat indolent nature I will finally give up completely. . . . do not forget your devoted recluse." This state of depression when she was subject to seizures, both of which she was experiencing at the time, is confirmed twenty years later in an overdue reply to Victor Cousin: "Neither illness nor trouble have I lacked this winter, and when I am tormented beyond a certain point, even the most agreeable activity is unbearable for me. I withdraw into my shell and remain there until the first bright day." Such confessions were not common, however. Cousin was particularly close to her and to Mignet. In fact, when he died in 1867, after a life of parsimonious bachelorhood, he willed Mignet a considerable income. The contrast between her letters to Mignet and those to other friends is demonstrated by a letter to Liszt, with whom she had a very affectionate relationship: "About me? Everyone is usually inexhaustible on that subject and I could perhaps find something to relate . . . but what for? My *me* is not gay, not amusing. I cough . . . so much for the physical. My morale is better than that. It is sometimes anxious, tormented, uncertain, even downfallen, *but it knows where to find a direction and follows its path"* (italics added).

In the spring of 1839 Cristina returned to Paris, reopening her salon with concerts of pre-Romantic music which were so remarkable that Liszt, then in Italy, read about them in the *Gazette Musicale*. In June she left for England, ostensibly to attend Victoria's coronation, with her sisters, her brother, and "the whole colony of the rue d'Anjou," as she wrote Liszt. There is no mention of the six-month-old Marie. Cristina rented a manor house near Kenilworth, where she remained until November, leading a spartan life, up at dawn, riding, reading, occasionally sight-seeing but with little enthusiasm: "Do you think me rococo enough to sit amid the ruins of Kenilworth with Walter Scott in hand?" she wrote Liszt. "I do sometimes go to ruins because they are beautiful, but I do not look for rooms, towers, or windows of this or that fictional character. I have the further shortcoming of being totally insensitive to the historical memories attached to places. I was in London without visiting Anne [Boleyn]'s axe or the room of Edward's children. . . . I prefer a book to pictures."

The only extant letters from this period—to Liszt and from the celebrated preacher l'abbé Coeur—reveal a curious state of mind. Coeur, profoundly influenced by Lamennais, shared his celebrity in the pulpit with Lacordaire, another Lamennais disciple. Coeur's sermons attracted a vast audience of liberals and often converted apostates to the new Christian democracy. Cristina found in Coeur a compatibility of religious conviction and progressive ideas and counted him among her friends. He was certainly one of her greatest admirers. In a dithyrambic reply to a missing letter from her, he asks: "Why do you say I know you little? It is true that you let me see a grandeur so unusual in your judgment, in the noble simplicity with which you speak of the daughter of Eve, that someone other than myself might be astonished. . . . I, Princess, would almost defy you to surprise me, so great is my certitude that you possess an inexhaustible wealth of grandeur. I have the delightful satisfaction of never having been mistaken about you for a moment, for I have studied you with the care one applies to rare things, with that impassioned love inspired by divine mysteries, when one has the privilege of encountering them on this globe. Yes, Princess, a divine mystery; it is you I mean."

Cristina's reference to "the daughter of Eve," which reappears in a later letter to Mignet, hardly suggests pride in herself, a sentiment one might expect in the new mother of a healthy child. Rather it evokes her heritage of Eve's moral weakness. Coeur's fervent vindication allows us to reconstruct her remarks. She evidently told him that he did not really know the truth about this "daughter of Eve," who was unworthy of his esteem. His arguments against her apparent self-deprecation—in terms more evocative of Heine than of a prelate—imply that she was not as euphoric about her motherhood as Malvezzi would have us believe. That biographer quotes a letter to Ernesta Bisi written, he says, shortly after Marie's birth but he does not give the date. The letter itself, however, clearly indicates a time lapse between the event and the reaction described: "For a while now a joy has developed in me and I have a happiness that is all my own. What shall I tell you about Maria? Nothing, dear Ernesta, since I cannot tell you enough. I can only tell you that she is well and that the only thing I ask of God is that He keep her that way for me."

In her letters to Liszt and to Coeur she does not even allude to the child, although Coeur had been informed of her own ill health, for on October 7, 1839, he writes, "I am very sad that you are still unwell; I do not like that sickly English sun for you; could you not have chosen a better climate for your solitude?" To Liszt, in the same month, she declared, "I am thirty-one and as soon as I have married off my youngest sister I shall live for myself, that is, withdrawn from the world." She had in fact taken upon herself the responsibility of settling her sisters, one of whom married Count Charles d'Aragon, a friend of George Sand and son of a peer of France. Cristina's brilliant salon opened new horizons for her young sisters, who would otherwise have been condemned to the narrow circle of Milanese aristocracy, devitalized by the continuing Austrian occupation. Was it to protect her still unmarried sister that she tried to avoid the scandal of an illegitimate child? The remark to Liszt would seem to imply this.

She returned to the rue d'Anjou in November 1839, remaining until July. During those tumultuous six months Musset fell seriously ill and seriously in love with her; a storm of jealousy broke in Marie d'Agoult over Liszt's friendship with Cristina, and violent quarrels between Mignet and Cristina resulted in a new rupture. It is highly curious that among all the letters exchanged between the principal parties and their friends, among all the nasty gossip circulated by spies and diarists, there is not a word about the princess's recent motherhood. It would surely have suited Austria's purposes, and those of her Parisian rivals, to spread rumors of an illegitimate birth—the ultimate confirmation of spies' assertions that she was a Messalina. And yet she, whose only known liaison was with a man mocked as impotent, whose image of noble sacrifice and vestal virtue could have been shattered by this one stone many would have cast, was accused by no one but her own husband, and at that privately. One can only assume that society accepted the child as Emilio's . . . or that the birth was kept secret. From available documents of the period—late 1838 to early 1840—references to her physical state merely speak of poor health, but in terms that do not infer the natural discomforts contingent to childbirth.

The first mention of Marie on record is in an intriguing letter to Caroline Jaubert that relates with considerable irony Cristina's reconciliation with Mignet, revealing at the same time an unresolved discord between them. The letter, undated,* was necessarily written in the late spring of 1840, since it refers to the recent death of Mignet's nephew, Etienne Marcel, who died on May 4 at the age of twenty-eight. This young man, whom Mignet loved as a son, served as a link between the family in Aix and Mignet's life with Cristina in Paris; Etienne was a frequent and informal visitor at the rue d'Anjou. Mme Jaubert, writing from the country, had evidently asked for confirmation of the rumored reconciliation, for Cristina answered:

I received your sweet little letter, which is however a poor compensation for your absence. Well then, yes, the *secrétaire perpétuel,* as Heine calls him, has come back, but do not believe that he swallowed his pride, admitted his mistakes, or took the great step of recanting them. Not in the least. Non-Christian philosophers are infallible. This is what happened. M. Mignet suddenly lost his nephew whom he loved very much, that is, over whom he made a great fuss. I learned

* Letters written to friends close by, as one would telephone today, were frequently undated.

that he was deeply grieved and wrote to tell him that I shared his grief and how I regretted that he denied me the opportunity to show it. My approach moved him and he came to thank me. I asked him to come back and he did. But he is convinced that I am worthless and esteems himself more than ever; he is proud of his conduct and ashamed of mine, etc. How does that affect me? When he enumerates all the countless faults that make me an abject creature, it pains me because I am not certain enough of the error of his judgment; but once he has left, I return to better views of myself and find it perfectly evident that he is mistaken about me. I like to see him because I am deeply attached to him and for me such attachments are immortal. But I no longer trust his, and you can count on my memory to keep me from ever trusting it again.

Further in the letter, she refers to Musset's convalescence, alluding humorously to Mignet's jealousy, and in successive sentences reveals a striking sequence of thoughts—at first glance unrelated. However, her very sizeable correspondence discloses a consistently logical mind, not at all given to non sequiturs. In her mind, and doubtless in Mme Jaubert's as well, the transition between the sentences in italics (added) was perfectly natural.

I saw Mme and Mlle Musset, who gave me excellent news of one whose health had been distressing me. The country is doing him great good they say, and he plans to stay for some time. *I know someone who will not be upset by this. Marie is very well and is the constant object of my adoration. She has the goodness to distinguish me somewhat in return for my cult, which is a great joy for me. Apropos, you wrongly applied to Mignet's visit the remark I made to you one day.* The visit I wanted to tell you about, or rather not tell you about so as not to appear too weak, was not his. . . . I am impatient to see you again . . . and am very sad to think it will only be for a few days. But why not come to see me in Milan? I would be so happy to receive you in my retreat.

The rapid transitions from Mignet to Marie and back to Mignet surely confirm their intimate association in Cristina's mind, just as her decision to leave Paris was equally related to both of them. In July, Cristina left for her first visit to Italy since the beginning of her exile, although the amnesty of 1838 would have allowed her to return sooner. This was more than a visit; as her remark to Mme Jaubert about her "retreat" indicates, this was a well-considered break with her life in Paris, a withdrawal into solitude. Whatever transpired between them before her departure, her subsequent letters to Mignet make clear that he knew why she left, that new factors which she could not explain in writing obliged her to prolong her absence, and that Mignet's initial resignation to this decision turned into bitter resentment as the months dragged on. Until Cristina's trip to England, Mignet had always remained near her. From then on he began spending vacations in Aix with his family, to whom he turned for sentimental consolation as he sought distraction in his work: "I live for long hours each day in the greatest and most interesting company," he wrote to Thiers, "so that deep in history I am little concerned with the miseries of today." As Cristina moved closer to Italy, taking with her the only personal happiness Mignet was ever to know, she kept him informed of her impressions ("Germany suits me. . . . the country is rather beautiful but does not compare with mine or with England") and of her health. Her tone seems to suggest that they parted on amicable terms. However, by the fall, when it appeared she would remain indefinitely on her estate near Milan with Marie and her English governess, Mrs. Parker, Mignet apparently decided to end his suffering and stopped writing to her. A year later he repented and sent a message through a friend, to which she quickly replied with unbridled feeling.

> I waited a long time for a reply to my last letter and resigned myself painfully to being deprived of one. But how could I believe that you still thought of me and nevertheless left my letters unanswered? I was obliged to believe that you did not care about continuing relations with me, and painful as that conviction was, I had to accept it, having no other choice. If I was mistaken, if you still think of me with something that resembles friendship, if the negative attitude that prevented you from answering me nearly a year ago was transitory, thank you. You have no need to ask me not to forget my friends in Paris. I very often think of them and sometimes feel the violent need to return among them. Interests which are at the same time duties keep me from Paris and I do not doubt that if you knew what they are you would encourage me not to neglect them. . . .
>
> When I left Paris you did not seem to believe in the firmness of my resolutions, and you were right, for my past conduct did not offer you sufficient proof. But God has assisted me and the path I now follow already seems much easier than when I started out. I live with God, with Marie, with the poor, and with my books. I do not allow myself the slightest distraction outside of these things for fear of not stopping in time, and I even resist M. Récamier [her Parisian doctor] who predicts a very imminent death if I do not leave my retreat from time to time. His prognosis inspires no confidence in me whatsoever; what I do know is that I would risk losing my taste for this retreat by leaving it and that taste is necessary. I study a great deal and think I have made some progress. Sometimes I think that if I were near you again, you would be more pleased with me and would

have fewer reasons for impatience with my ease in taking sides, my lack of impartiality and composure. Will my dream never be realized, and will I never again be subjected to your criticism? Let me hope this is not so. You have never traveled and this is either a mistake or a misfortune in your position. Why not remedy it? Must you always stop in Aix and not cross the sea or the Alps one day, at least to descend into our Lombardy and see this countryside that enchanted Charlemagne and many others? Tell me you will come. I can offer you an immense library, rich above all in historians and chroniclers still in manuscript, and a welcome such as you cannot receive elsewhere but in my house. Let yourself be moved and promise me you will come.

A month later he was moved to answer her warmly, but never left the borders of France despite entreaties that should have moved a stone.* There was no obstacle of health or work so great in 1841–42 that it prevented him from giving her the counsel she repeatedly requested, on a matter she could not discuss by mail. If he resisted her appeals to come to Locate, it must have been because the reasons that detained her there were not in his interest. Her second letter of 1841 confirms that his "totally inexplicable" silence was the result of his bitter rumination. When she speaks of "this frail adored object that keeps me far from Paris," there is no ambiguity as to whom she means. Marie is what keeps her from Paris and from him. To impress upon him the urgency of his presence, she even uses sentimental blackmail, reminding him of Dr. Récamier's dire predictions.

November 6, 1841

I have just received your excellent letter, which I must answer without delay, so deeply did it move me and do me good. . . . I did not believe that you had forgotten me, but your silence, totally inexplicable as it was for me, obligated me to imitate it. . . . Can you believe that the thought of returning to Paris does not often torment me? Do you believe that I can dream without deep emotion of the happiness of being once again close to people I not only love but who know me and whom I understand? To find the necessary strength I must ask God's help, must bury myself in books, and above all contemplate the frail adored object that keeps me far from Paris. It is impossible for me to explain by letter the gravity of my motives for remaining here. But if I were fortunate enough to see you in Locate, not

---

* All letters from Mignet were apparently destroyed by Cristina or, after her death, by Marie. Marchesa Niccolini has assured me that she has none, and I myself have checked the letters held by Marchesa Valperga, who learned from her mother-in-law (Marchesa Niccolini's mother and Cristina's granddaughter) that a quantity of correspondence was destroyed. It is most fortunate that Mignet could not bring himself to destroy Cristina's letters to him.

only would I reveal them to you in full confidence, I would also ask
you to help me put an end to them. And you could do this better than
anyone, certainly better than I. Having always had a weak character,
I am now employing the little strength I have against myself, reserving none against or for others. . . . Dr. Récamier's prognoses do not
really frighten me, not because they seem unreasonable, but because
they are expressed with revolting brutality. Another doctor less
knowledgeable and less bizarre advised me to travel for distraction.
Is it a distraction to travel alone, or is it not rather a bore? . . . In
that case, I am told, why not live in Milan rather than Locate? Why
not see people? I cannot tell the Milanese, but it is impossible for me
to be pleasantly distracted among them. There are certainly people of
merit there, but they live as I do, not even seeking each other out,
having lost the habit of even wanting to meet. *Besides, what do they
know about me?* That I lived a number of years in the high life of
Paris, and they conclude that we are not suited to one another. . . .
I can only choose between Paris and Locate. . . . [Italics added.]

Do not postpone your visit too long, and remember once in a
while that Dr. Récamier's prognoses . . . could turn out to be true.
From Marseille to Locate takes thirty-six hours. With what joy I
would meet you, would guide you through my library, show you my
school, accompany you to our lakes and mountains. With what trust
would I explain what keeps me from Paris and work with you to conquer all the obstacles. Come! Mercier often speaks of you and always
in order to convince me that you love me. I am too eager to believe
it for him to have to perorate at length. . . . Allow me to tell you
that you will never have friends [*amis ni amies*] more tenderly or
more solidly attached to you than I—neither more, nor as much.

Her relations with the Milanese, already tenuous because of her dubious situation as exile and estranged wife, had become embittered earlier
that year. In July, Manzoni's mother, Donna Giulia, was on her death-
bed. Until Cristina's departure in 1828 she had been like a daughter in
the family. However, when she rushed to Milan to see Donna Giulia she
was denied entrance on Manzoni's order. Lacking the courage to face her
himself, Manzoni asked Father Ratti—rector of the patrician parish of
San Fedele who had performed Cristina's wedding ceremony and was
then attending Donna Giulia—to turn her away. In his biography, Malvezzi explains this as provincial narrowness: whoever held a salon in
Paris and had been admired there by poets or, worse still, republicans
could not be redeemed from "trans-Alpine sins." What sins could have
denied her entrance to a friend's house? Was it a sin to receive celebrated
writers and musicians in her salon? Manzoni was a celebrated writer
himself. It would seem, rather, that rumors of Marie's illegitimacy (a
subject Malvezzi did not wish to raise) had been spread by the Belgio-

josos. (Manzoni's own rumored bastardy may have made him excessively touchy about such situations.) Cristina's remark to Mignet—"What do they know about me?"—and her choice of Paris or Locate over Milan become clearer in this light.

Before leaving Paris, very probably during the long months of seclusion surrounding Marie's birth, Cristina had begun her investigation of the origins of Catholic dogma. By November 1841 she had already written a number of chapters and received Mignet's plaudits: "My heart beat very fast on reading that you were pleased with my introduction. . . . I cannot thank you enough for the kindness with which you correct my saints." Until its publication in 1843 she continued to submit the manuscript to Mignet's penetrating criticism, which she respected above any other. As though that were not enough to occupy her, she also undertook major social improvements on her estate, to the irritation of neighboring landowners who had received her circular letter reminding them of their moral obligation toward their peasants, "those poor neglected creatures." She continued to suffer from recurring syncopes and other discomforts, but was then under the care of a young doctor in Varese, a pleasant town near Milan where Cristina had a villa. From her letters to this doctor, Paolo Maspero, for whom the main street of Varese has been named, we learn in detail the extent of her suffering, the treatment he prescribed, and the extraordinary medical attention she gave to others on her estate. Maspero, in addition to his early interest in epilepsy, was also a classical scholar; his translation of the *Odyssey* was dedicated to Cristina. In a letter to Maspero, written two weeks after the one quoted above to Mignet, she says: "I have no pretension of ever enjoying good health, or of erasing the traces of past maladies. I shall be content with a few years of life, during which I hope to retain those faculties that can make me not only independent of others, but useful to them." She then writes at length about Maspero's career and her care of an ailing servant. Her letters to Maspero are a necessary corollary to her other correspondence, for they alone reveal how sick she was, yet how readily she detached herself from her own suffering.

By February 1842 neither Cristina nor Mignet had crossed an inch of the distance separating them, but she was less guarded. She even proposed to write her reasons for remaining in Italy if Mignet was certain her letters arrived with unbroken seals, and considered returning to Paris when "receptions and balls are over" and "the do-nothings have left," that is, in the summer. It was not the projects for her estate or her health that kept her in Locate. There was an overriding necessity for establishing beyond a doubt her moral caliber—a curious undertaking for a beautiful woman of her fortune and title. Yet this is what she had been doing over the preceding eighteen months. She organized an elementary school

for her peasants' children, provided a social center, was setting up vocational training for adolescents, and was making plans to build decent
houses for her peasants, who had never known anything but squalor. She
was apparently living out an expiation within herself, while placing herself beyond moral reproach from without. A reply to Mignet of February
21, 1842, pinpoints these issues for the first time, and to him alone
among her correspondents.

> Far from boring or tiring me, your sermons, dear Monsieur Mignet,
> gave me real pleasure for they took me back to those times, which I
> never recall without emotion and regret, when you recited similar
> ones. If I did not always listen to them it was not that I misunderstood
> their wisdom or the sentiment that inspired them—it was because I
> am naturally too weak to maintain my balance and necessarily fall to
> one side or the other. *It is for that, knowing my direct descendance
> from our first mother, that I have thrown myself into the life I lead
> at present.* I know well its inconveniences, and feel them only too
> much. But it was the only way for me not to make any more mistakes.
> *I cannot make sacrifices to convention; I can make them to duty.* I
> prefer to suffer and seek pleasure. I suffer after exposing myself to
> labors beyond my strength or when I have repulsive things to do . . .
> but I suffer most of all when I look back on the years that have gone
> by, the friends I have left, and remind myself that the former will
> never return and that I may never see the latter again. I find pleasure
> when I see the happy changes that have come over this place during
> the last year, and tell myself that I can still do much more; when I
> tell myself that age can take nothing more from me; when I see my
> little Marie grow, become strong and deeply attached to me and, con-
> sidering her a proof of God's favor, I tell myself that He might take
> her away from me if I did not live according to Him. You will ask me
> if I truly believe that all the sacrifices I impose on myself are com-
> manded by God. I shall reply that I have no idea, but the surest way
> to please God is to think of Him and do good. . . . Here is the whole
> moral message of my catechism.
>
> The occupations I have created for myself here and the projects
> I formulate for the future would not prevent me from coming to Paris,
> for there is always a season when Locate is not habitable. That is pre-
> cisely the time when Paris would be most pleasing to me. . . . The
> receptions and balls are over, the do-nothings have left, and I could
> spend summers in the environs of Paris as I did before. It is thus not
> Locate that keeps me. If you had come I could have told you directly
> what keeps me from Paris; it is more difficult to write, but if you are
> certain my letters are not unsealed before reaching you I shall write
> about it. *I do not see things with a magnifying glass. This time I
> see with experience. I tried for more than a year to accustom myself to
> the life Bianchi wanted me to lead and could not do it. I would prefer*

to settle in the heart of Africa rather than begin again. That life was repugnant not only to my feelings but to my idea of duty as well. It would have been a lack of courage and dignity to conform to it and would have been a torture every moment. Judge for yourself if that was possible. The difficulties could be attenuated if Bianchi decided to seek employment outside of France, with which I would help him in any case. Bianchi, completely identified as he is with Paris, would be forced to come to that if I cut off his income. I lack the courage for that and wish this decision, necessary in so many ways, came from him. [Italics added.]

THIS MYSTIFYING REFERENCE to Bianchi has been the stumbling block to any hypothesis regarding the father of Cristina's child. Living descendants of the family regard Bianchi as the father on no stronger evidence than a story handed down: Bianchi's son gave Marie's elder daughter a case that reputedly contained the secret of Marie's birth. Out of respect for her mother, still alive at the time, she destroyed the case without examining its contents.* Even if the evidence were less tenuous, the supposition of Bianchi's fatherhood raises more questions than it answers. Could Mignet, rigidly correct, jealous even of the spurned attentions of Musset and Heine, have maintained a close relationship with a woman who had betrayed his love so flagrantly? Would Cristina have reproached him with neglect, burdened him with the problems of legitimizing Marie, which was finally achieved with his help and through his friends, and kept him informed over the years of Marie's development, if she was Bianchi's child? And if Bianchi was the father, why would he have written to Mignet in April 1843 in the hope of extorting more money from Cristina? Why would Mignet reproach Cristina for her sudden severity toward Bianchi's request for the fourth quarter of his stipend (which in fact he had already received)? Cristina replied: "This cannot go on like this. I set Bianchi's stipend at 4,000 francs, and will not go beyond that." She even paid some of his debts in addition to the fourth quarter, which had been paid in advance at Bianchi's urgent request. "I deeply regret it now for I see that he does not view my resolution toward him as definitive and considers the 4,000 francs a minimum."

This was a very considerable sum at the time, but insufficient for Bianchi's newly extravagant tastes. A very sternly worded letter to

---

* I myself have heard this story from two members of the family, both of whom accept it as irrefutable proof! However, they have not seen Cristina's letters to Mignet; nor of course does anyone know what the case contained. Another member of the family—more familiar with Cristina's private papers, and who graciously let me see them—is not at all convinced by this argument.

Bianchi, among Cristina's unpublished papers, reprimands him for the box at the opera and other such luxuries that he and his wife were enjoying at Cristina's expense. It is curious that she was paying him a stipend at all, since she had left Paris more than two years before and the services Bianchi had been employed to perform were necessarily being performed by some one else in Milan. Why then was Bianchi still on her payroll? A detail that has been consistently overlooked is Bianchi's marriage only a year before Marie's birth. A letter from Cristina to Liszt, dated November 6, 1837, announced this event: "Bianchi, you surely know who Bianchi is, is married. His wife is staying here [La Jonchère] with him." It does not seem probable that Cristina would carelessly fling herself into her secretary's arms with his new bride in the house. Nor does it seem likely that after seeing her retainer almost daily for six years, she would suddenly discover irresistible charms in him.

If Bianchi was readily accepted as Marie's father, it may be because, apart from his known role in Cristina's life, the Italian patriot Pietro Bolognini, alias Bianchi, had good credentials. His sixteenth-century English forebear married into the distinguished Emilian family of Malvezzi.* Mignet—whose relationship with Cristina was either never understood or deliberately concealed—was the son of a locksmith. Certainly the secret of Marie's birth was well kept, even in France, for not even A. Augustin-Thierry—Thierry's descendant and biographer—who never missed a chance to denigrate Cristina, seems to have discovered any trace of it in her correspondence with Thierry.

Too many clues point to Mignet as the father. The child's name, for one, seems significant; it was the name of Mignet's revered mother. For another, precisely because it is so common a name, it was not common among Lombard aristocracy except as one of the multiple names usually given. Marie, however, was the child's principal name since her name day was the Feast of the Assumption, as attested by Cristina's letter to Mignet of 1846: "Apropos Marie, I warn you that her name day was on August 15 and I do not count enough on her discretion to believe that she will not reproach you for having forgotten her, if in fact you do forget her on your return. I would blush deeply if she came straight to you in front of everyone saying, 'Didn't you bring me anything?' I prefer to warn you in time." No letter on record shows that Marie had such pretensions toward anyone else in Cristina's entourage, not even Thierry,

* Cristina's biographer Aldobrandino Malvezzi dei Medici was not only a descendant of Bianchi-Bolognini but indirectly of Cristina as well. He was the son of Marie's stepdaughter Costanza, one of three little girls Marie brought up after marrying their widowed father—which accounts for his silence on the subject of Marie's illegitimacy. He surely had access to the legal documents pertaining to her later recognition, though he never saw Cristina's letters on the subject to Mignet and Victor Cousin.

with whom they virtually shared the same roof in Paris. A subsequent letter speaks of the kind of gift Marie would like: "The result of my conversation with Marie is that you go to Giroux and find an educational toy; for example that construction set which amused her so much." Hardly an expected concern for the stiff-backed "secrétaire perpétuel." Marie was evidently of great importance to him. To most others, Cristina only mentioned Marie in passing. To Mignet—"with you I let my heart and mind go"—she told everything: Marie's health, her character, amusements, impressions, later on her choice of husband, difficult child-birth, even the post-partum complications.

The letter of 1842 quoted above becomes clear, and Bianchi's role comprehensible, if one hypothesizes that Bianchi, as her "homme de confiance," learned of her pregnancy and presumed, or knew, that Mignet was the father. To remedy the situation, he would have proposed that Cristina remain in seclusion for the necessary period—her poor health was a credible pretext—and that the child be raised in secret by foster parents, perhaps even offering to pass her off as his own.* This could explain her "repugnance" for the life Bianchi tried to impose on her for more than a year: she left for Versailles in the fall of 1838, when her pregnancy could no longer be concealed, returning to Paris, after six months in England, in November 1839. If Mignet was not the father, why would she tell him that to submit to such a life was undignified? What she was paying Bianchi, no longer in her employ, was evidently hush money. And Bianchi, always in debt, was not one to overlook a golden goose. Once Cristina decided to live openly with the child she was exposed to Bianchi's blackmail and Mignet's resentment. For she was determined to gain the Belgiojoso name for Marie rather than condemn her to the shame of bastardy. To achieve this, she had to divorce herself from Mignet's sentimental hold, from the threat of gossip, which fortunately has a short memory, and from Bianchi's bothersome presence. Once in Locate she was a week's journey from all that, and Bianchi, persona non grata in Austrian dominions, would hardly risk crossing into Lombardy.

When Emilio eloped with the comtesse de Plaisance, he was completely indifferent to the scandal caused by her abandonment of husband and daughter. But toward his own wife, he was as self-righteous as a Pharisee, refusing to recognize her child—not an uncommon practice

---

* Marchese Brivio-Sforza maintains that Marie "called herself Signorina Bianchi." It is unlikely that anyone but the Belgiojosos called her that since Cristina, desperate to have her legitimized, would not have tolerated anything so prejudicial. The family's hostility is understandable: once recognized as Emilio's daughter, Marie was heir to the entire fortune he possessed as eldest of the three brothers. Marchese Brivio-Sforza, descended from the Belgiojosos through his grandmother, and only briefly separated from the events—himself over eighty, his father was a close contemporary of Cristina—reflects even today that old hostility.

among high-born spouses who lived separate lives. This was the grave
motive that kept her in Locate. Her exemplary behavior as a devoted
mother, scholarly recluse, philanthropic landowner, living out a pious
existence far from the frivolities of Paris or even Milan—this was the
price she felt she had to pay for the legitimation of her daughter. Who
would believe any woman resolute enough to leave a lover, the father of
her child, and live like a hermit when she could have enjoyed all the
pleasures of life? By remaining in Locate she was openly disavowing
whatever rumors had been spread in Milan. If Mignet was not the father,
why would he be concerned about her sacrifices or reproach her for
seeing things with a magnifying glass? And what woman would tell a
betrayed lover—with whom she continued a deep sentimental relationship for the next thirty years—of the sacrifices she was making for a
child conceived with another man?

Having placed her fate in the hands of God, Cristina placed her trust
in time. In 1856, as revealed for the first time in Cristina's unpublished
letters to Mignet and Victor Cousin, Emilio finally succumbed to the
disease he had communicated to her thirty years before. His remarkable
constitution had remained intact, but his mind degenerated into total
dementia. Writing to Mignet on December 3, 1856, Cristina says: "You
know into what condition the Prince has fallen. It worsens from day to
day and the poor wretch is no more than a ruin, a child of two, without
will and without the means to have it respected if he had any. But before
he lost all sense, he often expressed the desire to see me, to be reconciled
with me, and even to recognize my daughter. One of his friends came to
see me . . . asking if even now . . . I would be willing to help him
end his painful existence. I replied that I was amenable but since the
Prince is no more than a child in the power of his brothers,* the proposition would have to come from them. . . . From another source, the
report of this friend is correct and the Prince has expressed his intentions
toward me and toward Marie before so many witnesses, and in so positive a manner, that his brothers would be ungracious to oppose them.
. . . Will he recover enough lucidity before the end to accomplish the
act of reparation that this hapless creature meditated? Will I finally see
this net, in which I have silently struggled for eighteen years, become
untangled? . . . Or will I simply witness a dreadful agony . . . see
him die with the word on his lips that would end all my torments, but
without the ability to pronounce it?" To call the legitimation of her
adulterine daughter an "act of reparation" may seem incongruous. However, Emilio's uncountable adulteries entitled her to this one noble act on

---

* The prince's nephew, son of his eldest brother, had been designated Emilio's heir. He
died suddenly at the age of twenty-one in 1859.

his part, an act that for centuries had been taken for granted in similar situations.

Mignet tried to dissuade her from any trust in Emilio's intentions, for she answered on December 31: "You are right, the poor wretch is utterly incapable of thought or action. He no longer recognizes his brothers and falls into attacks of violent frenzy during which the doctors withdraw holding their ears, the blasphemies and curses he shouts being that horrible to hear. Other times, when the fury has abated, he declaims the most disgusting obscenities. . . . Some are sorry for him; others see in this leprosy of the mind the hand of God. I am of this number. And when I see demonstrated in broad daylight the malice and depravity I have always known in his heart, it seems to me that divine justice has not allowed him to continue his play-acting all the way to the end. Nevertheless, if I could help him in any way I would be happy to do so, but in his present state I cannot come near him." Cristina's harshness is not unjustified, for on top of all his other wrongs, Emilio tried to extort money from her by forcing her to pay him an annual income, or return under the conjugal roof. "The Prince himself dropped the suit," she told Mignet, "which the sequester [of 1853] had suspended, but now that . . . his brother has been named his guardian, it is he who informed me that if I do not agree to pay this income he will pursue the case. . . . If he summons me to return, I shall tell him to prepare suitable lodgings for me and will go there for twenty-four hours, after which no one . . . can prevent me from going to the country or on a trip; for the guardian replaces [the Prince] in his business affairs but not in his private ones, and my brother-in-law has not become my husband because he has become my husband's guardian." Two months later the prince's agitation gave way to imbecility. Reporting to Mignet that when Emilio's confessor spoke of her, "the Prince, with that smile that never leaves his face, exclaimed 'Oh, we are great friends, especially now that Turks and Christians are united.' The priest then asked if he remembered his name. 'I am king,' was his reply. Oh, to die like that!"

In June 1857 Cristina was about to leave for Paris when she developed an ulcer of the urethra. Explaining to Mignet in full medical detail the cause of her delayed departure, she also told him that before leaving she would visit Emilio, whose end seemed close. Her relationship with Mignet, now that she was approaching fifty and he was a decade beyond, had weathered all the storms and was anchored in loving harmony: "I do not ask you to answer me since I hope to be in Paris soon. . . . Do not forget me, love me, and see that on my arrival I be pleased with you."

After Emilio's death on February 17, 1858, Mignet's friend Charles Giraud, a distinguished lawyer, assembled the brief for legitimation. Included were Cristina's testimony and that of witnesses that she had cohabited with the prince before her pregnancy. Her brother-in-law tried to delay proceedings by requesting a trial, which her Milanese lawyer, Pastori, assured her she had no reason to fear. Reporting this to Mignet she remarked: "I know that very well, but you, mon ami, you cannot know that for there is a brief period of my existence [the four years of her marriage] which you know only by hearsay. If the trial takes place, you will be astounded by what emerges. I would nevertheless wish to avoid it because of the delays. What does the rest matter? Have I not accepted the judgment of society? Let it remain what it is and let me marry off my daughter when the time comes."

The trial did not take place, but to end her brother-in-law's temporizing she was asked to swear to her declaration that she and the prince had been living together under the same roof at the time of her pregnancy—which was true, since Emilio had stayed at the rue d'Anjou in 1838. "I replied that I would swear, since I attach almost as much importance to not lying as to not perjuring myself, and having affirmed nothing but the truth, I will not back away. However, I would rather be a total Quaker and abstain from this ceremony." Cristina and her lawyers had evidently seen to it that the wording of her statements did not exceed the truth. Finally on December 11, 1860, a triumphant letter to Mignet. "My great affair, the affair of my daughter, is completely terminated and with full success. . . . The day after the verdict was communicated to my brother-in-law, I received two little envelopes, one to me, the other to Mlle la Comtesse Marie Barbiano di Belgiojoso, containing my brother-in-law's calling card. He was the only one who had not yet recognized my daughter, for no one else waited until the court's decision. . . . For twenty-one years I dragged that ball and chain telling myself that the day it was removed, and I would no longer fear that my rights as a mother could be taken from me, would be the most beautiful day of my life. It seemed to me that only then would I enter into full possession of my child.* That day has come; but already now my daughter no longer belongs to me as

---

* As an illegitimate offspring, Marie would have had no rights to any inheritance, Trivulzio or Belgiojoso, since her birth had not been registered under either name. In the eyes of the law she was not even her mother's child, having never officially been declared as such. A manuscript genealogy of the Belgiojosos—generously given to me by Count Franco Arese, distinguished historian of Milan's patrician families—lists Marie as: "Maria Valentina, si vuole figlia di Doller, riconosciuta dalla famiglia Belgiojoso" (claims to be the daughter of Doller, recognized by the Belgiojoso family). There was, among Cristina's friends, an Austrian pianist born in Naples, by the name of Theodore Döhler, whom Heine called "the greatest among the small." A long letter from Döhler, among Cristina's unpublished papers, attests to their close relationship, for, writing in Italian, he uses the familiar "tu." He mentions Marie with tenderness, but most of the letter is devoted to his forthcoming marriage. Could his name have been borrowed? Not even this name, however, appears on the registry of Versailles's archives under the date of Marie's birth. Furthermore, Marie's second name was Gerolama, which only adds to the confusion.

she did. She is engaged, and although the marriage satisfies me completely, it tears away a great chunk of my life."

Cristina paid dearly for her triumph. She acceded to the demands of Emilio's brothers that Marie renounce all rights of inheritance for herself or her heirs to Emilio's estate. Emilio's income may often have needed bolstering from Cristina's coffers, but the estate itself was very considerable. The only part of it Cristina wanted for Marie was La Pliniana, for which she paid her two brothers-in-law their share. This was an ironic requital for the pleasure she had never had there with Emilio, this villa bought for his idyll with Anne de Plaisance. Marie's possession of it, expensive as it had been, was a manner of recompense to Cristina. The villa, almost the symbol of her degrading marriage, would never again be peopled with Belgiojosos, but with the family of the daughter they had so reluctantly recognized. (La Pliniana is presently owned by the widow of Cristina's great-grandson. His mother, Marie's first-born, was Cristina's namesake.) A copy of the portrait by Lehmann looks down on the rooms Cristina never lived in. Yet in the end, it was she who took possession of the villa.

TOWARD MIGNET her affections remained perpetually young. In 1867 she was still coaxing him to come to Italy, using the new argument of his recent inheritance from Cousin. "Now that you are no longer forced to account to yourself for every item, who knows if one of these days you might be taken with the caprice to see how the world looks beyond the borders of France. And if you once crossed those blessed frontiers, Italy would naturally be your first stop after Aix. Who knows . . . if a servant brought me a card saying it was from a Signore wishing to see me, and on glancing at it I saw F. Mignet . . . My God! how happy I would be!" Throughout most of her life, every pleasure, every success, every tragedy, was shared with Mignet even at a distance. "My letters are of a revolting egoism; but what can I do? In times of crisis we think above all of ourselves, and when one turns to true friends one counts on their indulgence. That is what I do with you."

Many of her letters were exclusively devoted to Mignet's personal concerns. On March 7, 1848, barely a week after the revolution in Paris had toppled Louis-Philippe, she showed remarkable foresight in her concern over Mignet's position.

The news I have received this very moment makes me tremble for you. Where are you? What are you doing? What will become of you? Do you think you will have to leave your post? If I were you I would

not think so; but you do not think as I do in all things. If you have
left your post, leave your country as well for a while. Come to me and
wait for a return to peace. . . . Come and travel across this country,
which is so beautiful and whose awakening is so grandiose. Come.
During that time passions will quiet down and you will return home
to offer your country the services it has the right to expect of you.
I am so upset I cannot write more. If I knew you were safe and sound
and Director of Archives I would be relatively calm.

She anticipated by more than three months Mignet's misfortune under
the republic, although her subsequent letter of April 13 reveals her sympathy for this system, as yet unsuitable in Italy. Recounting her return to
Milan from Naples with volunteers for the insurrection against Austria,
she tells him how Lombardy achieved in five days what had been thought
impossible.

Now it is the turn of all of Italy to show that the lessons of the last
thirty years have not been wasted. . . . Everyone urges me not to
leave before our fate has been decided. . . . Our first step was a great
triumph but we can still encounter failures. It is not so much the
Austrian army that frightens me; it is the mood of the province. The
republican party is very strong in Lombardy. You know how attracted
I am to this form of government, which furthermore permits superior
minds to exercise all the influence they can capture. It is not the republic that frightens, nor does it in any way repulse me. What we
need is union and strength. The south of Italy is concerned with the
idea of forming a single nation and a single state, so that with a little
encouragement from us [Lombardy], Tuscany, Naples, and perhaps
Rome would yield to Charles-Albert. If, on the contrary, we set ourselves up as a republic, each of the cities which comprised the Lombardo-Venetian kingdom would separate from the whole and become
a state. Genoa would detach itself from Piedmont, and once the idea
were implanted that Italy's aim is a federation, and that a federation
of twenty states is as good as a federation of ten, there is no further
reason for two cities to remain together. . . .
    You understand how an influential and sympathetic voice can be
useful at this moment. I shall remain here, shall write, speak, neglect
nothing that can lead my country toward the solution I wish with all
my heart—its union with Piedmont. . . . As to you, I understand
your resolutions. As long as you think you can be of some service to
your country you are right not to think of leaving. Remember however that there are some circumstances in which one is defeated with
no advantage for anyone, and if that were to happen come and join
me. You would live by your pen without difficulty, I know that; you
would climb back into an attic, I don't doubt that either; but you
would not coolly watch your country commit acts that revolt your

ideas of duty, of decency. You would speak out freely, and if minds are irritated you would irritate them more, at your own risk. That is what I fear for you, and implore you to avoid. Remain at your post as long as your presence is useful; but if an adverse current comes along do not try to swim upstream, or let yourself be carried by it. Come to the bank and wait. . . . Let your bank be Milan, Locate, your friend's home. We will spend peaceful, happy hours together, talking of the present, the future, exchanging our regrets, our views, our hopes, and will agree more than we did before, for our old subjects of dispute have disappeared before the judgment of facts. . . .

When in May 1848 he was forced to resign the post he had held for eighteen years, Cristina rushed to defend him, and at a time when some of her more romantic biographers present her in necrophilic exaltation over the death of her young secretary. The coincidence of Mignet's calamity—his loss of income, dwelling, and the documents so necessary to his historical writing—and Stelzi's death helps clarify one of the more lurid aspects of Cristina's notoriety. On her return to Locate in December 1844 after one of her usual six-month stays in Paris, she had hired Gaetano Stelzi, a young scholar of good family but little means, as a tutor for Marie. In time Stelzi also helped her with research for her book on Italian municipalities, and became an editor on the *Gazzetta Italiana,* which she founded two years earlier. Cristina announced her great find to Thierry, who came to know Stelzi well as did Mignet, since he accompanied her yearly to Paris. "I have made a real find. A young man of the highest distinction, studious as an ancient scholar and particularly versed in charters, statutes, manuscripts. . . . He will teach Marie and help me with my work. When you have conquered his timidity and reserve you will find in him what you appreciate so much: a clear-thinking, cultivated mind and a passion for work. He has only one drawback which you, poor dear, will not notice, and that is a handsome face. After all, I am approaching the age when such drawbacks no longer matter. A few more years and no one will suspect me any longer of looking at a handsome face, while on the contrary, the view of whatever is beautiful will always please me were I a hundred years old. Everything is thus to my benefit in this matter and all the more in that my scholar is as honest and simple as he is knowledgeable." A more significant drawback, which she neglected to mention, was tuberculosis. Stelzi's health was a constant preoccupation, and despite all the comfort Cristina provided and all the care Maspero gave, Stelzi's health deteriorated inexorably. Cristina's need to prove the superiority of her own strength was once again satisfied by the challenge of caring for this young man. Just as Maspero and she began to think they had cheated the fates, Stelzi suddenly died.

Cristina's letters to Mignet often speak of "mon malade," who, dur-

ing periods of remission, worked tirelessly for the *Gazzetta* and collabo-
rated with Cristina on all aspects of her patriotic activities. For some
time, she and Mignet had not seen eye to eye regarding Italy's future. He
was convinced that states so jealous of their autonomy could never be
forced into a political entity but did envisage the possibility of a federation such as Switzerland had recently adopted. Cristina, impatient for
Lombardy's liberation, had supported Mazzini as a means to the only
solution she considered valid—total unification. At no time did she abandon her conviction that a united Italy should be ruled by the House of
Savoy. When in five days of March 1848, *Le Cinque Giornate,* Austria
was evicted from Milan, Mignet, convinced at last by Cristina's arguments for unification under Piedmont, wrote to an Italian friend in Paris
who was about to leave for Milan. The letter was intended only for
private circulation. "Please give this, as soon as you arrive in Milan, to
your celebrated and excellent compatriot [Cristina], whose opinions
after having been so courageous are so wise today. She thinks with as
much good reason as patriotism that Lombardy should unite with Piedmont. This is the considered feeling and ardent desire of all friends of
Italy." Reflecting that only a unified northern Italy under a constitutional
monarchy could guarantee freedom and independence, he added, "Lombards hold their fate in their own hands. . . . Providence has placed
beside them, in Charles-Albert, the instrument of their definitive liberation and their national greatness." The letter, first printed in Italian
newspapers, was reprinted a month later in Paris with an outraged editorial in *La Réforme:* "The candidacy of Charles-Albert, hangman of the
Italians in 1821, is now recommended to them as their king by an employee of the Ministry of Foreign Affairs of the French Republic." The
new Minister, a confirmed republican and supporter of Mazzini, was still
more scandalized that a subordinate should publicly advocate a policy
contrary to his own and asked Mignet to make a public retraction. He
refused. His resignation of May 23 was accepted "with regret" four days
later. Cristina, learning of this from the newspapers on June 1, wrote at
once: "In the name of our friendship keep me informed. . . . I wish I
were as rich as I once was, but even today I would be happy if you
accepted my hospitality until serener days shone over France. Your
temper, as the English say, is not calm; you will be exacerbated by this
injustice; your words, your acts, your writing will show it against your
wishes and unbeknownst to you. You will make enemies for the first time
in your life, because it is the first time that fortune is adverse to you. Let
the storm pass, come to me. . . . You will forget your vexations and
make me very happy during that time."

Two weeks later Stelzi was dead. Before taking the body to Locate
for burial, Cristina mobilized all her distinguished friends to write a

letter for immediate publication in Paris, expressing their sympathies to Mignet "for the misfortune which your attachment to our cause has brought upon you," she told him in her covering letter. "One of the names was written for the last time. Yes, mon ami, I have just suffered a terrible loss whose traces will not disappear. It happened most unforeseeably, for the sickness that caused me so much anxiety seemed to be waning; his increase in weight had been returning along with his strength when the other evening, feeling ill, with Mrs. Parker beside him after the discomfort had subsided, he suddenly called her in a perfectly strong and peaceful voice to ask for something. She quickly got up, approached the bed; he expired. Not a complaint, not a gesture, not a spasm. I am too stricken to write more; and all the more so since I am writing beside the coffin which contains the finest of beings, whom we shall keep until his final resting place is ready. Oh, how I need to see you! But how impossible for me to come to you!"

In his 1902 biography of Cristina, Barbiera published an account of Stelzi's exhumation that is worthy of any Gothic novel. As related by him, the embalmed body (later said to have been prepared by Cristina and Mrs. Parker) was secretly brought to Locate, a tree trunk placed in the coffin for burial in the cemetery; the corpse, attired in a tail coat, was kept in a closet and later discovered by Austrian troops searching the house. In 1926 Augustin-Thierry inserted this story, slightly embellished, in his biography of Cristina, supporting it with her letter to Thierry that relates the details of Stelzi's last hours and closes with: "I did not know I loved him that much: I did not know that his life was so intimately bound and so necessary to mine. I feel it today. I have brought him here, in a tomb that is within the grounds of my house, so that Mrs. Parker and I have the sad consolation of decorating it with flowers and keeping it more like a room than a sepulcher." This Augustin-Thierry calls "a veritable paroxysm of insanity . . . the exacerbated necrophilia of a lover [*une amante*] wishing at any cost to keep near her the body of her beloved."

Were this true, one would have to assume that Mrs. Parker, Thierry, Mignet, Stelzi's own family, were all necrophiliacs to have condoned such an act. It was Stelzi's own father, overseer of the estate, who informed Cristina on September 12, 1848, that fourteen gendarmes were billeted there to prevent the vandalism that had become rampant after Austria's recapture of Lombardy. When they found the coffin, there was apparently nothing inexplicable about its presence or a scandal would surely have followed. The story of the corpse in the princess's closet would instantly have been spread all over Europe, for Cristina was once again an Austrian subject and a political refugee, having fled to Paris on August 5, after the collapse of Milan's short-lived independence. Her

active role in the provisional government, her intrepid articles, which had
continued to appear after Stelzi's death, made her all the more vulnerable
to Austria's reprisals. And yet, there was no scandal to defame her. Had
there been even the slightest stir, Mazzini would certainly not have
chosen her as his emissary to the French government, precisely in that
autumn of 1848.

Any memories of Stelzi's death that remain among the older citizens
of Locate are tinged rather with melancholy. As told to me by a senior
employee of the Town Hall, a resident for the last fifty years, whose
information came from a still older native, the princess stayed beside the
coffin for three days until it was taken to the cemetery, a few minutes'
walk from her villa. The villa, known as Il Castello, is now a shambles, a
tenement dwelling for numerous families who commute to Milan's fac-
tories. All that remains in Locate of the once-glorious Trivulzios is a handsome brick tower, with elaborate window friezes, flanking the baroque
villa whose frescoed emblems have not yet faded, and the family name on
the town signs: LOCATE DI TRIULZI. The cemetery, neglected and incongruous on the main street of this now proletarian suburb, holds Stelzi's
grave and the raised sarcophagus of Cristina's tomb,* seen from the street
through the wrought-iron gates. Cristina and Stelzi are barely remembered by this village, which would surely not have forgotten the story of
an embalmed corpse in a closet—the village has few distractions. The
surviving memory, though imprecise, is a far cry from grave-robbing and
necrophilia.

In a minor masterpiece of innuendo, Barbiera established the legend
that, more than any other, undermined Cristina's reputation in Italy and
vouchsafed her notoriety in France. After inserting a fictional dialogue
between an Austrian soldier and one of Cristina's servants, a device
which immediately discredits the material, Barbiera adds, "It is not possible to establish any affirmations since precise documents are lacking."
Yet that is precisely what he goes on to do by negative inference:

> The princess, although stricken with terrible nervous afflictions . . .
> was not demented. . . . It is thus improbable that she could have
> kept in her house for a number of weeks (as was said) the embalmed
> cadaver of poor Stelzi; and that, on leaving Milan, had it clandestinely
> transported to Locate, to her own villa, with the order that it be locked
> in a closet so as to be able to have it at her disposal on her return from

---

* The inscription on it reads: "To Princess Cristina Trivulzio Belgiojoso, whose
vast talents, force of spirit, and devotion to country made her deservedly illustrious in
politics, in exile, in travels, during the hazardous times and great moments in which she
lived. Here the Marchesa Maria Belgiojoso Trotti placed the remains of her beloved mother,
invoking from her, who was a constant and generous helper of the poor, that blessing with
which God rewards charity."

the Orient; it is improbable that she herself would have ordered a tree trunk to be buried in place of the pitiful corpse deserving of piety. . . . Surely this funereal event seems a macabre tale out of Hoffmann, Poe, or Radcliffe. . . ."

Equally improbable is the clairvoyance which would have allowed her to see in June 1848 that Rome would fall a year later and that she would have to leave the country. As to the "Orient," she had no idea she was going to the Near East until after she left Rome.

The tale does indeed become macabre as Barbiera tells it, and as it was repeated in French and English by later writers. Hardly surprising that it entered the chronicles of mad passions still read today. However, Cristina's letters to Mignet and Thierry leave no doubt about her perfect lucidity. As she told them, she planned to keep the coffin on the estate until a fitting tomb was ready. Furthermore, documents published by Malvezzi prove that Stelzi's body was transported to Locate not only with every regularity but under escort of the Department of Municipal Health. The parish register of Locate reads: "Gaetano Stelzi aged 27, doctor of law, deceased the 16th of June 1848 in Milano, at one in the morning. Buried the 19th of June in this cemetery. Reason for death: Tubercular suppuration." The entry was made in 1849, probably after the coffin was found, with an appended note to explain the lateness of registration: "The registration was not made at the time because it was thought to have been done in Milano."

That Cristina's own coffin is in a raised sarcophagus indicates her wish not to be buried; she must have felt as strongly about Stelzi's grave, which would account for the time needed to prepare "his final resting place." Had his intended monument been just a tombstone, he would have been buried and the stone placed later on. But rather than have him exhumed after conventional burial, she evidently arranged with the parish priest to provide a temporary sepulcher within the precincts of her villa. If Stelzi's coffin remained unburied for a few months (by order of the health department, there was a sealed lead coffin inside a wooden one for transportation from Milan to Locate), it was more a question of negligence than aberration. Though deep in grief, she was nonetheless writing her usual quota of editorials for *Il Crociato:* one appeared on the day after Stelzi's death, June 17, another on the twentieth. In fact, after bringing the coffin to Locate, she returned to Milan to look after the paper, and in July was more overwhelmed by the reversals of Lombardy's military fortunes than by her own bereavement. Her hasty departure when Milan capitulated six weeks later left her no time to worry about Stelzi's tomb; she had to get Marie, Mrs. Parker, and herself safely to Paris.

The very fact that she wrote to Mignet and Thierry about her provisional arrangements for Stelzi indicates that there was nothing unavowable about them. For had he been the lover she now kept in her bedroom closet (that is where he had landed by the 1920's), she would certainly have kept it to herself. For that matter, had they even had an affair, she would not have written about her loss so openly to Thierry and Mignet, who would surely have been embarrassed. She was by then forty years old; Stelzi was twenty-six. Though modern and independent, she never lost sight of the decorum required by her status as a princess and a woman. Her letters to Mignet and Thierry reveal the nature of her attachment to Stelzi and the true connotation of "I did not know I loved him that much." In English and in French, one can "love" in many ways. Stelzi filled the void in her life, not with passion but with the moral and material support of a companion and collaborator. He provided the political solidarity and helping hand that Mignet could not. One has only to recall her pathetic "Oh, how I need to see you!" on Stelzi's death, and her outburst over Mignet's silence in 1852, quoted earlier, to recognize that her relationship with him had never been betrayed: "Whatever you do, I shall never forget that I loved you."

Deprived of a father's love, denied a husband's love and, out of duty to her daughter, separated from the only man she seems ever to have loved, Cristina lived like a nun in the company of Marie and Mrs. Parker. Stelzi and Dr. Maspero were the only men in her entourage, and the only ones she could rely on. The letters written to Mignet during Stelzi's three-and-a-half-year employment amply demonstrate her unchanged attachment to Mignet. In October 1847, a month after leaving Mignet in Paris, she already complained that he was neglecting her: "I am hardly surprised that absence accelerates the process of detachment . . . but I am not philosophical enough to avoid suffering from it." These are not the words of a woman involved in a fresh love affair, nor does her letter of July 18, 1848, a month after Stelzi's death, give the impression of "exacerbated necrophilia." Quite the contrary, it is an incisive analysis of the reasons for her grief and the nature of her bereavement. "Mon ami," she writes in response to Mignet's condolences (would he be so compassionate if she were Stelzi's mistress?), "you try to stifle my pity for the dead by tracing for me a devastating portrait of the agitations of life. . . . If it is not sad to die it is atrociously sad to leave life when one loves it, when one is impatient to know it. . . . Ah, mon ami, how often, seated alone where I was so often seated beside him, do I suddenly seem to hear his weak and yet expressive voice ask me: Will I die without knowing what it is to live? . . . And how often I replied: No, my child, you will not die, you will live, you will be happy, and it is you who will close my eyes."

Her pain over Stelzi's suddenly extinguished youth is first of all maternal, the sadness of an older person seeing a younger one robbed of the pleasures of life. Only after this expression of altruistic grief does she confront her personal loss.

> Never had I experienced the pain of losing someone dear to me, living near me. The isolation in which I live is dreadful and the company I could procure for myself unbearable. Marie is very dear to me, but she has an overabundance of vitality, which makes her incapable of conforming to my sadness. My existence is deplorable. Not a soul with whom I can converse without displeasure; one bores me, another irritates me, a third tires me, and so on. Milan is as gossipy as ever and my retreat in the country provides it with a good pretext for unleashing itself against me, under the assumption that I will know nothing about it. Would that it were so! . . . I had never known the void left by death. My mother was very dear to me, but when I lost her I had been away from her for many years. Another loss cost me many tears, but although the one for whom they flowed held a very great place in my heart, he had not yet gained any in the reality of my existence [her father]. I had always dreaded the effect that would be produced by a misfortune such as the one that crushes me, and now I know I was right.

Despite her courageous choice of isolation, she had lost her will to work now that she had to work alone. On the one hand she was being pressed to remain in Milan, on the other she was being calumnied.

> I require good will to remain in possession of my abilities, and here they are trying to get rid of me through the most absurd calumnies. I do not have the strength to fight for myself. . . . I can do nothing but cross my arms and let the storm break. Why can't I be left in peace? What have I done? . . . I only see two or three old friends; I do good for my peasants, I try to dissuade them from civil war, and I write my newspaper. Is there anything in that to excommunicate me? How I would like to leave! But there are people who oppose this on the grounds that I am rendering great services. . . . My God! what are those services? I offer a surface for their darts; is there no one but me for that function? In short, I am tired, disgusted, worn out.

This confession to Mignet suggests that—perhaps to explain her mournful seclusion—rumors of a liaison with Stelzi had been circulating. This, added to the earlier gossip of Marie's illegitimacy, marked her with a very scarlet letter.* Her very isolation made her all the more blame-

---

* Hostility toward her still runs high among the Belgiojosos. In addition to her "immoral behavior," she is accused of having been a *Mazziniana,* thus a terrorist. When I asked

worthy in that Emilio, on the other side of Milan, candid, carefree, ebulliently happy at La Pliniana, generously shared his voice and his table with his compatriots. Far more acceptable—because a man and a jovial one—although more deserving of opprobrium, he was even forgiven his disallegiance to the Italian cause, which went beyond political inaction to entertaining such Austrian notables as Princess Metternich and Marshal Radetzky. Who wanted to share Cristina's sadness and her dogged pursuit of national liberation when there were balls in Milan and parties on the lake? She was only a thorn in the side of those who preferred to accept the Austrians' and Emilio's invitations with an easy conscience. And who, after all, did this woman think she was, setting herself up as the political conscience of Italy, when distinguished men were still pondering the danger of falling into republican hands if Austria were expelled?

In the depth of her melancholy she nonetheless accepted her responsibility to continue, and looked for something to revive that inner energy, which had always survived each crisis. "If something does not pull me out of the state of depression into which I have fallen, I am done for. I say this without exaggeration," she told Mignet alone. No one else—not even Thierry or Mme Jaubert, and certainly not those around her in Milan—could have guessed how dejected she really was, for her pen was untiring. During all of July she wrote daily articles for her newspaper *Il Crociato,* protesting the ineptitude of the provisional government, berating the partisan squabbles that defied any organized program, imploring Charles-Albert's support, and incurring the wrath of all. Never a dupe even of her deepest commitments, she foretold the end of Milan's newly won freedom and saw the futility of her efforts. "What I need is some compelling work; not just the work of the pen, but of action. But where to find such a thing for a woman?"

The events of the next months provided her with the action she needed. And it was precisely the work a woman could do, particularly one who had already proved herself in the arts of healing. Mazzini called her to Rome to organize and direct the hospital services of the city. When Rome fell a few months later, she was no longer safe within her own country and hastily fled with Marie and Mrs. Parker to points east, beginning with Malta. Unwilling to return to Paris because of France's intervention against Italy, unable to return to Austrian-reoccupied Lombardy, she was once more an exile. However ungraciously Mignet had accepted her 1840 departure and two-year absence, he came to terms with the

---

one of the oldest descendants if Emilio's behavior had ever been criticized within the family, he instantly replied, *"Ma certo, però è lei che ha esaggerato"* (Certainly, but it is she who behaved outrageously).

compromise solution of her six-month stays in Paris. Cristina's letters from 1845 to 1848 further prove that their re-cemented relationship had been unperturbed by Stelzi's presence in her household. However, her departure for the Near East, with little hope of a foreseeable return, exhausted his patience. He had grudgingly adjusted to his half-year life with her; now he was denied even that, and was offered a correspondence in its place. Her need for him, her trust in him were unchanged. But what in fact was he deriving from this relationship after so many years? Each reunion, each departure, each letter meant only another heartache for this man whose emotions were not easily shaken. Better to be finished with it. In 1840 he had tried to forget her, or punish her for leaving him by not writing for over a year. In 1850, once she announced her intention to settle in Turkey, Mignet saw no reason to expose himself to further pain. He was then fifty-five, their liaison had ended more than a decade before, the only benefit he culled was that of adviser on the proceedings to make Marie a Belgiojoso! He had long ago resigned himself to bachelorhood; no other woman could replace this one.

For fourteen months, unable to bear Cristina's bitter resolution to stay far from Europe, Mignet remained silent. They had reached an impasse. He was powerless to alter her attitude, and her attitude was made very clear in letters to Mme Jaubert and Thierry, who could be more understanding because less intimately affected. To Thierry she wrote: "There is unhappily between France and me a sea of blood." She had exposed herself to danger in Rome during the siege; Mignet admired her courage and even championed her cause. She had risked her life and Marie's on a year's trek across barbarous lands and uncharted deserts to reach Jerusalem for Marie's first communion. He may have thought her foolhardy, yet he also understood the rage that propelled her far from France's treachery and Italy's defeat. But when she returned to Ciaq-Maq-Oglou and stubbornly settled into a life of privation, rejecting the entreaties of all her friends to return to Paris, he withdrew in mute anger. To survive at Ciaq-Maq-Oglou required the ingenuity and determination of a Robinson Crusoe. Mignet was not interested; after all, he was not forcing that life on her. With the limited means available to her—money, equipment, books, always arrived irregularly and inadequately—she engaged a few Italian exiles, a small staff of local servants, and proceeded to turn her barren valley into a self-supporting farm. She healed the sick, supervised the planting and harvesting, sold the embroideries Marie and she made at the local market, and began writing stories on Turkish life and legends, which were published in the *Revue des Deux Mondes* and the New York *Daily Tribune*. As in 1831, she was again eking out a livelihood with her own talents, but this time with the benefit of greater experience in hardship and the additional responsibility of a child. To all this, Mignet maintained a deaf ear, but detailed accounts nonetheless reached him via Mme Jaubert and Thierry, and he read her articles.

Her wrathful outburst of March 24, 1853 (see page 117), against Mignet's self-righteous silence was followed four days later by an anguished letter to him that makes no reference to his neglect or her tirade, but reads as though their correspondence had never been interrupted. A pointless insurrection in Milan had been ordered by Mazzini, then in London. As yet unaware of the personal consequences of this event, Cristina berates Mazzini's foolishness. "Twenty years of pitiful, bloody experience, have they taught nothing? Has Mazzini sworn to continue making victims, to discredit his party in the eyes of sensible people, to ruin the cause he claims to serve? Will he never be convinced that an émigré is only a man, that, try as he may to pile conspiracy on conspiracy, stretch the threads of his secret societies across the entire universe when it is no longer a question of plotting but of action, he is without influence, without authority, without power?" Her views on conspiracy in this letter, as in the others that follow in rapid succession over the next week, demolish once and for all the ridiculous scenario written around her as an extravagant conspirator hatching plots in dark corners. Even Marie d'Agoult—herself a countess turned republican and a friend of Mazzini —contributed to this image by portraying Cristina as a Borgia figure in her memoirs.

Cristina, perhaps to the disappointment of some, was a rational politician who approved of organized insurrections but not clandestine operations, and had always sought the open intervention of liberal governments in Italy's cause. "I have always had a horror of conspiracies," she told Mignet on April 5. "I consider them the expedients of bad causes; even when they succeed, their ultimate results are usually deplorable. And conspiracies woven from the outside are to my mind the most absurd of human inventions. I have therefore, since the age of reason, always taken care not to touch them. Emigrés have only one thing to do: write, and publish works with the purpose of enlightening their fellow citizens with regard to their interests, their rights, their duties, their powers. This is what I did until the revolution of 1848." The disorganization within Italy and the treachery from without made her recognize the futility of her efforts; other means and other leaders would be needed to accomplish her goals. Accused by her compatriots of deserting the cause, she tried to justify her position to Mignet:

> I see now that God truly inspired me by leading me to this desert and keeping me here. What would I do in Europe? Could I hold my tongue over such follies [Mazzini's latest plot]? Certainly not, and I would make enemies among my companions in exile. On the other

hand, the Austrian government would always suspect me of uniting with its enemies and I would be tormented on all sides. Here at least I live outside of factions, their extravagancies, their wraths. My separation from friends and relatives is surely very painful, but can peace of mind be bought too dearly? Though I no longer count on human wisdom, I continue to count on divine goodness and tell myself that sooner or later it will lead me back to you. While awaiting that happy day, keep your friendship for me which is one of the things I cannot do without. Give me news of yourself and tell me what you think of this pitiful tragedy in Milan.

Before Mignet could answer either of her letters, Pastori (her attorney) informed her of Mignet's distress over her new calamity. Austria, convinced of her involvement in the Milan conspiracy, once again confiscated her revenues and sequestered her property. This time, far removed from friends and family, she was totally destitute. Heine and Mme Jaubert, alarmed over the situation, immediately advised her to write an open letter disclaiming any participation in the insurrection. This she did, and in her covering letter to Mignet she expresses the unchanged depth of her feelings toward him.

Mon ami,

I know everything. Pastori wrote me about your compassion over my misfortune and all your anxiety. And his letter arrived the day after I had unburdened my heart of all its bitterness, irritated as I was by your incredible silence. It is thus I who ask your pardon. And I ask it sincerely for the interpretation I gave your silence, while reserving the right to complain of it, at least until you have given me a satisfactory explanation. I will only add that the joy I felt on learning you had not withdrawn your friendship was so intense it absorbed the displeasure which the rest of Pastori's letter was bound to cause. Let the wicked attack me. I can endure the effects of their malice so long as I have the love of my friends. Mme Jaubert and Heine advised me to send you a letter on the subject of Mazzini's coup, which you will be kind enough to have published in *Les Débats* [*Le Journal des Débats*] or elsewhere . . . and since you know that I do not lie, let me tell you on this sheet of paper, destined for you alone, that I was completely ignorant of Mazzini's wild project, and had I been informed would have blamed it loudly without mincing words. . . . I shall write again in a few days but I warn you, I expect a reply to each of my letters. . . . And now adieu, adieu mon cher ami. Give me your hand across the mountains and the seas. Love me, and consider me as always your devoted

Christine

It would take six weeks before his first letter reached her but she continued to speak to him across the miles, reassuring him that she would bear this new reverse of fortune as she had the others. "It is true that I have more years on my head than at the time of the last sequester. But it is also true that I have spent almost three years now in solitude, and solitude strengthens the soul. . . . I have learned to do without many things I once considered necessary. And so, do not be pained for me. Tell those who speak of me that I had nothing to do with that wretched attempt in Milan, for I do not wish to be accused of absurdity . . . and do believe that there is neither happiness nor unhappiness that can change a single one of my feelings. Least of all, the one that for more than twenty years binds me to you." A day later she sent Mignet another letter destined for publication, leaving it to him to choose between them. The first had been written as though news of Austria's punishment had not yet reached her and she merely disclaimed any connection with the conspiracy; the second did the same but in the light of the sequester. She was no less opposed to Austria's presence in Lombardy: "I would admit it to the Emperor of Austria in person, but my intervention is limited to that." Cut off from Europe, she was unable to judge the diplomatic expedients necessary for her reprieve. "All I know," she told Mignet in the same letter, "is that one of my buffaloes is limping and I hesitate to shear my sheep this week. Imagine what a capable defense I would make."

Finally on June 8 an answer arrived from Mignet. Her anxiety over his reaction to her first indignant letter was so relieved by what she read that she at once dashed off a contrite reply. "I said to myself, while M. Mignet is worried about me, distressed for me, preoccupied over my misfortunes, I, after fourteen months of patience, take it into my head to lose it and begin fulminating. Finally I received your response . . . and saw to my great satisfaction that you had not sent me packing. Thank you, mon ami. I won't say that your explanations are very persuasive, but what is good about your plea is the assurance that you never forgot me. And since you say it, I believe it. Ergo, peace is all the more binding in that we were never at war." In the long letter that ensues she tells him candidly of her situation, which could hardly be worse. For two full months before the sequester she had received no money from Pastori, so that she was unable to pay off the debts incurred before her journey to Jerusalem. Now, in view of the sequester, she has lost her credit. Yet despite her woes, she finds the equanimity to discuss her current readings, among them his recently received biography of Mary Stuart. "You have achieved a tour de force, for without writing a historical novel you have created a piece of history a hundred times more interesting than the best novel." And she closes with a delightful commentary on the travel book of J.-J. Ampère, a worshipper at Chateaubriand's feet in Mme Récamier's salon and a friend of theirs: "It is amazing to see the pain he takes to be poetic without ever achieving it. He runs through Greece and Asia Minor in Homer's wake; through Italy on Dante's heels . . . but without catching a single inspiration, a single one of the pearls with which those roads are littered. . . . The atmosphere of L'Abbaye-aux-Bois, and the need always to move around in it on stilts, lyre in hand, was fatal to him." The remarks are astute, for Chateaubriand can be said to have destroyed his disciples.

A month later her financial problems looked insignificant compared with the latest calamity. An employee, enraged when Cristina put a stop to his flirtation with Mrs. Parker, attacked her with a dagger. Miraculously able to doctor herself, she had recovered enough five days later to write an account to Mme Jaubert that runs to four thousand words, a shorter one to Thierry, and a still shorter one to Mignet, referring them both to Mme Jaubert for details (see pages 210–11). For the rest of her life she would carry her head to one side because of one of those wounds. Thierry, Pastori, and Mme Jaubert had been writing anxiously about the imminent war between Turkey and Russia. The events that would turn into the Crimean War frightened her less than the dangers she had just survived, and less so for her sake than for Marie's. For herself, as she told Mignet, this dreadful experience confirmed her faith in God's protection and cured her fear of death. "It often upset me, this instinctive revulsion I had for the inevitable end, but now I know that the aversion disappears as the thing draws closer." Her only fear had been for Marie. "What worried me most was the total lack of money, which, to begin with, prevented me from calling for a surgeon, and would have plagued me in my final agony, for I desperately desired that Marie not remain here an extra minute after I had closed my eyes." Now the torment was over. The local governor came to her rescue with a few thousand piasters, 3,000 francs arrived from Paris, and her brother sent her some money. The Turkish government offered to pay the debts incurred before the sequester and send the bill to Austria. "If that works out, I can use my bonanza for my departure. But I have to find someone to replace me here, the strength for such a long voyage, a sea free of Russian warships, and the certainty of being received somewhere."

THE LONG JOURNEY finally ended with her return to 28 rue du Montparnasse in November 1855. They were all waiting to welcome her: Mme Jaubert, the faithful friend to whom the confidences of so many years of exile and separation had been entrusted; blind Thierry, who had de-

spaired of hearing her voice again before he died; Heine, in the last
months of his agony, whose paralyzed eyelids spared him the sight of his
dream love bent by wounds and cares; and Mignet, whose solitude had
been peopled with Thiers's family and with his "immortal" colleagues of
the academies, but with nothing of his own outside his books. He was
once again united with Cristina, the only woman to have understood
and shared the privacy of his sentiments. For the next few years they
would recapture some of their earlier happiness, now muted into autum-
nal sympathy. Cristina's letters of this period are frequent, rich in detail,
and infinitely tender. One of them, written when Mignet's mother died,
is particularly moving for its expression of a woman's sentiments after
time, trouble, and separation have left their patina on a bond that never
tarnished.

> Never, as long as I live, will you ever suffer or be happy alone. When
> at times the sadness and weariness that accompany age weigh on you,
> you will always know where to find a heart that saddens with you.
> Never will the malady of isolation afflict you. From close or afar, at
> any hour of the day or night, you may tell yourself that a friend
> awaits you, arms and heart open, a friend who thanks God for having
> left her in ripe age with all the freshness of young affections, if that
> gift can make her more endearing or more useful to you, if she can
> thereby inspire in you an affection strong enough to attach you to
> life. . . . Come, mon ami, come rest your pain beside me, come tell
> me that my friendship for you is not an object of luxury, like gala
> attire, cast aside on days of mourning.

In Paris he came daily. But once she left for Italy, her pleas to break
his habit of the yearly pilgrimage to Aix, her reproaches for his desultory
letter-writing began all over again; reproaches that are touching for the
youthfulness they reveal. Nearing fifty, aged by illness and the wounds
that left her bowed, her tone was still that of a girl recriminating against
a negligent lover. "You acknowledge your wrong in not writing sooner,
which is good of you; but since you do not tell me what caused the
delay, I conclude that there was no real cause and that it resulted quite
simply from the little need you have to think of me. . . . Far from
repaying you in kind, I write today because . . . despite your lukewarm
manner I know you take interest in what affects me." "Lukewarm" does
indeed characterize Mignet's manner toward her or his closest male
friends. Rarely are letters to lifelong friends so uneffusive, so imper-
sonal, as are his to Thiers or Cousin. He could nonetheless rise to the
occasion when it was pressing or personal enough. So with the lengthy
imbroglio over Marie's legitimation, when he served as zealous intermediary between Cristina's Parisian and Milanese lawyers; so with her

publications, when he served as editor of her manuscripts and go-between with her publishers; and once as her banker, in a comedy of errors that records the only laughter in their correspondence. On one of her trips to Italy she stopped along the Loire to await a thousand francs that Pastori was to send her via the Rothschild bank in Paris. Assuming the letter lost after a few days, and not willing to wait for another draft from Milan, she wrote to Mignet asking him to send her the sum, or borrow it for her, "anything to get me out of here for I feel imprisoned." He replied immediately enclosing a postal check, but the covering letter was addressed to a "Cher Monsieur" whom he was thanking for a re-print. Vastly amused, she related her surprise: "Monsieur Mignet is very ceremonious, I thought; could he be annoyed by the liberty I took? And why does he call my letter 'pages'? Hmm. I continue, I reach Pope Hadrian and think I must be dreaming. Can you believe I had to read to the end not once, but two or three times before I was convinced that you, Monsieur Mignet, the very model of exactitude and precision, were guilty of a total mix-up such as I have made more than once, but would have sworn you were incapable of. . . . 'Mon cher monsieur' was the last thing I saw, I who was born scatter-brained and will die that way." Hardly true, but another of her charming deferrals to his superiority.

After Marie's marriage in 1861 to an attractive young widower—reported in an interminable letter to Mignet—Cristina's morale sank for the first time. The years of passionate struggle were over: Italy was united under Victor Emmanuel; her "grande affaire" over Marie's legitimation was settled; Marie's future was assured. Her son-in-law, knowing the deep attachment of mother and daughter, proposed that they live together, but her own discretion made her doubt the wisdom of such an arrangement. All this she wrote Mignet, adding, "She is happy! That is what I desired above all, and now that this desire is fulfilled, I would be ungrateful to complain. The truth is, however, that I no longer find any reason to live, and am consequently afraid that I am no longer obliged to do so. I would leave life with great regret, but am much less convinced of having many years ahead of me than I used to be, that is, before the wedding. If you can reason me out of this you will be doing me a great favor."

A year later, little Cristina was born. The happy grandmother hastened to write Mignet that she was "just emerging from a temporary hell and one of my first thoughts is to share with you my great joy." Mignet was kept informed of everything and everyone: Marie's health; "Christinette," as the baby was called; Mrs. Parker, now the baby's nurse; Dr. Maspero and his expert assistance during Marie's terrifying post-partum complications. This alone should prove Mignet's special relationship with Marie. One does not write an aged bachelor such intimate news unless it is of special concern to him. In this light it becomes clearer why Mignet served as accessory to Marie's legitimation, and why Cristina turned to him, and to their mutual intimate, Victor Cousin. She certainly had better placed and more expert friends than these two elderly bachelors. Evidently, it was a matter of great importance to Mignet. As a legalized Belgiojoso, Marie's chances for a dignified life were assured. The ultimate recognition of society was Marie's appointment as Lady-in-Waiting to the Queen of Italy.

Nonetheless, Mignet's letters became more and more spaced. In May 1862 Cristina once again complains of his neglect. Despite her many resolutions, she cannot keep him out of her life and writes half a dozen pages on the baby's progress.

> You see that I am beginning to regulate my letters to your replies. You always let three or four months elapse between a letter from me and your answer, and this time I waited four or five months before inciting a new one from you. If our correspondence becomes established on this basis, I will at least spare you the displeasure of beginning all your letters with excuses for lateness. For one who knows as I do your orderly life, your schedule, your habits, the idea that you vainly seek, over months, an available half-hour to give some sign of life to an old and absent friend like me is inadmissible. You have decided to slow down our exchanges, and perhaps to untie ever so gently the bonds that have existed so long between us. Having now reached this conclusion, it would be unfitting for me to oppose your will. As for myself, let me tell you frankly, this manner of treating a friendship does not suit me at all. When I love someone, I am impatient to know everything that concerns him, I often wonder how he is, and would like to follow him every moment of the day. I also feel the need to have him share in what happens to me. . . . Even today, despite all my resolutions, I cannot write you without telling you about myself and my family. . . . I have a granddaughter who is a miracle of beauty, health, and intelligence. . . . I do not think I have become more playful with age, but my little Christinette finds my face very much to her liking and when she sees me, she laughs, shrieks with delight, kicks her little feet and clenches her little fists to shriek louder.

Her last letter to Mignet, consoling him over Cousin's death, still holds out the vain hope that his new fortune will change his habits and bring him to Italy. Realizing that her affectionate impulse falls on deaf ears, she sadly concludes: "But I forget while writing to you that you have chosen to erase me from your memory and that I have even stopped fighting it. You can forgive this letter as having been dictated by the thought of your grief and by the need to tell you I shared it. Adieu, take good care of your health, and believe me always what I am in fact, your devoted Christine."

Mignet survived her by thirteen years. At eighty he was still as active and elegant as he had always been. Spared material hardships and family cares, he was able to follow her counsel: he took excellent care of himself, avoiding political strife and personal entanglements. His self-contained existence had been the perfect complement to Cristina's need for commitments; he had been a refuge from the agitations around her and the frustrations within. In his lukewarm, limited way, he seems to have given her the things she most deeply wanted: the faithful, albeit parsimonious, love of a man she respected; the daughter who allowed her to love with unrestrained exuberance and provided her with a family. However remote, however protective of his emotions, he could still be visibly moved at the age of eighty-seven by the mere mention of her name.[7] Their personalities, their characters, their views, the events around them—everything conspired against a stable intimacy. And yet, what they shared was greater than the sum of their differences. Not even politics, the great passion of their lives, had managed to sever their bonds. In 1860 Cristina reminded him that "we have differed on politics for a long time yet our friendship has held fast in spite of it." It was not the relationship dreams are made of, but it had the lasting devotion and affection of a mellowed marriage. Mignet does not emerge as a striking figure. He was precociously middle-aged, prematurely temperate. He seems to have been what someone once called "a first-rate second-rater"—as a historian, a man, even as a friend. He was nonetheless of major importance in Cristina's life, and to a lesser degree in the nineteenth century, not so much for what he did as for what he demonstrated. His writings, largely forgotten today, reveal the currents of nineteenth-century thinking in history, politics, and philosophy, to which he certainly contributed. But more important to the present task, the intimate side of Cristina—the woman, in love, anger, distress—emerges strikingly through her attachment to him.

6

Pro Patria

WHEN CRISTINA RETURNED TO PARIS in the spring of 1843 for her annual visit, she found Thierry faced with a tragedy more dreadful than his own infirmity. His wife, Julie, was dying of cancer. For days Cristina did not leave their apartment. At the very end, Julie called her to her bedside: "Don't abandon him, take care of my poor Augustin." These were her last words, according to Thierry, "spoken in a strong and penetrating voice."[1] From that moment, Cristina assumed responsibility for him as she would a member of her own family. Had she not, in fact, been their "sister" since 1831?

She took him first to the house Mignet had found for her the year before in Port-Marly, then in October settled him in the garden cottage of a property she rented at 36 rue de Courcelles, at that time still a bucolic suburb. Thierry's means were adequate for his basic needs—and he insisted on paying rent—but it was Cristina who saw to his comforts, from furnishings to servants, providing him with what he described as "a life of family intimacy and affectionate care." Five-year-old Marie added the gaiety of her companionship, filling his sightless immobility with the delights only a child can offer. Cristina's house could have accommodated him, but to protect his privacy she arranged the cottage for him, just as she would include an adjoining pavilion when she had a house built for herself a few years later on the rue du Montparnasse.

Considering that Thierry was far from destitute, thus not a financial burden, and had a brother, Amédée—two years younger and a historian himself—it seems curious that Amédée's grandson should have made so acrimonious a case against Cristina for not devoting every day of her life to the care of his ancestor. This grandson, Albert, who took the confusing name of A. Augustin-Thierry, wrote two biographies, one of Cristina and another of Thierry, in which he published their extensive correspondence. In the latter work he said, "She doubtless meant to carry

out the final wish of the dying Julie, but this role of consolatrix
. . . of Egeria to an illustrious writer [was] to admire herself in the
beauty of her own work."[2] This is a cruel evaluation of a woman whose
own pitiful health and personal problems were more than enough to
occupy her, and whose vanity was well satisfied by her own accomplish-
ments, not to mention the other illustrious writers who pleaded for her
attention. When she returned to Italy that winter—her presence there
having become indispensable to her estate, her work, and the assurance of
Marie's place in society—she was accused by Thierry's descendant of
having abandoned him: "Within a few months, having recovered from
that first intoxication of charity, now captivated by other chimeras, she
shed her costume of the moment. Seized by another passing whim, her
beneficent ministry would be exercised from afar and sporadically."[3]
There was nothing capricious about her departure; it had been foreseen
from the time of her arrival in Paris. Cristina begged Thierry to come
with her to Locate, assured him the same care, the same comforts he had
in Paris, and a trip so carefully planned that no day's journey would
exceed his energies. He could not be made to budge any farther than
Versailles in the summer. He preferred her absences to any change in his
own habits.

The frequency and length of her letters to him from Italy are staggering. For one winter alone, 1844–45, there are thirty-eight extant letters,
an average of more than one a week. In one letter she told him, "I am
certain, my dear brother, if I live, of devoting the better part of my life to
you, of surrounding you with care, of always loving you as a good sister
loves, and of never regretting the commitment I undertook to you." To
this his biographer retorts: "Lulling music of sweet words, at the moment absolutely sincere, but one cannot repress a feeling of irony to see
them always in a state of intention!" Like most of his interpretations of
Cristina's character or motives—and for reasons as incomprehensible as
those of other similarly hostile writers—this one is purely malevolent.
For until her second exile, in 1849, she spent six months of every year
with Thierry, taking him to Port-Marly in the summer and resettling him
in Paris before her return to Italy. And in her absence, he was cared for
by her own staff in the pleasing atmosphere she had created for him. He
was not an easy charge, as his own biographer admits; moody, unsociable
much of the time, offending his own friends, who visited him largely
because of Cristina's urgings, he was certainly an obligation she could
have done without.

Their relationship, difficult as it may have been at times for them, is a
great boon to a biographer. Already in their lifetimes, this friendship had
become a legend. Charles Monselet, writing in 1849, recorded what was
common knowledge in Paris: "The profound friendship that unites Prin-

cess Belgiojoso and the author of *La Conquête d'Angleterre* is one of the most beautiful and noble things we know."[4] And their rich correspondence reveals today what Monselet and others saw in her at the time: *"une femme politique, une grande dame, et un homme de lettres."* Her letters to Thierry are a unique document of her life and work in Italy, reflecting at the same time certain aspects of her personality that would otherwise remain unseen. Always perceptive, brightened with anecdotes, they often provide a remarkable analysis of events, of herself, and of their friends.

In her first letter, she described the festive welcome she received from her peasants, for whom she had provided schools and housing during her tenure as chatelaine of Locate.

> Almost 10,000 people were assembled in my little village, which consists of only a fifth of that number. All those people walked through my garden, my house . . . and there was not a drunkard, not a quarrel, not the slightest disorder. . . . The young men thanked me for the instruction I had been giving them. . . . Locate has taken on another look. The children are clean, the young people polite. . . . This letter is confidential, my dear Thierry. I would not like to be suspected of taking pride in these demonstrations. I do, on the contrary, find in them great cause for humility. I tell myself that among all these people there are only a few whom I have obliged. If gratitude can extend this far, what can one not do or expect! I know only too well that I am a thousand leagues from doing all that I should. I have the charge of these souls, who give themselves up to me with such enthusiasm. Let God grant that I not return to whence I came before I have accomplished my duty.

It might be possible to dismiss this as false modesty, or delusions of grandeur, were it not for the fact that she indulged in such showing off with no one else.

Her concern for improving social conditions on her estate was more than merely philanthropic. She saw in these neglected peasants the future of Italy. A united Italy, responsible for itself, had to draw from its lower classes. First of all, they had to be educated. Unlike the French, they had never benefited from the Napoleonic Code, which standardized education and made it obligatory. By restoring human dignity to these people, who had been traditionally kept as serfs, she could envisage a time when civil dignity would be restored to a nation divided and oppressed by popes and conquerors. A people held in virtual serfdom was furthermore counterproductive to a healthy economy. This was what she tried to point out to her compatriots in a circular letter she sent to the landowners of lower Lombardy: "Frequent marriages, unhealthy air [the marshes bred malaria and the humidity of the region caused chronic respiratory diseases], and the nature of their work result in a greater population of orphans here than elsewhere. Entrusted to the uncertain custody of distant relatives, often to strangers, employed in the most wearisome tasks, mistreated, undernourished, badly raised, they create a weak and delinquent population that consumes more than it produces, falling on the charge of proprietors or tenants or the well-to-do, thus diminishing the revenues of those who could benefit from those lands."

Her letter was ignored, her arguments ridiculed. Why improve the conditions of a class that was more animal than human? Decent houses would be turned into stables in days. And education? For what? To make them lazy and demanding? These were the utopian ideas of Saint-Simonians. Rubbish! Cristina did not agree. She forged ahead with her ambitious plans and set up a nursery school for children under six, where they were dressed, fed, and taught rudiments of civility, including catechism. She instituted a soup kitchen in a ground-floor room of her own villa, where for a token sum her peasants could eat and gather in a heated place. In this simple refectory—luxurious for the peasants, accustomed to the unheated hovels they shared with their animals—there were discussions of community projects, readings, and prayers. For older children, there was now a school that taught them basic skills, and for adolescent boys *and* girls there was vocational training; carpentry and ironwork, sewing and embroidery, printing, higher mathematics, and agronomy. In addition, Cristina herself taught the girls music and singing. This was more than enough to keep her busy for six months a year, but she also found the time to write books, articles, and innumerable letters.

In another letter to Thierry during the same winter of 1844–45, she made a pungent analysis of their mutual friend Mignet, who had advised Thierry to "profit from your solitude to work"—a counsel Mignet could give from the heart since he too suffered from Cristina's absence. Nothing, in fact, prevented Mignet from spending a few weeks with her in Locate, as she repeatedly asked. But his rigid character was as paralyzing for him as was Thierry's ataxia. Seeing deeper into Mignet's remark than Thierry, who had innocently quoted it, she was incensed by his advice. She too had urged Thierry to work, had in fact succeeded in getting him to resume his work on the Third Estate (which resulted in *Monuments du tiers état,* his first publication in five years), but not in those words. Thierry, in fact, had complained: "The remark of a strong man; alas, it is hardly for me." Her homily, inspired by Mignet's remark, had less to do with Thierry's work than with her basic incompatibility with Mignet. "Today marks a month since I left you and it is a sad anniversary . . . a month spent in solitude, in shadows, in immobility, without the resource of cherished work, is very long and very oppressive. Monsieur Mignet's remark is one that makes for the delight of character analysts. Profit from your solitude—that is magnificent! Monsieur Mignet does not know that to profit and to enjoy are mutually exclusive verbs. To profit is to turn things on all sides, to take them apart, to find the good and leave it at that. To enjoy is an act that analysis destroys. To enjoy something is to accept it with eyes closed, with suspended judgment, and if there is bad mixed with the good, as there always is, it passes with the rest and one is not suspicious of it. Thus . . . the habit of profiting makes one incapable of enjoying . . . and that is perhaps why M. Mignet is not the happiest of mortals." This contrast between the two verbs reveals the bitter disappointment of her relationship with Mignet. Her spontaneous affection and perhaps exaggerated sense of responsibility were in constant friction with Mignet's restraint and egoism. He was suspicious of her friendships, resentful of her duties, rigorous in his standards, and secure in his convictions, thus making compromises all but impossible between them. She was, of course, equally convinced that right was on her side.

Thierry's descendant, in both biographies touching on their relationship, contributed greatly to the image long held of Cristina as eccentric, fickle, alternately playing the contradictory roles of grande dame, priggish intellectual, madonna of charity, breaker of hearts, revolutionary firebrand. Fortunately, he published their correspondence, as well as other related letters, which provides better testimony than his denigrations. Thierry himself had said, "A person whose heart and soul are above all praise surrounds me with care and affection as would a sister." And Guizot, minister of state, eminent historian, and close personal friend of Thierry, wrote him a year after Julie's death, "I am grateful to Princess Belgiojoso for her care of you. She is good, a quality most rare indeed and, it must be said, quite different from mere airs of goodness." Within her power, she was as constant in her goodness to Thierry as she was consistent in her projects.

One of the invaluable aspects of her correspondence with Thierry is the close record it provides of her thoughts and sentiments, disclosing a compulsive rather than an impulsive personality; she took on one obligation after another and all but drowned in work as a substitute for the private life she could not have. In December 1844 she lucidly traced her life for years to come in the kind of letter she wrote only to Thierry. Speaking of her future projects for Locate, she says:

> But all this is not the matter of one day. It required my somewhat magical influence on these poor people to make them accept closed dwellings which they have to keep clean. . . . They consider me strange, but well intentioned, and someone from whom one does not escape. The land belongs to me from all eternity; I am a single

woman and not yet too old; I have visited distant lands. . . . I am afraid of nothing, I speak their language; I sometimes heal their children and their wives; and to boot, I have not yet given up any of the things I undertook to do here. There is sorcery in all that. I shall leave [for Paris] as planned, the last days of March, but I shall leave without having accomplished much. You will not scold me for coming back here when necessary to settle my peasants in their new lodgings, teach them to take care of them. . . . The meeting room would soon degenerate into a tavern if I did not reappear from time to time. . . . All these reforms require my personal supervision, and although I neither wish nor am able to plant my stakes here, I must at least come to see what progress is being made and to help as best I can. You see, dear brother, repose is not yet within my reach. Movement, change, separation, absence, regrets, and anxieties constitute my lot for some time still. I need you to help me get through this agitated future bravely and patiently.[5]

It was Thierry's bravery and patience that she needed. Perhaps also, she hoped that Thierry's understanding of her position might be communicated to Mignet, in whom she had found no real solidarity since her first return to Italy in 1840. Torn between sentiment and duty—a conflict that pursued her most of her life—she invariably sacrificed her own peace and often her own happiness. Aware that Thierry's prolonged mourning and loss of interest in his work made her absences all the more intolerable, she tried to stimulate him by writing about her own research for a history of Lombard cities. Speaking of a compatriot who had written a work similar to the one she was contemplating, she said, "His is a rivalry I do not fear. I suspect him of having done his work with Sismondi and Gibbon. When I asked him if he had used any new document, he enthusiastically replied, *Not one.* I admit I do not understand re-doing a work of history only to say what has been said. A historical work is not just a work of literature in which style takes first place. It is not enough, to my mind, to recount better than one's predecessors; one must recount something else: present new facts or new ideas." Ironically, Thierry's own reputation was finally to rest on the literary quality of his works, despite the freshness of his approach.

In her attempt to people his solitude, Cristina filled her long letters with accounts of local events such as the performance of Rossini's *Stabat Mater* given by the girls of Locate: "Even my co-workers thought that for once I was exaggerating my powers; for me, who think that with enough volition one can live indefinitely, the execution of the *Stabat* was a trifle. I thus persisted in teaching my young girls—who do not know a note of music—one of the most difficult ensemble works. . . . The most famous organist of Milan came to help me with the inevitable fiasco that awaited me. . . . The whole piece was performed without a mistake and we were showered with compliments." She also offered him perceptions of her private sentiments, as admirable for their psychological insight as for their expression. When Marie, then six, fell ill she wrote: "How often, my dear brother, when I preached courage and resignation to you this summer, when I disapproved of the constancy of your pain, how often did I tell myself that I would deserve far greater reproaches if I lost what I love! But believe me, the love of a mother makes any other seem pale. There is no passion, however fiery, that can compare with this affection—in appearance, tranquil, steady, radiant—that a mother has for her child. . . . One loves not as one loves oneself, but a hundred times better and more. Qualities are superfluous, for even defects are dear, and if they are corrected, it is with an eye to the harm they could do the one who has them. There is only one thing that could undo me. Pray, my brother, that this will not happen." Cristina's anxieties were not the fantasies of a melodramatic mother, but those of an insecure one. Seeing Marie almost as a proof of divine favor—a gift of love to fill her lonely life—every illness held the threat of taking the child she was still legally prevented from calling her own. She may also have feared that syphilis was hereditary.

It was during this same winter of 1844 that she hired Gaetano Stelzi to help her with her historical research and to tutor Marie, who, a year later, was translating Latin themes assigned by Thierry into French, English, Italian, and Milanese dialect! According to Augustin-Thierry—who claimed to have seen through "the half-confessions that abound between the lines" of Cristina's letters—this twenty-six-year-old consumptive, with less than four years left to live, was the last great love of Cristina's life. These "half-confessions" are his own very personal interpretation, since Cristina was perfectly forthright about the young man's attractions and the nature of her attachment to him. A letter Cristina wrote that very winter is a far truer index of her emotional state: "One finds security in love only on seeing it disappear. One breathes and relaxes when one knows it is no longer. And do you know why one is so secure then? Because one knows it will not return." This disenchanted view of love is hardly that of a woman who has just discovered a great love with a younger man; it is rather the bittersweet musing of one who has renounced love. Thierry, often an intermediary between her and Mignet, surely caught the allusion to Mignet, with whom she was then having the worst falling-out since their reconciliation in 1836. Her letters of this period—none to Mignet; she apparently stopped writing to him that winter—reveal not the exhilaration of a new love affair, but the numb bereavement of a lost one, and above all her concerns for Thierry, for Marie, and for their future together. She informed him that she had purchased a large property on the rue du Montparnasse, whose middle strip "will be for the two of us and the rest for speculation. . . .* Yes, my brother, that will be your share, the tranquil, smiling, secure retreat where we will grow old together, barely separated in time or space, where you will accomplish your great work."

By the first of March, despite an unusually severe winter, she had almost accomplished her own herculean task. Her estate had become a veritable community, almost a phalanstery: "Locate really looks a bit as though it emerged from the hands of the Fourierists." There was a workshop for painters, restorers of paintings, and bookbinders, and four schools, one of which taught singing. In addition, she began to learn Greek, continued her research on Lombard municipalities, and was adding notes to her recent translation of the *Scienza nova*. On her return to Paris later in the month, she at once launched into the building and decorating of their "tranquil retreat," which was slowly rising under the shade trees of a vast park.

Montparnasse was then a quiet wooded quarter into which a few artists and writers had recently moved. Sainte-Beuve, Henri Martin, and Edgar Quinet were neighbors on the same street. Henri Martin, historian, lifelong senator, for whom one of the most beautiful streets in Paris was named, had been a frequent visitor since the rue d'Anjou. Two years younger than she, Martin was stimulated by her salon and influenced by her ideas. The impression Cristina made on him and on his younger contemporary, the historian-statesman Gabriel Hanotaux, is recorded in a tribute to her personality and her work of that period: "No one did more than she, in France, for the propagation of the Italian cause. She devoted to it her life, her fortune, her heart. In her house men were reconciled, came to know each other, loved one another, and loved. . . . Her life was a struggle. Even her loves were combats. The weak and the delicate could not stand up to her superb energy and perished. The strong and valiant were fired by its flame and acquired greater virility. Only egoists and the cold-hearted triumphed over her. . . . There is no doubt that [Henri Martin's] frequentation of Princess Belgiojoso's salon contributed to confirming his belief in the principle of nationalities. This idea was, so to speak, in the air one breathed at the princess's house."[6]

WHILE DASHING TO SHOPS, supervising masons, submitting samples of fabrics to the approval of Thierry's fingers, and enduring his endless questions and indecisions, Cristina was also embroiled in the financial

* Liszt was negotiating with her to buy a lot and build a house for himself on it.

and editorial problems of the *Gazzetta Italiana,* the Paris-published tri-
weekly she had taken over as director. With a publicist's genius for attract-
ing the right people to disseminate the right ideas at the right time, she
succeeded in convincing many of the major figures of the day to contribute
articles. But when it came to giving money or time to her editorial board,
she found them less cooperative. Giuseppe Massari—secretary to the
charismatic abbot Vincenzo Gioberti,* one of the great moderates of the
first Risorgimento—a young Neapolitan writer-patriot, was one of the
people she approached. His unrequited infatuation with her made him a
hypocritical collaborator. First he defamed her behind her back, then he
withdrew his support when his own calumnies precluded further participation. Years later, Cavour still referred to him as Cristina's lover.
Terenzio Mamiani apparently refused to join the board because a woman
was directing the only journal concerned with Italian affairs. In his memoirs of those years in Paris, published fifty years later, he mentions Cristina only once, and then in connection with her friendship for Liszt. Not
a reference to her work or her generosity toward Italian exiles. Yet this
was the same Mamiani, captured with General Zucchi, who was released from the prison of San Severo in Venice through Cristina's relentless efforts in 1831, and who was patronized by her when he arrived in
Paris later that year. Apart from health, the other gift she seems to have
been denied in life was gratitude from others.

The *Gazzetta's* objective of awakening political consciousness and
transmitting a broad spectrum of liberal ideas was compatible with the
goals of the Italian moderates who wrote for it. But Cristina's profound
belief in the need for Italy's independent unification unwillingly placed
her in Mazzini's camp. She had no sympathy for his conspiratorial tactics
and republican ideals, but she could not accept the premise of Austrian
hegemony, however loose, or the presence of foreign masters on Italian
soil, as proposed by Cesare Balbo.† This placed her in a political no
man's land in terms of the lines drawn at the time, but allowed her a
sibylline lucidity in terms of future history. It was Cristina's unwavering
belief in an Italy united under a constitutional monarch, specifically from
the House of Savoy, that finally triumphed. Balbo's utopian dreams of a
benevolent Austrian dominion were never realized; Mazzini's republic
lasted only a few months. Metternich, however, saw less of a difference

---

* His *Primato morale e civile degli Italiani* of 1843, widely esteemed though not very
practicable, saw the supremacy of Italy as based on the moral sovereignty of the Church.
Cristina epitomized his beliefs as "a temporal monarchy for Charles-Albert, a federated state
for the other princes, and a theocratic republic for the Pope."

† His *Speranze d'Italia* (*Hopes for Italy*), immediately translated into French and
widely read, urged the repudiation of secret societies and local uprisings, and advocated
a federation under Austria. His naïve hope was that Austria's interests in the Balkans would
eventually loosen her hold on Italy.

than Cristina between these two factions: "Between a Balbo, a Gioberti, an Azeglio . . . those champions of Italian liberalism, and a Mazzini and his acolytes, there is no other difference than that which exists between poisoners and assassins, and if the *will* of these men differs, that difference disappears on the terrain of action."[7]

Thanks to the feeble support of Cristina's prudent compatriots, probably unaware of how little their moderation was appreciated by Austria, the *Gazzetta* became a bottomless hole for which all her subsidies and ingenuities were never enough. She had tried to make it a viable commercial enterprise by selling shares. Liszt, not Italian, or titled, or politically minded, or even rich, turned out to be the only important shareholder after Cristina. The Italian noblemen in exile, the well-heeled patriots in or out of Italy approached by her, were not prepared to support the initiative of this female energumen: better no propaganda than hers. Thierry had warned her about her editor, Falconi, indicted for fraud in 1837. But she preferred to believe in the dubious honesty of an Italian patriot than in the suspicions of French friends. Ever since the inauguration of the journal, Cristina's cold appraisals of Louis-Philippe had been chafing Thierry's idealism. He still saw in the king his cherished principle of constitutional monarchy, a victory so great for a man of his generation and temper that nothing could tarnish it. When the monarchy fell in February 1848 to republican forces exasperated by the inertia of their seventy-four-year-old "bourgeois" king, Thierry could still write Dr. d'Espine, "1830 marked for me the accomplishment of all my political hopes and dreams. I have understood nothing of the heated opposition against the most sensible, most patriotic king France has ever had."

With Mignet, Cristina had more serious quarrels, making her all the more resentful of French attitudes toward Italy. France's growing isolationism only strengthened her arguments in the *Gazzetta* that Italy had no alternative but to rally its own forces and make use of the lower classes by educating them. The French bourgeoisie was enjoying too much wealth and power to be interested in nationalist causes outside of France, and Louis-Philippe was too concerned for his throne to risk offending Austria. Where Thierry was merely complacent about France's political achievements, Mignet was deeply distrustful of the participation of lower classes in any revolutionary movement and, to his greater guilt in Cristina's eyes, was convinced that Italy's geography defied unification. This unsympathetic view on the part of her closest friends, whom she bitterly named *"les gens de la raison glacée,"* and particularly Mignet's doctrinaire opposition, left a chilly corridor between her and Paris when she returned to Locate in December 1845.

Thierry had been right about Falconi. While Cristina was trying to raise more money for the *Gazzetta,* and secure a franchise for its publication in Piedmont, Falconi cleaned out the till that she had replenished before leaving. After much reflection, she concurred with Thierry's suggestion that instead of being terminated, the *Gazzetta* should be transformed into a monthly. It first appeared under the name of *Rivista Italiana,* later becoming the more successful *Ausunio,* and continued to be published in Paris under her direction. Wanting to offer her young artisans in Locate another career possibility, she set up a printing press and at once received the business of two Milan newspapers. Because the original arrangements for the *Rivista Italiana* had included her taking over another floundering monthly, she informed Thierry, "I will thus find myself at the head of three periodicals in Italy, plus one in Paris, which will make the propagation of my ideas very easy and will add to the influence I already enjoy." This was not vain posturing, for she produced reams of articles on political, social, and agrarian reforms, and supervised every detail of publication herself. Stelzi proved to be her stanchest ally, proof-reading, editing, soliciting articles, arranging for distribution. The frenetic pace of their work probably hastened his death and certainly undermined Cristina's health. But she was convinced of a duty she had to accomplish, and Stelzi must have known he had little time to live, with rest or without. Cristina told Thierry, "If I do not act, if I die leaving this as I found it [her estate and Italy], no one will persuade me that I have no reproaches to make myself."

Her overextended energies finally collapsed. The nagging fatigue she had mentioned to Thierry earlier, but had tried to ignore, heralded a violent return of epileptic seizures, at first not recognized for what they were. As she told Thierry eleven days after the onset, she suffered from "continuous vomiting, pain in the stomach and intestines so intense I screamed out loud, icy cold and a general feeling of anguish which excellent Dr. Maspero thought at first was inflammatory colic. But the truth soon struck him and he no longer thought of anything but tranquilizing and sustaining me until the end of the seizure. . . . I am still unable to eat or sleep and live enveloped by clouds that I haven't the strength to chase away." These symptoms are classic for her form of epileptic seizures, as are the "clouds," corresponding to the confused dreamy state of the post-seizure period, first recognized in the 1860's.[8] There were times when the high fevers accompanying the seizures left her as debilitated as would have some virulent infectious disease.

Symptoms described in medical literature never sound as dreadful as when recounted by a patient who has experienced them. The ones most commonly known—lip- and tongue-biting, frothing, flailing members— are less significant, because the patient is often unconscious, than the intense discomforts that can precede and follow seizures. Some of them (elevated blood pressure, tachycardia, high fever) are violent enough to cause cardiac failure. Cristina, it would seem, suffered from many of the more unpleasant symptoms, such as olfactory hallucinations: an odor of ammonia so strong and persistent as to cause nausea; a terrible sense of anguish that gripped her chest, this being her characteristic aura; palpitations and trembling of the hand; intermittent fevers. During a seizure period, sleep became a major problem. After the first hour or two, she would be awakened by that familiar anguished feeling which left her afraid to go back to sleep. "That nervous pain in the chest and stomach has returned with great intensity. My pulse disappeared under the violence of the spasms, which netted me a blood-letting from which I gained little benefit."

This state of anxiety, vividly rendered in her own words, was misunderstood by her earlier biographers as a fear of the dark, a terror of death, and other *bizarreries,* as they were called. Augustin-Thierry attributed these eccentricities to "her highly superstitious nature," stating that she saw "fantoms," and that the story of Stelzi's embalmed cadaver (which he had read in Barbiera's biography) was a certain proof of her attempt to conquer death, which so terrified her. Who would not be terrified of such precursory symptoms as that anguish in the chest, knowing that one's pulse disappeared during an attack, that death was a constant danger during a seizure? She seems to have anticipated the ignorant interpretations of her symptoms. In a long letter to her brother, describing a seizure that had occurred in her own house, when she was found on the floor by her servants, she concluded, "Here then is the detailed report of the event which will be interpreted and explained God knows how by those not familiar with the history of my health." Had Barbiera understood more about epilepsy, he might have left a truer picture of the woman he transformed into a ghoulish heroine. As to Augustin-Thierry, more than fifty years before he wrote his biography of Cristina, French neurologists had made significant discoveries in the field, but he evidently preferred to consider her "possessed" rather than examine medical literature. Malvezzi, in his attempt to rehabilitate her reputation, understandably chose to juggle away the whole subject.

In the same letter that described her condition, Cristina, weak as she was, returned to an old subject discussed with Thierry many times before: her desire that he stay with her in Locate for at least a three-year period. It would cost him virtually nothing, the house on rue du Montparnasse would not be ready for another year, and in Locate he would have every comfort as well as an excellent library. "Alas, whose fault is it if we are separated," she complained. "Did I not smooth away all the difficulties? Did I not promise you my care, my company, and that of friends on whom you and I can count? And what were your objections? Trifles! . . . The unsettling of your habits? In the last two years, how many habits that seemed deeply rooted have disappeared without your even noticing? If it were merely a question of sparing myself a few hundred leagues, I would not breathe a word of this. It is because I know you to be sad, alone, disheartened, that the thought of sparing you this solitude returns to me with force." The "friends on whom you and I can count," when one has become familiar with the occasional insidiousness of her style, is a slur against Mignet, on whom she could not count for moral or ideological support, and against Mignet and other friends who, when she was not in Paris, tended to neglect Thierry. It was Julie's charm that had attracted a wide circle of friends; Thierry was admired, but he was a difficult man to know. Cristina even chided him for refusing to be alone with visitors, which made them feel like intruders, and for making no effort to see anyone when she was not there to invite people.

Throughout that winter and spring, her letters to Thierry carried little barbs against Mignet. It is, by the way, interesting to note the difference between her correspondence with these two men. Each of them occupied a privileged position in her life, yet the one with whom she had the greater intimacy was the one with whom she was less at ease and far less expansive. Where Mignet received the confidences of certain private matters, Thierry benefited from her humor, her irony, her gift for narrative, and even for polemics. The vivid accounts to Thierry of her achievements and successes—told with the enthusiasm and ingenuousness of a child trying to please a parent—rarely, if ever, appear in her letters to Mignet which are, on the contrary, sober, intense, often embarrassed, even more often self-deprecating. She constantly deferred to Mignet's superior abilities and judgment whereas with Thierry, her role of protector allowed her to show herself in a more favorable light and even to judge Mignet: "Monsieur Mignet likes to see in history the effects of the development of the human spirit. He always writes the history of progress: the Revolution, the Reform. He does not think of uncovering the existence of the spiritual causes behind actions, precisely where they are not apparent. Which is what I will try to do when talking about Italian municipalities." Again a little barb: Mignet never stopped to examine the reasons behind her actions, and if he did, they were not judged in their moral or psychological perspective. Whatever did not suit him, was not a positive factor in his life or ideology, he rejected or ignored.

Their shared knowledge of Mignet, his rock-like constitution, his puritanical working habits, his rigid nature, permitted her to make ironic allusions Thierry could surely appreciate: "Fatigue weighs on me in the morning and does not let me follow the precious example of Monsieur Mignet." In the most intriguing of all her letters to Thierry, she offered a parabolic explanation of her rift with Mignet. Such diametrical and stubborn opposition to her ideas, whether patriotic or maternal, was intolerable coming from the one man she seems to have loved and who never loved anyone but her. Thierry, apparently fearing that her bitterness extended to him as well, queried her anxiously. Knowing that her mail was intercepted, she answered in metaphors only he could understand, which allude to Emilio as well as to Mignet.

> I kept for the end my answer to the question you put to me because I fear you are concerned about my reply. Yes, there is something in me that erodes under the thousand little collisions of *la vie à deux.* . . . When I was urged to enter into an association with another person and was promised all manner of happiness, I took the makers of promises at their word and entered into the association for my own satisfaction and for the pleasure I was assured to find in it. I was then disarmed and the smallest pebble under my foot made me bleed. Little by little the pebbles began to multiply. . . . To suffer and endure, there has to be a motive. What motive is there in this? I see a flower, I pick it because I am sure it smells good, and hold it to my nose; but then it stings me and poisons me. Why would I not remove it from my face? If I am very nice I will not throw it away, that poor innocent flower, but will put it gently in a vase, on my window, in a hothouse, but not under my nose, unless I am convinced this is useful to someone. This experience I had, alas, more than once! I did not grimace at once so as not to wound the flower's pride; I made no complaint, convinced that said flower could not change its scent at will. I tried to put up a good show when the game was lost . . . but finally I said to myself: "Am I not fooling myself? Why have I taken this flower? To do good, render someone a service? My God, no! I thought it smelled good; it smells bad. Is it not natural that I should get rid of it?" There are other associations that one forms for better and more serious purposes than pleasure. When I have pledged myself to those nothing can make me break with them, for I have a motive for enduring what displeases me, and that motive is the very one that determined me to enter into the association. I lived as long as was necessary with persons whom everybody fled. . . . You are not among them, and if we have some subject of quarrel, they are quarrels of no importance or gravity, while the motives I have for remaining attached to you are a thousand times greater. I know, dear brother, that I am useful in helping you endure life; do you not believe that such a thought would make me tolerate collisions infinitely harsher than those that alarmed you? I have unhappily had the time to get to know myself, and I know with certainty that I love you tenderly and that it will cost me nothing to prove it to you. . . .

Mignet's love was a flower with too many thorns. And her experience with Emilio, with whom she "lived as long as was necessary," a person "whom everybody fled" as a would-be husband or a reliable friend, had made her feel that two failures "for the purposes of pleasure" were enough. Emilio was a voluptuary and understood nothing but pleasure. Mignet, however, was just the opposite, and yet when she needed him most—just as when, so pitifully ill in 1828 through his fault, she had needed Emilio—Mignet was as unyielding in his habits as Emilio had been in his. As an "association for pleasure" it was no more successful than the first had been. If love could be so ungenerous, then friendships or working relationships were surely more satisfying. If, after Emilio, she had still held the hope of discovering passionate love with another man, her affair with Mignet cured her completely.

This may explain her willing commitment to Thierry for the "more serious purpose" of helping him live out his pathetic existence. It may also explain the meaning of her attachment to Stelzi, who stood by her when others only discouraged or betrayed her.

Cristina had good reason to remain in Italy. She was swamped with work, which could best be done on the spot, she may have hoped that her new-found prestige in Italy might further her case for Marie's legitimation, and three years away from Mignet would be a welcome relief. She was tired of bickering, profoundly hurt by his refusal to come to Locate, and was perhaps above all peeved at French indifference to Italy, which Mignet seemed to condone. Paris was no longer enjoyable; nonetheless, keeping her promise to Thierry, she made the annual trek with Marie, Mrs. Parker, Stelzi, servants, horses, carriages, and endless baggage, for five years running. "It is for you," she wrote Thierry as she was about to begin another six-month stay in Paris, "that I leave my *chez moi* just now when my presence would be absolutely necessary." Her ambitions for a modernized estate were slowly being realized. The heated community room, the soup kitchen, the schools, the new houses, were so appreciated by her peasants that they were willing to abandon their age-old habits of filth and ignorance to this "sorceress" who was teaching them self-respect.

On her way back to Italy in 1845, Cristina stopped to visit Louis-Napoleon, who had asked, through Buchon, to see her. Since his attempted coup at Boulogne in 1840 he had been held in the fortress of Ham, near Amiens, in the province that borders on Belgium. Discouraged by his failure to gain the throne of France, he fell into complete apathy. Recalling this visit four years later, after the troops under his presidency had forced her into exile, she wrote from Athens to Caroline Jaubert:

> The prison and the prisoner made a very painful impression on me. He was almost crippled with rheumatism; the prison was indeed a real prison . . . and not one of those cells one sees in the theater. Imagine a small room with barred windows, its walls filthy and damp,

miserably furnished and smelling of mildew. You can imagine what went through my mind, I who cannot hear of a place of confinement without immediately thinking of escape. My first words were therefore these: "How can you tranquilly stay here without trying to get out?"

The prisoner declared that he could have done so a hundred times, since all the officers and soldiers of the guard had proposed it to him. "But," he added solemnly, "I prefer prison in my country to the perpetual exile that escape would necessitate. Here at least I am in France; I breathe French air; I tread the soil of France." I interrupted him. "Prince," I said, "allow me to point out that a prison is no one's homeland. Furthermore, you can hardly feel a wild and unreasonable love for a country you left a few days after your birth and with which you renewed acquaintance through the windows of a dismal prison."

Abandoning his tone of affected patriotism, he argued it would be cowardly to leave his comrades in misfortune who were imprisoned for having served his cause.

To this Cristina countered that they were being held because he was there; if he escaped they would be released, for without him they posed no threat. However, she knew the secret reason for his inertia—censored in the 1850 publication of *Souvenirs dans l'exil,* in which this letter appeared—to be the ingenious distraction arranged for him in his confinement. "A young laundress [Alexandrine Vergeot, later wittily nicknamed *La Belle Sabotière**] was placed in his prison to distract and console the prisoner." Louis-Napoleon had two sons with her. "The prince thus found himself with a sizeable family that cost him a fair sum but which in turn made his life less hard. There was much laughter in high circles over this manner of preventing prisoners from escaping." In the spring of 1846 he finally did escape in a mason's work clothes and reached London, where Cristina saw him again during the summer. She had gone to London with a letter of introduction to Disraeli from Thierry in the hope of gaining from England the help France had denied. She achieved nothing. England was as unwilling to alienate Austria as was France. She did, however, get Louis-Napoleon's assurance of solidarity: "Princess, let me first put things right in France; then we will look to Italy." This was hardly an encouragement, since at that moment Louis-Napoleon was the only one to believe firmly in his destiny to rule France. There were Bonapartists aplenty, but they were powerless.

Still convinced of Italy's destiny, Cristina returned undaunted to spend the rest of the summer with Thierry. Before her departure for

* *Sabotière* is both a woman-wearer of the peasant's traditional clogs (*sabots*) and a female saboteur.

London a fresh reconciliation with Mignet had taken place, and this one so tender that, for the first time in a decade's correspondence, she addressed him as "mon cher ami." Writing to him about very personal feelings—her disappointing reunion with her sister, who had married George Sand's friend Count Charles d'Aragon—she laments the fact that blood ties, which should be stronger, are less reliable than others: "You have not changed, mon ami, nor do I think I have; why have others?" Perhaps to tease him, or unable to resist a touch of irony, she added, "Your letters give me great pleasure; they portray you exactly as you are: satisfied, strong, serene; understanding many things, and pleased with the results of your intelligence. You have an admirable constitution. I hope you will long keep it as it is today." He was then fifty and eager to prove the sincerity of his affections—but as always, prudently. He did not give up his summer holiday with his mother and sisters in Aix to be with her, but wrote touching letters from a spa in the Pyrenees where he was then taking a cure, to which she replied in kind. Her two-week trip to London restored "the forces that my illness had taken from me and that inactivity did not renew. I have returned to my normal state, and work still appears to me as a sweet refuge from many problems. Thierry greeted me with great pleasure after that fortnight's interruption and demonstrates his pleasure by reducing his usual dose of teasing by a few measures." Evidently delighted to be reconciled with Mignet, even if the contact was merely postal at the moment, she tells him that "with you, I let my heart and mind go," and confides her innermost feelings. "My life continues in a uniform, muted shade. I have completely stifled those feelings of impatience that Thierry's moods used to cause me, and he himself seems gratefully aware of this. The fact is, I am certain of never falling out with him and never leaving him. I also have more extensive projects, which I will communicate later. But what use is all that! Merely to wait, alas, and to await old age. . . . As for you, mon ami, it may be that you are fifty, but certainly you have nothing that goes with fifty years. You have strength, beauty, hope; what makes one old is the loss of those marvelous gifts."

At thirty-eight, Cristina felt that her personal life was over. All her frenetic activity was merely a palliative, however useful, to fill the time until life ended. Love, the *amour-passion* she may have dreamed of long ago and may briefly have shared with Mignet, was an abandoned ideal. Its present avatar was friendship, the special kind she now had with Mignet, almost like that of spouses obliged to live apart. She had told him, on her return to France in 1842, when she was at Port-Marly and he in Paris, "Do not forget me, I beg you. Do you know how much your friendship means to me? There are very few things that I place above it, and all of them are duties." Her letters of 1846 reveal the very same sentiments. With Thierry she had the material day-to-day relationship of a facsimile marriage. "I am certain of never leaving him" suggests that her commitment to Thierry was a guarantee of her fidelity to Mignet. No one would ever take his place; no one ever did. Her plan to grow old with Thierry, "barely separated in time or space," meant that her heart and her house would always remain open to Mignet.

BACK IN LOCATE in November 1846, she found herself the target of violent invectives over a work that had appeared in Paris a few months before: *Etude sur l'histoire de la Lombardie dans les trente dernières années, ou les causes du défaut d'énergie chez les Lombards.* Published anonymously, its title page advises that it is the work of an Italian, with an introduction by a Parisian lawyer, Lézat de Pons. To this day, the work is catalogued in the Bibliothèque Nationale under the name of Lézat. There is not even a cross reference to Belgiojoso. Nonetheless, all her contemporaries were convinced that she was the author, as she doubtless was. Her papers, when Malvezzi classified them, were overflowing with notes, drafts, corrected proofs, letters, prescriptions, even hotel bills; it would seem she threw nothing away, or almost nothing. Of the *History of Lombardy,* Malvezzi—also convinced it was her work—found only the fair copy, identified as being in her handwriting, but no draft to trace the work in progress. There is no mention of it in letters she wrote during the period of its composition. More curious still is a letter to Thierry, dated December 3, 1846, in which Cristina categorically denies responsibility for the work—a letter Malvezzi chose to omit* from his biography, except for two innocuous sentences: "Not a person comes to visit me without talking of the book (which none of them has read yet) or trying to extract a confession from me. The general version is that the book is very good but is very harsh on the hero."

The hero in question is Federico Confalonieri, whose carelessness after the foiled conspiracy of 1821 implicated scores of others, including Cristina's stepfather. The portrait drawn of him in the book is respectful but critical. It attempts a psychological explanation of his actions. Easily exalted but without clear principles, he lacked the resolution needed for leadership, simultaneously obeying a number of contradictory impulses. Warned that the conspiracy had been uncovered by the police, he courageously declared he would remain in Milan. At the same time, he prudently had an opening cut into his attic to allow him to escape across

* The letter was published in full by A. Augustin-Thierry in his 1922 biography of Thierry.

neighboring roofs. When he finally decided to flee, as the police were
invading his house, he discovered that the opening had been resealed.
Once imprisoned, he confessed his own participation but refused to reveal his associates' names. However, he foolishly entrusted a guard with
a letter to his wife in which he named his collaborators, who were
promptly arrested. "Is this not," the writer asks, "the behavior of three
different men? It is not at all unusual to find united in the same man the
most contradictory qualities and sentiments; and if such characters are a
stumbling block which novelists must avoid, the historian, a slave of
facts, must retrace them faithfully while taking care to warn the reader
of the bizarre spectacle he is obliged to reveal." This is a sound precept
that Cristina's own biographers should have taken to heart, instead of
trying to squeeze her into the mold of a Romantic heroine. What did not
fit they rejected; what they could not explain they attributed to flighti-
ness.

Well into the twentieth century, Italian historians did not forgive her
the carefully worded and sensitive analysis of Confalonieri, a pathetic
hero who languished for years in the Spielberg because he had lacked the
good sense to escape to Switzerland when he could have walked safely
out of his house and ridden across the border. The book was even held
responsible for his death. Cristina's crime was to have put into print what
many others confided in private correspondence. The *History of Lombardy* does indeed have the crisp style and narrative flow of Cristina's
other works. Furthermore, its indictment of Austria's repressive methods,
meticulously compiled from all the events after April 1814, and its account of Lombardy's degenerative will to resist, unmistakably evoke Cristina's thinking and sentiments. The book carries the pungency and
immediacy of good journalism—a *J'accuse* addressed both to hangman
and victim—evidenced in all of Cristina's political writing. According to
the writer, Austria's system of fear—"fear of committing a cowardly act,
fear of appearing to have committed it, fear of exposing oneself to
trouble by not committing it"—finally led to an amputated upper class,
taught by mothers who had been widowed in 1821 to believe that politics
was a vice on a level with drinking, gambling, and wenching. "The first
generation [of the nineteenth century] resisted bravely and did not give
in without a fight. The second, raised for obedience, submitted more
readily. . . . It is evident that Austria today is gripped by terror inspired
by the discontent of the Lombards; it is also evident that the Lombards
are gripped by a terror no less violent and no less puerile, inspired by the
memory of Austria's vengeance." One learns from this dramatic work of
little more than two hundred pages that Austria had already perfected
police-state tactics. Humiliation, mass arrests, spies, agents provocateurs,
solitary confinement, threats of execution during long years of relentless

interrogation, confessions extracted by claims that a fellow prisoner had already confessed—these were but a few of the techniques used. After thirty years of effective repression, a once-dynamic upper class was reduced to paralyzed compliance. "There is no people," says the writer in defense of the Lombards, "however enlightened, who can escape the effects of habit. He who today was indignant to the point of fury will tomorrow for the same cause feel no more than a twinge of impatience." This goes far to explain not only the apathy of a repressed upper class, with much to lose by resisting, but of lower classes as well, with nothing to lose but personal safety. The habit of fear and the enforced ignorance of any different existence atrophy the will to resist.

When Cristina wrote Thierry that "it is not difficult to deny what is false and, by virtue of repeating that I had nothing to do with the book, I will be spared the blame and honor of authorship," she was manifestly quieting his fear for her safety. (She was also exculpating herself in the eyes of the police who censored her mail.) Thierry's anxiety can only have been caused by his previous knowledge of the book's true author and its inflammatory contents, since no mention of the work appears in her letters before December 3. Reassuring him that there was no cause for concern, she offered a very convincing argument: "The sagacity of my compatriots is not great since they think that an Austrian subject, living and owning property in the Austrian empire, could commit the folly of writing and publishing a book such as the one attributed to me. The supposition is so unreasonable that it must soon collapse."

"The folly of writing and publishing such a book" is perfectly coherent with her contempt for Austria. It is also characteristic of her courage and wit. Under the thin veil of anonymity, she was flaunting her loathing and openly inciting her countrymen to rise up. Had the book been written by an exile safely outside Austrian borders it would never have had so great an impact. But Cristina, an hour's ride from Milan, was exposing herself to reprisal while pretending to be an obedient subject. The authorities could not prove she was the author (perhaps that is why she destroyed her drafts of the book), but they were surely aware of rumors to that effect. It is a pity that she never officially claimed the book as her own, for it is a brilliant piece of polemical writing, thoroughly documented, expertly organized, and to her greatest credit. Having steadfastly denied its authorship at the height of its notoriety, she may have felt that the author's identity no longer mattered once Lombardy was liberated, except perhaps to Confalonieri's defenders who never doubted it was she.

The advent of Pius IX to the Holy See appeared to usher in a new era of liberalism. When he appointed—over Vienna's opposition—an Italian as archbishop of Milan, patriots throughout Italy were heartened, for this post had been traditionally held by an Austrian. Metternich clairvoyantly saw the consequences of such conciliatory policies. His criticism of Pius IX is being echoed today by critics of John XXIII and the whole spirit of ecumenism that emanated from his reign: "It is the democratic element that is coming to light and that proclaims Pius IX as its Messiah. From that element, applied to the Catholic Church, to civil radicalism and atheism there is but one step, and the Head of the Church who awakens that element is preparing a very sorry future of reproaches and combats for himself."[9] The appointment of an Italian archbishop was indeed viewed by patriots as a papal blessing of their nationalistic goal. Charles-Albert, at long last and doubtless encouraged by the Pope's action, tacitly manifested his support of national independence by allowing the publication of Camillo Cavour's newly founded newspaper, *Il Risorgimento,* which advocated constitutional reforms and later, war with Austria. Metternich quickly reacted to the analogy between these two sovereigns, foreseeing at the beginning of December 1847 what would come to pass within the next year and a half.

> A liberal pope is an impossible being. A Gregory VII could become master of the world; a Pius IX cannot. He can destroy, but not build. What this liberal pope has already destroyed is his own temporal power. . . .
>
> It will be the same for King Charles-Albert. This prince offers a new example of what is produced by characteristics that should remain in constant opposition, yet appear together no less often: ambition and weakness. The king is the prototype of these two faults. He has the hopes of enriching himself with Austria's booty, and the foolishness of imagining that Italy can be placed under the Japanese system of two emperors, religious and lay.[10]

Cristina's return in November 1847 was not to a tranquil Locate but to an Italy seething with nationalistic vigor and noisy with incoherent programs. By then a noted journalist and writer, she set out on a tour of Italian cities, addressing vast crowds who hailed her as a modern Bradamante.* Everywhere she was ceremoniously received by municipal officials and political leaders. There were many others who were scandalized by this lack of decorum, this woman interfering in the *serious* (meaning masculine) business of politics and exposing herself to crowds of rabble rousers. In Rome she was acclaimed by the newspapers even before her arrival: "Awaited these days in Rome is Princess Cristina Belgiojoso, paragon of Italian women, venerated for her lofty ideals no less than for the noble integrity of her principles, and for the devotion and sacrifices

---

* Warrior-heroine of Ariosto's epic poem *Orlando furioso.*

sustained by her at every moment pro patria" (*La Speranza,* December 23, 1847). She was the guest of honor at a banquet tendered by the Circolo Romano, which had never before admitted a woman within its portals. "This is a great satisfaction for me," she wrote Thierry, "who love my country so passionately and have so often seen myself the object of vile and stupid calumnies even on that subject."

At the beginning of January the wind of reform began to blow from the south, all the way to Rome where she could feel it herself. On the twelfth an uprising in Palermo scoured Sicily of Bourbon troops. By the end of February, Ferdinand, Bourbon king of Naples and Sicily, lacking adequate forces to support his conservatism, granted a constitution patterned after the one promulgated by Charles-Albert two weeks earlier. Cristina finally obtained the right to distribute *L'Ausunio* in Piedmont. Now she raced to Naples, that last bastion of retrograde authority outside Austria's provinces, hoping to diffuse the journal there too. "My position here," she informed Thierry on February 13, "is even more brilliant than elsewhere. I do not think anyone has ever enjoyed *so suddenly* a popularity as great as mine. . . . The only difficulty of my position is to maintain it." *L'Ausunio,* incorporated with two local papers, was to appear twice weekly to inform the public of the great work ahead. "Now that we have freedom of the press, it is in Italy that Italian problems have to be treated." It was no longer necessary to publish from Paris; she could now operate directly from Italy with greater efficiency. Two weeks later, she announced the first number of a new daily. The brevity of the announcement makes it all the more striking: "Its title is *Le National.*" This was the title of the newspaper Mignet had triumphantly launched in 1830. It is typical of her self-consciousness with Mignet that she wrote this to Thierry and not to him.

The moment was intoxicating but she kept her head, even between the two major factions, each gaining momentum and on a collision course. The moderates, consisting largely of upper-class liberals, had not altered their program of a federation of already existing states that could mollify Pope and princes. Mazzini was determined to abolish every internal boundary and integrate every separate fief into an Italian republic. This radical program was not likely to win support from the top, essential to any program of unification; even the more liberal moderates saw republicanism as synonymous with anarchy. Cristina's goal, though basically Mazzinian, had one significant difference: she was a confirmed monarchist, not out of aristocratic principle, but because she felt that a republic required prepared citizens. Italy was as yet too backward for such sophisticated government. With all his irresolution, Charles-Albert, already on the throne of Piedmont and a proven nationalist, was the only reasonable choice as national ruler. Cristina did not think too highly of her natural comrades-in-arms, the moderates, and unequivocally stated her opinion to Thierry: "The moderate party is certainly large, speaks loudly and volubly, but does not have two cents' worth of judgment in its head, and dreams of accomplishing miracles while diminishing anything and rejecting everything. The radical party is better by far. I am impartial in this since it is not my party, but it is the only one that has my sympathies, and if my own party continues to reveal itself as increasingly inept I may well lose patience with it."

Relieved about Thierry, who preferred to remain in Paris without her rather than move to Locate, and who applauded her work in Italy, she was able to devote all her energies to the events erupting around her. By March 1, fifteen million Italians were living under constitutional governments. Conditions for the Lombards, however, were very different. Vienna, exasperated by Torresani's persistent requests for retribution against the seditious princess, finally yielded and issued a warrant for her arrest. In Milan, Marshal Radetzky—whose brutal slogan, "Three days of blood will give us thirty years of peace," has gone down in history— sent a cavalry charge against protesters in the streets. The Milanese, in an action reminiscent of the Boston Tea Party, had been boycotting tobacco because of a new increase in already exorbitant taxes on that commodity. Military and civilian police, ordered to provoke the populace, blew smoke into their faces and hurled insults that finally led to rioting. A veritable massacre took place on March 3. Cristina learned of this appalling event and of the revolution in France at almost the same time. Fearful of the consequences for Mignet and Thierry, both of whose incomes depended on government agencies, she hastily wrote each of them, begging them to come to Locate as her guests until the situation in France was settled. She evidently disregarded the warrant for her arrest —valid only at Lombardy's borders—unless she herself did not intend to join them in Locate. Thierry, moved by her offer, replied that he would live and die in his own country; Mignet felt that he should not leave just then. Both of them were, in fact, too much creatures of habit to consider so radical a change. It was easier to adjust to a revolution at home than to a residence abroad. Given the events that followed, it was fortunate that they remained in Paris.

Within those first months of 1848 European history was written on a new page. Louis-Philippe was replaced by Lamartine at the head of a republic. Hungary revolted. Metternich fell to an uprising of Viennese constitutionalists. In Milan the moment to strike had come. During the memorable five-day insurrection of March 17 to 25, *Le Cinque Giornate,* the Milanese succeeded in driving Radetzky's superior forces from the city, fighting at times with nothing more than pitchforks and unbridled fury. On April 6, Cristina arrived from Naples with one hundred sixty volunteers and entered the free city of Milan to cheering crowds. This episode has occasioned more comment and more discrepancies than almost any other in her public life.* Her own former collaborator and disappointed lover, Giuseppe Massari, was responsible for the most vicious attack, published four days later in a Florentine newspaper (although unsigned, its author was later identified).[11] His sanctimonious reproaches were ostensibly directed against the theatricality of the event, and his outrage exacerbated by her criticism of Confalonieri in *The History of Lombardy*. The fawning letters he wrote her (published by Malvezzi) suggest that the real reason for his ire was to repay her disdain. One did not refuse a handsome Neapolitan, who moreover wielded a powerful pen, with impunity.

> No need to speak of the enthusiasm with which those young men were welcomed. The only displeasing thing was that the entrance of these Neapolitan volunteers offered an occasion for one of those theatrical spectacles . . . that are always unsuitable, but on certain solemn occasions are intolerable scandals. With the volunteers came the principessa di Belgiojoso. . . . La signora principessa . . . appeared at the balcony [of the provisional government's offices] accompanied by Count Casati and Count Borromeo. Very many people were reminded of a certain book written against the great Italian martyr, Federico Confalonieri, and were overcome with outrage and pain to see the authoress of this work beside the brother of Teresa Confalonieri [his widow, née Casati]! One is unable to understand how men of the stature of Casati and Borromeo can have tolerance and gentility to such a degree. . . . The Italian cause is a sacred cause, very sacred, and immorality and scandals are the greatest outrage that can be perpetrated against it. . . . Men of good sense who are concerned for their dignity and have true affection for Italy are disgusted beyond expression by such a spectacle.

And one speaks of the wrath of a woman scorned!

The simple truth of this "theatrical spectacle" was told in Cristina's articles in *La Revue des Deux Mondes,* and corroborated by numerous other documents: "No sooner did news of my departure begin spreading through town than I was able to see how much warm sympathy the Lombard cause inspired in the Neapolitan population. Volunteers of all

---

* An example of how this incident was used to mock her as recently as 1972 is in Indro Montanelli's book on the Risorgimento. Quoting what may have been a hyperbolic figure in her account—"ten thousand young men presented themselves and since the boat I chartered could only hold two hundred. . . ."—he dispatches her from Italian history in two derisive pages as "a friend of Mazzini," "a would-be cross between Mme de Staël and Joan of Arc," and *"questa scocciatrice"* (that nuisance), in the words of Ferdinand of Naples, who certainly did not relish the enthusiasm she aroused among his subjects [Indro Montanelli, *L'Italia del Risorgimento* (Milan: Rizzoli, 1972), pp. 254–55].

classes came to beg me to take them with me to Lombardy, and during the forty-eight hours preceding my embarkation, my house did not empty itself." They came, as their proclamation to the Milanese stated, "not as deliverers, but as the armed deputation of a people." It was a gesture of solidarity intended to show the Milanese that the rest of Italy would fight for the expulsion of Austria. Volunteer armies from Rome and Naples did in fact reach Milan later to join Charles-Albert.

While Piedmont's army, now joined by the volunteers, continued to fight Austrian strongholds in Lombardy and Venetia, Cristina channeled her forces and her publications into a campaign for the provisional unification of Lombardy with Piedmont. She walked a dangerous tightrope trying not to alienate Mazzinian republicans while maintaining her own position as a monarchist, and trying to make her party understand that the enemy was not the republic but Austria. Within a few short months the exalted pride in her country's new-found energy, the fevered hopes for its future, her own tireless contributions to that end, all collapsed around her like a house of cards. On June 14 Stelzi died, depriving Cristina of her only reliable collaborator. She nonetheless continued her crusade without him, driving herself without mercy, articles and editorials flowing daily from her pen. It was all for nothing. On August 5, Milan was handed back to Austria by an ill-advised and insecure Charles-Albert. Having already sustained heavy losses elsewhere in Lombardy, the king did not feel he could protect the city against the Austrian offensive and was apparently led to believe that the Milanese would not provide adequate support. Cristina's account of these disastrous events appeared in the fall, after her return to Paris. From that distance it was possible to write, if not dispassionately, at least with some restraint. But writing to Thierry on August 8 from Turin, she voiced the authentic violence of her first reactions.

> I am safe and sound; Marie too, who never let go of my skirts, not in the midst of troops and barricades or in the effervescence of popular fury. Fury well motivated, for we were ignobly sold out by Charles-Albert who, the very day the city was attacked, when we were all ready to fight to the last man, cravenly capitulated by giving up everything and sparing the city nothing but pillage.
>
> The people, the people of our five days, protested as the people can. They took the king prisoner, forced him to tear up the capitulation and swear he would fight with the Milanese to the last drop of blood. The promise concealed a new betrayal. The regiments most devoted to the king's person were secretly called to deliver him. They arrive. The people are busy with defense preparations against the Austrians. The regiments try to carry off the king. The guard around him resists. Piedmontese and Milanese start to fight. The king is fired

at, his horse is killed, and he is obliged to fling himself on an old nag that someone instantly offers. Someone else cries out "The Austrians are coming!" and the people abandon his capture to rush to the barricades. The king takes off. That day the Austrians do not enter.

The next day all the troops are gone, having taken cannons, munitions, treasure, everything; the people do not know what to do. The Austrians make it known that they will enter at noon and will grant the entire day to those who wish to leave.

The whole population emigrated! *

We no longer have any hope except in France and in the republican party. The House of Savoy has become as impossible as the Bourbons in France and Naples.

I am leaving for Grenoble, where I hope to find General Oudinot and convince him to bring his army across the border. If I fail, I will come to Paris at once, present myself before the Ministers, the Chambers, in the popular districts if need be, but I will bring saviors to my poor country.

Have this letter published. It contains the exact truth and I want it known that I have broken all ties with the king of Sardinia and the principle of monarchy. With the republic we will embark on a career of agitation that will outlast us; but only this is possible.

The "exact truth" was made known in the fifty-four closely set pages of her article "L'Italie et la Révolution Italienne de 1848," which appeared six weeks later in the September and October issues of *La Revue des Deux Mondes*.[12] Her honesty cost her the good will of almost everyone who had participated in Milan's five-month independence. Republicans doubtless viewed her with as little trust as Bakunin later viewed intellectuals. An aristocrat, a defected monarchist, what could she understand of the aspirations of true republicans? Yet it was her vigorous support of the people—whose incredible heroism had defied thirty years of Austrian despotism and conquered Radetzky's disciplined army in five days—that stirred up the animus still hovering over her memory in Italy.

Lamenting Europe's inability to understand Italian affairs—"there are [in Italy] as many interests and as many men to represent them as there are cities, and consequently, as many different versions of the same facts as there are systems to which these events are made to conform"— she tried to explain Milan's calamity and the reasons for it. Kept out of administrative functions by Austria, ordinary Italians, "who might have

---

* Though this claim is somewhat exaggerated, it is true that more than half the population of greater Milan crossed into Switzerland that day. The city had been notified by the Austrians that all men between eighteen and forty would be conscripted into Croat regiments. Those who preferred exile had from 8 A.M. to 8 P.M. to leave. The choice was evident. Close to one hundred thousand fled to the canton of Ticino, including members of the provisional government.

distinguished themselves by their character and their talent," turned to the nobility for leadership. "There are doubtless men in Lombardy capable of leading the nation . . . but their names are unknown to the people, whereas those of noble families . . . are in every memory." The republicanism of these remarks is unmistakable; this was as much a pamphlet of disassociation from her former cohorts as it was an informative essay. The president of the provisional government, which soon became a provincial and not just a municipal government, was Count Casati, who had been mayor of the city under Austria. Of the other members, very few (Borromeo, Porro, Litta, this last singled out as "a man of rare distinction") were worthy of their position in the government. Baretta was "generally known for his attachment to Austria," and Fava, the replacement for Torresani, who had escaped with the Austrians, was totally inept: "Never was a post more in need of the rare mixture of penetration, skill, and firmness; never was a man less suited to fulfill it than the new director of police, Dr. Fava." She names every individual who participated in the government and comments on his lack of ability, preparedness, or trustworthiness, or the government's misuse of his talents, as in the case of Achille Mauri. Had the people been consulted on the choice of their leaders? No, she answers. "While the noise of cannons, rifles, tocsins, and drums filled the air, while death roamed our streets, most of the men we have named distributed among themselves their parts and their share of power." More damning than her criticism is her suggestion that these men, in the event of Austria's return, could justify their positions "by pretending to be faithful subjects who devoted themselves to maintaining order and to containing public furor." She does not say this was their motivation, but merely wishes "to establish that the people were not asked to choose them, and their cause was never combined with that of the people." Cristina evidently felt that diplomacy no longer had a place in journalism. Is it any wonder that her compatriots preferred to write her out of their history?

Not only did she enumerate the personal failings of individuals, she made a catalogue of the policy errors committed by the government—fiscal, military, moral, political—which undermined public trust, turned the people against the upper classes, sapped the enthusiasm of volunteers. Assumed to be of wealthy families, volunteer soldiers were neither equipped nor paid; thousands died of exposure and hunger before they had had a chance to fight. An untrained army was rapidly conscripted and sent off to engage Radetzky's crack troops, whereas a corps of partisans could have been organized in the same amount of time and would have "advantageously replaced these improperly disciplined regiments." In fairness, she added that Charles-Albert apparently wanted to fight the war with his army, well trained and well equipped. "For that reason, he refrained from requesting French intervention, rejected the offers of foreign officers and even generals who were drawn to the Italian cause, was ill-disposed toward the Lombard volunteers, and received the soldiers sent to him from other Italian states so ungraciously." The implication is that his ulterior motive was the annexation of Lombardy through a military victory.

Charles-Albert, on entering Lombardy with his army, had proclaimed that he had no personal ambitions, and was merely "the sword of Italy." Lombardy would decide its own political future after the Austrians were expelled. Ironically, the republicans were more amenable to Charles-Albert's offer than the monarchists, who suspected such altruism. Torn between the fear of becoming a province of Piedmont and the fear that a plebiscite would result in a Lombard republic, they did nothing. Seeing her own party too weak and too reticent to further its cause, Cristina launched a newspaper, *Il Crociato,* whose credo appeared on May 16:

> It is time to declare ourselves openly because, one, our opinion must triumph or be vanquished in a few days, and, two, because the opposite opinion has an eloquent defender [Mazzini]. *Il Crociato is monarchist.* Not that it considers the sovereignty of one person more . . . legitimate than the sovereignty of . . . many. Not because a republic frightens it as one of those fantastic entities whose name alone makes one shudder. . . . A republic, in my eyes, is rather the most perfect form of government. . . . [We are monarchist] because a people to whom [a republic] is introduced should have arrived at a level of civility not easily achieved. . . .
>
> The unity of Italy as our goal; the monarchy as the means of obtaining it first and conserving it later; Piedmont as the center of attraction around which all the peoples of Italy will gather. . . ; the House of Savoy as the instrument designated by Providence . . . the only Italian House reigning in Italy. . . . This is the *Crociato*'s profession of faith.

She began a campaign for a public sounding, convinced that the republicans were less strong than her cohorts believed. Two weeks later the government finally agreed. In each parish of Lombardy adult males were invited to register their preference: immediate union with Piedmont, or a political decision after the war. The government was bankrupt. Without Piedmont's army they could not survive. In the vote 561,000 were for fusion against 681 for postponement. Mazzini, warmly welcomed by both sides on his arrival in early April (each side hoped to win his support and exploit his popularity with the people), had been opposed to a plebiscite of any kind before the war was won, but had no objection to provisional fusion with Piedmont; it was a military expedient that did not endanger his long-range strategy of total unification. There would be time for the republic once its foreign enemies were vanquished.

None of the leading actors in this great drama seems to have been suited to his role. The House of Savoy may indeed have been Providence's gift to Italy, but Charles-Albert was not. It would take another scion of Savoy, Victor Emmanuel II, with an inspired condottiere, Garibaldi, to fulfill the *Crociato*'s goal. Although Cristina had little sympathy left for Charles-Albert, she tried to explain his betrayal of Milan: "If the king did not dismiss his generals [some were suspected of collusion with Austria], if he did not devise a more energetic plan of attack, one must accuse his weak and irresolute character, and . . . if he capitulated, it is because the intentions of the Milanese were not presented under their true light." However, the primary purpose of her account was to "defend Lombards rather than accuse those who prepared their ruin. . . . If a terrible disaster has terminated the war of independence, it is not, I repeat, the courage of the people that is to be accused; one must find fault with a few men whose acts are easier to determine than their intentions."

Unable to relinquish her dream because of this first defeat, she chose to hope that the Venetian republic just re-established after fifty years of Austrian rule, and Garibaldi's leadership of Lombard volunteers, would bring the new French republic to Italy's side. "These are forces that can suffice, if well directed, to erase the traces of our recent disasters. . . . Let us hope that the honor of Italy will finally obtain reparation . . . and that our independence, once reconquered, will no longer be placed in jeopardy."

Once again émigrés were flocking to Cristina's house, convinced like her that France would come to Italy's aid. All of Europe was exasperated by Austria's abusive power. Paris and London seemed on the verge of an agreement. About the time her articles appeared, Louis-Napoleon, correctly gauging his chances for the presidency of the young republic, left London for Paris, where he called on Cristina. In her *Souvenirs dans l'exil,* she described this visit to Mme Jaubert: "For my country, suspended between liberty and slavery, honor and shame, life and death, it was then the supreme moment in which France was summoned to decide her fate. 'If you succeed,' I said to him, 'what will you do for my country? Do you remember the anathemas you hurled against Louis-Philippe in 1831 regarding the popular uprisings in Italy?' 'Can you doubt me?' exclaimed the nephew of the great man, 'your country will be one of my first objects of solicitude,' and he added in a tone full of unction, 'you will be pleased with me.' " On December 10 Louis-Napoleon was elected president with an impressive mandate. Former Carbonaro, for whom Italy had been more of a homeland than France, who had furthermore given her his solemn assurance, surely this was the savior she had waited for. "No sooner in power," she bitterly concluded, "he abandoned us."

The closing months of 1848 were filled with promise. The dramatic simultaneity of events marking great epochs in history seemed now to be converging on Italy's long-awaited deliverance. A few weeks after Louis-Napoleon's election, Emperor Ferdinand of Austria, having satisfied no one with his April constitution, abdicated in favor of his nephew Franz-Joseph. The duchies of Tuscany, Parma, and Modena revolted. A massive uprising in the Papal States forced Pius IX to flee to Gaeta, leaving Rome to a chaotic popular government, eventually organized under a triumvirate (Mazzini, Carlo Armellini, Aurelio Saffi), headed by Mazzini. Piedmont was now ready to attack Radetzky's armies, and Charles-Albert set out to erase the bitter memory of his defeat at Custoza the previous July.

The evil demon that seemed always to mock Cristina's trust in "saviors"—those idealized figures in her private or political dreams—now prepared a crippling blow. In February 1849, at the time of his escape from Rome, Pius IX had appealed to the Catholic kingdoms of Austria, Spain, and Naples (within whose territory he had taken refuge) to restore his throne. In April, Louis-Napoleon, in an exemplary piece of devious diplomacy, rejected the Austrian offer of a joint expedition against the Roman republic, thus satisfying French nationalists, who had not forgotten Austria's intervention in 1831 or forgiven France's tolerance of it. At the same time, he gained support of France's extreme right by arranging with the Apostolic Nonce to occupy Rome with French troops and bring back the Pope; gulled the Piedmontese into believing that France's intervention was merely to keep Austria at bay; and assured the liberals that his motive was to reconcile the Pope with Mazzini's republic. With this multipurpose strategy, worthy of Metternich himself, he sent an expeditionary force under General Oudinot to Civitavecchia.* It appears that a month earlier, when Charles-Albert was definitively routed by Radetzky at Novara and abdicated in favor of his son, Victor Emmanuel, Louis-Napoleon considered declaring war on Austria. (He finally did so eleven years later with Victor Emmanuel as his ally.) The adviser who dissuaded him from this idea was Thiers, the great liberal of 1830 and Cristina's devoted friend.

On April 26 General Oudinot sent a message to Mazzini telling him that he planned to enter Rome to mediate an agreement with the Pope in order to prevent an Austro-Bourbon punitive expedition. Mazzini's assembly, doubtful of a French occupation without guarantees, voted

---

* This was the same General Oudinot whose help Cristina had hoped to obtain when Milan fell eight months earlier.

unanimously to resist. They had rightly smelled the rat, for Louis-Napoleon was intent on restoring not just the Pope, but pontifical power, thus assuring himself support from the rest of Europe's monarchs for the crown he coveted. Cristina had arrived in Rome early in April and was assigned the directorship and organization of the city's hospitals and ambulance services. It may not have been the position she imagined for herself, but as it turned out, hers was the only sector of the provisional government to function efficiently during the dreadful months to come. Oudinot, surprised to find her there, asked, "What are you doing in Rome, Madame? You are Milanese, what do you care about the affairs of Rome?" To which Cristina, never at a loss for repartee, snapped, "And you, mon général, are you from Paris, Lyon, or Bordeaux?"* Throughout the implacable siege she remained at her task, gaining not only the admiration of all present, but long after, the only unequivocal praise Augustin-Thierry ever gave her in either of his biographies: "She organized her services with the veritable genius of a commander, decreeing strict rules, introducing everywhere order and discipline. She demonstrated the most total abnegation."

THE AMERICAN WRITER-SCULPTOR William Wetmore Story was a witness to Cristina's activities in Rome. His diary, much of which appears in Henry James's book about him,[13] honors Cristina's work in Rome, and fortunately so, for her own compatriots neglected to do so. "May 2 . . . We went to carry out money to the Princess Belgiojoso, directress of all the hospitals, whom we found sitting surrounded with men and women, giving her various orders with calmness and clearness and showing the greatest practicality and good sense in all her arrangements. She had laid down strict rules and reduced the establishment to order and discipline; for three days and two nights she has been without sleep and still is strong." Four days later, he reported: "Went this evening to the Trinità dei Monti [hospital] to carry the American subscription for the wounded in the late battle. Everything was in complete order, clean floors and beds, good ventilation, attendants gentle and without confusion. These the hospital owes to the Princess, who has a genius for ordering and systematizing. She said that nothing was more pleasant to her than to attend to the sick—it was indeed a sort of passion, for she added that in

---

* This anecdote has been attributed to Cristina by French writers and to Luciano Manara, in slightly different form, by Italian writers. It is not improbable that Oudinot would have teased Cristina in this way, knowing her and doubtless irritated by her presence in Rome. It is also possible that he used the same line more than once, since Manara's Lombard contingent only added to his problems.

the sick-room one is *sure* of doing good. All efforts of charity in other directions may fail of their end—money may be squandered or do injury; but the relief of physical pain is a thing definite and certain." Margaret Fuller Ossoli, who died with her husband and child in a shipwreck on her return to America after the fall of Rome, was another American who knew and admired Cristina at the time, having been placed by her in charge of one of the hospitals.

It was through Story that Henry James first learned about Cristina. What he then discovered about her in Barbiera's biography of 1902 only added to his fascination. A year later his stunning vignette of her appeared in *William Wetmore Story and His Friends.* Just as Story—who lived most of his life in Rome and died there in 1895—interested James as the forerunner of his own experience as an American in Europe ("the American consciousness of the complicated world it was so persistently to annex"), so Cristina intrigued him as the prototype of his romantic vision of the artist in society, with all the connecting links of new ideas in the Old World, the glamour of aristocracy in a revolutionary setting, the tension between authenticity and self-creation. James was sensitive to the anomalies and ambiguities in her personality, as she had been when writing about Confalonieri, recognizing, as did few others, that all those disparate aspects may well be responsible for the dynamism and allure of such individuals. Cristina's remark that the contradictory qualities and sentiments of an individual are a stumbling block to the novelist raises the very problem James attempted to overcome in developing his characters, for whom Cristina could have served as a magnificent model. The Princess Casamassima, whose Christian name is Christina, is one such example.

An American married to an Italian prince, from whom she is separated, in search of vital ideals outside the sterile atmosphere of Italian nobility, she becomes involved with a vaguely defined revolutionary movement. The movement remains ill-defined (although Lionel Trilling chose to see it as the anarchist movement of the 1880's) because James seems to have been more interested in revolution as background than as historic fact—a background, furthermore, associated with his model. Christina Light, Princess Casamassima, bears many other interesting resemblances to her model, not least of which is her motivation for political involvement. James astutely opted for psychological rather than physical traits, though granting his heroine Cristina's dark-eyed beauty. When the prince, unsuccessful in his attempt to see Christina, judges her behavior "crazy," her companion, Madame Grandoni, replies: "The Princess is no more so than the rest of us. No, she must try everything; at present she's trying democracy, she's going all lengths in radicalism." The reason behind this "crazy" behavior is that "at bottom of much that

she does is the fact that she's ashamed of having married you. . . . She
has thrown herself with passion into being 'modern.' That sums up the
greatest number of things that you and your family are not."[14]

This quest for independence, for asserting herself outside the conventional role of wife, even with so brilliant a position in society, for vindi-
cating past errors through "humanitarian" activities is not only suggestive of Cristina Belgiojoso, it is resonantly echoed in James's nonfiction
portrait that grew out of Story's diary. When James says of his fictional
heroine: "The Princess was an embodied passion. . . . her behavior,
after all, was more addressed to relieving herself than to relieving others
. . . and now that she had tasted of the satisfaction [of helping others
with her money] she regarded her other years, with their idleness and
waste, their merely personal motives, as a long stupid sleep of the conscience. To do something for others was not only so much more human—
it was so much more amusing!" One recalls Cristina's explanation to
Story that her "passion" for tending the sick was a sure way of doing good.
Though speaking of social and political agitators in the novel, James
seems to be referring to artists as well, particularly his and Story's kind of
artist who found their esthetic (read *ideological*) identity outside their
native society. Perhaps what first attracted James to Cristina is that her
personality holds many of the artist's deepest tensions: her compulsion
to work for an ideal, divorced from life in her private existence, restless,
uprooted, in need of an audience to reflect her creation, fragmented in her
struggle to be and to do. James might well have been the artist to paint
her definitive portrait had he known her better. Certainly his miniature
in *William Wetmore Story* is an admirable likeness:

> We feel it a pity . . . that we have so scant a title to recruit for our
> faded company one of the figures intrinsically the most interesting
> and most marked we are likely to meet. It would unquestionably have
> taken . . . but a slightly less limited acquaintance with the Prin-
> cess Belgiojoso to have made me not hesitate to seek for our pages
> the benefit of her remarkable presence. Her striking, strange name
> . . . was in the air, when we were young, very much as that of
> Garibaldi was to be a little later, and with the note of the *grande
> dame* added for mystification, to that of the belligerent. The history of
> this extraordinary woman has lately been written . . . by an Italian
> investigator [Barbiera, cited in a footnote], whose portrait of his
> heroine . . leaves us in depths of doubt . . . as to the relation, in
> her character, of the element of sincerity and the element we have
> learned . . . to call by the useful name of *cabotinage*. A Lombard
> of old race, a Trivulzio and essentially a great lady, an ardent worker
> for the liberation of her country, was she not . . . at once a sincere, a

passionate crusader and a "bounder," as we elegantly say, of the real bounding temperament? Nothing is more curious, as we read her story, than the apparent mixture in her of the love of the thing in itself and the love of all the attitudes and aspects, the eccentricities and superfluities of the thing; a mixture which . . . may represent little more than the fact that she was romantic, so to speak, in spite of herself, that the romantic appearance at least, in a life of eminent exile, of conspiracy, of all sorts of adventurous fellowship, was forced upon her by the general connection. The incoherent facts of her origin and person, moreover, greatly added to it; the strange, pale, penetrating beauty, without bloom, health, substance, that was yet the mask of an astounding masculine energy; the "social position" so oddly allied with her perpetual immersion in printer's ink, with the perpetual founding, conducting, supporting, replenishing, from her own inspiration, of French and Italian propagandist newspapers. Not the least interest she would probably present to a near view would be by freshly reminding us that the great political or social agitator is most often a bird of curious plumage, *all* of whose feathers, even the queerest, play their part in his flight. We must take him, in either sex, as the wild wood produces him; he is not to be plucked as for preparation for the table.[15]

ON APRIL 30 the French attacked with six thousand of the ten thousand troops that had landed at Civitavecchia, apparently convinced that the Italians would not fight. To Oudinot's surprise, they did, led by a Lieutenant-colonel Garibaldi, until then still a very marginal figure, who suddenly revealed himself to be "a devil, a panther."[16] While awaiting reinforcements from France, Oudinot discovered himself with unwelcome allies: the Spanish had landed at Gaeta and were moving north; the Austrians were heading south toward Ancona. Two French armies were preparing to attack. The Republic, actually consisting of no more than Rome, was about to be crushed in a four-pronged offensive. The French plenipotentiary, Ferdinand de Lesseps, remembered as the originator of the Suez Canal, proposed that Rome be peaceably occupied and its citizens assured the rights of political determination. Mazzini accepted. Oudinot, however, rescinded this agreement on the authority of his government, placing Lesseps in a very embarrassing position, and informed Mazzini that the city would be occupied on the fourth of June. Garibaldi, as military commander-in-chief, undertook to defend Rome not only against superior forces, but against cannonades that rained over the city for twenty-six days. By June 30 there were three choices open to the provisional government: mass suicide, capitulation, evacuation of the army. Garibaldi chose the last, informing his assembled troops: "I am leaving Rome. Whoever wishes to continue the war against the foreigners, come with me. I offer no pay, no billet, no provisions: I offer hunger, thirst, forced marches, battle and death."[17] Four thousand followed him on his crusade to Venice.

With Mazzini's resignation, the fall of Rome, and the dead and dying who passed through her care went all of Cristina's hopes and efforts of the previous eighteen years. From the "felonous Bonaparte," as she now called him, to her friends "de la raison glacée," France had betrayed her. Italy, poor blundering massacred Italy, had also betrayed her through the divisiveness of its factions and the ineptitude of its leaders—Gioberti's gullible idealism, Mazzini's inefficacy, Charles-Albert's disastrous vacillations. Instead of deciding for or against his generals' battle plans, which might have turned the tide in August 1848, Charles-Albert pointed to the Virgin on his desk and told one of his generals: "You see, the one who wins battles is she."[18] Clearly, heaven was not on his side. Cristina had foreseen the futility of the carnage around her long before the end in a letter to Vieusseux: "The triumvirs are committing many and various stupidities. The people remain silent because a movement against the triumvirate would be construed as opposition to the Republic. It is nonetheless certain that they have cooled and do not work actively to support these men with whom they are displeased. Instead of intervening, the Romans will, I fear, remain immobile, not out of indifference, as some are saying, but out of a lack of trust in those who lead them."

Thierry, without news from her since April, understood only too well her silence. On July 13 he wrote to a friend: "She has stopped writing to her friends who, like Mignet and myself, did not sympathize with the party she espoused out of despair. I learned that after the capitulation of Rome she was still there. No one knows if she will return to Paris soon. I desire it and at the same time fear it because of the mutual thorns of political conversation; and what other can there be now?" On July 31 Cristina received an unsigned note of warning: "Flee as fast as you can, a file concerning you is on the cardinal's table, and in his hand is written in the margin: *irreligious sentiments.*" A few weeks earlier, a priest had been stabbed by an angry Roman crowd shouting *Traditore!* when the French occupied the city. Brought to her hospital at the point of death, he was nursed back to health by Cristina. In his gratitude, all he asked was an occasion to prove the sincerity of his devotion to her. She knew at once that the note was from him; he had been placed in Cardinal Antonelli's service after his release from the hospital.

A few days before, she had obtained a British passport, so that when the note arrived, she left her house on foot, hailed a cab some distance away, and went directly to Civitavecchia, where she was able to board the *Mentor,* bound for Malta and points east.* As she later wrote Mme Jaubert, "You are right, I must change the course of my ideas and momentarily break with politics. . . . To wallow in regrets is something abhorrent to my nature. If I must renounce the realization of my hopes for Italy, I want to embrace a way of life that offers me new sources of interest; the new existence must kill the memory of the old, or at least what is too painful in that memory." Everything was too painful to remember: the devotion, the tireless sacrifices of the Roman people, the friends who had died in her arms. And yet, all she had left were those memories. "Are you not astonished, très chère, to see me looking back into the past. . . . I who, before, totally immersed in the present or the future, never made my memory do any retrospective exercises. This transformation is a blessing of nature. The present is cruel, the future very grim. I no longer sleep."

It was not insomnia that plagued her, but a long procession of gentle phantoms who smiled at her, recalling the care she had given them; "but an oblivion of the present that conjures up a past like that, does it deserve the name of sleep?" No stretch of the imagination, she tells Mme Jaubert, could capture the painful reality of her life under the bombardment, which was not an ordinary spectacle of death. Those young men who sacrificed their lives for the love of freedom were all heroes. How, she asks, could she have yielded to sleep, exhausted as she was, when she knew she would not find in the morning those who had wished her a restful night the evening before. "Did I know how many hands had pressed mine for the last time?" To their heroism was added the incredible devotion of Roman women. Recruited hastily, Cristina relates, they were not selected with peacetime care: "I soon discovered that I had unsuspectingly formed a harem. And so, I sent away the young and pretty aides, enrolling from then on only the toothless and deformed. But to what end? These old ones had daughters, and if they did not, they borrowed them. . . . After sifting through my personnel, I began to play the role of stern dueña, armed . . . with a rod to put a rapid end to conversations that could become too intimate." And yet these women of the people, blissfully unaware of any conventional morality, were capable of the most total self-abnegation.

> I saw the most depraved, the most corrupted, remain at the bedside of
> a dying patient without leaving him to eat or sleep for three or four
> days and nights running. I saw them accomplish the most arduous and

---

* Marie and Mrs. Parker left with her, and since her passport included two servants, she took two other refugees under its umbrella: a count, who passed as her footman, and an artillery officer as her valet.

disgusting tasks, saw them bent for hours over gangrenous wounds that exuded a fetid stench; saw them endure the gross caprices of miserable men exasperated by their suffering, without showing disgust or impatience. I saw them remain unmoved and immobile while bullets, shells, and bombs crisscrossed over their heads and whistled in their ears. In almost all the women I placed in the hospitals I saw this same contrast operate between the past and the present. . . . When pity enters their hearts, they sweep away or at least silence the vices that until then exercised absolute empire over them. . . . Were this dying man your brother or your son, you could entrust him without fear to the samaritan who cried, for she would care for him as though she were his sister or his mother. Can you understand, chère amie, how my heart bleeds to see prolonged indefinitely this state of degradation among a people capable of heroic virtues and noble faculties? Until when will all education be denied them?

Once again Cristina found herself the target for the slings and arrows of public outrage. When Caroline Jaubert asked her permission to have the letters from Malta and Athens published in Paris, she had no idea what a storm of protest she would raise. When *Souvenirs dans l'exil,* —first published in two successive issues of *Le National*—arrived in Athens, Italian refugees as well as Athenians protested vehemently against what they considered insults to their national pride. The Athenians found that her remarks about the city lacked the gratitude befitting a guest; the Italians resented her depiction of lower-class Roman women and published an open letter to her in *Le Courrier d'Athènes,* which ended with: "To betray in this way truth, Christian charity, patriotic love! No, it is not possible!" To these invectives, Cristina could make no reply. A text can be read any which way, but those letters, written to a friend, not intended for publication, and containing personal impressions and reminiscences, were certainly not meant to insult. However, when Pius IX, on returning to the Vatican, published an encyclical to the bishops of Italy, in which he lamented the unfortunate victims who had been refused Holy Sacrament and were obliged to die in the arms of prostitutes, Cristina felt the need to defend the women who had served under her. Her letter to the Pope, published in the *Giornale di Gorizia,* is a minor masterpiece of irony and aggressive defense.

Holy Father,

I read in a French publication a part of the Encyclical of Your Holiness to the Bishops of Italy. . . . It is not on my behalf that I respond [to the accusations]. Among the women . . . who voluntarily accepted me as their directress, there were many who, less noted than I, are no less honest than I, and have no less right to the respect of the virtuous. I will not maintain that among the multitude of women who, during May and June of 1849, dedicated themselves to the care of the wounded there was not a single one of reprehensible mores: Your Holiness will surely deign to consider that I did not dispose of the Sacerdotal Police to investigate into the secrets of their families, or better still their hearts. It happened, I admit, that I was informed that one or another of the hospital aides was known to have formerly exercised a dishonest profession. Had this warning reached me before these aides were admitted to the hospital, I would doubtless have excluded them, but such was not the case. The women who were denounced to me had for some days been . . . vigilant at the beds of the wounded; they did not withdraw from the most enormous labors, not from the most repulsive sights or functions, or from danger, since the hospitals were the target of French bombs.

No one could reproach these women with a word or an act less than decorous and chaste. Perhaps I might nonetheless have expelled them, did I not adore the precept of that God who, in human guise, did not disdain that a woman of perverse habits anointed his feet and dried them with her long plaits. Remembering this sublime parable . . . I replied: what this woman was before I do not know, but I do know that from the moment she assumed this pious task, she behaved piously, nor did I need to know any more.

The women who were in this manner denounced to me were five, whereas the number of those who frequented the hospitals during the siege were always a few hundred. . . . As to the priests who are supposed to have been expelled, and the Sacraments refused to the dying, I affirm that nothing of the sort occurred. The hospitals were regularly served by priests, and not one of the victims, rightfully lamented by Your Holiness, died without the assistance of a priest or the comfort of the Sacraments. If Your Holiness is unaware of this, Your Delegates are not, for no sooner were the Cardinals reintegrated into the positions conferred by Your Holiness, than the priests who had exercised their holy ministry in the hospitals were incarcerated in the prisons of the Holy Office.

I have respectfully responded to the accusations contained in the Encyclical of Your Holiness because I believed I had contracted the obligation to do so toward the accused who do not wish, are not able, and do not know how to respond.

I take this occasion to lay at the feet of Your Holiness the humble obeisance of my respectful veneration. . . .

Cristina Trivulzio di
Belgiojoso[19]

The Furies had descended on her, beating their black wings on all sides. No longer a voluntary émigrée from Austrian states, as she had been in 1830, she was now a fugitive from certain arrest and probable

trial for treason. Her compatriots viewed her with little more amity. She
had managed to offend them all by telling truths they had no wish to
hear, especially from a woman. She had criticized the provisional government of Lombardy after the *Cinque Giornate* for its inadequate organization and factionalism; she had condemned the inefficiency and ill will of
the medical administrators in Rome, whom she held responsible for lives
that could have been saved. Now that she was on the losing side, her
former friends among the moderates could voice their horror over her
support of Mazzini, although her position had been perfectly logical. On
June 13, 1848, in her newspaper *Il Crociato,* she had said, replying to
Mazzini's encomium in the republican paper *L'Italia del Popolo* of the
tenth, that she and Mazzini had been on opposite sides though fellows-
in-exile. Now they were still on opposite sides: Mazzini's Giovine
d'Italia wanted "L'Italia repubblicana ed Una." Her party wanted a constitutional monarchy as a means of achieving unity. "Time and events
have to judge between us. . . . let us see if one day . . . directed toward the same goal, it will not be possible to follow the same road." She
concluded by saying that if Charles-Albert proved unequal to his task,
"then I would take the last position in your ranks." Charles-Albert's
inadequacy more than justified her "apostasy," nonetheless, Gioberti and
his followers turned against her viciously. Even Mazzini—who had
written on June 10 for all to read: "A woman who for patriotic zeal,
gifts of intelligence, sincerity of her own opinions and tolerance of
others, deserves, even when she disagrees with us, much esteem and
much affection from us"; who further said: "Perhaps the only [news-
paper] that explicitly advocates the idea of unity coupled with the monarchic principle is the *Crociato*",* who in September wrote her: "I have
in you not only a collaborator in the national enterprise, but an honest
and loyal friend"—even Mazzini wrote his mother: "In Rome she was a
torment for me because of her continuous litigations with the surgeons,
doctors, and nurses. As for that feuilleton [*Souvenirs dans l'exil*], she
would deserve at the hands of Roman women the punishment one gives
children; and if one day she returns to Rome, I am not sure that the
trasteverine [women of Trastevere, the most plebeian district of Rome]
won't treat her that way, if they are informed."

There was nothing for Cristina to go back to, not even France. So
long as Louis-Napoleon remained in power, France was more a torment
than a refuge. The farther she could go from Europe, the better. She had
become an outcast, a tragic figure driven from her home and friends for
what at one level was no more than imprudent candor and integrity, but
at another was the sin of hubris. She had, in truth, placed herself above

---

* The other monarchist papers supported federation.

the laws of society by speaking, writing, and acting—however justly—according to absolute tenets of her own making, as though she were beyond the judgment of her peers or inferiors. Pettiness being more common than magnanimity, there were few to defend her.

In November, learning from Mme Jaubert that Cristina was in Athens, Thierry wrote a long and sympathetic letter that bordered on contrition. He explained that because his two letters to Rome had gone unanswered, he thought she had turned away from her friends in Paris, himself among them.

> Mignet also thought so and the error of one augmented that of the other. . . . I sympathized with your suffering as a patriot. So many lost hopes that I shared in order to console myself for the state of my country, so many years of your life devoted to that great cause which now seems lost. . . . I understand your attitude toward France and the French; you are entitled to resentment, and even if I saw in this some offense to my opinions and to myself, I would respect this injustice and not complain.

Cristina's reply confirmed her unabated bitterness toward Mignet and France, but once again assured Thierry of her constant affection.

> You were wrong to believe I could leave your letters unanswered. There are two entities in each of us: the political one and the loving one. The first have been at war for a long time, and for my part, I have been willing for no less time to keep them apart while we lived under the same roof. The second persevere and will continue to do so despite the din of the first. . . . Neither your letters nor Mignet's ever reached me, although Mme Jaubert's did. I did not have the strength to write to those Frenchmen who applauded our murder while blood flowed around me, that blood which you and your friends poured yourselves. This same sentiment, even more deeply felt, prevented me from writing to Mignet, but would not have prevented me from answering either of you. There you have an explanation as categoric as it is sincere. . . . Alas, between France and me there is a sea of blood which I cannot cross without imperious motives. Does it follow that you can only expect me at your deathbed? No dear brother, let me hope better of God's justice. A great crime has been committed in France and its authors are triumphant today. When the wheel has turned (and it turns quickly in our day), I shall come back.

7

The Last Odyssey

T HE WHEEL TURNED, but not as she hoped. When Cristina assured
Thierry of their reunion, she had in mind the end of Louis-
Napoleon's three-year term as president. But she was mistaken. The man
she now rancorously called *"à moitié idiot et à moitié infâme"* (half idiot
and half villain) was not repudiated by his electorate at the end of his
mandate; he became instead their emperor. Cristina's exile thus proved to
be twice as long as she had planned, but it offered her the only effective
balm for her painful memories.

Malta, her first port of call in August 1849, was no Shangri-La.
Filled with refugees like her, it provided no distraction for her mind or
for her eyes. Its drab monotony made her long for Lombardy's lakes and
woods, but there was one marvelous thing there, the sunlight: "I could
become idyllic about it," she wrote to Caroline Jaubert, "I understand all
those lovely ladies who allowed themselves to be caught by Apollo."
What was needed to endure exile was either a place "as similar as possible to the one that you wished not to have left, or . . . [one] whose
originality forces your attention. Similarity mellows regrets, difference
numbs them."[1] Cristina's destination was in fact Constantinople, where
she hoped to lose all track of Europe. But getting there was not as
simple as it had seemed. Cholera had broken out in Malta, making
the refugees unwelcome anywhere they went unless they managed to
arrive before the news reached their destination. There were also rumors
that Turkey would extradite two noted Italians who had sought asylum
there. Athens therefore seemed the safest place until she was sure of her
reception in Constantinople. However, a quarantine in Egina stood between her and the Acropolis, since news of the cholera outbreak had
preceded the *Mentor*'s arrival.

Sequestered in a squalid hut, but in sight of "the most beautiful sea
and sky on earth," she discovered "an infinite charm" in her enforced

solitude, which evoked the memories she communicated to Mme Jaubert. She recalled one day the Camaldulite nuns in Rome, comparing their egotistical resistance to leaving their convent, when it was requisitioned for a hospital during the siege, to the generous altruism of the Roman people. The rich gave money, the poor shared their bread. A man insisted on giving Cristina his shirt, telling her he had no money for bread the next day, but the one shirt on his back was enough for him; the other could serve a wounded soldier. "Do you think I refused it, or gave him money?" she asked Mme Jaubert. "Not at all; but I made the mistake of asking his name. By refusing, with simplicity and dignity, to tell me, he made me feel my error. Yet, while such things were happening outside the walls of Rome, it was said that the Roman people would capitulate because of their terror of the republic and of republicans!"[2]

Finally released from quarantine, she was surprised to discover the reality of Athens: "For me until now, Greece had been no more than two points in the past and nothing in the present. Ancient Greece was the homeland of all cultured people at a time when culture was not in common currency." Modern Greece, the Greece born after Byron's death, sported a royal palace "of Bavarian construction [Otto of Bavaria was the first king of modern Greece] that looked more like a Belgian spinnery." And Athenian women, visible in the streets for only a few hours on Sunday, followed three steps behind their Western-suited husbands, while they wore Eastern costumes. "One might wonder that, given the profound humility required of women in national costume, there are still some who consent to wear it. However, the Greek costume is much appreciated by foreigners and their admiration compensates for the husband's boorishness."[3]

In Athens there were still more refugees, 1,700 of them, many of them dying of hunger. Outraged by Athenian indifference, Cristina wanted to aid them but realized that she could not help settle them in Greece. "Perhaps the Turkish government will be more Christian," she remarked ironically to Mme Jaubert. The furor of those very refugees toward her *Souvenirs dans l'exil* prompted her first and only disagreement with her dearest friend. It was Mme Jaubert who had wanted to have the letters published in *Le National,* not the other way around, as Cristina's detractors believed. "Do you need to ask my authorization to do what you wish with my letters," she replied to Mme Jaubert, "they are yours, and you may dispose of them as you like." First serialized in the daily paper (which is what arrived in Athens), they later appeared in a supplement of thirty-nine pages set in two columns, tabloid format, and running to more than forty thousand words. Faced with the violent reaction of her compatriots to her treatment of Roman women, and of her Greek hosts to her remarks on certain local practices, Cristina published an open letter protesting that her statements had been taken out of context from a private correspondence. She may even have written this in good faith, since she probably did not have copies of the letters. Mme Jaubert, finding herself indirectly accused of having edited the letters to Cristina's disadvantage, was understandably incensed. Happily, the rift was soon healed through Thierry's mediation. There is, in fact, nothing in those letters that Cristina had reason to retract or defend. Had they been written for publication she would doubtless have been more cautious and in some cases less irreverent, which would have been a great pity. But there is no malice in any of them.

When she wrote about the curious institution of allowing prisoners to buy their days at home, or their nights as well at double the price, she was only informing Mme Jaubert of a local custom she had witnessed, not mocking the Greeks. Learning that the country's extreme poverty made it desirable for prisoners to eat at home while paying for that privilege, she noted: "From our prisons, so well locked, what scoundrel emerges an honest man? Here at least, family ties are maintained, and the culprit may better himself."[4] And when she compared the preparation for political careers in England, France, and Italy, it was not to denigrate but to exonerate Italy. "In England, men destined for a career in politics receive in childhood an education oriented to that end, so that even the youngest statesmen have a professional assurance that seems to come from experience. In France, men reach office filled with ignorance. They learn to conduct the business of state . . . at the expense of the country which pays dearly the tuition of their experience. Leaders already toppled are continually brought back in the hope that their past mistakes will not be repeated. Alas, it happens that evil becomes routine and, moreover, the intoxication of power, the arrogance that accompanies it are obstacles impervious to any betterment. In Italy, there is neither schooling nor practical experience. One can therefore not be surprised by the disorder which accompanied our revolutionary movement."[5]

For the rest, the letters abound in delightful anecdotes, descriptions of people and places, a constant interplay of past and present laced with personal perceptions. Commenting on the absence of gaiety in Athens, and facetiously remarking that All Souls' Day seemed to be the gayest of the year, she described the procession to the cemetery, picturesquely placed in the valley between Hymettus and the Acropolis: "Do not think, my dear, that because of the above my philosophy has turned black. It pleases me that people should have no fear, and consequently no horror of death or graves. From such a state of mind it necessarily results that one speaks of those who are absent and does not dismiss them from one's memory. What horrifies me is oblivion. Tell me, I beg you, who speaks of me now and then. Is not oblivion premature death?"[6]

The numberless deaths she had witnessed in Rome, all those young patriots robbed of their chance to grow old, had dulled the pain of Stelzi's premature death and her own fear of aging. To Thierry she wrote that same month, *"I am haunted* [in English and italics in the original] by the memory of the dead. They are not, as for Macbeth, the phantoms of those I killed . . . [but] those I helped to die. *They don't frown* [in English and italics]; they smile sweetly and seem to await me at the terrible passage they have crossed and that I have still to cross."[7] All the upheavals she had suffered had robbed this woman, not yet forty-two and still beautiful, of youth, of vanity and of all fears but one—that of being forgotten. She could endure any hardship, any privation, but to be forgotten by those who had loved her was intolerable; it was her only remaining connection with the life and the living of her past. To Mme Jaubert on the twenty-seventh of that same November, Cristina spoke with the serene resignation of an anchorite:

Yes, chère amie, I have aged. Not yet physically noticeable, but I feel that moral transformation which I long ago guessed to be the cause of all aging. All said and done, this transformation is infinitely sweeter than I imagined. It consists principally in that I live in the past much more than in the future. The contemplation of the future is naturally disquieting and agitating . . . whereas that of the past, when it does not awaken regrets, calms and composes the soul. The images that provoked in me fierce terror and aversion now attract me and seem to be filled with charm. It is that appeal which will continue to grow until it bends me to the ground, bares my head and wrinkles my face. If the feeling that accompanies old age is no more bitter than this, I greet that inevitable hour by saying, welcome! How I dreaded its arrival. How wrong I was to believe that anything in nature could be totally bad!

At the end of the spring of 1850—a strange and timeless year since that nightmarish spring in Rome—Cristina left Athens with Marie and Mrs. Parker for Constantinople. She rented a house along the Bosphorus, a few kilometers outside the city. There were three rooms on each floor, one of which was destined to be the living room, as it can accurately be called. Strewn with divans and rugs, it had none of the accoutrements of European living.

To work, chat, or dream, one snuggles into a corner of a divan with one's legs tucked under. If sleep overcomes you, you stretch out your legs, lean back, close your eyes and you are asleep. Are you hungry? You clap your hands and are brought a platter of sliced roasted meats, garlic, raw onions, soured milk, an infusion of boiled grapes. You place the platter on your knees . . . [and after being brought] an

egg cup of coffee, you smoke through a carafe of water. This simpli-
fication of life delights me. What madness, I told myself, is the life
of Europeans who claim they cannot do without a room for dining,
another for chatting, for sleeping, etc., which require a multitude of
furnishings. Each day I recognize the advantages of living in the
East when one is exiled and has little money.

But the heat was ferocious. She spent her days, "deserving a Legion of
Honor for bravery," on a couch between two windows in search of a
breeze, wearing only a cotton shift under a muslin robe, legs and feet
bare, surrounded with handkerchiefs "to mop the sweat that streams
down my face and shoulders."[8]

The years of action were over. This was truly exile, her first real
exile, far from the heated discussions and bright society of Paris; equally
far from her self-imposed exile in Locate, where she had continued to
work for her ambitious projects of social and political improvements. In
Turkey she found a world remote from the one she had known and
suffered in. All the great ideas of Europe, the refinements that so often
conceal hypocrisy and cynicism, yielded here to the unretouched beauty of
man and nature, to a directness of speech and manner that made Europe
seem artificial:

A few years ago, I might have hesitated to tell you my honest feelings about Easterners. Released from the childish prejudices that are
so often mixed into the education of women, I have acquired the
courage to state my opinions sincerely. Asiatics,* in their manner
toward women, lack what we call deference, delicacy, and reserve;
they are not respectful. . . . But their spontaneous homage seems
more flattering than that of the very refined Lovelaces of Paris and
London. Here they address themselves directly to beauty. Nothing is
less ethereal, true, but nothing is more real.[9]

In October she left for a month's excursion into Asiatic Turkey "to
visit superb countrysides where one finds no trace of human work. I shall
rest at night at the foot of a tree where I staked my tent. By day, I shall
cross hill and vale on an excellent horse." With Marie, Mrs. Parker, and
two Italians (one a carpenter, the other a pharmacist), she set off in
search of paradise. "When one has seen what I have seen, experienced
what I have experienced," she wrote Mme Jaubert just before leaving,
"believe me, chère amie, there is only one thing left to do. It is to lock
oneself in a convent, if one can; if not, to leave the world or society and
go live in forests or deserts, in the heart of nature and far from civilization."[10]

The purpose of her trip was precisely to find such a place, and she

* Asia technically begins east of the Bosphorus.

found it—a property, a *çiftlik** in Turkish, near Safranbolu, a few days' journey north of Ankara, offered to her by an influential Turk in the capital. Originally leased to her for 1,200 francs, she was able to buy it for 5,000, with rights of inheritance, despite an official ruling against foreign ownership. Ciaq-Maq-Oglou, as the property was called, lay in a valley four kilometers long by two wide, framed by wooded hills and crossed by a river. The land was good, watered by numerous streams, and on it stood an abandoned shack, a water mill and a sawmill. When Pastori came in November with bedding, furniture, and money, the shack was transformed into a European house. Only one room had been equipped with windows and doors when Cristina first arrived, but the mild climate had allowed her to camp until her carpenter turned it into a proper dwelling. With a buffalo cow for milk and two pairs for work, four horses, and a dozen workmen, mostly Italian exiles, she undertook to apply in Asia Minor what she had learned in Locate about farming and administration. Her purpose was twofold: she wanted to help as many of her compatriots as she could, and she hoped to provide Marie with some manner of inheritance. Because the child was not yet legitimated, and Cristina's means had been drastically reduced by Austria's imposition of a fine that exceeded her revenues, Maria would remain a nameless pauper if Cristina died.

The experiment started out successfully. Her little community worked with enthusiasm, and the local Turks were eager to help the mistress of Ciaq-Maq-Oglou who had such marvelous powers of healing. Her fame as a doctor had begun to spread. As she informed Thierry, "God comes in aid of men of good will, and here good will is lacking neither in patients nor doctor. I have achieved recoveries that amaze even me." The climate was superb, Marie was deliriously happy as "sovereign of the hen coop," and Cristina's health was better than ever before. All her maladies—the neuralgias, palpitations, suffocations, fevers, syncopes—had magically disappeared once she left the tensions of personal and political life in Europe. Her only serious problem was money. It arrived so sporadically from Pastori that she was often forced to live on the generous credit of her Turkish suppliers. In her memoirs and letters, she left a grateful tribute to Turkish kindness and hospitality, adding that as a woman she felt safer in Turkey than anywhere in Europe. The esteem in which the Turks held her was greatly enhanced by her care of

---

* Since the Arabic alphabet was still in use at the time, Cristina transliterated what she heard: *tchifflik* for *çiftlik* (*çift* means a pair; *çiftlik*, a plot of land that can be plowed by a pair of oxen—thus the word came to mean a farm or property of any size). Ciaq-Maq-Oglou is Cristina's Italo-French spelling of Çakmàk oğlù (*c* before *i* in Italian is pronounced *tch; q* is more common than *k* in French); *çakmàk* is a flint or, today, a lighter, and *oğlù* translates as son.

the local peasantry. They brought their sick and dying to her as though to a clinic. One of her more remarkable cures, related to Thierry, was of a woman "paralyzed for six months on her right side, who can now move her arms and legs thanks to the massages, belladonna, and sal ammoniac I gave her. Now people believe that I can cure anything." Perhaps the greatest benefit Cristina derived from her medical ministrations, apart from the credit extended to her, was her exemption from property taxes, which the local governor refused to levy, in recognition of her care of his people.

Her enthusiastic letters did not satisfy Thierry. He continued his pleas for her return, unable to understand why she persisted in this folly. "Why have you bought a domicile and made investments outside of Italy and France? Why, why?" The same question was echoed by most of her friends. Despairing of moving her, Thierry finally evoked Lamartine, "who, perhaps wiser than you, returned from Asia Minor without building or planting." To this she replied in terms that left no doubt about her own wisdom. Lamartine, she explained, had come to Turkey not as a refugee, but to speculate in real estate. In contrast, she, in the seven months since she settled on her *çiftlik* with less than 10,000 francs, had bought rice fields, four pairs of buffalo, six cows, two mules, five horses, two hundred Angora goats; paid her workers, two of whom she had brought at her expense from Europe; and maintained thirty people on her property, while at the same time "refusing myself and others nothing . . . lending to one, giving to another, in short, living as though I had the means of Monsieur de Rothschild." Anticipating Thierry's argument that she could also live within her means in Paris, surrounded by friends and comforts, instead of exposing herself to untold dangers, she retorted:

> As I lived in Paris during the winter of '48 to '49? Working twelve hours a day, sacrificing my feelings to the caprices of a crude boor like Mʳ Buloz [publisher of *La Revue des Deux Mondes*] or a pommaded one like Mʳ de Mars [his editor] to earn a few hundred francs a month? Going on foot because a cab was too costly, mending my dresses to avoid buying new ones, closing my eyes when I passed a theater so as not to be tempted, even denying myself a bouquet of flowers because it cost something? And the refugees who held out their hands, and whom I had to refuse. . . .[11]

After Austria's recapture of Milan, all Lombards of means who had participated in the rebellion were heavily fined. Even though she was technically entitled to her revenues, the exorbitant fine of 800,000 Austrian lire imposed on her left her in much the same situation as in 1831, when her revenues were under sequester. But the refugees, with far less, who came begging at her door on the rue du Montparnasse, did not understand. In their eyes, so long as Austria had not confiscated her property she was rich. She might even have endured their bitter calumnies and resigned herself to penury again had her political aspirations not been annihilated. As it was, her return to Paris would mean "a life of material and physical privation only to undergo a multitude of . . . tortures." "You who love me," she beseeched Thierry, "congratulate me, congratulate yourself that the wind of adversity brought me to a friendly shore." She promised to return when the men "who now triumph in their perfidy" are no longer in power, and when the peace of her valley has calmed "the violent agitations and made bearable the regrets that will never disappear."

Six months later her bitterness was still running high. Mignet had finally written to her, largely about Thierry's health in the hope perhaps of persuading her to return. But she was still incensed enough in October 1851 to write Thierry: "Let M. Thiers beware and M. Mignet too; they halted the history of the Revolution without mourning their martyred king* or denouncing the assassins. They are men without heart or soul, they are conniving demagogues; no salvation for them or pardon either. Shame on M. Cousin, who dares reproach Louis-Philippe with a few wrongs, among others, that of having fallen from power and having deprived France of his excellent government." It was not that she lamented the deposed king, but that Mignet and Thiers did not. In her view, they had betrayed their own ideals—their king, their revolution of 1830—by not denouncing the revolution of 1848 and Louis-Napoleon. Mignet, had he the courage to emigrate and the flexibility to alter his inveterate bachelor's habits, could have joined her in Turkey, thus protecting his principles and her at the same time. And Thiers, a confirmed Orleanist and Louis-Philippe's last Prime Minister, could have taken a public stance against Louis-Napoleon's candidacy. But few people have the dynamism or volatility of a Cristina Belgiojoso, or the habit of great wealth which, even in distress, allows them to think and act on a grand scale. Mignet was fundamentally a petit bourgeois, despite his lordly carriage and elegant frock coats. As to Thiers, Cristina's warning was prophetic. Two months after her letter, Thiers was arrested for opposing Louis-Napoleon's coup d'état of December 1851† and sent into exile. Bitterly discouraged over the events in France and the backbiting of her compatriots, Cristina informed Mme Jaubert that she was leaving for the Holy Land, "to change the lugubrious course of [her] thoughts."

* Louis-Philippe had died in exile the year before in England; her terms are metaphorical.

† Although in 1848 Louis-Napoleon had sworn to uphold the constitution, when he seized power in 1851 he dissolved the Assembly, brutally suppressed a popular uprising in Paris, and proclaimed a plebiscite, which ratified his coup d'état largely through the armed persuasion of his army and police.

A long letter, written on December 3, just before her departure, explained to Mme Jaubert why Paris was impossible for her even if she tried to follow Caroline's excellent advice. Her situation was as complicated as it was insoluble. Cristina, whose determination and lucidity were often given short shrift by her biographers, recognized the hard necessity of her continued exile. There was neither irresponsibility nor exoticism in her decision to remain in Turkey. The courage needed to make it and maintain it surpasses the imagination. In 1830, at the age of twenty-two and alone in Paris, she could better afford to have been headstrong. At forty-two and in Turkey, without the Lafayettes and the Mignets of those earlier years, she had the charge of her twelve-year-old child and an English governess. To those who saw her as flighty and reckless, her letter offers an explanation that could not be further removed from the spirit of adventure.

> Let us leave aside the aversion which that man [Louis-Napoleon] and his conduct toward my country inspire in me. By living withdrawn, by not seeing everyone and not saying everything one thinks, one can live in Paris, you tell me, but that means you, you who are surrounded by relatives and friends who share your feelings or respect them too much to offend them, you who are French and owe no thanks to anyone, you have need of such restrictions to endure the life of Paris as it has been fashioned by politics and its passions. How different my situation would be from yours!
>
> In the present state of affairs, it is in no way certain that I can set foot in Paris again. Austria, from which I am no longer a voluntary émigrée but an exile in the full sense of the word, would exercise her diplomacy and would either win her case, in which case I have lost mine, or would lose it, in which case I would become obligated to the French government. Such obligations hardly obligate one, you will say. But the one who does the obliging does not think so and does not fail to make his charity felt. . . .
>
> *By speaking little and not seeing everyone* one can live. . . . As to speaking little, I have never been talkative, and if I ever was, I have learned to hold my tongue in my valley where no one hears me. However, speaking little does not mean saying few words, but only saying the right ones. . . . It is thus prudence in conversation that you advise me. But I who never knew how to use it when Austrian confiscation and imprisonment hung over my head . . . do not know if I would be wiser and cleverer in Paris. It is above all the second part of your sentence that seems to me to hold an impossible goal. *Not to see everyone,* but those whom I would see are precisely the ones I should not see to live peacefully. Could I not see Mignet, or Thierry, or Thiers . . . or Lamartine? I might add that in the case of the first two I would be crushed not to see them, but admit at

the same time that placed between those two gentlemen there could be no peace for me. I know that during the first days following my arrival each of them would avoid irritating subjects; but such subjects are in the air; they preoccupy one's thoughts, especially ours, and we would soon be as uncomfortable about our silence as opposed in our discourse.

Then comes the question of my compatriots, which is no less arduous, no less sad. Since we are on this subject, I cannot hide from you or from myself that I am on their black list. If I belonged to a party, I would soon be back in their graces for the services that I could render, but my compatriots do not ignore the fact that I do not share the wild illusions of some or the grim warnings of others. They know that once action is undertaken they will find in me a zealous helper who will even consent, when necessary, to close my eyes to obstacles . . . but when the crisis is over and it is time to prepare the setting for a new act in the perpetual tragedy, they know they will find in me a straightforward mind and a stalwart heart, which sees their mistakes and is not afraid to inform them out loud.

A friend like me is very inconvenient, and people are delighted to be furnished with an opportunity to flatten him out in the dirt without appearing to have had any part in it. They will even weep over his fall, but will take great care to keep a foot on his chest for fear he might get up. This, then, is my situation. I am on the ground, and the great Italians of the party that has, if not my trust, my sympathy, have their paws on my ribs. If I came back to them they would be at my heels, barking at me and making life difficult.

You say I must be superior to their yapping, that I have the testimony of my conscience, etc. . . . . If *superior* means indifferent, then I am not superior to calumny; I would be attacked in the newspapers; my actions, my words, my relations with this one or that would be under suspicion. And what of it, you ask? Nothing, except that I would suffer terribly. And money, my dear, how would I do without it in Paris, among all those émigrés who think they have a right to live off me? I can tell them I am poor; will they believe me? The sequester is lifted, my lands are mine, is any more needed for the mendicants to see me as a Croesus?"[12]

While work went on at Ciaq-Maq-Oglou under her Alsatian overseer, Cristina set out for Jerusalem with Marie, Mrs. Parker, and a small retinue led by the youngest son of the Turk from whom she had bought her *çiftlik*. In addition to articles, short stories, and a play (all of which appeared in *La Revue des Deux Mondes*), three books resulted from her extraordinary eleven-month journey across Turkey and Syria: *Asie mineure et Syrie; Emina,* a collection of oriental tales beautifully retold with the psychological insights of a novelist; and *Scènes de la vie turque.* Later translated into Italian and English—some of them had been partially serialized in the New York *Tribune*—these works capture the fascination of her discoveries while revealing her keen eye for detail, humor, and the "human interest" universally sought by journalists, among whom Cristina stands as a master. Elegantly written and related with much wit, her observations of Near Eastern life are still delightful to read even though the world is much smaller now and exoticism barely possible. She gratefully discovered that a guest, a *müsafir*, is God-sent, therefore it is a host's sacred duty to receive him well. A host will consequently "tolerate the total consumption of his larder, the destruction of his dishes, and even being sent out into the rain."[13] But the guest on leaving, no longer a *müsafir* once he has crossed the threshold, is expected "to pay twenty times what he received," or be pelted with rocks and stones.

The mufti of Cherkess—a host with no such expectations of remuneration—offered Cristina his winter apartments, preferring for himself the damp floors and frozen fountains of his summer residence to a night in the harem. At ninety, he still visited his harem as he did his stables, to admire his possessions. But he could not bear the dirt and noise of the harem, which Cristina discovered to be a far cry from the fantasies of the Thousand and One Nights. She was the first to offer the West a description of harem life on the basis of personal experience. She not only visited harems, on occasion she slept in them, sharing fleas and smoking chimneys with their inhabitants. The walls were generally cracked and soot-covered, the ceilings festooned with cobwebs, the couches worn and filthy, grease and wax stains on everything. In the absence of mirrors, the women used each other as guides for the application of make-up. But since many were rivals, they often delighted in producing grotesque masks on each other, deliberately misplacing lines and colors. Scarlet on the lips, rouge on cheeks, nose, forehead, and chin, white in between, blue around eyes and nose, and eyebrows drawn from nose to temples or even in a straight line all across—the possibilities for hideous effects were limitless. The deplorable result of such artistry, aided by natural sloth, was the rejection of all cleaning materials. "Each feminine face is a work of highly intricate art that one can hardly begin again each morning. Even hands and feet, striped with orange paint, resist water as harmful to their beauty." Living in semi-dark boredom—only a feeble shaft of light filtered through the chimney—smoking, drinking tea, and beating children became the only pastimes for "those mortal houris of faithful Moslems."

When called upon to perform for their masters, the women presented their only dance—the same for all of the Ottoman Empire, Cristina sadly noted, whether Turks, Arabs, Armenians, or Greeks—the belly

dance. "What is graceful about this dance escapes me, but what is indecent about it strikes the least prudish of spectators." Food, on the other
hand, turned out to be more varied, at least within a single meal if not
from meal to meal. Some fifteen or twenty hors d'oeuvres—meat balls,
"tiny squashes in clotted sour milk" (yogurt?), honey, fresh, dried, and
candied fruits, oatmeal in milk and honey, "everything that can satisfy
the heartiest of appetites and the least delicate of tastes"—preceded a
whole roasted sheep or goat served with a lemon-flavored soup. Her
greatest hardship was being "condemned to go through the meal without
drinking, since Eastern usage forbids mixing solids and fluids." At the
end of the meal, a large bowl containing *sherbett,* fruit syrup and water,
surrounded by wooden spoons, was passed around. "Each guest takes a
spoon and plunges it in turn into the *sherbett* and into his mouth as often
as he likes." (She does not comment on it, but *sherbett* would seem to be
the origin of the water ices that, in English, still go by the same name,
minus one *t;* the French *sorbet* and Italian *sorbetto* are equally recognizable from the same source.)

Struck by the beauty of the animals she saw—the cats and goats of
Angora, the horses (her own, a magnificent white Arabian named Kur,
seems almost mythical in her tales of his intelligence), the Turkoman
sheep with tails so heavy they are attached to a kind of wheeled scaffold-
ing to support the cumbersome appendage—she was even more
astounded by the attitudes of their masters. No Turk or Arab would
mistreat an animal. The flock led the shepherd, buffalo and oxen worked
how and when they liked, a different language was spoken to each animal, private murmurings that changed sound and tone according to the
animal. Dervishes, those ambulant healers who designate themselves as
such merely by stringing up some relic—a stone from Mecca is sufficient
—were perhaps more important as veterinarians than as doctors, since
they cured the evil spirits that haunt herds and the barrenness of cows
and mares. (The identical therapy was used for women.)

On April 10, after three months of travel across uncharted or ill-
charted lands, Cristina reached Judea. Except for a few intrepid English
missionaries and Lady Stanhope, Europeans rarely ventured into these
lands. Bandits roamed freely, there were constant uprisings against the
Turks or between rival tribes, and maps were more often than not inadequate. As she told Thierry, "all the way to the outskirts of Caesarea,
where the anti-Taurus begins, the map is colored to suggest that the land
is entirely desert. I have just crossed this territory and am writing to you
today from a town with a population of nearly forty thousand souls,
situated in the heart of this supposed desert. I can also assure you that
there is no country less flat than Cappadocia. We traveled for seven days

across mountain after mountain covered with snow, and not one is shown
on any map." At ten in the morning of April 10, her diary reveals, the
little party stopped under olive trees to rest from the heat.

> At eleven we remounted. Water is rare. However, after four hours
> of travel we found a cistern every hour. The sun is almost at the
> zenith. We hasten our laboring horses. One more climb and we can
> see Jerusalem. I remembered the emotions of those poet-travelers
> who, on seeing the Holy City, shed tears and I asked myself where
> they found those effusions of piety. Involuntarily, I urged my horse
> into a gallop and reached the final summit that still separated us from
> Jerusalem. "There it is!" cried the guide. There it was indeed! My
> eyes filled with tears, my heart swelled in my chest.

Here is a fine example of Cristina's chiseled style, even in her personal
diary. From irony over the lack of water for tears, implying affectation in
the "poet-travelers," to her own emotional response is a span of a few
brief sentences, all so understated that the climax is truly a surprise.

During her month's stay, successfully timed to coincide with Holy
Week, Marie was prepared for her First Communion. Cristina's reputation had evidently preceded her, for when she and Marie went to confession, the priest treated her to a political homily. "I asked him to limit his
reproaches to the sins I had confessed. He apologized." Much as she tried
to escape politics, her antennae, as it were, were so keen after years of
practice that on receiving a letter from Thierry, remote as she was from
the climate of Paris, she was able to evaluate his news perceptively.
Thierry told her that as an Italian she could safely return to France: "The
persecuted of the day are the Orleanists and the red republicans. Orleanist you can hardly be called, if I am not mistaken; republican you were
for three months and it was not for France." She did not share Thierry's
optimism about her return or his acceptance of Louis-Napoleon as emperor. Augustin-Thierry's appraisal of her judgment—"If Mme de Belgiojoso did not lack literary judgment, she was and always remained totally
bereft of political clairvoyance"—is belied by her Cassandra-like reply to
that letter, written on her return to Turkey. Receiving only sparse news
during her double trek across the mountains of Anatolia and the deserts
of Syria, she nonetheless evaluated the situation in France with uncanny
foresight; the new and more violent upheaval she predicted did indeed
take place, and still within her lifetime. (In 1871, a few months before
her death, the Paris Commune rose up against the provisional government led by Thiers, which had been formed after the French defeat in
the Franco-Prussian War. Unwilling to lay down arms or accept the
humiliating treaty that Thiers had signed with Bismarck, the Commune
of Paris began a fierce insurrection that was finally suppressed by troops

loyal to Thiers. In August 1871, a month after Cristina's death, Thiers became president of the Third Republic, which marked the end of Napoleon III and monarchy in France.) Cristina's letter, only partially quoted here, reveals how modern, how realistic, and how clairvoyant her thinking was.

I do not share your view of the position that would await me in Paris. . . . Your reasoning, your memories tell you that you should regret the parliamentary regime to whose support you gave your finest years; but your heart saw it disappear without pain. The parliamentary regime bore fruits that frightened you and made you lose taste for the tree. The tree was uprooted and you like to think that the seed of those blood-colored fruits disappeared with it forever. You see tranquillity and congratulate yourself that you need no longer tremble for society. Your resignation is more facile than commendable. I see things differently: I am not afraid for society, which is as old as the world and will last as long. I believe that certain kinds of progress have to be accomplished and I cannot hope they will be achieved without turmoil. But the turmoil will be in direct proportion to the resistance. The reactionary regime that triumphs today cannot last any longer than the ancien régime, the Empire, the Restoration, or the House of Orléans. A new upheaval will take place, have no doubt, and will be all the more violent for its delayed arrival. The form of government established in France today is repugnant to all my feelings, all my opinions; no prestige surrounds it, and the means employed for its triumph are reprehensible to me in every way. . . . You are not French, you tell me, and what happens in France does not concern you. You are mistaken, my friend. Surely, had it been that my country was free while yours was not, I would go and live in Italy and close my eyes to what happens in France. But the enslavement of one necessarily involves the servitude of the other, and this thought would be enough to foster in me the deepest resentment against that middling faithless man who plotted the first and caused the second. This letter will probably be read by the police, but since it is an argument against you, I cannot compromise you; as for myself, I am not prepared to give myself up to the clemency of your chief of state.[14]

Pastori, even more eager than Thierry to see Cristina back in Europe, given his difficult task of managing her affairs from Milan, told her that Paris was not for her at that time. And Mme Jaubert, as lucid as she was sentimental, advised her: "If you are still the same, you cannot live in Paris; and would I wish you changed?" The Second Empire is usually associated with Napoleon III's waxed mustachios, heavy-legged furniture, and academic art. But far more important, it was a period of reactionary repression. For twenty years all of France's ideals since 1789 were trampled by the retrograde ambitions of Napoleon III, a course of events foreseen in Cristina's wrathful jeremiads of 1851–52.

PERSONAL MISFORTUNES were to change her thinking about returning. In March 1853, after the attempted coup engineered by Mazzini from England, Austria once again sequestered her estate, this time leaving her virtually penniless. She had known nothing about the plot, but all Italians living abroad were indiscriminately punished to prevent émigrés from subsidizing future insurrections. Four months later, one of her own employees almost killed her. Her voluminous letter to Mme Jaubert, written five days after the assault, relates an incredible tale of horror and melodrama.[15]

Her storeroom manager, an irascible Italian from Bergamo, had apparently seduced Mrs. Parker. One day, after he had broken her nose and blackened her eye, the poor lady came to Cristina for protection, confessing her desire to break off relations with him. When Cristina confronted him, he promised never to go near Mrs. Parker again. Cristina would have liked to fire him at once, but unable to pay his back wages, she felt it unfair to dismiss him. Although he became increasingly agitated, threatening to leave victims behind him, no one took him seriously enough to warn Cristina.

After dinner one evening, he brazenly followed her to her room. Convinced that he was a coward who would do her no harm, she continued calmly up the stairs while he muttered behind her that she had insulted him. Suddenly, he raised his arm shouting "Die, perfidious one!" and stabbed her. She was too startled even to feel the two thrusts to her lower abdomen. A third, to her left breast, revealed the dagger she had not seen earlier. Stepping back to ward off another blow, she broke the window behind her. Her left hand, protecting her chest, received a fourth wound. The staircase rapidly filled with servants alerted by the shattering glass. The assailant, behind her as she fled, managed a fifth stab to her back before the servants surrounded him. He managed to struggle free and escaped from a balcony.

Cristina's voice, until then frozen in her throat, suddenly shrieked, "He has killed me!" Marie sobbed, "No, Mama, you won't die. Don't die, Mama. What should we do? Think! Talk!" "I still felt no weakness," she wrote Mme Jaubert, "but my blood was flowing in torrents. I calmly returned to my room and put myself to bed. From there I could hear sobs echoing throughout the house. . . . What I felt just then cannot be described. It seemed that I was coming out of a nightmare, that my strength and intelligence had tripled, and that nothing was impossible for me at that moment."

Checking her wounds to make sure no arteries were severed, she found a huge gash in the thigh and a smaller one in the groin. The bleeding was soon stopped with cold water and the wounds bandaged. The breast wound was the most frightening, until she probed it and found it had not reached the chest cavity. She applied leeches to the region of the heart and left lung, had herself bled, and asked her pharmacist to make pills of aconite, a cardiac and respiratory sedative. Within twenty-four hours she was without fever or severe pain.

The next day, the assailant was apprehended at the market. The governor tried to convince her that he had been hired by Austria, but she rejected the idea, convinced he was merely a "ferocious beast." To her own surprise, she felt no loathing for him, "but," she added, "I will not make the mistake of interceding for a man who could make new victims." Her highly detailed account to Mme Jaubert had been written with a precise purpose: to ask a surgeon in Paris for a prognosis of possible complications. Her long practice of consulting Dr. Maspero by mail had taught her what information to supply.

CRISTINA SURVIVED, as she had survived so many lesser calamities, but this time she was physically and morally broken. Her friends in Paris militated to have the sequester lifted; Heine—whose widely read political satires made him a formidable opponent—appealed directly to Metternich. She was finally advised to make a formal request for repatriation —an act she would earlier have considered beneath her dignity. Now she was not unwilling, but was hesitant about any direct negotiation with Austria in view of a required oath of fidelity to the empire. "It is not that I would bring into my country the project of conspiring against whatever government is imposed on it, but oaths are repulsive to my nature," she explained to Thierry. "I have taken only one in my life and cannot say I kept it, whereas I have never broken my simple word, and if I had had the honor to be born a man, I would never have accepted any engagement that was contingent on an oath." After so many years, the bitter memory of her wedding vows was still not forgotten! It not only made her uneasy about oaths, it made her extremely sensitive to the condition of women and to society's expectation that they uphold vows men could break with impunity.

Her determination not to return to France under Napoleon III was of no avail. She recognized the physical and material need to leave her *çiftlik* and end her exile. For Marie's sake as well they had to go back

to Europe. She was then fifteen; it would soon be time to think of marriage, her civil status was yet to be settled. The stabbing had shown
Cristina how defenseless Marie would be without her, far from friends
or family. It nonetheless took two more years before her affairs in Turkey
were settled and she obtained the money needed to set sail for Marseille.
She finally arrived in Paris in November 1855, and at the beginning of
February returned to Italy, having been granted repatriation and repos-
session of her property. Italy was not yet independent and united; she
would see that dream realized in another five years. But Lombardy under
a new viceroy was enjoying relative freedom, and Cristina was given a
compassionate welcome by Milanese society. The odyssey had ended at
last. As she reminded Thierry, "Ulysses took longer to return from Troy
to Ithaca yet the distance was shorter and the countries more peaceful."
Thierry was not to benefit long from their reunion. In early May 1856
she returned to Paris to spend the summer with him in Port-Marly as in
the past. Ten days later, she was awakened during the night and was at
his side when he died of a cerebral hemorrhage.

Over the next three years she continued to spend half her time in
Paris as she had in Thierry's lifetime. (Previous biographers reported
that she had sold the house in Paris in order to raise capital after the
sequester of 1853, but her unpublished letters to Mignet and Victor
Cousin, written after her return, bear the address 28 rue du Montparnasse, in her hand. It was not until 1860, as stated in a letter to Mignet in
November of that year, that she decided to sell the house. What she may
have done in 1853 was to mortgage the house and rent it.) Settling back
into her old routine, she worked industriously at her writing, now unin-
terrupted by political activities. Between 1856 and 1858 she published
half a dozen stories and her three books on Turkey, and began work on a
history of the House of Savoy, which appeared in 1860, a hefty tome of
over five hundred pages. Her chief concern at that time—one wonders
where she found the time and energy for anything but her writing—was
her daughter, and Mignet's importance in this concern was to grow over
the next years as Marie's future became more of a preoccupation. Cristina's unpublished correspondence with him provides a unique view of
her as a mother, and of this troubled period in her life.

In August 1856 she wrote to Mignet, then in Aix with his ailing
mother: "The waters [of Vichy] did Marie's health much good, for
though apparently prospering, it worried me at times, above all just
before our departure for Vichy. She is well now and the amusements she
enjoyed at the spa did not spoil her cure. I suppose I shall have to return
next year and shall feel recompensed if the results are the same." After a
long digression on his mother's health, inspired by "the sentiment that is
always so strong when it comes to you or to what touches you," she gives

Cristina, pastel by Vincent Vidal, c. 1836

Watercolor by Ernesta Bisi, 1824　　　　　*Medallion, 1835*

Oil by Francesco Hayez, c. 1840

Oil, attributed to Hayez, painted c. 1856, after Cristina's return from Turkey

Alfred de Musset's caricature: "She is pale and, although pale, is beautiful."

Photograph of Cristina, 1868

The salon at Blevio. Cristina is in the foreground, her daughter and son-in-law beside

her; the 1840 Hayez hangs on the left wall. Watercolor by Ernesta Bisi, c. 1861

General Lafayette, engraving after
a painting by Ary Scheffer, 1831

François Mignet, lithograph
after a photograph, c. 1860

Augustin Thierry,
pastel by Cristina

Heinrich Heine, oil by
Moritz Oppenheim, 1831

Franz Liszt, oil by
Henri Lehmann, 1840

Honoré de Balzac,
pastel by Cristina

*Napoleon III, from an oil
by Hippolyte Flandrin*

*Emilio Belgiojoso, oil by
François Bouchot, c. 1840*

*Alfred de Musset,
pastel by Cristina*

him some startling news: "I have heard from Milan that the P[rince] has fallen into complete idiocy. His youngest brother does not leave his side for fear that he will kill himself by accident or design." This letter holds the first indication in her correspondence that Emilio's luck had finally run its course. The disease that had spared him during the many decades Cristina suffered now destroyed his brain as he fell victim to paretic neurosyphilis. Another letter written after her return to Locate in December, carries still more details about Emilio's dreadful condition and raises the question of Marie's legitimation. In February she reported to Mignet, who had earlier warned her against trusting the prince's good intentions, that *"le pauvre P^{ce}"* often spoke of her and of a house he wanted to build for them to live in together. "The thought that in his present state he is uncomfortable under his brother's protection and turns to me for help moved me. I asked the priest who ministers to him (alas, completely useless now) to explain, in case a ray of intelligence should reappear in those heavy shadows, that my absence during his illness is not the effect of indifference or rancor on my part."

Marie now appears in one letter after another, presented with maternal pride or anxiety. "I am very pleased with my daughter this year. You know how she loves entertainment; the poor child has none here. Neither theater, nor balls, nor society; nothing but Locate and her lessons. I must say she endures her seclusion with a courage and good humor I would not have believed her capable of. I bought her a Turkish horse that delights her; she rides every day whatever the weather . . . and has regained the gaiety and healthiness she had in Turkey." Sick herself, frightened by what seemed to be cardiac symptoms, she was suddenly cured of her discomforts by cod liver oil. "I am tempted to believe that this is the famous elixir vitae so long and so uselessly sought over the centuries. But nothing in this world is perfect, not even cod liver oil. My stomach has declared itself in permanent hostility with that good oil . . . and so here I am, enchanted to breathe freely and no longer feel my heart, but forced to buy that pleasure with an almost constant state of seasickness."

To entertain the poor girl who at nineteen still led the life of a child, Cristina had a little theater built for her in Locate ("there is place in the house for ten such theaters"), and organized a troupe among her personnel: Marie's teachers (she studied music, drawing, languages, and literature), the doctor, and anyone else available.

My daughter, still kind enough not to enjoy completely entertainments in which I do not participate, and I, not entirely at ease about leaving her backstage without me, even in Locate, have joined the company, myself in the role of *noble mother*. I wish you had

seen my sweet child. With what grace and simplicity, what natural-
ness and reserve she played her parts! Except for Molière's *Tartuffe,*
she has only seen tragedies, I think, but to hear her and see her play
Goldoni, one would say she had studied very long and finally achieved
a perfect blend of gaiety, innocence and reticence. All that comes
naturally to her because hers is an unusually straightforward and
sensitive nature.

The plethora of intimate details concerning Marie and herself leaves
little doubt about Mignet's unique importance. Victor Cousin, who might
seem to have been just as close a friend, never received such news, nor did
he receive greetings from Marie, as did Mignet. Even her queries about
Mignet's health are in terms she used with no one else, just as no other
man was addressed as "Cher ami," "Mon bien cher ami." Having heard
from an unreliable source that he was ill, she writes: "It seems to me if
you were sick I would have known it from Mme Jaubert or Mme Mohl,
who wrote me a few days ago. In short, I am unwilling to believe a report
that would plunge me into atrocious anxieties, and it seems to me that I
have recently had enough sorrow without adding to it your illness. A
letter from you would do me much good. God grant that I receive it
soon. *Mille et mille tendres amitiés,* Christine."

Mignet was once again the go-between with her Parisian publishers,
receiving and transmitting her manuscripts, hearing her complaints, submitting her arguments. The most prominent figure in her literary life was
François Buloz—founder and publisher of *La Revue des Deux Mondes,*
for which the entire Romantic generation wrote—who was often seen
"sleeping at the opera as though in his bed; people step on his tailcoat,
on his hat, on his feet. He wakes up long enough to mutter 'Sacré nom de
Dieu!' and goes back to sleep."[16] Buloz had a near monopoly on his
writers' production and often total control of their purses. Angel of
mercy or demon of avarice according to the promptness and generosity of
his advances to them, he was on Cristina's black list in 1857. "Buloz
wants to count me among his properties and dispose of me as he likes.
He would not leave me alone until I gave him the manuscript of two
Turkish stories before I left [Paris]. It was useless my telling him that
they did not suit the *Revue,* that they were too long, that I would not
consent to their being cut, etc. He wanted to see them, and to my great
surprise accepted them at once, promising to publish them intact. Now he
has them; he is certain they will not appear elsewhere and that is all he
wanted." It was also Buloz who urged her to let Lévy (the major book
publisher of the day) publish her *Asie mineure et Syrie.* Although Lévy
paid her in advance and received from Mignet's hands the corrected
proofs sent from Locate early in January, the book was nowhere near

ready by the end of the winter and Cristina was furious. Had she given it to another publisher who wanted it, she complained to Mignet, it would have appeared long before. "If you find the occasion to tell these gentlemen what I think of them, I authorize you to make no mystery about it."

Victor Cousin, one of Mignet's oldest friends and very close to Cristina, was another important correspondent during the period between her return to Europe and his death in 1867. Eclectic philosopher, author of *Du vrai, du beau et du bien,* target of Heine's endless jibes for his borrowings from German philosophers, he was one of that very small circle, comprising Mignet and their lawyer-friend Charles Giraud, who gave advice and was kept informed of the proceedings for Marie's legitimation. Of twenty-two unpublished letters from Cristina, covering her thirty-six-year friendship with Cousin, the longest and most interesting date from the late 1850's. In two of them she speaks almost exclusively of Alessandro Manzoni, then over seventy, whom she had not seen since 1841, when he refused to let her see his dying mother. Cristina had not forgiven the dean of Italian letters his uncharitable attitude toward her, which dated, in fact, from the time of her separation from Emilio. Manzoni's miserable old age seemed to Cristina a mark of divine punishment, yet she was compassionate enough to ask Cousin, a friend of his brighter days, to write to him. Disgraced by his sons, harassed by his wife, he had become an object of pity.

> Philippe* is the worst of the three scamps who carry his name. Pierre is no more than the husband of a dancer and a bad son. Henri is a forger and a thief; but Philippe outdoes them by far. His wife's lover, who pays the couple's bills, had the stupid audacity of going to ask Manzoni to be reconciled with Philippe. Manzoni told him to get out or he would leave the house himself, and once the scene was over, he fell on the ground in dreadful convulsions. However slow and often mysterious is God's justice, I have always noticed that it seems never to overlook bad sons and punishes them . . . in their own children.[17]

Awhile later, in response to Cousin's questions about the propriety of suddenly writing to Manzoni after so long an interval, she wrote even more emphatically. Her letter offers a pathetic image of Manzoni's old age, quite different from the common view of this righteous patriarch whose *Promessi sposi* was almost as sacred as the Bible for generations of Italians.

---

* Because she was writing in French, the names were gallicized.

April 14, 1857

Mon cher Cousin,

. . . I think you would do well to write a few words to Manzoni. His mother's last moments are too deeply etched in my memory for me to see him with the feelings of affection and veneration I once had for him. But his situation pains and upsets me, and I wish him all the consideration that it deserves. I know that he has aged and shrunk beyond recognition, that he wanders in deserted places accompanied only by the faithful Rossari, that he is in need or would be without the generosity and goodness of his stepson, Mr Stampa, who has more or less taken over the care of the old couple. This finale is the work of Pierre (the best of his three sons) who had Brusiglio* and the adjoining properties ceded to him with the promise that he would pay his father a pension, and who, since the transfer, has paid him nothing. . . . Pierre is a heartless person and the husband of a dancer, but he has not overstepped the bounds set by law, nor even those of honor as it is understood in a certain society. Prison does not lay claim to him and one can carry his name without shame. This is not so for Henri or Philippe. The first is in hiding for forgery, the second lives off his wife's lovers. . . . The current Mme Manzoni (alias Mme Stampa) spends her time dosing herself with medicines and lecturing her husband who, in her view, totally lacks savoir vivre and good manners. I have seen Manzoni's friends who stay away because they can not bear in silence the stupid nagging of this woman who harasses him. Think what the affectionate greetings of a friend from his better days would do for this unhappy old man. The memories are indeed old, but they would be a ray of light in a dungeon. Tell him vaguely that you have heard about his chagrins (nothing is less secret), and felt the need to tell him that he still has friends who follow him in thought from afar and suffer with him. You know better than I how to turn a phrase. I only wanted to say that you can, without indiscretion, allude to his misfortunes as the cause for this renewal of your correspondence. I am convinced that you would give him a moment of joy and, for my part, would be very pleased to have contributed to it.

One may accuse Cristina of self-righteousness for seeing divine retribution in Emilio's madness and Manzoni's chagrins. However, this is less the view of a religious zealot than that of a true believer who applied to herself the same threat of punishment for her own sins. Whatever else she was, she was sincerely devout, and although forgiveness came hard to her, goodness was something she had in superabundance.

Two years later, writing from Paris on April 28, 1859, she announced

* Manzoni's estate near Milan.

to Cousin the death of Emilio's nephew who was to inherit the title and properties of the prince.

> That death, so premature (he was twenty-one at most), will necessarily delay the progress of my case, but delays hardly surprise me. They would have taken place anyway. The brief for the hearing that will order the rectification of the birth certificate has to be written and presented by all the parties concerned, and before presenting the first petition, all the evidence we intend to use has to be completely approved by these same parties . . . given the obvious bad faith of our natural adversaries. . . . There are endless sentences to modify, words to change, etc. This, according to Pastori's letters, is what is slowing down progress. . . . My duty is to see my daughter settled, but she is not in a hurry and I am no more than she.

Progress was indeed slow, for the previous year she had informed Cousin that the Belgiojosos had "finally yielded to the truth: you have every reason to be pleased, in view of the results that we will achieve from now on. My joy is extreme. I have just spent a half hour pacing back and forth in my room unable to say anything but Thank God! Thank God!, and even now I can hardly hold the pen." Only one brother and his wife had in fact capitulated; it would take two more years before the other brother also recognized Marie and her birth certificate was finally registered in Milan in the name of Contessa Maria Barbiano di Belgiojoso. The great victory was finally won in December 1860, with the help of Mignet, Cousin, and Giraud in Paris, and the faithful Pastori in Milan. Revealed here for the first time through her unpublished letters to Mignet and Cousin is the twenty-two-year battle she waged to gain legal possession of her own child—not for Emilio's title, which Marie could not inherit as a girl, or for his estate, but to call her daughter her own, and assure her a place in society.

Cristina's last letter to Cousin gives us a pitiful reflection of her in the early 1860's:

> Mignet came to tell me that last Wednesday a number of people thought I looked very poorly and were of the opinion that I should give up my Wednesdays. I protested and am writing to you, still protesting, in case you are one of those who advised complete retirement. I protest because it is the only day of the week when I have some pleasure; because I am doing nothing that can harm me, not changing temperature and knowing that if talking tires me I have permission to be silent. My hand on my conscience (my ungloved hand), I do not think I had anything more than a bad cold. But even if I had something worse, to think about it constantly and deprive myself of all distraction, would that be refreshing or salutary? No, no,

do not take away from me my three or four hours a week of contact with the living, which I prefer, and be assured that I will not be the worse for it.

SHE DOUBTLESS HAD MOMENTS of weakness, and her beauty had not been enhanced by her years of suffering and hardship, but her energy, her spirit, and her optimism do not seem to have flagged. Nor for that matter was she as devastated in 1860 as Louise Colet's malicious pen, in *L'Italie et les Italiens,* would have us believe: "The princess in ruins passed before us. Her body, bent under the flaccid folds of her white gown, was horrible to see. The vertebra pushed through the neck. The spine curved prominently under her parchment-like skin. The head was even more ravaged than the body; a toothless mouth, envious and sinister, smiled. The eyes, staring, hollow, and haggard, burned avidly; sparse hair grew patchily on her denuded head on which diamonds gave off their ironic luster." A photograph, taken in 1868, when she was sixty, shows a wizened old woman who is nonetheless recognizable as the one-time beauty in Lehmann's portrait.

When Colet traced her ugly caricature, Cristina had recently resumed her journalistic career. Colet, determined to wrest for herself the laurels of political journalist and Italian specialist (Marie d'Agoult, under the pen name of Daniel Stern, had in fact preceded her), was considerably annoyed to discover that her former rival for Musset's attentions and Parisian celebrity had re-emerged among the living. That was also the year Cristina's *Histoire de la Maison de Savoie* appeared and was well received, even by such former antagonists as Terenzio Mamiani, now Minister of Education under Victor Emmanuel II: "I did not delay a moment to read the book and to rejoice with you and with our country, which claims you and glories in your lofty mind. The House of Savoy has indeed found its historiographer, and through your pages will teach Europe not only to admire it, but to perceive in it . . . the secret instrument of Providence." In a letter written a few months earlier, he tried to make amends for his previous attitude toward her: "I take this occasion to thank you for the kind and affectionate memory you keep of me. I am little enough in this world, but I was nothing and less than nothing. You, however, not heeding external demonstrations, always and invariably wanted to show some esteem for my intellect and my pitiful works. This corresponds perfectly to the nobility of your heart, and I will always be pleased to be in the good graces of the first woman writer in whom our country prides itself."[18]

Cristina's book traces the dynasty with an eye to the fulfillment of its

destiny as the first *Italian* crown of an Italian kingdom. Of major importance are the chapters devoted to the years after 1848. Surprisingly
enough, she attempts to rehabilitate Charles-Albert's reputation by explaining that as king of Piedmont, he did not have the right to sacrifice
his army or the people of Lombardy for what was a strategic impossibility: Milan could not have withstood a major attack from Radetzky's
armies. Had the king won the confidence of the Milanese, he might have
been able to lay before them his position and their risk (a defeat would
have provoked terrible reprisals). But lacking their trust, he did not even
try to speak to them candidly. "His only objective was to calm the Milanese by promising to perish with them. The populace then regretted its
distrust, but while hope was reviving, a closed carriage drawn by six
horses left the palace at a gallop." Before fleeing, the king had signed
the order for capitulation in the hope of saving the city. But not for a
moment, Cristina maintains, did he renounce his dream of delivering
Lombardy and Venetia and of making peace with Austria. In March
1849, at the battle of Novara, he saw his last hopes collapse and tried to
bare himself to a bullet on the battlefield. He was saved in spite of
himself, only to die in his bed later that year.

In the ten years since Victor Emmanuel II had become king of Piedmont he accomplished his father's dream. Lombardy was now part of his
kingdom. But he had not achieved this alone. "It was Providence again
that placed beside this loyal king . . . a minister who cannot be compared to any of those honored by history. . . . He surpasses all of them,
some by the grandeur of his thoughts and views, others by the purity of
his methods, and all or almost all by his selflessness and abnegation."
This hyperbolic praise of the man who had written so offensively about
her two years before was in fact sincere. Never did her admiration for
Cavour diminish, in spite of his public indifference and private carping
before he became her friend. He came once to her salon in Paris in the
1830's and never again. He apparently believed the gossip he had heard,
for in his unflattering letter of 1857 he told his Director of the Interior:
"I am sending you one of her ex-lovers, the Neapolitan Massari, so that
you can inform him what the princess must do to saturate herself as
quickly as possible with her narcotic [tombeky]."

By 1860, world-wise and world-weary, Cristina did not find it in her
to bear grudges against those who had slandered her. She knew perfectly
well that Massari had vilified her in print, that Mamiani had all but
sabotaged the *Gazzetta Italiana* out of hostility to her as its director, that
Mazzini, Gioberti, and others had mocked her or disparaged her efforts
because she had spoken out against their ineptitude or misguided ideas.
As she had told Mme Jaubert, she knew she was "an inconvenient
friend" and knew the price of such integrity. It no longer mattered. She

could as easily forgive them as she could not absolve Emilio or Manzoni. Her pride was expendable, her principles were not. To Massari, with whom she had renewed acquaintance since her return, she wrote in 1859: "Remember me to Cavour who treated me very badly during his last hurried visit to Paris. But he can do with me as he likes and remain certain that I will not get angry with him for it." It was after 1859 that Cavour came to know her in Turin, en famille so to speak, through her sister Giulia, who had married his cousin, Count di Rorà. Until then, he had known her through malicious hearsay rather than firsthand acquaintance; he admired the patriot and was grateful for her support, but the woman was to be avoided. His later letters to her attest to his discovery of a person he respected and with whom he shared a warm friendship until his sudden death in 1861.

Cavour had gained for Victor Emmanuel the trust of most Italians as well as France's alliance. Austria unwittingly fostered the Italian cause by incurring Europe's wrath for her ferocious repression of her own states, her insolence to weak ones, and her cunning toward great ones. The stage was set for a military encounter by early 1859; only the pretext was lacking. France's armies were ready to cross the Alps and land in Genoa; Piedmont's army was on the alert. In April 1859 Austria crossed the Ticino and a series of losing battles brought her to the peace table: Montebello on May 20, Melegnano on June 8, and Solferino on June 24. The treaty of Villafranca—the last time Italy's structure was decided by foreign powers—left Rome, Venetia, and the kingdom of Naples still outside a unified Italy. But Lombardy was no longer Austrian and the ultimate goal seemed within reach. "If the House of Savoy were to die out, it would not be before one of its scions is hailed King of Italy," Cristina prophetically announced near the end of her history of the dynasty. The event occurred less than a year after her book was published.

The treaty, which marked a political and military victory for Napoleon III, had cost French lives. Public opinion in France became deeply hostile to continued support of Italy. Some saw Piedmont as a threat to France's influence in Italy, others still found laughable any attempt to assemble Piedmontese, Romans, Neapolitans, Tuscans, Venetians, and Lombards into a single political framework. There were also those who considered the aegis of Cavour and Garibaldi a shield for republicanism. They did not know that Cavour wanted Garibaldi stopped before he reached Rome, or that Garibaldi called Cavour "Napoleon's lackey." France had very good reasons for an armistice rather than a total victory. The war against Austria, though brief and successful, had not been a ride to hounds. French soldiers lay on the fields of Magenta and Solferino, many of them young officers from the upper classes, and for a cause that was not ostensibly French. Had the war continued, and Austria seen the need to accept Prussia's offer of intervention, France could have run the serious risk of losing it. What interested Napoleon III was not Italy's war of independence but rather the political substitution of French for Austrian influence in the peninsula. Which meant keeping the Pope in power, preventing Garibaldi's followers from turning a war of independence into a revolution, and placing Bonapartes in the vacant duchies of central Italy and perhaps even in Naples. Cavour's master plan for Italy did not include French hegemony, but he needed Napoleon's support as he hoped to profit from Garibaldi's victories. In a letter to Cristina, Cavour succinctly stated his policy: "To take advantage of the revolution to level the terrain; dominate it when it is time to build." Until 1849 Cristina had seen Mazzini as the same means to the same end.

The French public was unaware of the complicated power politics behind Napoleon's support of Italy. All they knew was that a French general had suffered defeat at Castelfidardo and that French youths had died there. When a French publicist decided to launch a French-language newspaper, *L'Italie,* in Milan to counteract French hostility, he turned to Cristina. Thus began her second career in journalism. While addressing a French audience, she was once again pleading for Italian unity. Cavour had been forced to resign over the treaty of Villafranca, which undermined his policies by allowing Austria to retain Venetia, and the duchies of Tuscany and Modena to return to their rulers. For Victor Emmanuel, however, the treaty was a godsend: in one fell swoop he was rid of his overbearing Prime Minister who had been exercising almost dictatorial power for years, even interfering in his private life; Lombardy was now part of his kingdom—undreamed of by any previous king of Piedmont—as was the duchy of Parma; and he had asserted his will over Cavour, although Cavour had had the temerity to say that to sign the treaty would dishonor him forever. No, the king was quite satisfied. The conquest of Italy would have to wait.

In January 1860 Cavour was back in power and Cristina pledged her total support. In August, Garibaldi completed the liberation of Sicily. In September, Cavour sent an expedition to stop him before his republican comrades reached Rome.[*] Cristina, in one of her first articles in *L'Italie,*

---

[*] With Napoleon's secret blessing, Cavour sent 18,000 men under General Cialdini against the papal army led by General Lamoricière, a bitter opponent of Napoleon who had been exiled after the coup d'état of 1851. Cavour's purpose was to have the Piedmontese army invade the papal states surrounding Rome (under the pretext of protecting the Pope from Garibaldi's *Mille,* since it was feared that some of its republican elements might foment a revolution if allowed to continue to Rome) and stop Garibaldi before he reached Naples. On September 18 Lamoricière was defeated at Castelfidardo, in the Marches, and a month later Garibaldi turned his conquests over to Victor Emmanuel, who was crowned king of Italy on January 14, 1861.

testily asked what it took to satisfy the French. They had reproached Cavour for allowing Garibaldi to aid the Sicilian revolt against the Bourbon king; now they reproached him for intervening at Castelfidardo. "There exists in France a category of wise and liberal men who love order with such unbridled passion that anything that disturbs it, however transitory, seems to them . . . a crime and an irreparable disaster. The word *revolution* has so odious a meaning for these sages that they pronounce anathema on anything related to it, and recognize in no case the necessity or legitimacy of any revolutionary act."

So long as any part of the peninsula remained outside the kingdom, it was not yet time for victory balls or factionalism. Those who were more concerned with adding new territories to the states of Piedmont than with adding Piedmont to the unified state of Italy were as nefarious to Italy's future as the republicans they feared. Rome had yet to be conquered. Once again Cristina felt obliged to raise her voice against Italy's internal enemies, no less dangerous than her foreign ones. "We want unity because we know it to be the only means for attaining independence and nationhood, because we are tired of the nauseating seesaw of Germanic domination to be free of French domination, and of French domination to escape the Germanic one. . . . We want unity as one wants life. . . . That unity we have achieved in part, but we have still to surmount the most arduous obstacle and obtain the most vital part of ourselves. We are still without our capital, which the temporal power of the Pope contests."[19]

CRISTINA'S RENEWED INVOLVEMENT in Italian affairs was fortunately timed for her personal needs. Marie's marriage to Marchese Lodovico Trotti was held in Locate on January 24, 1861. She was now in possession of her long-disputed birthright and had an assured future with a man eminently pleasing to Cristina, who was furthermore deeply sensitive to the attachment of mother and daughter. Cristina's hopes for her child were finally fulfilled, but this happiness had now to be paid for with her own loneliness. In the past, her work had helped her through personal crises, Italy's future had served her almost as a religion, and her own deep faith had set goals for her to attain. Now, nothing seemed to hold any meaning. Her life, consistently deprived of personal happiness outside of her child, seemed emptied of any reason to continue. How would she live out the days remaining to her without Marie to fill her heart, to worry about, plan for, laugh with? Everything she had worked for, suffered over, was now accomplished. She could have died a happy woman. The problem was how to live.

Two months before the wedding she all but begged Mignet to come for the event. As so often before, she needed him, needed him in Locate, where the drama of her life was being enacted. She had every reason to be satisfied, she told him. Her future son-in-law was an honest, charming man; he had not even wanted to wait for the court's decision before marrying Marie, whose title and dowry were unimportant to him.

> Marie loves him very much and she would, in truth, be very difficult indeed if it were otherwise, for he has everything one needs to please even the least inflammable person. And yet, mon ami, I confess it to you humbly, I am in despair; which is to say that I cannot imagine how I will endure the separation. I hope God will give me the strength necessary when the time comes, but it is like death. Those two moments, that of dying and that of leaving my daughter have the same effect on me when I consider them at this distance. Oh, how you ought to devote a fortnight to me at that time which will be in two months. You have never given me the tiniest little week [in Italy], and when I limit myself to asking for a fortnight it seems very little for a friend of such long date.

It has generally been assumed that only middle-class women, condemned to the sole occupation of housewife and mother, suffer from this "empty nest" syndrome, so often synchronous with menopause. When their children marry and their fertility ends, their youth, their very life appears to have ended. Cristina, a woman without a husband, who had a cause and a vocation, and whose life had not been geared to the constant care of house and family—there had always been a Mrs. Parker and servants to free her from the tedium of such chores—should therefore have been immune to this affliction. Not so. Rarely, in fact, has a mother's sense of loss and loneliness been more poignantly expressed than by this active, independent woman of rank and wealth. Two weeks after the wedding—an eleven-o'clock ceremony at Locate, attended by both Belgiojoso brothers and fifty guests, despite the hour's drive from Milan on bad roads rutted by winter rains—Cristina wrote again to Mignet.

> The great change has taken place, the crisis experienced; my daughter is married. She left for her honeymoon . . . and should be back in Milan tomorrow. I am leaving Locate tomorrow to meet her. How often during that extraordinary day I remembered my agonies and terrors of the past two or three years. A marriage such as the one she has just made was what she needed to be happy. A large prestigious family that receives her with tenderness and honor, a distinguished, respected husband with a charming face and a singularly gentle character, cold and taciturn with strangers, loving, full of abandon and attentions for her; this is what her heart and her pride needed.

Without all that I endured and risked for the past three years, the twenty-fourth of January would never have gone as it went.

Cristina's reminder of all the legal tangles for Marie's legitimation, the risk of scandal, trial, and perjury to achieve this end, seems to be a tactful justification of having deprived him of his child. Without all that she endured and risked, and that he was morally obligated to assist, Marie could not have made the dignified marriage that established her place in society, and that "her heart and her pride needed"—an allusion to Marie's awareness of her situation? To whom but the man most interested in Marie's welfare would she say this? "Pastori savored his triumph, and I delighted in it for him and for *my daughter as well, who does not know what it cost us.*" Cost *us?* The pronoun must refer to Mignet and herself—the cost of their happiness together to assure Marie's future and her respectability.

Is it possible Marie knew nothing about all this? It is difficult to believe that Cristina never talked about Marie's father during the long years of seclusion in Locate and Turkey. What child would not have asked about its father? It stretches the imagination to think Marie accepted the prince as her father. She was twenty when Emilio died. Not once had she seen him; nor had she received anything from him but his name, and that after years of litigation. On the other hand, Mignet had not only offered gifts and affection, he had remained her mother's dearest friend and a constant figure in her own life until her marriage. Even as a child, Marie cannot have been unaware of the contrast between this kindly man, so devoted to her mother and her, and the prince, who clearly shunned them both. Whatever little she knew, Marie must have known that her name was not Belgiojoso until her twenty-second year. (An unbiased relative maintains that she was called Signorina Trivulzio until her legitimation.) Cristina, however, chose to believe, or wished others to believe, that Marie had been spared all embarrassment. A letter of 1858 to her brother's wife—as close to her as her brother—states this unequivocally: "I have the consolation of receiving all the blows myself, and of having protected my daughter from every distress or agitation. She suspects nothing [*Di nulla sospetta*]."[20]

The great affair of Cristina's life was happily resolved, but she now felt bereft. "I feel very much alone," she complained to Mignet, "and sadness often hovers over me; but I tell myself repeatedly that Marie is precisely where she wanted to be; that she is happy and satisfied from morning to evening and from evening to morning, without my having to wrack my brain to find amusements for her. In your last letter you put your finger on one of the tautest strings of my heart . . . the possibility of avoiding separation and living as one family."

She had examined this possibility in every which way, weighing the obstacles against the benefits, balancing Milanese custom—traditionally opposed to such an arrangement—against sentimental necessity, and finally decided "to make my sacrifice simply and completely rather than share it with others. . . . My son-in-law was very moved when saying goodbye to me [after the wedding]. . . . He assured me that he would never try to take my daughter from me and that his greatest desire was to form a single family. If he wishes it and my daughter does too, it will soon be done. If it is otherwise, should I desire it? She is happy! That is what I desired above all, and now that this desire is fulfilled, it would be ungrateful of me to complain. The fact is, however, that I no longer find any reason to live and am consequently afraid that I am no longer obliged to do so."

Here is the pitiful, perennial lament of the middle-aged woman, conditioned by nature and society to feel that her only true function is maternal. But who would have believed that Cristina, a woman so free in her thinking, so unconventional in her behavior, would also feel that her only raison d'être was her child? Certainly no woman was more sure of her rights or lived more completely according to her own dictates than Cristina. Unlike George Sand, mistakenly considered a "liberated woman" but who in fact entered into one "marriage" after another—successively subjugating her needs, her habits, even her children, to those of her lover, and unconsciously perhaps seeking society's approval for her affairs by making them domestic whenever possible or at least long-lived when not—Cristina rejected any infringement of her privacy or her freedom. Yet she was as bound up in her motherhood as the least cultivated of her compatriots.

This "great crisis" was survived as were all the others, and happily at that. Her life was now divided between her little villa at Blevio, a short ride from La Pliniana on the same shore of Lake Como; the Trotti villa at San Giovanni di Bellagio, farther up the lake; and Milan, where she eventually gave up her small apartment and joined the young couple. During all of 1861 Cristina wrote with her habitual fire against Italy's domestic enemies who were willing to jeopardize total fulfillment of the dream for partial satisfactions or petty ambitions. And near the end of the year, on November 11, Marie presented her with a namesake. Cristina had gone to stay with Marie in Bellagio as the event approached. But the joys of the grandmother were quickly tempered by the anxieties of the mother, for Marie developed puerperal fever two days after a difficult breech delivery. The poor girl had been obsessed with thoughts of death, and precisely because of this very infection, to which her husband's first wife had succumbed, and which remained the constant danger of childbirth decades into the twentieth century. Dr. Maspero was called in at once and as soon as Marie was out of danger, Cristina wrote to Mignet: "Now that I barely begin to breathe again, I feel the need to have you share in my agitations and my happiness. For on my side, material separation has no power; and my friendship for you is as intense as though I saw you every day. Tell me the same, if your truthfulness allows you to." Those days when Marie's life hung by a thread and Cristina could do nothing "but tremble and pray," were recounted to Mignet in every detail, medical and emotional, so that even removed in time and place, he could relive all the drama of the event. One of Cristina's political colleagues wrote her on learning that Marie was better: "I do not know why you, who have a nature so disposed to hope for the best in public affairs, are so susceptible to grim terrors in your domestic affairs." This is an interesting view of her personality, for optimism was indeed one of her outstanding characteristics, sustaining her during the many reversals of her private life as well. Only Marie aroused an uncontrollable fear in her, the fear of losing this one being in her life whom she could love freely.

FIVE YEARS LATER, by then a grandmother for the second time, Cristina was offered an unusual opportunity to reflect on her experience as a woman. Terenzio Mamiani, her one-time adversary, invited her to contribute an article to the first issue of a new review he was directing, *Nuova Antologia.* This may have been the greatest recognition she received in her country, for in this way Mamiani publicly demonstrated his esteem for Italy's "first woman writer," as he had called her in his letter the year before. Many a lady had written poetry and even philosophical essays in the past, but Cristina was Italy's first professional woman writer, first woman historian, first woman publicist. For this first issue, which appeared in January 1866, Cristina wrote about women. In a seventeen-page article entitled "On the Present Condition of Women and Their Future,"[21] she addressed herself to a subject which she said she had always fled, because "a woman treating this question is never held to be impartial and disinterested." Moreover, any amelioration of the situation seemed to her so fraught with difficulties and perils that it was hard to find adequate justification for incurring them. Astutely sidestepping the pitfalls of militant feminism, she dispassionately surveyed the time-honored subjugation of women and the reasons for and against its reform.

From her unique position of social and intellectual prominence, joined to her universal experience as a woman and mother, she could examine the situation with uncommon acuity. She had been beautiful and desired, had left a husband and a lover, had soiled her hands with earth, blood, and money, had lived in princely opulence and mended her clothes, had been heaped with celebrity and derision. How many women had gone through so much in one lifetime? Written more than a hundred years ago her words seem uncannily apt today, even though one of her basic arguments—education for women at all levels—is no longer an issue. But all the other major problems she raises have remained untouched by time, which is why the article (written in Italian) deserves expanded attention here.

Although it is generally admitted, she points out, that a woman is neither morally nor intellectually inferior to a man (except for the effect of physical strength and education), "a woman always was and still remains in a social condition far inferior to that of a man." With all the pretensions of modern society to being different from its primitive past, when man's superiority was determined by his greater physical strength, "the new society is not completely divested of the prejudices of old. One need only observe the habits and customs of existing barbarous cultures to see woman treated like a slave and the appendage of man, without any regard to her needs, desires and rights. As to her duties, they are limited to servile obedience to masculine commands." Her clever use of the word "barbarous" is not to be confused with "aboriginal" or truly "primitive," for even civilized societies are as barbarous in this respect as the ones she ostensibly refers to.

Why then did, or does, woman not protest against this "usurpation of her rights and claim them for herself? Because woman herself accepted the condition imposed on her and reached the point of preferring it to the condition of her lord and master. For centuries deprived of intellectual training, severed from any responsibility in public or domestic affairs, she did not covet an equality that would have imposed serious and tiring duties on her." Is this not still true of women who today are opposed to the Equal Rights Amendment, who are unwilling to assume the obligations that such equality would impose, and thereby condemn themselves to continued subservience? Cristina, speaking of her "today" seems to have prophesied our own when she said: "the few female voices that are raised to ask of men the formal recognition of their equality have an even greater majority of female adversaries than male."

Shocking as it is, Cristina saw the secret reason behind this remarkable absence of self-respect and self-affirmation: it is the "singular artifice" adopted by men, either out of shrewdness or natural instinct. They succeeded in convincing women that absolute difference was the essence of a woman's appeal. "Cowardice is despised because courage is demanded of man, but this virtue is not granted to the woman who seeks a man's admiration. Scholars, scientists, poets, statesmen, enjoy universal respect, while ignorance and frivolity are held in contempt. But of women is asked the most perfect ignorance; and who is unaware of the ridiculous nicknames for cultivated women, the deplorable effect of a beautiful finger smudged with ink, etc."

How familiar Cristina was with just such abuse, the nasty epithet of "bluestocking" hurled at her, not by ignorant men of "barbarous" societies, but by the Mérimées, Gautiers, and Balzacs of sophisticated Paris, not to mention the more insulting remarks of her less enlightened compatriots. Balzac, it will be remembered, made a point of telling Mme Hanska that Cristina was "horribly bluestocking. The day before yesterday, she left her study to receive me; she came with ink spots on her dressing gown!" As though this were scandalous behavior. And it evidently was, or he would have used other means to denigrate her to Mme Hanska. George Sand, more famous and more appreciated throughout the century than any male novelist except Balzac, was called *"une pisseuse d'encre"* [ink-pisser]. Was any male writer of lesser stature ever called *"un pisseur d'encre"?* No. He was simply a writer, good or bad, prolific or not. *"Un homme de lettres,"* however insignificant the literature he produces, is a man of some distinction. (The Académie Française was and is filled with members of this vague nomenclature, and they are all "Immortals.") *"Une femme de lettres"* carries about as much prestige as *"une précieuse."* With or without Molière's qualifier of *"ridicule"* she is an object of mockery. Nor is this attitude a thing of the past. When Simone de Beauvoir's *Le Deuxième sexe* appeared, a reviewer (male) began his article with "Encore une intellectuelle!" In the masculine, this highly charged noun denotes the hero of the liberal world, the crusader against bigotry and obscurantism. In the feminine, it is clearly a put-down, as low and as disparaging as "bluestocking." It would seem that a woman who thinks can't be feminine; and if she's feminine, she can't think. This was the axiomatic view that caused Cristina difficulties during and, to an even greater extent, after her lifetime.

"The greatest harm that resulted from so much masculine deception is, in my mind, the fictitious character women have donned to please men. And why? Because they learned that men liked weak women . . . and that nothing was more distasteful to them than feminine forcefulness." Women became so convinced that a man's admiration and affection could only be bought at the price of intellectual inferiority that "they hid their culture for fear of being placed among *superior women,* pedants, and other similar abominations." Even Stendhal, champion of superior women, warned his sister to hide her superiority, for most French males would not tolerate a woman who eluded their domination. "The frivolity, inconstancy . . . and submissiveness of women became proverbial . . . and yet, I hold for certain that a woman is the most tenacious, the most constant, the most unmovable of creatures when it comes to her convictions. She has devoted all her strength to the ultimate aim of pleasing and being loved. Her present state in society is best suited to obtaining that end, and for that reason the greatest majority have absolutely no wish to change it." After a century of hard-won victories, Cristina would be not at all surprised to discover that the "greatest majority" is still on the side of those women who do not want change, who are afraid that equality will deny them the masculine devotion that provides for the family and guarantees the only position in society they feel to be securely theirs.

Cristina's article raises all the grave questions surrounding this knotty problem instead of charging blindly ahead, like so many feminists of yesterday and today, with slogans flying. We have no better answers now than she had then, but the questions remain. When Cristina attacks the crucial problem of her time, education for women, the question of the family immediately arises. "What would happen to the family as it is presently constituted," she asks, "if women were initiated into masculine pursuits, and shared with men public, social, and literary activities?" A father's love is awakened when the child's intelligence begins to develop; the concerns and duties that go into child care are tedious and distasteful to him, whereas "a mother's heart becomes constantly more attached for the very reasons that alienate a father. A mother's existence is absorbed in the love of her offspring, and whoever would deliver her of those tiresome cares would appear to her as an enemy rather than a liberator." But then, supposing women of intellectual capability and professional ambition were given equal opportunities, a new problem arises. "If women of inferior mentality are the only ones destined to domestic, conjugal, and maternal cares, who would respect them? How would they respect themselves? How could they respect those obscure but sacrosanct duties that are imposed on them as an almost dishonorable task, a punishment, or at very least a proof of their incapacity or inferiority?"

The situation is indeed so difficult that one can only sympathize with Cristina's dilemma. "Wherever I try to find a path for the radical reform of the present condition, I discover difficulties so numerous, so varied, and so serious, that however much it seems an improvement over the barbaric past and an indication that we are still not entirely free of that barbarity, I would never raise my voice to ask for its reform." What is striking about this statement is not her apparent resignation to an unsatisfactory situation, but rather her astute realism. She, who had lived and worked thirty years for a political ideal which she saw realized, knew, with the certainty of one who had experienced the joys and sorrows of womanhood, the impossibility of idealism when it came to the feminine problem. "The benefits that make a woman's youth happy diminish with

the years and leave her alone and disconsolate as age approaches."
Daughters marry, become mothers themselves, transfer their interests
and affections to new objects. Sons, "who in childhood knew no protection but the maternal," as soon as their studies and social activities take
over their lives, become contemptuous of the mother, who knows so little
of their interests, stays home all day, and worse still, continues to fuss
over them. "The mother becomes a secondary person, loved yes, but as
part of the past, and without participation in a future that will probably
be realized over her grave."

Cristina tactfully refrained from the subject of a husband's infidelity,
but the implication is there when she asks what remains for the older
woman. "The condition of woman is only tolerable in youth. The men
who decided her fate only looked to the young woman; her mature years,
or her old age, were not considered or provided for. When a woman no
longer procures pleasure or distraction for a man, who is concerned about
her?" Here again, Cristina touches on an issue as painful today as it was
then. There are few emeritus posts for retired wives and mothers, except
as continuing housekeepers and babysitters for grandchildren. But the
physical demands of such activities are often too great for an older
woman, and the emotional satisfactions often too few for the effort. All
that remains for many an older woman is the church, a secure refuge for
her solitude. On this subject Cristina openly berates those clergymen
"who are less concerned with the afterlife than with wealth and power
on earth." The poor woman, who has been led to believe that all God's
ministers are equally worthy, entrusts her family along with her soul to
her new master, who "teaches her to judge her husband and children,
censure them . . . or lead them to saner thoughts." She who until then
was submission itself soon incurs their greater contempt and loses them
completely. Was this only in Cristina's time?

And if virtuous women are so rarely offered a modicum of happiness,
or "if they achieved it, even more rarely retain it," what of those "more
ardent, more indomitable, more resistant to the yoke"? Such women are
even more pitiful once their youth and beauty have faded. "If they were
offered other goals in life besides beauty and admiration, one could eliminate the perennial and dangerous desire to please." With ill-concealed
irony toward all the humanitarian causes then in vogue, she asks: "Is it
not time that society, so eager to stamp out all tyrannies and extend its
hand to all the oppressed . . . remembered that in every house, in every
family, there are victims more or less committed to . . . procuring the
greatest possible measure of happiness for those who condemn them to a
life of dependency and sacrifice, many of whom would cheerfully buy at
this heavy price the benefit of being constantly loved by those to whom

they devote themselves? And yet, only a few obtain this inadequate recompense." Can anyone reading this appeal today find it dated? On the contrary, it is all the more moving because of its unbroken link with the present.

In many ways Cristina held women responsible for their plight. The few women in the past who had forced doors open for themselves, such as the rare university professor or physician, did not have enough successors to keep those doors open. Each new victory seemed to be followed by a new loss of ground. "Women themselves, who in recent years have demanded what they call their own *emancipation* [her italics], have, in my opinion, made the satisfaction of their desires more difficult. . . . They ask for radical and prompt reforms, provisos and laws that would disturb the peace of the family and produce deplorable confusion in society. . . . The very expression, so often uttered in those requests, of *liberated woman* [her italics], has, and not without reason, something unappealing and distasteful about it that arouses the laughter of men and the disdain of many women." The point she makes is that the feminine condition is so weighted by instinct, societal habits, and psychological patterns that the whole structure cannot be torn down in one fell swoop.

> Let us leave aside declamations. The condition of women today . . . is almost the same as the one imposed on them in the first dawnings of civilized society; and since today everything . . . progresses and is transformed, the immobility of the feminine condition is contrary to the nature of things. . . . However, it is more fitting to place well-cemented supports to hold up the structure as one removes one by one the stones that compose it and that will be used to build a new one, in which the needs of men and women will find equal satisfaction . . . for reforms enacted in haste almost always have unhappy outcomes. . . . Many women who would be liberated from their yoke disdainfully reject a liberty they did not request, whose name seems to them synonymous with vice and libertinism.

Some of her words may sound quaint, but the ideas could not be more modern. Then as now, the question of sexual freedom tends to becloud the greater issue of social equality, which, once achieved, necessarily entails sexual equality. It is a tribute to Cristina's modernity that she raised, however delicately, a subject that has assumed inordinate proportions today.

What she does want is open education for women in any field for which their intellect qualifies them, opportunities to exercise their training, just compensation for their work, and all honors accruing to them for their achievements. Cristina never loses sight, however, of the danger of undermining society and opposing certain irresistible laws of nature. The article closes in an apotheosis of optimism as she foresees the men of the future, marveling that an educated woman does not cease being a woman or living the life of a woman; that a cultivated woman remains an enjoyable companion after her youthful attractions have left her. And women, when they have acquired the status in society that they deserve, will have learned that the influence they have always exercised surreptitiously over men should be exercised openly, honestly, as equal partners, instead of catering to masculine vanity by pretending to be less than they are. "Let the happy and esteemed women of future times turn their thoughts to the pain and humiliation of the women who preceded them in life, and remember with some gratitude the names of those who opened and prepared the way for their never-before-tasted, perhaps not even dreamed of, happiness."

IN 1868 ANOTHER IMPORTANT WORK appeared from Cristina's pen; it was her first book in Italian. She had written reams of articles in the language, but never before a work of this nature: her observations on Italy now that Rome was the capital of a unified nation. Her correspondence with Italian friends reveals her lack of confidence in her handling of the language, especially in this book, intended for a large audience without historical background. Entitled *Osservazioni sullo stato attuale dell'Italia e sul suo avvenire* (Observations on the Current State of Italy and Its Future),[22] its 154 pages overflow with ideas and information. Drawing on her earlier historical works, she recapitulates the years of foreign tyranny and its effect on the already disparate populations of the country. But, most important, she discusses the character of this multifarious nation (the chapter is called "Character of the Italian, Its Varieties and Its Consequences") in an attempt to debunk the various provincial myths that contribute to Italy's psychological fragmentation. The ultimate purpose of the book—seen in the final two chapters, "Our Duties" and "Goals Toward Which We Must Strive"—is to foster a nation no longer divided by foreign influence or regional misconceptions. Alas, the forces in man that defy reason would seem to be as opposed to her ideal for Italy as they are to her ideal for women. Just as atavism seems to be antagonistic to social equality for women, so Italian regionalism resists all attempts to achieve a national mentality. Cristina's hopes have still not been fulfilled, but her efforts were noble.

Her portrait of Mazzini, leading to her benevolent and perceptive criticism of the Italian personality, succinctly captures the man's enormous appeal.

The first to address the people, until then indifferent to ideas but hardly to material benefits, was Giuseppe Mazzini. The liberals had been so convinced of the inertia of the masses that no attempt was made to inflame them against their trans-Alpine oppressors. Mazzini spoke to the people as the only class worthy of liberty and capable of the energetic efforts needed to secure it, flattering them so that popular passion, always ready to vituperate against those who have more, was easily inflamed. His style, often too poetic to be readily understood, nonetheless had a magic power that aroused enthusiasm.

He apparently had fewer original ideas than felicitous expressions: "Prudence is vileness, moderation is weakness, the title of king a tyranny." Mazzini believed that the only form of government suited to a people worthy of freedom was a republic, which, Cristina snidely remarks, "did not include the ministers of God who had always been the prime instrument of royal tyrants." Her experience in Rome after Mazzini's provisional government collapsed certainly strengthened the anti-clericalism she shared with him.

Her disenchantment with France after 1849 was not so confounding that it stamped out her early fervor. Though her tone is often cynical, she is too objective a historian not to credit France with the impulse that mobilized the Italian nation. And it was Mazzini who had known how to make the doctrines of the French Revolution clear and exciting, although no clear idea of an Italian republic evolved. There were those who wanted a republic like that of medieval Venice or Genoa; others, a republic like that of France in 1793; not to mention the Gioberti followers, who wanted a political papacy under Pius IX; or Cavour and Cristina, who believed in a liberal monarchy under the House of Savoy. "Those who repeated the maxims of Mazzini thought to conquer the world with a few high-sounding words devoid of meaning. The native complacency of Italians was bolstered by such rhetoric, so that the idea that *l'Italia farà da se* [Italy will manage on her own] contributed greatly to the calamities that followed."

Cristina tried to show the necessity for total re-education, since Italians had been taught by their long history as a conquered people to be suspicious; to criticize with fantasy rather than with cold logic; to be exalted by anything that assumed the dramatic aspect of heroism, of *sublimità*—as though re-enacting the epics of Ariosto—without determining whether the substance corresponded to the appearance. "We were taught . . . to confuse swollen vanity with the awareness of our true strength, and not to doubt our superiority and the triumphs it guaranteed, and when, instead of triumphs we met with reversals, to exaggerate them and fall into despair, to impute to others the misfortunes of our arrogance and inexperience." It is hard to believe that these lines were writ-

ten so long before the Italian experience of fascism, when this very
arrogance and inexperience led to disasters blamed on England's betrayal. The foibles of the Italian character outlined by Cristina were
evidently destined to perpetuate themselves.

Her homily to a budding nation is perhaps no less appropriate today,
when Milan is as distant in sympathy and interest from the south as it
ever was; when Tuscany stands alone on the rock of its past glory,
mocked by the rest of Italy for its perhaps not unwarranted sense of
superiority; when disgruntled voters seem prepared to rush headlong into
a new extremist experience instead of improving the democracy they
finally achieved.

> We were taught . . . to pride ourselves on our ingenuity, our wit,
> which knows everything through intuition, without suffering the bore-
> dom of learning. We were taught by those who wished to keep us
> in slavery . . . to be incapable of accomplishing our duties as citizens
> or sacrificing our private ambitions and interests to the salvation and
> prosperity of a common country. . . . The institutions that England
> jealously defends over the centuries, that France has bought at the
> price of many revolutions and much blood, that created America in
> two centuries to the amazement of the rest of the world, Italy has
> judged in seven years and condemned as childish, vain, unfitting. Italy
> still does not understand the need for educating its people at all levels.
> . . . Southern Italy is still bound to its clergy. The landowners of the
> north could easily combat the influence of the clergy but that requires
> effort, and effort is what is most repugnant to the present generation
> of Italians. . . . Those who governed . . . until 1859, governed a
> small and intelligent population. Since then it has become a country
> of twenty million and only a rare individual would have the gifts to
> lead such a nation. . . . Providence gave us such a man and then
> took him away—Cavour.

CRISTINA HAD GIVEN the better part of her life and her energies to this
country she loved. Her work was now over. She had done her best,
prodding, encouraging, perorating, vituperating in journals, newspapers,
letters, books. The nation would stand or fall; she had more than fulfilled her duties as a citizen. Her frail figure supported by pillows in her
salon at Blevio, where a steady stream of visitors came to enjoy her
conversation, her eyes bright and still captivating, her mind as acute as
ever, she could look back on a life well spent. She had seen and done
more things than most people, and had missed out on only one, perhaps.
She had surely been loved, by many, but had she ever loved? There was
no husband or old lover with whom to share the memories of a life gone

by, but five granddaughters (Marie's three stepdaughters and two daughters, Cristina and Antonietta) competed for her affection, and her house was never empty.

At fifty-two, when Louise Colet portrayed her as having one foot in the grave, Cristina told Mignet: "I do not think that my daughter's marriage or the sale of my Montparnasse house will succeed in separating me completely from Paris. That is reserved for age; but that time has not yet come, or so it seems to me. I do not feel the years at all, and I begin to find that extraordinary. My mirror tells me that we are indeed in 1860, but my mind completely ignores it." In fact, she never yielded to the gentle repose of old age. Until the end, she continued writing and arguing. Found among her papers were drafts of articles, on subjects as current as the Franco-Prussian War and the fall of Napoleon III, begun only months before her death. Afflicted at the end with dropsy and heart trouble, she closed her great sphinx eyes forever on July 5, 1871. She was much older than her sixty-three years, for she had lived many lives. And yet none of them was enough to protect her from her one great fear—oblivion. At the time of her death, the then Minister of Education wrote to her son-in-law: "There are few lives in these times of ours, filled with grief and glory, more proudly lived, more virilely spent, more nobly concluded than that of Cristina Belgiojoso. This name, I hope, will remind our Milan that it should and can take first place in the education and preparation of women, and as the finest monument for l'Agnesi* and la Belgiojoso, let there be built a *liceo* for girls, that will rise up under the salutary auspices of those two great minds." The *liceo* (a secondary school for classical education, like the French lycée) was never built, but a nursery school and a street carry her name in Locate. In fact, Cristina left a trust fund in real estate to assure the continuation of the school.

For thirty years she was all but erased from the public memory, until Raffaello Barbiera resurrected her as a vampiric Joan of Arc, leading the revolution but cringing in terror before death and darkness. Once exhumed, this ghost appeared in all manner of novels, biographies, authentic and fake memoirs, biased histories, sensational articles. And once again she faded away, a specter almost too ghastly to remember. Aldobrandino Malvezzi undertook the enormous enterprise of sorting Cristina's papers, many of which appear in his three-volume biography,

---

* Maria Agnesi, born in Milan in 1719, was already a philosopher-mathematician at fourteen. Président de Brosses in his *Lettres d'Italie* relates his astonishing discourse with her, in Latin, on the perception of objects, their communication to the brain, the emanation of light, etc. When her father, a professor of mathematics, fell sick in 1752, Pope Benedict XIV appointed her to his chair. After his death she became directress of the Hospice Trivulzio and later joined the sisterhood. She died in 1799. It was to her remarkable appointment that Cristina referred when lamenting the absence of successors to such rarely achieved positions.

expressly to correct the grotesque image fashioned by Barbiera, who, among other inaccuracies, insisted that Cristina did not keep letters. Malvezzi's work, to date not translated into French, widely cited but evidently too long to be read by hasty readers, did little to change the picture.

Now, decades later, she has reappeared again, so that her often expressed wish not to be forgotten has been fulfilled. Even after death she continues to live many lives as each portrait adds another highlight, another touch of color, to the pale beauty that held the Romantic generation in its thrall.

Part Two

THE VISIONS

8

Tannhäuser's Crown of Roses

THAT NOBLE AND UNHAPPY LAND which is the homeland of beauty and produced Raphael Sanzio d'Urbino, Gioacchino Rossini and the princess Cristina Belgiojoso . . ."[1]—this was one of the last tributes Heine paid to the woman he loved until the end of his life. The memoirs in which this line appears, written in his final years "to satisfy the gracious curiosity of a lady," were dedicated to the "Erlauchte Seele,"* who had embodied his poetic ideal for over two decades. His remarks to her and about her resounded in his poetry, his image of her underwent the slow refining of an art work. Hers was the ideal beauty, mysterious and compelling, an enigma to be unraveled, the venerated object of a cult that Heine served with unwavering constancy.

> Keep for me, Madame, the friendship with which you honored me one day when perhaps I did not fully deserve it, for at that time I was only the courtier of your beauty and could easily have listened to any ill remark about you, any misinterpretation of your actions, so long as one did not blaspheme against your eyes or the grace of your lips. Since then, Madame, things have changed greatly, my feelings of admiration have become a cult, a religious cult of *everything* that pertains to you . . . I dare not believe that this fanaticism will cost me . . . I do not say what . . . I do not say anything at all.
> Things in Denmark are not in their proper state, says Hamlet, who

* *Erlauchte* is both the conventional title "Highness" and, as applied to *Seele* (soul), means "noble."

was the maddest of all men, with the exception of your humble servant

Henri Heine*
[April 30, 1834]

Heine had discovered in her the Romantic Ideal, that unique beauty which transcends the merely beautiful, Venus, to become the eternal feminine, the Madonna.[2] For Heine, this Madonna was quite specifically Italian with quattrocento traits. As early as 1828, his first contact with Italy, this woman-idol appeared to him in the cool refuge of a cathedral: ". . . during a pious *dolce far niente,* one prays and dreams and sins in thought, the Madonnas bend forgivingly from the niches, their womanly nature forgives even the intermingling of their divine features with sinful reveries."[3] Already then, his notion of Italian beauty was formed: "I love those pale elegiac faces whose great black eyes radiate love and longing. . . . I love them as I love poetry itself."[4] Hardly surprising that when he met Cristina three years later he should have seen her as an apparition, a fabrication of his imagination, and, once familiar with the mind and character that accompanied her beauty, should have become obsessed with her.

Of the many portraits drawn by her contemporaries, Heine's is the most exalted, the most moving. Its brilliant highlights of unrelenting love have survived the dust of time and neglect, and can still be seen by anyone willing to look carefully. He was unable to arouse in her the emotions he felt, but he was the one man among those who desired her with whom she had the most in common. Both were dedicated to the freedom of their countries, both were given to the same black-edged idealism, both remained unfulfilled in their need to love. Like her he was homeless, a voluntary exile from a country where freedom had been eradicated after Waterloo, by the same Austrian tyrant.† For the Jews of Germany, even more than for the enlightened nobility of Lombardy, Napoleon had been a liberator; he made them equal in civil and political status to any other German. "Perhaps one day," he remarked ironically in his Italian *Reisebilder* of 1828, "an ingenious schoolmaster will prove irrefutably . . . that Napoleon Bonaparte is identical with that other Titan who robbed the gods of light and for that fault was chained to a rock in the middle of the ocean, to be the prey of a vulture who daily lacerated his

* Letters to Cristina were written in French and signed with the French spelling of his name. Ellipses in this letter are in the original.

† Napoleon's Confederation of the Rhine was dissolved by the Congress of Vienna and reformed into a German Confederation under Austrian domination. Heine did not live to see the liberation of Lombardy, which galvanized Prussia to victory over Austria seven years later.

heart." The vulture in this case was the Imperial Austrian eagle, who confined Napoleon to St. Helena, rescinded the rights of Jews, and destroyed freedom of expression. Heine's earlier *Reisebilder,* of 1826, had contained a daring discussion of social and political subjects: the Church, class struggle, Napoleon. Banned from all German states, it quickly became a clandestine best-seller.

Like Cristina, Heine arrived in Paris in the spring of 1831 (he in midMay, she at the end of March) believing that Austria's victims would be rescued by the July monarchy. Like her, he would suffer the disappointment of its unfulfilled promises. His love of Italy had already committed him to the Italian cause, which was the same as Germany's. And his pages on Rossini, which incidentally offer an uncommon interpretation of opera buffa, must have endeared him to Cristina even before she knew him well.

> The detractors of Italian music . . . will one day in Hell be unable to escape the richly deserved punishment of hearing nothing but the fugues of J.-S. Bach throughout eternity. . . . Rossini, *divino maestro,* Helios of Italy . . . forgive my countrymen who do not see your depth because you have covered it with roses. . . . Speech is forbidden to the poor Italian slave, so it is through music alone that he can give expression to the emotions of his heart. All his hatred of foreign domination, his longing for freedom, his rage at his impotence, his sorrow on remembering his former lordly greatness . . . all this is embodied in those melodies. . . . This is the esoteric meaning of opera buffa. The exoteric [Austrian] sentinel would never suspect the meaning of those joyful love stories.[5]

(Balzac, who had learned this lesson from Cristina, Heine, and the maestro himself, was to teach it ten years later in *Massimilla Doni.*) Heine understood how sick Italy was and proclaimed—with tragic foresight of his own future suffering—his admiration: "The entire Italian people is inwardly sick. Sick men always hold a greater attraction than those who are healthy. For only the sick man is a man; his limbs express a history of suffering."

Born January 1, 1797,* of a merchant father with more charm than business sense and a cultivated mother, Heine (named Harry for an English friend, not Heinrich) reached manhood in an atmosphere of political and intellectual enlightenment. By 1823, when his concern for a career became pressing, Napoleon was dead and so were civil rights for Jews. Heine's father could offer little help: "Between my father's heart

---

* During his lifetime he claimed to have been born in 1801: "I was the first man of my century."

and his pocket there was a kind of railroad. It goes without saying that stocks in that line did not make him richer."[6] Neither his millionaire uncle's business nor the law, which he studied, attracted him. Within the next six years, his fame as a poet and journalist grew as the opportunities for a livelihood decreased. Not even his conversion to Lutheranism ("the certificate of baptism is the entrance ticket to European culture") provided him the university post he sought. His last hope for such a position, the only one that would have enabled him to continue writing, was finally denied by a man who admired him—Ludwig of Bavaria. Though some of his finest poetry (*Buch der Lieder, Intermezzo*) had appeared by 1829, it was his prose (in the *Reisebilder*) that attracted the greater attention, particularly that of the Censor.* Like Cristina, Heine turned to Paris as to the Promised Land.

"Liberty is the new religion, the religion of our time," he wrote in 1827. "The French are the chosen people of that new religion; it is in their tongue that the first gospels and the first dogma took root. Paris is the new Jerusalem." In Paris, Cristina and Heine and thousands of refugees like them found the standard-bearer of this new religion in Lafayette. "The world marvels that an honest man once lived—his place is vacant," Heine lamented after Lafayette's death. It was probably in Lafayette's salon that Cristina and Heine met. The aging general, in a short brown wig, his tall frame bowed by seventy-four years, concealed beneath an old man's joviality the political passions of a youthful firebrand. Sharing his passions were the young and old of Carbonaro spirit exiled from all of Europe: generals without armies, writers without readers, princes without kings. France alone supported the cause of nationhood, and Lafayette was then the spirit of France. Italophilia was nearing its zenith—"Italian exiles distinguish themselves from all other people; not one among them is stupid."[7]—and the striking figure of the princess represented Italy's martyred greatness. Though Heine's republicanism was not exactly harmonious with Cristina's monarchism, he was entranced by the magic of her eyes and the fervor of her arguments: "You waged a battle worthy of the *juste milieu;* you shelled the masses, it was a terrifying barrage. It would have taken little for my heart, which is a republic, to become a monarchy." Occasions were not lacking for these two foreigners to come into amicable and polemical contact. And Cristina doubtless heard about Heine's works long before she read them, from her early acquaintances Victor Cousin, the Germanophile philosopher and Heine enthusiast, and Jules Mohl, the German orientalist. By the time she had her own salon, a few doors away from Lafayette on the

---

* "It was said that my book would stir up the intimidated spirit of freedom and measures were taken to suppress it" (conclusion to *Reisebilder*, November 29, 1830).

rue d'Anjou, she and Heine were close friends. Later, they also became fellow contributors to the *Revue des Deux Mondes.*

Among the many friends Heine acquired during his twenty-five years in Paris, many of whom he shared with Cristina, no one was closer to him than his "belle princesse," as he usually addressed her. According to Joseph Dresch, Heine's letters to Cristina occupy the most important part of his Parisian correspondence.[8] Jules Legras, Heine's first French biographer, said of his relationship with her: "Among his Parisian relations I know of none that had such permanence or inspired such expressions of sincerity in him."[9] And among the women Heine had loved, Legras correctly noted that the only significant ones were the two who "in different ways exercised great influence over him: Cristina Belgiojoso, his protector, and Mathilde Mirat, his wife."[10]

Heine had many reasons for "such expressions of sincerity." By 1834 Cristina's salon was rivaled by few others in all of Paris. The most celebrated names in politics, letters, philosophy, music, were attracted by her charm, her generosity, her prestige—and each other's presence at her weekly receptions. It was she who enabled Heine to meet some of the most influential figures of the time, and she who arranged for his pension from the French government through her close friends Mignet and Thiers. The tenderness and protection she offered him were very different from the attention he received from those who feared his tongue or admired his pen—both indefatigable. Hoping to efface Mme de Staël's bucolic image of Germany, which had largely distorted France's vision by 1830, he wrote feverishly for both sides of the Rhine, serving as cultural ambassador for each: "The Rhine is the Jordan that separates the land consecrated to liberty from the land of the Philistines." Risking his future return to Germany, he published in the *Revue des Deux Mondes* of December 15, 1834, a prophetic article on the inevitable eruption of a united Germany, "more to be feared than the Holy Alliance with all its Croats and Cossacks. A drama will take place in Germany compared to which the French Revolution will seem an innocent idyll."

JUST AS HIS LITERARY SUCCESS was inadequate to satisfy his material needs, so his social success was unable to fulfill his emotional needs. He was tormented by a thirst for love, for the ideal love, unquenched by the nameless women of a night or the titled ladies of an evening. And that ideal love had a face he instantly recognized in Cristina Belgiojoso. Caroline Jaubert has described Heine's esthetic predilections: "Pale women with regular features, of a somewhat phantasmal beauty, interested him particularly; a bizarre face, having something of the sphinx."[11]

No other woman in Heine's life fits this description. Nor was he the only one to respond to her unusual beauty. Musset was similarly captivated by her sphinx-like quality: "She had the terrifying eyes of the sphinx, so large, so large that I got lost in them and cannot find my way out." Delacroix was another who was struck by the mysterious beauty of this living sculpture. *"C'est beau, c'est beau!"* he exclaimed, although he remained unmoved by "that marble pallor, that body tapered like a Gothic saint, those enormous eyes whose lids never blink; only the smile makes her alive and feminine."[12] Arsène Houssaye echoed the master: "A Gothic saint forgotten in her niche, of marble whiteness, her body frail and slender like one of Angelico da Fiesole's angels."[13] Heine's admiration surpassed them all. He was in ecstasy over her and told her so in a letter of April 18, 1834. "I have never seen anything so fabulous, so poetic, so fairy-like, as those black locks that fell in natural waves on the transparent whiteness of your face!" It is worth reproducing the remainder of this letter, for two years later it became the amplified portrait in *Florentinische Nächte.*

> And that face—you stole it from some painting of the fourth century,* from some old fresco of the Lombard school, perhaps from your own Luini, or from some poem of Ariosto, how do I know! But that face haunts me day and night, like an enigma I should like to solve. As to your heart, which is doubtless beautiful enough, it is of little concern to me. All women have hearts, and some have truly magnificent ones. My grandmother, for instance. But no one has your face.
>
> In truth, Madame, I am not joking. Day and night I wrack my brain to guess the meaning of that face, of those symbols, those incredible eyes, that mysterious mouth, all those traits that do not seem to exist in reality, but seem rather to be the creation of a dream. So that I am always afraid all of this will evaporate one fine morning.
>
> I beg of you, Madame, do not evaporate, and accept the assurances of the perfect respect and devotion with which I remain
>
> > Your very humble and very obedient
> > Henri Heine

Here was the dream made real, the acme of esthetic and moral perfection. He never wrote such dithyrambs about any other woman, never tired of writing them to her or about her: "Before knowing you I imagined that people like you, endowed with all bodily and spiritual perfec-

---

* Heine evidently means the quattrocento. Bernardino Luini, Cristina's compatriot from Lombardy, was a pupil of Leonardo da Vinci. It is a curious coincidence that the fresco auctioned at Cristina's famous bazaar in 1837 was by Luini, whose Madonnas she did in fact resemble.

tion, existed only in fairy tales, in a poet's dreams." For Heine the poet, she was a perpetual spring of inspiration; for Heine the man, she was an unending torment of Tantalus. Her inability to respond to his appeals imprisoned them both in desperate isolation. And with his uncanny sensitivity he seems to have fathomed better than anyone the mystery of her unyielding nature. Where others found her cold or coquettish, a bluestocking or even a Sapphic initiate, Heine appears to have guessed the truth. "You have certainly seen her in Paris, the ideal form that is, however, merely the prison in which the holiest soul of an angel has been confined. . . . Yet this prison is so beautiful that everyone, as though bewitched, stops at the sight of her and gazes at her in amazement."[14] It was a spell that held him so fast, so long, he could contemplate at his leisure the nature of that "prison."

The very word "prison" suggests hidden meanings. It is hardly the metaphor one would normally apply to a face and body that inspire such ecstasy. If a woman's virtue is unbreachable, one might speak of a fortress; if her ardor is dormant, one might use *tomb* or *corpse,* as Musset did in his vengeful poem about her, "Sur une morte." Chivalric resonances of the *cárcel de amor,* the prison of love, may have been intentional, and surely apply to Heine, who was and remained the prisoner of his love for her. But he is speaking of her in these lines, of her body as the prison of her soul, not of her soul imprisoned by her love. In this case "prison" implies that the woman was locked into a beautiful but confining form within which she became the pure chaste creature evoked by the "saintly soul of an angel." Given the context, the attribute though metaphysical implies the physical through a negation: angels do not have bodies. Cristina had in a sense become disembodied. She was the prisoner of an irresistible body that resisted all approaches; only the eyes still burned with longing. Many men were drawn to her but few remained gracious once rejected. One such was Arsène Houssaye, who decades later called her "that strange woman whom one wanted to hate and whom one loved desperately. . . . That great lady was not quite sure of having a heart for she had only the passion of the mind; she was quite willing for one to give oneself to her, but she did not give herself. She served with adorable grace the feast of love, but flew off when it was time to partake of it."[15]

The tributes of the men who desired her make it hard to believe she was just a dyed-in-the-wool bluestocking. It is equally hard to imagine a sphinx inspiring the kind of fervor she aroused. Epilepsy may have illdisposed her to the pleasures of the senses, yet a powerful sensuousness apparently emanated from her eyes, her mouth, her hair. A patient husband might have freed her, but Emilio had no time to waste on reluctant novices when willing Venuses were at hand. However, a man of Heine's exquisite sensuality, whose poetic imagination was inflamed by the woman-sphinx, the woman-idol, was excited by her very reserve. For such a man, desire is more inebriating than conquest. If Heine's ideal was "a woman chaste and cold, but hiding beneath her chasteness and coldness unassuaged ardors,"[16]* it becomes evident that Cristina was his model for such dream-figures as Diana in "Atta Troll":

> *White as marble was her face*
> *And as marble cold. Startling*
> *Were the rigor and the pallor*
> *Of those stern and noble traits.*
>
> *Yet in her black eyes*
> *Gleamed an awesome*
> *And wondrous sweet flame*
> *That dazzled and consumed the soul.*[17]

The tenor of their relationship suggests that Heine must have understood Cristina with as much insight as despair. The facts of her marriage were common knowledge. Emilio was in Paris often enough, carousing with Musset and other lions so openly that gossip was superfluous. And given the candor of her letters to others, she probably made no secret of her epilepsy to Heine. However little was known about the disorder, it had been identified as a nervous disorder, and in such matters Heine was well versed. Hypertension, neuralgia, headaches had been familiar problems throughout his own youth. This much, and perhaps more, he shared with his "belle princesse." (If Balzac knew that she had contracted a venereal disease from her husband, it is not unlikely that Heine, much closer to her, also knew.) Like her, he was an avid reader of medical literature and was reputed to have saved the life of a friend's child by recognizing the gravity of the symptoms. While there is no certain diagnosis of the paralysis that buried him alive for eight years, Heine himself believed it was syphilitic in origin.†

When Cristina first met him he was "a germanic Apollo," according to Théophile Gautier:

His white forehead, pure as a marble slab, was shadowed with great masses of blond hair. His blue eyes sparkled with light and inspiration; his round full cheeks, elegantly contoured, were not hollowed by the Romantic pallor so fashionable then. A slight curve altered, without spoiling its purity, his nose's intention of being Greek. His har-

---

* Yet the author of this observation seems unaware of Cristina except as a salonnière.

† Later opinion has ascribed it to atrophy of the spinal cord or multiple sclerosis, but Heine had all the more severe symptoms of tabes dorsalis, many of which he shared with Thierry.

monious lips . . . had a charming expression in repose; but when he spoke, their red bow shot sharp barbed arrows. . . . no one has ever been more cruel to stupidity. He was a charming god—clever as a devil—but very good, whatever has been said."[18]

By 1832 Heine's sight was beginning to fail and two fingers of his left hand were paralyzed, which did not prevent him from quipping: "I am losing my sight but, like the nightingale, I shall only sing the better for it." He and Cristina were of the same heroic temper, which allowed them to transcend their miserable state. Their remarkable capacity for idealism whether in politics, friendship, or love, their ability to mock their own suffering, to devote themselves to others with the same indulgence the sick usually lavish on themselves—all this brings to mind Michelet's remark about Joan of Arc, whose "pity was so great she no longer pitied herself." Such bonds they shared with no one else. Nor did Cristina have with anyone else a relationship of such equality, tragic in many ways. Lafayette was her protector as she became Thierry's; Mignet's moral and intellectual rigor often placed her in an almost filial position, making her seek his approval. Other men in her entourage may have loved her, admired her. Only Heine shared with her the torments of an exile; the dreams of a liberated homeland; the need for an idealized love, but which for her had to be platonic; persecution by Austria; condemnation to sickness. Most often called his "protector," her intervention on his behalf was the help of a loving friend rather than the benevolence of a patron. He was in the prime of his beauty during the decade they were in greatest contact, his refinement of taste and manners was as suited to her aristocratic elegance as her intellect and wit were deserving of his admiration. Mignet's status of *cavaliere servente* did not preclude her intimacy with Heine, although she never became his mistress. It was an intimacy of thought, of feeling, and of humor. To have elicited such confidences from Heine as she received, she must have been similarly candid with him. Of course Heine was jealous of Mignet's privileged position, but he manifested his jealousy in the subtle way of incorporating Mignet into his love for Cristina. He accepted him as her alter ego, and as his own friend and benefactor. Toward the blind and paralyzed Thierry, who later enjoyed her care, Heine showed fraternal commiseration: "Our disease has the same origin—an excess of work, as kind souls call it. Excess is the word. But is it the right one?"

IN THE EARLY 1830's there were gayer moments with the regulars of Cristina's inner circle—at La Jonchère, her summer residence, or her apartment on the rue d'Anjou. Among them were Caroline Jaubert, who became Heine's lifelong friend, Mignet, Thiers, Cousin, Jules and Mary Mohl, Balzac, Liszt, Bellini, Musset, Rossini. Heine had no patience for Cousin, whom he considered a pilferer of German philosophy and whom he often interrupted rudely when Cousin was purloining German ideas and passing them off as his own. "Yes, yes," Heine would explode, "I know just what you mean! This is Fichte's theory, elaborated by Schelling!" Heine's deviltry toward Cousin was particularly gratified by a story Cristina told him,* which he adored hearing repeated. Cousin, walking in her garden one day and gesticulating with his cane in support of his argument that "reason is totally heterogeneous and separate from personality and sensibility," was suddenly attacked by Cristina's bulldog, Kisch, who felt personally threatened by the raised cane. "The eclectic philosopher, in his vast knowledge, knew that the distinguishing trait of a bulldog is never to let go once it bites. . . . One has to have seen the illustrious writer to know to what degree a human face can express terror." Everybody rushed to help but only created more confusion. Mignet alone remained in possession of his faculties, giving orders to grab Kisch by the tail and pry his mouth open with a stick. Cousin, finally released, was carried half dead to a couch. Heine found this scene hilarious. "How Cousin must have gazed at that threatened arm," he mused to Cristina, "at the end of which were the fingers that held the magic pen that fluently translated languages unknown to the brain that guided it!" He was more generous toward Mignet, whose sober scholarship he was obliged to respect: "Never does *he* hide the veins he digs in! Now there is a writer! Honest, fair, serious, a beautiful soul." Then, unable to resist the biting flattery that betrays his jealousy: "Yes, I say a beautiful soul! Graced with that particular beauty that is immediately understood by women because it is manifested in the purity of the lines of his face; it strikes one at once, speaks all languages, constitutes a cosmopolitan soul."[19]

Heine's choice victim among Cristina's friends was Bellini. The cherubic composer, then at the height of his fame, was ill-equipped to ward off Heine's sallies. His French was faltering, his admirers always indulgent. Only Heine dared tease him, and diabolically. An evening at Cristina's house—always cited from Caroline Jaubert's *Souvenirs* but in fact first recounted by Cristina in a letter to her†—was their last meeting and the background for the scene in *Florentinische Nächte*. Reminiscing from Athens in 1849, she wrote Mme Jaubert: "Bellini's melodies are often on my lips and I run my fingers over a piano that, bad as it is, helps me render my musical thought. I often recall with sadness the premature

* Told in her *Souvenirs dans l'exil*, from which the quotations were taken.
† Later published in Cristina's *Souvenirs dans l'exil*, p. 19. Heine's remarks are quoted from her account.

death of that great composer, not with the egotistical feeling of regret over the masterpieces he carried to the tomb, but because death was something so frightening to him." As a Sicilian, he was atavistically sensitive to the notion of a *jettatore*—one who gives the evil eye, *la jettatura**—and thought Heine was one because he wore glasses and had reddish glints in his blond hair—legendary attributes of the devil. A month before Bellini's death, they were together at Cristina's country house, La Jonchère. Heine, greatly amused by the idea of such satanic power, knew Bellini's weakness and invariably joked about death, especially the death of young geniuses. "They all die so young, those men of talent," Heine lamented mockingly. "Tell me, how old are you? Thirty-two, thirty-three? Hmmm. Mozart only lived to thirty-five." Bellini, horrified, immediately made the exorcizing horn gesture (pointed index and little finger) behind his back, which only encouraged Heine and provoked glances of hilarity between him and Cristina. Then to console him, Heine added: "But perhaps you run no risk. Who knows if you have the genius attributed to you? I personally am unaware of it; I don't know any of your works and so shall remain in my ignorance. I find you charming and am too much of a friend not to feel deeply distressed were I to discover in you that gift of heaven so fatal to its possessors." Small consolation for Bellini to have his genius doubted and learn that his "friend" had never heard his operas!

Cristina was contrite in retrospect:

Those jokes would have seemed terribly cruel had the future been known to us. I myself was the first to laugh heartily at the terrified face of our beloved composer. Only a few days passed before he fell sick. He was to dine at your house, I remember, when at seven o'clock a letter arrived containing his regrets. A sudden indisposition, he said, deprived him of the honor. Turning the note over in your hands, on scented colored paper with a very elaborate envelope and seal, you said to your guests, "I am not really anxious; one can hardly be very sick when one sends such elegant health bulletins." Two weeks later Bellini was no more. You probably received the last words he wrote. During his brief and violent malady no one was admitted near him. With great difficulty I succeeded once, and believe I was the only one among his friends who managed to see him. . . . He expressed the deep desire to see me again. I promised to come back but was no longer admitted; the door remained stubbornly closed to all.

Even after his death Heine did not desist: "I warned him, I warned him," he told all their friends.

---

* Benedetto Croce, a philosopher but first a Neapolitan, was asked what he thought about the *jettatura:* "I don't believe in it, but it's better not to joke about it!"

In Heine's account of this episode (contained in *Florentinische Nächte*), they were at the house of "a great lady with the smallest foot in Paris," where Bellini was, as usual, massacring the French language to everyone's amusement. Exhausted by his "Bellinisms" he sank to the feet of the beautiful lady, who was clearly enjoying his discomfiture despite her indulgent smile. In his "Sicilian jargon," Bellini protested to her that what he had been saying to her earlier, in his fractured French, was praise not foolishness.

> The beautiful lady barely listened to his explanations. She had taken the bamboo cane which Bellini used to support his feeble rhetoric, and was slowly undoing the graceful curls on the young maestro's temples. The smile that lent her face an expression such as I have never seen on a living face, was doubtless produced by her mischievous occupation. That face will never leave my memory! It was one of those faces that seem to belong more to the world of dreams than to the crude reality of life; contours that recall da Vinci; a noble oval with the naïve dimples and sentimental pointed chin of the Lombard school. The coloring rather of Roman softness, the matte luster of pearls, a distinguished pallor, a *morbidezza*. In short, it was a face such as can only be found in some old Italian portrait which depicts one of those great ladies of whom Italian artists of the sixteenth century were enamored when they created their masterpieces; of whom the poets of that time dreamed when they sang themselves into immortality; for whom German and French heroes yearned when they buckled their swords and scampered across the Alps. Yes, yes, such a face it was, and on it played a smile of the sweetest mischief, the noblest teasing, while she demolished Bellini's curls with the tip of the cane. At that moment, Bellini seemed to me as though touched by a magic wand . . . and my heart went out to him at once. His face gleamed in the reflection of her smile; it was perhaps the fullest moment of his life.

IN JUNE 1834 Heine wrote Cristina, "Farewell most beautiful, most kind, most admirable being I have met on this earth. Your memory balms my existence." Four months later he met Crescence Eugénie Mirat, whom he renamed Mathilde. Their liaison continued stormily for seven years until his jealousy and humiliation were legitimized by marriage. A Parisian shopgirl, eighteen years his junior, she was so ignorant that the nature of his work and of his celebrity remained outside her grasp to the end of his life. She even destroyed manuscripts, thinking they were scrap paper. She was gay, opulent, pretty, totally irresponsible. Her ingenuousness amused him; he was her protector, her benefactor, her lover. In an apparent transferral of roles, he became for Mathilde what Cristina had been for him, and what he could never be for her. And the diametrical contrast between these two women—physical, moral, intellectual—only accentuates this substitution.

Letters of the following spring show that despite Mathilde's lascivious charms, Heine's hopes for Cristina's love were still undaunted. It is curious that some of his biographers—ordinarily attuned to his wit and self-mockery, which served as gauze over a wound—should have read his letters to Cristina so literally, or carelessly, as to falsify their meaning. In April 1835, for example, he wrote her a letter that Legras offered as proof of Heine's trusting friendship: "The poet willingly used his beautiful protectress as a confidante of the vagaries of his heart. . . . Thus he spoke to her one day of *'une petite femme'* he had seen at her house."[20] This was indeed a confidence, but not about a third party. It is an enchantingly disguised declaration of love, which the addressee did not misconstrue, as a subsequent letter indicates.

> I have the honor of greeting the beautiful princess by sending her a copy of Sand's novel. The little lady [*la petite femme*] I saw at your house yesterday holds an attraction in her personality, a *je ne sais quoi,* that affects me in a singular way. Accustomed to examining everything I feel, I am at a loss to explain this sensation. I believe she has a mysterious agitated nature whose agitation is contagious to Germans with big blue eyes; she makes my soul ache and awakens slumbering regrets; she is painfully good, she is playfully naughty. I do not want her and yet I do [*je n'en veux pas et cependant j'en voudrais*]; it is a spell. If you promise not to laugh, I shall confess that I think she is a sorceress. But you, Madame, you have a rational mind and you treat as superstition anything that is not Chinese and eclectic philosophy.
>
> Your very humble and very tamed,
> Henri Heine

For a man whose genius was verbal, there is no doubt that he put as much artistry into such a letter as he would into a poem. Every word was selected with an eye to arousing her interest, but not her anger. And on this subject, hardly a new one, their only common tongue was humor. "La petite femme" is obviously none other than "la belle princesse," perhaps that day particularly receptive to the blue-eyed German's agitation. There is something exquisitely wishful about "I believe she has a mysterious agitated nature." Did she express a longing that revived feelings she had made him suppress? For her it may have been no more than a velleity; for him it awakened "slumbering regrets" over his failure to win her earlier. She would only laugh at him if he told her baldly that he loved her, wanted her; to tell her that he does not want her but would, could, if encouraged, is a very different way of putting it, and one that does not so easily arouse laughter. Furthermore, the responsibility is hers: she has bewitched him. His will, his reason, cannot fight a spell. Then, certain of provoking that smile he extolled in print, he closed with a chain of allusions to her interests and her friends: her "rational mind" refers not only to her analytical approach to politics and history, but to Mignet as well; "Chinese" refers to the orientalist Jules Mohl, another regular at the rue d'Anjou; and "eclectic philosophy" to Victor Cousin and her own "eclectic" studies of Hebrew, the Church Fathers, and early heresies, which led to her book on Catholic dogma. His final "very tamed" suggests earlier reprimands for going too far, and the assurance that he knows his limits, though he would like to extend them.

Six days later, his reply to her missing note suggests the contents of hers. She could not respond to him as he might wish, could not return the love he offered, but . . . one can imagine all manner of affectionate phrases. What she could, and did, offer was the help of her influential friends to obtain the pension that remained his only secure income until 1848.

> Your note, Princess, is very clear and I have understood it very well, very precisely, although it exudes a perfume of *amabilité** that goes to my head and confuses my thoughts. I have understood and will be at Monsieur Mignet's tomorrow at ten-thirty, and shall go with him to Monsieur Thiers. I am grateful that M. Mignet goes to such trouble for me; I am really most grateful. When one wants to be loved by someone, one must offer that person the opportunity to do one favors. Madame, one cannot be more beautiful in body or soul than you.

The matter of his pension is all that Heine's biographers have gleaned from this letter, or from the note it answers, which evidently communicated more than the related logistics. Heine's note is an exercise in subtlety, as hers must also have been; the matter of the pension is only peripheral. Thiers, as Minister of the Interior, was instrumental in obtaining the pension. And Mignet went to "such trouble" for Cristina's sake. This much Heine understood before. Cristina's note must have carried an implicit reminder of her attachment to Mignet, and this was hardly a time to offend him as her *primo cavaliere.* That was what Heine understood so precisely. His elliptic transition from gratitude to Mignet to the "someone" whose love he wants—that "someone" clearly not Mignet—implies his recognition of their union. But the beginning of the letter suggests that despite the clear call to order, her rejection was not

---

* As used here, *"amabilité"* is more "lovable" or "loving" than "amiable." Amiability would hardly go to his head. He may have intended a pun on *amabilis,* which is clearly what he means.

definitive: "although" marks the ambiguity he saw or chose to see. What heady perfume other than that of hope could have confused his thoughts? His closing formula, used many times in the next few years, confirms that all hope was not destroyed. And when it finally was, the formula continued to serve as a reminder that he still loved her.

A year later, when writing to her of "the domestic misfortunes" that prevented him from coming to La Jonchère, his tone is neither politely apologetic nor confidentially friendly, as has been generally thought. It is a cry of anguish, a plea for help: "Do not laugh too hard, beautiful princess, for it is highly possible that the consequences may become serious. It is now a question of draining the cup. I have forgotten my godliness, I have compromised my divinity, I am in the mud of human passions and find it difficult to extricate myself. In my great trouble, in my insipid torment, I sometimes find solace in thinking of you, of your smile, of your friendship." He was prepared for her teasing. It was her defense against the violation of her boundaries: love yes, passion no. But this time Heine dispenses with the usual pleasantries. He accuses her directly: her laughter is responsible for the serious consequences. Previously she may not have taken seriously his declarations to her, or his subsequent entanglement with Mathilde; now she must: this has the ring of an ultimatum. He has sunk into "the mud of human passions" because she rejected him. What good is his "godliness" if he is banished from Olympus? He begs her to save him from this degradation, from Mathilde, his "insipid torment."

He finally decided to go to La Jonchère in the hope of resolving his despair, and Cristina urged him to come in the hope that she might help him. Writing to a friend in September 1836, after his stay there, he offers a clue to his attachment for Mathilde: "I was in the country at the chateau of the most beautiful, most noble, most gifted woman in the world. I am not in love with her. I am condemned to love only what is most base, most inane. . . . Can you understand how this must torture a man who is proud and intelligent?" This statement has been commonly accepted as a solemn denial of his love for the princess.[21] And yet, the contrast between the superlatives for Cristina and the denigrations of Mathilde ought to be enough to give one pause, particularly in view of the rapid transition from one to the other. It is not that he does not love the princess; he *may not* love her. He wants Cristina but can only have Mathilde. Cristina cannot give herself to him nor can he win her, but Mathilde he can buy and keep. In fact, he did "buy" her for 3,000 francs from her aunt, who thought she had the better of the bargain.[22] Condemned he was, not by his own depravity but by fate, which denied him the woman he wanted. To rescue him from the mud of this substitute passion he needed Cristina the woman, not just "la belle princesse." If he

could not have her, then her reverse image—a black mass for holy communion, an expiation in hell for the paradise never won. That Mathilde
was indeed a substitute is made patently clear in the memoirs he wrote
for Cristina in 1854, his final testament to the woman he never ceased
loving. He had told her of his passion for Mathilde, perhaps even hoping
to arouse her through jealousy or compassion. Instead, she urged him to
leave Paris, to forget her, who could not be his, and Mathilde, who was
unworthy of him, and cure himself with solitude and writing. Nineteen
years later he still reproached her for the choice she had inflicted on him:
"The principle of homeopathy, according to which a woman cures us of a
woman, is perhaps of all remedies the best and most widely proved . . .
It is . . . senseless to advise a man who has *le mal d'amour* to flee his
lady and seek his salvation in solitude on nature's breast. Alas, on a
verdant breast he will only find boredom. The best antidote for women is
women themselves."[23]

This agon of contrasting loves, this Janus-woman, is dramatized in
Heine's dialogue-poem *Tannhäuser*. While adhering strictly to the
legend of the thirteenth-century Minnesinger—who after a life of debauchery on Venusberg leaves to seek absolution from the Pope, is denied it, and returns in despair—Heine embellished it with details that
identify his personal torment. Venus assumes the physical attributes of
Cristina and the moral attributes of Mathilde. Tannhäuser's crown of
roses, which becomes a crown of thorns, appears in his desperate letter to
Cristina of 1836, written at exactly the same time as the poem, when he
was in southern France. On Tannhäuser's enforced return to Venusberg,
he goes through Florence and Milan, both cities identified with Cristina.
And he comes back to "Frau Venus [who] goes into the kitchen to
prepare him soup." The Venus of his dreams, his crown of roses, has
Cristina's face, the enormous eyes and black locks described in his letter
to her of April 1834. The Venus of his damnation, his crown of thorns,
is an insipid Hausfrau who serves him soup and bread. His body is fed
while his soul starves. Even the Pope's admonition parodistically evokes
Cristina: "It is with your soul that you must now redeem the pleasures of
the flesh. You are damned as of now and condemned to eternal torment."
These lines recall Cristina's oft-quoted warning to Musset that expressed
her rationalization of platonic love: "The punishment of vulgar love is
to deny those who abandon themselves to it the aspiration to noble love."
Heine's dramatic portrayal of his plight, all the more striking because the
pleasures of the flesh were still very intense in 1836, has not been seen
for what it is: a poetic construct of his desperate love for Cristina, the
Italian redeemer who rejects him. Passing fancies such as his cousins
have been associated with numerous poems, but not Cristina, although
one of the most powerful of all his works is transparently evocative of

her. Viewed in retrospect, *Tannhäuser* is a dreadful prophecy of Heine's eight-year purgatory. Paralyzed in his mattress-grave [*Mattratzengruft* was Heine's own term], he had nothing more from his Venus-Mathilde than the meals she served him. As in the poem, the pleasures of the flesh gave way to vulgar cohabitation. His Italian pilgrimage—an unmistakable metaphor for Cristina—had denied him redemption; he was "condemned to love only what is most base, most inane."

His attachment to Cristina, unaltered by his liaison with Mathilde, is revealed by the moving candor of his correspondence during that first year of his "crown of thorns." To Cristina, in a recently discovered letter*—the most explicit and most pathetic of all his declarations—he not only says that she is supreme in his thoughts (*"Ma foi, j'ai fait de vous, Princesse, mon occupation principale"*), but that he remains hers, and delicately suggests that she will regret his loss (*"Vous ne retrouverez pas si vite un miroir comme moi"*). For no one has loved her, will love her, as he has, understood her, admired her. He does not even amplify her— most exquisite of compliments!—he merely reflects the truth. To enhance the beauty he sees in her, in her character, he stresses the sordidness of his entanglement with Mathilde—the "Phrygian grisette"—which she understood compassionately but ineffectively. One wonders how she could have resisted him after this letter.

Boulogne-sur-Mer
26 August, 1835

I hope, Madame la Princesse, that this letter finds you in good health. I myself am fairly well, fairly calm, and as resigned as is possible for me. I live apart from the *beau monde,* which is not *beau* this year. The lovely Englishwomen I usually meet here have already left. For hours on end I sit on the rocks near the sea and relate to the waves my unhappy loves, my sorry adventures. I no longer have the imagination to believe they are the Oceanids, the princesses of the sea, who rise up at times with their white shoulders and green locks to listen to the melancholy tales of a poet. Alas, princesses of the sea no longer exist for me, they have vanished along with so many other chimeras, so many other fanciful creations of my brain, I no longer believe in them. Barely do I still believe in princesses of the earth. No, I admit it to you frankly: I no longer have faith in them either. Doubt alone reigns and rules at present in my soul. Do I have a soul? If I do not, at least I have tears, I feel them flow, and yesterday I cried at the sea shore like Achilles when Agamemnon, that miserable Brazilian, took from him Briseis, the lovely Phrygian grisette. As you see, I am not yet cured of my ignoble folly . . . You laugh?

* Found in Mignet's archives by Mme Yvonne Knibiehler, who generously made it available to me, and subsequently published it in the *Heine JAHRBUCH* (1975).

Not really, you are not laughing yet, although this affair is becoming tiresome, although these reminiscences must be very offensive to delicate ears. You always remain the same, kind and intelligent. You did not laugh when you knew I was suffering. You understood very well that a wound deserves compassion when it bleeds. Blood is never ridiculous. Whether one breaks one's leg on the gleaming parquet of an elegant salon or on the filthy floor of a miserable garret, it is still the same pain. May the heavens repay you for your generous compassion. I recommend you to their particular protection; although no longer a god myself, I still have enough credit in Olympus, I am still on good enough terms with Jupiter, my father, to make him favorable to those I love. I kiss your feet.

I know that writing letters does not amuse you; it is for that reason I am not giving you my address. Do not write to me, but think of me. Never forget that when all is said and done, I belong to you, and I am worth something. You will not readily find another mirror like me, so true, so intelligent, a talking mirror which, while telling you how beautiful you are, can also give you the philosophic explanation of the wondrous nature of your beauty. In fact, Princess, no one in the world has pondered over you, has meditated on you with as much perseverance as I. Weeks on end, day and night, I have reflected on every detail of your face. I know now what your nostrils mean, how they flare with enthusiasm. I understand your lips and the smile that can appear on them, a smile whose type has disappeared from the earth and may only reappear in heaven. And your voice, what a mysterious organ, what a thrilling sound, and how many insomnias it cost me! Your hands are very pretty, more delicate than gentle, angelic yet very human, poetic and at the same time true, at once modest and distinguished, singularly touching; I cannot look at them without being moved. My word, I have made of you, Princess, my principal occupation. Would that I had seen you earlier! I lost the most beautiful years of my life in the study of jurisprudence. The time that those Roman casuists cost me I could have spent more profitably.

I kiss your feet, and if you permit your hands as well.

Your very humble and very obedient servant,

Henri Heine

That this letter was found among Mignet's papers is a sign of Cristina's eagerness to prove her fidelity. Not only would she not answer such letters, she would not keep them. Whatever she felt for Heine, and however indiscreet this gesture, her need for Mignet was more important. She could not trust men like Heine or Musset; their capacity for *amours faciles,* for *amoreggiare,* reminded her of Emilio. Mignet was as pure as an altar boy, as constant as a rock. Heine seems to have understood it all; perhaps she told him. In any case, he expected no reply, and invariably told her he was not giving her his address, which balmed his pride and eased her conscience. Instead, he wrote to Mignet who was honor-bound to answer. In December of the same year, still from his disconsolate exile on the Norman coast, he reveals his distress at being away from Cristina and not hearing from her, his melancholic attachment to her, and his revulsion for Mathilde. "You will readily guess," he writes Mignet, "and fully commend the reasons for this voluntary exile; when you see me again, I will be completely recovered, my heart purified of this painful filth. . . ." (References to Mathilde are most often in terms of "soiling," "dirt," "debasement," even when he was writing to his German friends, less familiar with his amorous calamities.) It is an open avowal of defeat to write about the woman one still loves to the man who has seemingly won her favor ("I kiss her beautiful hands a thousand times a day in my noblest dreams.") Yet only a sentiment of such depth can explain the need to establish an intimacy with the putative lover. In this light, quite apart from his gratitude for the pension, Heine's warm relations with Mignet can be better understood.

> Present my respects to Madame la Princesse. I know she does not think of me during my absence and, my word, I haven't the right to be angry. She already does enough for me by deigning to offer me a friendly smile when I am in her presence. I do not write to her so as not to provoke a reply. She is young and pretty, very pretty, and witty, and a princess, and the season of pleasure has already begun . . . and I would be a monster, a barbarian, a Hun, if I stole a single one of those precious moments by asking for news of herself. One day, when she will be only witty and a princess, and I will be her very own Ballanche,* then I will write her enormous letters and she will answer lengthy pages—but I pray the good Lord to delay that day as long as possible. Nonetheless, I must know how the princess fares, and it is you, Monsieur Mignet, who will write me that.

With Mathilde he had nothing in common save the pleasures of their bed, until he became confined to it. "She has never read a line of mine," he confided to Mme Jaubert, "she has no idea what a poet is:" Some time later, already incapacitated and temporarily without a secretary, he complained to Mme Jaubert of his despondency because he had no one to read to him, not even a newspaper. "Couldn't you ask this small favor of Mme Heine?" she asked. "No," he replied, "she can only read the selected letters of Mme de Sévigné, which is not what I need." These were among

---

* Pierre-Simon Ballanche, 1776–1847, a Lyonnais writer whose philosophy of history was influenced by Vico, was Mme Récamier's closest intimate, after Chateaubriand. The suggestion here is that Mignet, like Chateaubriand, holds first place, and that Heine will take Ballanche's second in Cristina's autumn days.

the texts used in elementary schools—the extent of Mathilde's education. What then could she possibly have understood of the anguish Heine suffered over his statelessness? In 1836, a year after the decree that banned the sale of all his works within the borders of Germany, there were subtle overtures for his repatriation, and urgings from his Parisian friends that he acquire French citizenship. "Had I been consulted on coming into the world, I would have preferred to be born in France, despite the lack of iambic blank verse in French poetry. Having been born German, one must be German."[24] To renounce his country he felt was "unsuited to a German poet who has written the most beautiful German lyrics."

The terrible tension between his nostalgia for Germany, for the language that was his artistic blood, for the readers who would be restituted to him on his return, and on the other hand his decision to remain in France, where artistically everything was frustration and compromise for him but politically and intellectually life was amenable, is revealed in one of the most remarkable letters of his voluminous correspondence. Germany meant a secure income if the ban were lifted, but it presupposed a retraction of his republican principles, a public obeisance to the government he had offended. How curious, along with their other affinities, is this analogy between their difficulties with their respective governments and compatriots. Both of them found their sources of revenue cut off for the same reason of subversion; both benefited from the intervention of Metternich, who remained a contemptuous intercessor; both were accused of appeasement by their compatriots; both refused to vow obedience or resume residence under the existing regimes; and both were equally vilified by countrymen, spies, and officials.

Writing from Aix on October 30, 1836, on his way south to Naples, he began with the ostensible motive for his letter—introductions to her friends in Naples—but in fact, merely an excuse to keep his memory alive and confide in her at great length.

Madame la Princesse!

For the last two weeks I have had the desire to write to you to ask a favor. . . . But on the eve of my departure I learned that cholera had broken out in Naples and was wreaking havoc there. Only fools rush toward useless dangers, and so I have wisely remained in Provence. I do not wish to *vider Napoli et poi morir* [sic].

Nonetheless, I regret having lost the opportunity of asking a favor; it will be for another time. I have the notion that the more one obliges someone, the more interest one takes in him. Do not forget me!

He goes on to describe his impressions of this southern city, Mignet's birthplace, surprisingly covered with snow. Among the tourist attractions visited, he was particularly struck by the four remaining columns of a Roman temple to Apollo, which now support the roof of the baptistery.

You see, even stone submits to the necessity of serving the conquering side, stone which does not even have the excuse of our human needs, which is not tormented by hunger, thirst or vanity . . . Shall I, Madame, soon make my peace, an ignoble peace with the authorities across the Rhine, so as to escape the miseries of exile and this tedious penury which is worse than total poverty? Alas! The temptations are growing of late . . . Am I not more candid than others who consider themselves Brutus or Regulus? No, I am not a Regulus. I have no desire to be rocked in a nail-studded barrel. Nor am I Brutus; I would never sink a dagger into my poor belly so as not to serve the Prussians. No. Given such an alternative, I would not kill myself, I would become benighted . . . But what do all these pointless words mean, and which might make you think that the man writing them has succumbed to the greatest misfortune, that of being unworthy of your friendship, Princess! No, most beautiful and most compassionate Princess, I am merely sick at the moment, sick in soul even more than in body: the jaundice is at present in my heart and all my feelings and and all my thoughts are tinged with that drab yellow you saw on my face on the eve of my departure, when I said goodbye to you at La Jonchère.

You would have a fair idea of the health of my morale if you knew what reaction my mind has of late to the religious doctrines I am known to oppose. My opinions are in contradiction to my feelings, I carry a garland of roses on my head and pain in my heart. I thirst for moral unity, for harmony between my opinions and my feelings; I must tear all the rose petals from my garland so that only a crown of thorns will remain, or else quell all the sufferings of my heart and replace them with new joys. But alas, I fight these agonies in vain; they are armored, and the sharpest weapons of reason are dulled against them.

And so what are you doing in Aix?

Good heavens, Madame, I have to be somewhere! I am only here in body, my thoughts are elsewhere; most often they roam around a chateau situated on a hill between Rueil and Bougival.*

I kiss your lovely hand.

You are the most complete person I have met on this earth. Indeed, before knowing you I imagined that people like you, endowed with all bodily and spiritual perfection, existed only in fairy tales, in a poet's dreams. I know now that the ideal is not a vain illusion, that some reality corresponds to our most sublime ideas, and while thinking of you, Princess, I sometimes stop doubting another divinity, which I also habitually relegated to the empire of my dreams.

* La Jonchère.

Farewell! I am not telling you my address. I spare you the trouble
of writing to me; it suffices that you do not forget me.

Your poor friend,
Henri Heine

Had the letter ended with the third paragraph ("the sharpest
weapons of reason . . ."), one might justly assume that the anguish
Heine refers to is solely related to the question of repatriation. But here
again, Heine makes a veiled analogy between his despair over returning
to his homeland and his hopeless passion for her. Critics have seen this
exclusively as an unconfessed—to anyone else—temptation to return to
Germany. He knows he can not have his garland of roses—her love, his
country—but reason is a useless weapon against such agonies. His
thoughts dwell on their leisurely days at La Jonchère, where he saw
confirmed in the reality of her being the perfection of his dreams. Having seen such a vision, he is almost prepared to believe in the supreme
being, that other divinity, who has eluded him so long. He is even prepared to love her unrequitedly rather than give her up altogether: "I
spare you the trouble of writing to me; it suffices that you do not forget
me." All he asks is that she allow him to love her, that she accept his
love. "The sufferings of [his] heart" are too deeply rooted to be replaced
by "new joys." Paris cannot replace Prussia, nor Mathilde, Cristina. He is
condemned to statelessness in art and love, to the insipid ersatz of a
borrowed country and a purchased intimacy.

There was no escape. He had already investigated the possibilities.
For Judaism he felt no affinity, and the Lutheranism he espoused out of
necessity offered no solace. Italy, much as he loved it, was even less
suited to his artistic needs than France, where he was published and
admired, where he was fluent in the language; England he had thoroughly disliked during his stay there, and America, though he had never
been there, he considered "an immense prison of Liberty" where there
was no aristocracy to fashion taste and where money was the only god.*
Short of humiliating himself before the German authorities, he had to opt
for France.

IN 1841, resigned to the impossibility of altering any aspect of his situation, he married Mathilde in an almost symbolic espousal of his fate.

* "All men are equal there except for a few million whose skin is either black or brown
and who are treated like dogs. At the same time, Americans pay great homage to their
Christianity and are devout believers. This kind of hypocrisy was taught them by the
English. . . . Profit is their true religion; money is their god, their sole and all powerful
god" (Helgoland).

Learning of Rossini's reaction to the marriage of a mutual friend—
"What joy! To think he too possesses a legalized woman, a legitimate
wife! Just like me! Now there's a thought that gives me as much pleasure as a good dish of pasta!"—Heine remarked, "Well then, let me add
to his joy that of learning that from now on, like him, I am exposed to all
the inclemencies of marriage; let him put it to music while I put it in
verse." According to Heine's doctor, who felt that medicine had no
remedy against his extravagant jealousy and insane possessiveness, his
marriage hastened the progress of his malady. As his health declined, his
jealousy increased. Mathilde's fidelity was his only collateral against total
mortification. If he could no longer keep her with his virility, he would
rely on material means. They had always been inadequate, but after his
marriage became even more so, when a cashmere shawl for Mathilde
assumed the proportion of an idée fixe. It was a life of perpetual degradation at the side of a woman who made no real distinction between her
husband and her parrot; they were treated with the same fondness. Heine
loathed the parrot so much he finally killed it, then in remorse got her
another one. "If I did not have a wife and parrot," he wrote with his
grimmest humor to a friend in 1847, "I would put an end (may God
forgive me!), an *end* as to a novel, to these nights when my chest is full
of glou-glous, and to all misery. But that is unfitting for the father of a
family."[25] Mathilde cared for him as one cares for a pet, and surely with
less comprehension. She had reduced him to less than a man three years
after they were married. Writing from Germany, where he had gone to
visit his family, he closed with *"Adieu, tranquillise-toi si tu t'ennuies trop
et conduis-toi comme le mérite/Ton chien et mari"* (Keep calm if you
are too bored, and behave as is due/Your dog and husband).*

Heine was mistrusted by his German compatriots and mistranslated
by his French friends. His private and public problems were com-
pounded by the litigation over an inheritance from his uncle which
would at least have solved his financial problems. Instead, his cousin
exacted the right to censor Heine's writings, for fear the family might be
besmirched, before handing over a pfennig. By 1850 the situation had
grown even worse. Learning about it from Mme Jaubert, Cristina was
outraged over his family's neglect: "I should like to tell Heine's relatives
that when one carries his name, one contracts two kinds of obligations—
the one that is due the invalid in care and thoughtfulness; the other, that
of gratitude toward the man whose celebrity, eminence, and glory are
reflected in the name they carry." The family did not think so. Heine fell
deeper and deeper into bitterness. His family abandoned him, his friends

* From an unpublished letter, N.a.f. 13503, ff. 1–2, manuscript collection, Bibliothèque
Nationale, Paris.

neglected him. Cristina, herself in exile far from friends or family, was horrified. "How can friends and visitors shy away from him when his intelligence has retained all its power and his imagination all its richness? Men are willing to be moved by fiction but not be saddened by the deeper impression made by reality." Mathilde was no compensation. Her tireless appetite for chatter inspired in him a yearning for a German fortress "with a sentinel before the door to keep her and other torments out. I thirst for silence." Her ill-tempered disappointment over the awaited wealth that never came only added to his misery: "My domestic Vesuvius, who was calm for the last three years, is now spitting fire." Before total paralysis set in, he complained of being drained by Mathilde's appetite for sex and money: "I always thought that in love one must possess . . . but platonic love has its advantages; it does not prevent one from dreaming by day and sleeping by night, and in any case is not so costly."[26] His sight, his body were failing him; only his wit and his lyric genius survived until the end, along with his inalterable yearning for Cristina. In 1847 he wrote to Mme Jaubert:

> In the final analysis, flesh hides beauty, which is revealed in all its ideal splendor only after sickness has enhanced the body; as for me, I have agonized to the point of skeletism. Pretty women turn in the street when I pass; my closed eyes (the right one is only one-eighth open), my hollowed cheeks, my delirious beard, my faltering walk, give me a moribund look that suits me to perfection! I assure you, at the moment I am enjoying the success of a dying man. I devour hearts, only I cannot digest them. I am now a dangerous man, and you will see how the marquise Cristina Trivulzio will fall in love with me: I am precisely the funereal bones that suit her.

This was written a year before Stelzi died. Cristina had not yet acquired her reputation for necrophilia—that was Barbiera's contribution. Nevertheless, Rudolf Leonhardt, writing today, juxtaposes Heine's quote and Stelzi's cadaver, after inverting their sequence, to make his own contribution: "Of course this is not a metaphor to be taken seriously and in no way an accusation of necrophilia. But that Heine, who was fatally ill . . . could make no better joke . . . is not a matter of chance." Ergo, she *was* the keeper of his title's skeleton, "Die Leiche im Schrank."* This despite his exonerating first sentence. What Leonhardt has failed to mention is that Heine's remarks were patently humorous, grimly humorous, in the very German style of *Galgenhumor*. His allusion is to her excessive pallor and slimness, which had long been satirized

* *ZEITmagazin*, March 1975, pp. 26–31.

as cadaverous, and to his inability to seduce her when he was still young and handsome. Under the jocular surface, with all hope of health or happiness abandoned, his ache for her still throbbed. Mme Jaubert understood this very well, for she commented: "This remark, addressed to the princess, was a bit of vengeance for the teasing that [Heine's] complaints were received with, when he tried to kindle the platonic admiration of which the princess was the object into an amorous flame. It was not without considerable jealousy that he viewed the deep interest that was awakened in [Cristina's] feminine heart by the sight of physical suffering, among others, that of the illustrious Augustin Thierry, blind and a widower. She took him to her side and interested herself in his historical writings with devoted friendship. Later, however, Heine profoundly appreciated this friendly charity and often lamented its absence during Mme Belgiojoso's long exile in the Near East."[27]

Jules Legras bemoans the fact that her counsel, the only one he says Heine ever heeded, and her influence, "which would have kept him in a more select world than the one he fell into," were so brief. This he attributes to Heine's sensuality and bad luck, "which led him to a woman as unworthy of his mind as of his heart." Were it merely a matter of the senses, then his sybaritic relations with Mathilde should have obliterated his longing for Cristina. He did not continue to yearn for George Sand, to whom he had turned in 1836 as a homeopathic cure for both his passions. The easy familiarity of their correspondence, in which they call each other "cousin," reveals nothing more than the fondness of "adopted relatives." In fact, George knew that Heine's interests lay elsewhere. Writing to Liszt she quipped: "It is said that our cousin Heine became petrified in contemplation at the feet of Princess Belgiojoso"—a remark ever so slightly touched with envy, and the gruesome humor of unintentional prophecy. Ten years later, his body slowly turned into living stone. Heine never withheld his return address when writing to George nor was he afraid to trouble her for a reply; on the contrary, he expected one. The dream passage in the fourth letter of *Französische Szene*—unhesitatingly identified by Friedrich Hirth, without any clue whatever, as a night of love with George Sand[28]—is more probably an allusion to Cristina, whose country house he had visited and to which he so often referred.

> I was dreaming of her, whom I wish not to love, whom I must not love, but for whom my passion gives me great secret happiness. It was in her country house, in the somewhat shaded little apartment whose balcony window looks over wild olive trees. The window was open and the bright moon cast its brilliance into the room, shedding rays of silver light on her white arms which so lovingly embraced me. We remained silent and thought only of our sweet misery.

The healthy appetites and willing dispositions of George Sand or Mathilde do not fit at all this scene of "sweet misery" shared by the two
dream figures. But it clearly harks back to Heine's frequent mention of
La Jonchère in his letters. His statement of 1834, "I am not in love with
her," takes on its true meaning in the opening line of the passage: ". . .
her, whom I wish not to love, whom I must not love." There must
indeed have been moments of great tenderness between them for this
"sweet misery" to have lingered so long in his memory. It was this very
misery, this shared understanding, that kept the love unchanged over the
years. Otherwise it would have been a shallow wound that healed quickly
as such wounds do. Or it would have festered into such acrimonious
sentiments as Musset later addressed to Cristina in print, in "Sur une
morte."

Heine's devotion to Cristina was so great that after "Sur une morte"
was published he never forgave Musset, whom he had admired as a poet
and enjoyed as a friend until then.[29] If others had doubts as to the
identity of *La Morte,* Heine knew perfectly well whom Musset had in
mind, having observed over the years Musset's ridiculous attempts to
seduce her. So ungallant an attack as Musset's could not go unanswered,
if but for Heine's personal satisfaction. As a poet Heine was almost
unknown to the French public until 1847, when translations of his works
first appeared in the *Revue des Deux Mondes* and later in book form.
The only writings known until then were his articles in French on the
German scene. In his *Wintermärchen,* which appeared in 1844, two years
after Musset's poem, the river Rhine complains to the poet (Heine):
"Alfred de Musset, that nasty rascal may show up . . . as a drummer
and drum all his nasty gibes into my ears." To this the poet-narrator
replies: "Don't be afraid, we'll stop his mocking tongue, and if he drums
a vicious roll we'll whistle him a meaner one." Repeating the mocking
term "to whistle," he says *"Wir pfeiffen ihm vor, was ihm passiert/Bei
schönen Frauenzimmern"* (We'll show him what lovely ladies have in
store for him). Struck by the enormity of the words *"coeur stérile"* in "Sur
une morte"—the last reproach one could make to a woman of Cristina's
compassionate nature—Heine remembered an earlier poem by Musset,
"Les Voeux stériles," which later served as the title for his own verses of
bitter disappointment, "Verlorene Wünsche," his "vain hopes" in Musset.
The poem is a direct address in the first person. It recalls Heine's fondness for Musset, so great that "I would eat what you liked / And push
away at once / The dish that displeased you / I even learned to smoke
cigars." But these dreams of a fraternal *dolce far niente* in which words
were superfluous, a glance was enough; in which Heine hoped to live
vicariously Musset's better luck (*"An dem Herde Deines Glückes /
Wollt'ich meine Knie'rwarmen"*)—all empty dreams! Musset, by attack-

ing Heine's deepest love so shamelessly, had wounded him beyond recovery.

> *Goldne Wünsche! Seifenblasen!*
> *Sie zerinnen wie mein Leben*
> *Auch, ich liege jetzt in Boden*
> *Kann mich nimmerwehr erheben.*
>
> *Und ade! Sie sind zeronnen,*
> *Goldne Wünsche, süsses Hoffen!*
> *Ach, zu tödtlich war der Faustschlag,*
> *Der mich just in's Herz getroffen.*

> Golden wishes! Soapbubbles!
> They collapse just like my life,
> I lie now in the grave,
> Can nevermore arise.
>
> So goodbye! They melted away
> The golden wishes, sweet hopes!
> Alas, too deadly was the blow
> That struck me squarely in the heart.

By the time Cristina returned from Turkey in 1855, Heine was less than half the man he had joked about in 1847: "Alas, I can only chew on one side now, can only weep from one eye. I am only half a man. I can only express love, can only please from my left side. Oh ladies, in the future shall I be entitled to only half a heart?" Buried in his *Mattratzengruft,* barely able to distinguish forms when he forced open his lifeless lids, he could not see that this ageless beauty of his memory had now been touched by time. At last she was there beside his bed, that long-awaited presence Mme Jaubert had said was "the only one that really gave him joy." And he could once again hear the melodious voice that had made him thrill, as she related her trip to the holy places he had often imagined. Mistaking his interest in the Holy Land for a spiritual awakening, she offered to bring the noted prelate l'abbé Caron. Humorous to the end, he told Mme Jaubert: "The princess brought me l'abbé Caron . . . He did awaken a few religious velleities in me, but decidedly I prefer poultices. The relief is more immediate."

Aside from the visits of a few close friends, and morphine, there was no relief but death, which finally came in February 1856. Although remembered as a poet of unfulfilled loves, Heine was also "the cruel painter of happiness and love rendered impossible not for moral reasons, but because of a physical accident."[30] Legras's analysis is subtler than he may have realized, for "the physical accident" that denied Heine happiness also denied Cristina happiness. These two victims of their unwilling bodies shared a secret dialogue they had with no one else; the sweet misery of their frustrated love bound them like the body to its soul in Heine's *"Leib und Seele."* The afterlife was all they could look forward to. During her exile in Turkey, Cristina sent him a message via Caroline Jaubert, who saw him regularly and often served as go-between: "When my time has come, enough friends will receive me on the other side of the tomb so that those who still remain should make every effort to keep well and greet me when I am able to return.—Please read this passage, I beg you, to Henri Heine. It is my reply to what he had someone write me, that he strongly desires death."[31] Shortly before his death, concerned that Mathilde was too feckless to manage without him, he assured her he would return in some other form to look after her. Terrified of ghosts, she implored him to do no such thing. "There is a woman, however," he told a friend after relating Mathilde's terror, "to whom I recently promised, when bidding her farewell, that I would come back again if atoms can manifest themselves even after death, and she is one who has the courage for it: it is Princess Belgiojoso."[32]

9

La Belle Dame sans merci

ALFRED DE MUSSET sought to enter into a love affair the way the
damned enter hell, leaving all hope behind. Since a willing victim can always find a torturer, if need be of his own invention, Musset
found one in Cristina. For Heine, she was the ethereal made real, and he
was finally content merely to idolize her. For Musset, bruised by his
affair with George Sand, Cristina was an unhealing wound. The poetic
portraits left by these rejected suitors offer a study in contrasts and paral-
lels. For Heine, Cristina and Mathilde were variations on the same
theme of *l'éternel féminin*—the Madonna and Venus—and each was
sung in fitting major and minor modes. Musset saw Cristina and George
as the twin faces of the dominating mother-woman, industrious and
self-sufficient, producing books like Ceres her fruits, judge and consolatrix, whose love he sought with the ruses and tantrums of a spoiled child.
As a poetic inspiration Cristina appears to have won out over George, for
George had once been his, while Cristina was forever out of reach. For
both troubadours, Cristina represented the same dream of unattainable
love in the Renaissance décor of a mythicized Italy. In their individual
ways, each of these blue-eyed poets fell under the magic of Cristina's
black eyes, and each proffered his love like the annunciating angel his lily.

If Romanticism can be defined as the pursuit of the self, and the
Romantic writer the oracle of this self-revelation, then Alfred de Musset
is an exemplary Romantic. It seems fitting that he should have pined for
the woman known to her contemporaries as "The Romantic Muse."[1] In
his *Confession d'un Enfant du siècle*, Musset traces his lineage: "During
the wars of the Empire, when husbands and brothers were in Germany,
anxious mothers gave birth to an ardent, pale, nervous generation." In

December 1810, two days before the German states were triumphantly consolidated into the Empire, Musset the petty nobleman was born. Musset the poet was born in January 1830 with the publication of his *Contes d'Espagne et d'Italie* into which he poured all the essences that were inebriating the youth of the day: Mediterranean lands, home of dark-eyed beauties and burning passions; Byronic heroes; wasp-waisted dandies in fitted coats and pastel trousers; tortured lovers.

Within days of his twenty-third birthday, already sworn to passion and tears, he embarked on the pilgrimage that was to become one of the best-documented love stories of all time. The events of the Sand-Musset liaison were recorded first by the participants (Musset in his *Confession* and Sand in *Elle et Lui*), then by brother Paul de Musset in *Lui et Elle,* later by Musset's mistress of a season, Louise Colet, in *Lui,* and ultimately by every chronicler of the period. Its only significance in the present context is to recall the mutilated state of Musset's heart, which may have been his strongest faculty. Heine suspected Musset's inadequacies in other areas and told George a year later that "one loves only with the head and the senses; the heart means little in love."[2] Long after, Heine remarked to a friend that "Musset was already physically decrepit and incapable of any true love when they left for Venice. Ah, what a Romeo! Even near her [George] he could not give up his customary excesses. A saint herself would not have forgiven that!"[3] Musset blamed George, however, as she herself reveals in a letter written shortly after their separation: "One day in a state of fever and delirium you reproached me with never having given you the pleasures of love."

Musset often blamed the women he loved for their insufficiency or cruelty, and his biographers continued to do so for him.* Only one escaped his recriminations, Aimée d'Alton, who had not been cruel enough to keep him and finally married his brother Paul when Alfred died. Aimée was a charming girl who received little for her devotion besides the confession of his credo: "The first experience, Aimée, consists in suffering, in finding out and feeling that *absolute* dreams are almost never realized. . . . The heart, wounded in its very essence, in its first impulse, bleeds and seems forever broken. Nonetheless one goes on living and one must love to continue living."[4] He put it more succinctly in verse in his "Nuit d'Août":

---

   * Among the more impassioned was Emile Henriot, who in his *L'Enfant du siècle,* saw Musset as a foil for ambitious women and the victim of heartless ones, the most contemptible of whom was, in his eyes, the Princess Belgiojoso: "La Belgiojoso is enchanted with this victory that places the poor boy at her mercy and whom she uses perhaps to enrage or entice her lover, the honest Mignet. . . . The nasty woman, and even worse, the silly creature! And that lasted two, maybe more, years. Useless martyrdom, without glory for the coldly cruel woman who wanted it and whose honesty cannot be discussed here." The greater fool Henriot for understanding his hero so little!

Après avoir souffert il faut souffrir encore;
Il faut aimer sans cesse après avoir aimé.*

It was not the blond girl Aimée he wanted but a woman, with dark hair and glowing eyes, capable of cruelty like the Rachels and Pauline Garcías who flashed across his horizon. Having suffered with George, and made her suffer too—"*Pauvre George, pauvre chère enfant!* You were mistaken. You thought you were my mistress; you were only my mother; it is incest that we committed"—he needed a new hair shirt, a new tormentor.

Far more significant than his debacle with George Sand is the landscape of his sentiments, in which the women he loved were most often relegated to the role of tourists. He was less concerned with the fervor of their love than with the anguish of his own.

J'aime et je veux pâlir; j'aime et je veux souffrir
J'aime et pour un baiser je donne mon génie
J'aime et je veux sentir sur ma joue amaigrie
Ruisseler une source impossible à tarir.†

(NUIT D'AOÛT)

Musset needed to weep as Rabelais needed to laugh, and he constantly required fresh tears. The genius he was ready to give up for a kiss lay precisely in his tears:

Le seul bien qui me reste au monde
Est d'avoir quelque fois pleuré.**

(TRISTESSE)

Arsène Houssaye, perceptive critic of his contemporaries, sketched a vivid likeness of *"l'enfant du siècle,"* who always spoiled things because he was impatient for the next day or had been jealous the day before. "His restless heart dislikes repose, he seeks storm after storm, but at each thunderclap starts to cry like a child."[5] The conflicting aspects of his nature—exalted hedonist and lucid melancholic—are in perpetual dialogue throughout his writing. The Byronic model, "imitated so well that

---

* After having suffered one must suffer more;
  One must love without end after having loved.
† I love and want to grow pale; I love and want to suffer
  I love, and for a kiss would relinquish my genius
  I love and want to feel on my hollowed cheek
  An unstanchable spring flowing.
** The only good I still have in this world
  Is to have cried from time to time.

Byron no longer seemed a model but a brother,"[6] provided him with a libertine dandy for his personal use and a glib-tongued cynic for his plays. Another model, far more important though never discussed, casts light on a major poetic impulse in Musset and on the true nature of his love for the princess with the terrible eyes. No poet has sung more melodiously his hopeless love, and his pleasure in that hopelessness, than Petrarch, evoked by Musset in his "Nuit d'Octobre":

> *Aimerais-tu les fleurs, les près et la verdure,*
> *Les sonnets de Pétrarque et les chants des oiseaux,*
> *Michel-Ange et les arts, Shakespeare et la nature*
> *Si tu n'y retrouvais quelques anciens sanglots?**

If Byron was Musset's model for pleasure, then Petrarch was his model for pain. For Petrarch's glorification of his torment over Laura appears as the archetype of *"J'aime et je veux souffrir."*

> Oh blessèd be that first beloved torment
> That taking me in its hold gave birth to love,
> And that bow, and that arrow which struck me,
> And the wound made deep in my heart.

> (SONNET LXI)

The Petrarchan tradition with its suggestion of Italy—often the setting of Musset's plays—clearly left a strong imprint on Musset's imagination. The Laura figure appears constantly in his writing, no matter what face his biographers attribute to it; that distant, never-to-be-attained creature to whom the poet's genius, his youth, his happiness are sacrificed:

> *Tu perdis ta beauté, ta gloire, ton génie*
> *Pour un être impossible et qui n'existait pas.†*

When Petrarch complains that Laura "guarded her womanly honor . . . in spite of circumstances that would have softened a heart as unyielding as a diamond," one hears Musset in his "Nuit de Décembre" berating the *"faible femme, orgueilleuse insensée / Partez, partez, et dans ce coeur de glace / Emportez l'orgueil satisfait."* Cristina, Musset's "princess Turan-

---

* Would you love flowers, fields and grass,
  The sonnets of Petrarch and the songs of birds,
  Michelangelo and the arts, Shakespeare and nature,
  If you did not find in them sobs of old?
† You lost your beauty, your glory, your genius
  For an impossible being who did not exist.

dot," the impassive "mandarin" of his complaints to Mme Jaubert, seems to be the reincarnation of Petrarch's unmoveable Laura. The sentiments and language of Petrarch's bitter reproach:

> You see me suffer more than a thousand deaths
> Yet up to this day your eyes have let fall
> Only anger and disdain and never a tear.
>
> (SONNET XLIV)

are echoed throughout Musset's poems, plays, and letters wherever Cristina, or her Laura image, appears. Even Petrarch's view of Laura's alternating moods corresponds to Musset's bitter jokes about Cristina's *"jeu de la balance,"* her seesaw game of retreating when he advanced, recalling him when he withdrew, or so he believed.

Most of Musset's biographers have accused Cristina of being a cruel tease, which has not been said of Laura, although both women were better known through the poets who lamented them than as real women. However, it is less the real woman than the poet's vision that matters—when poetry is the subject. "The nature of the poet . . . is to take the reality he lives and extract from it a sublime ideal which fulfills his indefinable need for the dream."[7] Through Musset's art Cristina emerges as a necessary foil for his ambivalent nature and for the creative impulse which sprang from that conflict. Emile Henriot, while reviling Cristina as a *"sèche coquette,"* unwittingly discredited Musset in his eulogy of the ingenuous poet: "To read his letters to Mme Jaubert, so gay yet so tormented, torn as he was between Rachel and Pauline García, Augustine Brohan, the beautiful Mlle C., and so many other unnamed *amoureuses* . . . not counting the shadowy pleasures, one views with regret the pointless enslavement of that still childish being, always willing to be caught, subjected to the rude shocks of the heartless flirt who led him on."[8] Henriot thus justifies Cristina's opinion of Musset's loves, which she called his "easy conquests," and paradoxically vindicates her refusal to be numbered among them. Musset's closest friend, Alfred Tattet, corroborated Cristina's view: "Alfred continues to wallow in wenches." And so without this "heartless flirt," Musset would have had to find another such figure, since no other woman played this tantalizing role in his life. As it happened, Cristina was well cast, and Paul de Musset, writing to Caroline Jaubert long after Alfred's death, prepared the way for Cristina's unmasking: "Women have always been, and continue to be, his champions. To date I have known three exceptions, and they were women he loved* and who inspired his most beautiful poetry: George

---

* All three had been his mistresses; the only real exception was Cristina.

Sand, Rachel, and the ungrateful Pauline, as he called her. Will we see a fourth join the list?"

As early as 1833, the Laura-Cristina figure appeared in his play *Les Caprices de Marianne,* published in the May issue of *La Revue des Deux Mondes.* (He first met George Sand later that month.) Already then, at twenty-three, Musset had begun dramatizing the dual aspects of his nature in the twin protagonists of the play, Octave and Coelio, contrasting them through the person of Marianne, who is endowed not only with the national and temperamental characteristics of Cristina, but with Musset's conception of how she viewed him as well—revealed in their later correspondence. Coelio, the *patito,** enamored of Marianne, the beautiful but haughty nineteen-year-old bride of an aged magistrate (a mocking allusion to Cristina's liaison with the pompous Mignet and to the inexplicability of her stubborn virtue), confides his torment to his libertine friend Octave, who offers to plead his case. Like Petrarch, Coelio had only to see his lady pass to be smitten at once and suffer the pain of unrequited love: "Woe to him who, in the flower of his youth, abandons himself to a hopeless love! Woe to him who gives himself up to a sweet reverie before knowing where his chimera will lead him, and whether he will be paid in return!" (Act I, scene 1). His letters are unanswered, his serenades unheard. Octave, who finds immediate pleasure in wine and harlots, tries to dissuade him from his folly, but Coelio replies: "Love, which for those like you is a pastime, perturbs my entire life! . . . When I see her my throat tightens and I suffocate." (How reminiscent of Petrarch's Sonnet XVI: "My lips have often tried to speak / But my voice remained strangled in my throat.") Octave identifies the lady: "I know that Marianne; she despises me without ever having seen me." Later, Octave approaches her and accuses her of having been nursed too generously on "a certain milk." When Marianne asks, "What is that marvelous milk?" Octave replies, "Indifference. You can neither love nor hate."

A letter from Cristina to a friend in Italy, dated March 1832, indicates not only that she already knew Musset but that she had little interest in *"ce dandy de Musset."* While Musset, who evidently recognized at once that Cristina was the living object of his poetic ideal—his quest for the hopeless love—reminds her in a letter of 1841 of his old *coup de foudre* and the dismay her "indifference" has caused him, like Petrarch, like Coelio. He also echoes Octave's remark, "She despises me without having seen me," knowing that his own libertine reputation, like Octave's, had preceded him.

---

* The suffering lover of the Petrarchan and Troubadour tradition; a term Musset always applied to himself in letters to Mme Jaubert regarding Cristina.

My first impression on seeing you, as you know, was a feeling of irresistible love, the first of that kind I ever experienced. I am over it, so to speak, and you would be perfectly entitled to laugh about it; it is nonetheless that first impression which has made me in your presence what I believe I have not often been in the presence of any other woman, embarrassed and abashed. Every time I went to see you, it seemed that I was going, not to remind you of my forgotten folly or to attempt to please you in the slightest way, but—how shall I say it—to delight in your presence, to recapture that impression and abandon myself to it *in petto,* at my own risk. And I did indeed recapture it when seeing you, but as soon as I spoke to you, I felt not only that *you did not know me, but that you knew me badly, that when replying to me you were addressing someone who was not I, and through my own fault.**

It is not too extravagant to suppose that Musset, knowing that Cristina and all their circle read *La Revue des Deux Mondes,* hoped to explain himself and his love in the veiled reproaches of his play. He was to use this review again to reach her in 1842, but then to air his undisguised rancor in "Sur une morte." From the beginning to the end of his long obsession with her, Musset never varied his themes: her misjudgment of him, his pathetic love, and, at least when writing to her, his perfect understanding of her attitude—although his confidante in this affair, Mme Jaubert, heard a different tale.

In 1837, in a novella entitled *Les Deux Maîtresses,* which also appeared in *La Revue des Deux Mondes,* Musset again externalized his oscillations between the ideal and the earthly. The hero, Valentin, is attracted to the contrasting figures of Mme Delauney, a sweet and simple young widow who embroiders for a living and is as candid and colorless as middle-class poverty, and Mme de Parme, a marquise by birth and marriage whose name at once suggests Italy and whose every characteristic suggests Cristina. Living independently while her husband is away for a prolonged period, she is dark-haired, very pale, plays the piano admirably, and is the center of attention at the Austrian Embassy ball—all traits taken from life. Musset goes even further; after identifying the lady, he makes moral judgments that allow him to expose his griefs in print: "The marquise was more than proud, she was haughty. Accustomed since childhood to seeing all her caprices satisfied, neglected by her husband, the only counselor who directed her in the midst of such dangerous freedom was that natural pride that even conquered passions."

---

* My italics. These lines recall not only Coelio's sentiments and Octave's conviction of having been prejudged by Marianne, but Petrarch's Sonnet LXXVII: "But when I come to speak to her / She seems to listen to me rather kindly / If only she replied to what I say."

However heartless Musset's biographers make Cristina appear, Musset's letters to her, and Paul de Musset's remarks about her, reveal the meaning of his attachment to this unyielding creature: she could serve as the model for his dream-love, as the reason for his suffering, as the excuse for his debauchery.

> *Tu te livres dans l'ombre à ton mauvais destin*
> *Quelque fière beauté te retient dans sa chaîne.**

Between 1837 and 1842 a number of poems evoke Cristina herself, his hopeless love, and his preference for the kind of love that only she can inspire. In "Idylle," a poetic dialogue that recaptures the characters and situation of *Les Caprices de Marianne,* Albert (like Coelio, the *patito*) declares:

> *Je compris que l'amour était peine inutile,*
> *Et cependant mon coeur prit un amer plaisir*
> *A sentir qu'il aimait et qu'il allait souffrir.†*

As a poet, Musset knew that desire is the elixir of life, that only in his continued longing for the unattainable could he feel himself live, could he communicate with the best in himself. Alcohol and "the shadowy pleasures" were an escape into numbness. In his last letter to Cristina, dated August 6, 1842, two months before his despair exploded into the rancorous poem that delighted generations of literary gossips, he told her what she had meant for him. His charming candor reveals not only his own sentiments but his unquestioned acceptance of hers—"With my love and your friendship . . .":

. . . In the love I feel for you, for you know as well as I that I love you, there is not, there could not be any harm in a sentiment full of respect, based on the most genuine reasons, on the noblest and loftiest thoughts. That sentiment which was born a long time ago, made me live, made me face myself, corrected me, made me better. Who knows? With my love and your friendship, God could have done something, but did not want to. Now my suffering will perform its pointless and awful work on itself, I will go away and recover, which is to say that I will lose the sweetest, rarest memory of my life, and will regain a head clear enough to add a sum. Make fun of me if you

* You abandon yourself in the dark to your sorry fate
  Some proud beauty holds you in her chains.
† I understood that love was a useless anguish
  And yet, my heart took bitter pleasure
  In feeling that it loved and was about to suffer.

will, Princess, but do not take this letter for a declaration made by
a pair of polished boots to a pair of kid gloves. If you are kind enough
to reply, I beg you to forgive me in advance; when judging my foolishness, remember that my pain is real, remind yourself that you are good
and that I am half mad.

 Adieu, Princesse.

Alfd. Musset

WHEN MUSSET'S ADMIRERS slandered Cristina as a frigid tease who
made the adorable adolescent suffer out of sheer perversity, or for the
vain pleasure of snaring a "personal poet"—undervaluing their relationship because she never became his mistress—they overlooked a salient
point when condemning her for what is considered laudable in other
women. At the time Cristina first met him in the early 1830's, Musset
was a poet of middling note (his *Contes d'Espagne* had not exactly set
Paris on fire). His pastel trousers and high velvet collars, his assiduous
presence at the Café de Paris, surrounded by the *jeunesse dorée* of the
time—which often included Emilio—marked him as a dandy, a wastrel, a
débauché. He had little interest in French politics, even less in Italian
politics, and prided himself more on his tenuous connection with Joan of
Arc than on his volume of poetry. Sainte-Beuve, an early admirer, left a
glowing description of Musset at eighteen: "blooming cheeks still rosy
with childhood, nostrils flared with desire . . . convinced of his ability
to conquer, and filled with the pride of life, nothing, at first glance, gave
a better idea of the spirit of adolescence."[9] By the time Musset turned
twenty-seven, Sainte-Beuve lamented: "Too appealing and attractive in
face and complexion to be so corrupt and spoiled to the core and underneath."

One can hardly be surprised if the princess, already known in Genoa
as the "Signora Misopoesia," whose reading tastes ran to history and
theology, was as unimpressed by the poet as she was by the peacock. His
own brother Paul testifies to Musset's social posturing: "To dance with a
real marquise seemed to him the height of happiness."[10] And even later
in the decade, one may well ask which of the two seemed the more
outstanding—the young poet, overshadowed by the literary giants of the
day, or the beauteous princess, whose salon attracted Musset's superiors
in talent and titles and who argued the future of Italy with heads of
state? One of her rare champions, with a sin on his conscience to atone
for,* mused on page one of *Le Figaro* in 1929, "Was this just any little

* Marcel Boulenger, whose fraudulent *Mémoires du Marquis de Floranges* had contributed to her unearned reputation.

woman? And should she, at his first bidding, have given herself to the impatient Musset? . . . In 1836, was it the poet or the overwhelming and glorious exile who seemed to their contemporaries to have the greater gifts?" Still another chronicler of their relationship remarked: "In the eyes of la belle Milanaise, Musset cut the figure of a lettered gentleman. For the proud Trivulzio he was too much the petty nobleman; for the learned Urania he was not enough the man of letters."[11] It was nonetheless Cristina who acquired, largely through her relationship with Musset, the reputation of celebrity-seeker and flirt. That it was the other way around is confirmed by Arsène Houssaye, who had met Musset at Cristina's house and later wrote that one had to avoid humiliating Musset by reminding him he was a poet. He had a yearning for stardom, especially in women. In George Sand he found the star of letters, in Cristina the star of society, in Rachel and Pauline García, stars of the theater. The record of his stargazing is a sorry one: each brilliant asteroid sputtered out like a meteor leaving him each time more tearful.

He had reached his ideal age at twenty-five. By the time he was thirty, Heine called him "a young man with a considerable past." The best of his poetry was already written and his health was failing. His doctor told him he would never be like other people and was condemned to a state of limbo, neither sick nor well. Musset has long been a favored post-mortem patient for physicians and psychiatrists alike. He was thought to be epileptic; he was known to be alcoholic; his abuse of spirits and sex was held to be the cause of his poor health. In 1939, André Villiers finally wove together all the diagnostic fibers.[12] Musset was apparently a manic-depressive whose dipsomania was symptomatic rather than causative of his cyclothemia, just as compulsive eating is not the cause but the symptom of a nervous disorder. The malarial infection he contracted in Venice left him with an inflammation of the aorta, which eventually proved fatal, but also caused psychic disturbances that were aggravated by the emotional stress of his disastrous affair with George Sand. Musset himself was aware of these alternating states and was afraid of being one day committed as a patient: "an asylum—I have always been afraid I would be put into one."[13] To Caroline Jaubert, his "godmother," he wrote of an encounter with a beckoning sybarite whom he had to refuse because he knew he was incapable that night, just as certain days he was incapable of any mental activity, trying "uselessly to go, to want, to attempt." Given such attacks of moral and physical impotence, it is understandable that he could have no satisfactory relationship with any woman. Quarrelsome, compulsively talking or writing when exalted, plunged in poetic melancholy or drunk when depressed—these same alternations occurred in his relationship with Cristina, whom he accused of playing *"le jeu de la bascule"* with him. The seesaw was of his own making. He made himself objectionable, then reproached her for keeping him at a distance.

January 1840 proved to be the winter of his despair. He was thirty years old and looked back on his youth with the sadness of an old man: "It is a sad thing to look back on the past and see . . . the dead hopes and dead torments, an even sadder thing to look at the future and see . . . the winter of life."[14] Cristina tried to encourage him to do something worthy of his talent, to apply himself to a serious project, instead of dissipating his health in pleasure and his energy in melancholy. As an incentive she proposed that he study Italian poetry, Alfieri in particular, as she later convinced him to translate Leopardi. He obeyed. "I am up to the neck in Italian. . . . I have found superb things in Alfieri. . . . Believe me, I beg you, that your kind and friendly visit this morning counted for much of the well-being I feel, and be convinced above all that I will never forget how much you did for me during this tedious illness."

In an extraordinary letter of close to fifteen hundred words, written in May after his recovery, he told her in "this long confession" of his difficulties as a writer: "It is a great relief for me to be able to speak to you in this free way, for I feel I am talking to a mind as elevated as it is indulgent, which in truth is very rare down here. . . . My friends, or those who consider themselves such, understand nothing of my torments." Among them were his financial distress and his revulsion for the literary marketplace. "You don't know what it is, Princess, the material condition of Parisian literature. Never, perhaps, in any time has it been as shameful as now. It is the most disgusting market one can find. . . . To get mixed up with that, display my merchandise in a feuilleton, is impossible for me." To his professional integrity he adds his moral sincerity, in an attempt to persuade her that he can turn over a new leaf—all of which constitutes a moving plea for her participation in his life.

> Now that I am thirty I know where I stand on many things, I live alone, I would like to be serene—but unhappily my past blunders have mortgaged my future. . . . I do not want to be hypocritical, and least of all with you. I still like pleasure, I even like excess, that is my nature; but, willing or not, at the present time I do without. . . . There is yet another thing on the subject of which I have often had the desire to explain myself to you. It is that when you may have thought of me as habitually dissolute, even in the past, you were mistaken. I have never had, in regard to anything, what can be called *habits*. I have spent my life changing every year or two. . . . Thus it is that, for a certain time, I was truly what is called a libertine and, since I never hide things from myself, that is what gave me the reputation I have; but I have also been other things, passionately fond,

for example, of poetry, of social life, of solitude. . . . Therefore it remains true that to change is not a problem for me. . . . But how can I undertake anything if I do not see before me a period in which my peace of mind is untroubled? How can I feel that my mind is free and active if I do not begin by feeling that it is calm?

Disheartened by his inability at thirty to foresee a future different from his past, he allowed his health to yield to his morale. A serious case of pleurisy caused fevers so high he was often delirious. Barely recovered, he asked to see Cristina, who came regularly during his long convalescence. She coerced him into taking medicines others could not make him swallow, and endeared herself to his family—as Paul de Musset gratefully recorded in his biography. Her tender nursing, so characteristic of her need to care for others weaker than herself, renewed his hope of finally winning her love. However, in July 1840, to his great chagrin, she left for her first visit to Italy in ten years. "At last there was one good woman in Paris, and she had to go far away," he grumbled to Mme Jaubert. Musset's correspondence with Cristina during her absence discloses his perfect awareness of her attitude toward him, but his coy references to his own past sentiments indicate he still kept a foot in the doorway in January 1841.

You have been kinder to me than is generally the case for a woman, and as kind as those who show me the greatest friendship, without my having deserved it in any way. *I know perfectly well that when you came to see me during my sickness, you were inspired by your habitual charity rather than by your interest in me,* but should I be less grateful to you because there is no conceit in my gratitude? . . . Ever since, I have sincerely desired to suffer all over again, in the hope of seeing you as you were. . . . There you have it, Princess, that is what I wanted to tell you, and I beg you not to take it as clumsy flattery, for it is a fact, explicable perhaps but nonetheless bizarre, that I have always been embarrassed when talking to you, and I am even now, in spite of myself, when writing to you, even now that I think I may never see you again. . . . [Italics added.]

Cristina replied in a long letter that clearly reveals her attitude. There is nothing equivocal about her tone or words, nothing to indicate a nostalgia for his love or an encouragement for its continuation, not even a suggestion that she was once the object of that love. A flirtatious woman would hardly sermonize an admirer, talk to him like an elderly aunt or a worldly nun. Her insistence on his morale, on her isolation, even the reminder of "la petite Marie," all are intended to sound clearly the F of "friendship." If Musset's histrionic outbursts to Mme Jaubert have been taken as true evidence of Cristina's vicious teasing, then her letter should be read with at least as much credence.

Locate, 11 February 1841

Your letter, which in fact I was awaiting, arrived last evening. It is I who thank you for not having forgotten me, since forgetfulness is more excusable in you than in me. You live in the midst of noise and agitation, which can deafen at least. Whereas I, living in the most total solitude and enjoying an adequate and veritable happiness, but which surely has nothing intoxicating about it, can easily remember the friends I have left. This word *friend* may surprise you perhaps, because you like many others doubtless have the habit of applying it to serious and respectable people; and you do not recognize in yourself any of these qualities. This is not so for me. A friend is someone I wish well not just as a fellow-creature. I have friends whom I esteem and whom I respect; others whom I love and for whom I am merely sorry. All are not friends to the same degree: but it has never happened to me to remove one from the place I gave him. I thus think of you sometimes, and it is always to wish you more good than you wish yourself. You complain of a timidity that I provoke in you; what would you say if I told you that I share it? Ever since you called me to your side at a serious time, you gave me a manner of right to concern myself with you; I would often like to do so in a way that is profitable for you, but I feel hindered by the fear of intruding, and by the somewhat dry and peremptory quality in your manner that seems to say, "That is all very well, let us talk about the weather." And yet, when I think of all that you waste of life and talent to amass nothing, not even happiness or much pleasure; when I think at the same time that you manifested a certain trust in me, I blame my timidity. Let us strike a bargain; do not forget me and develop the habit of writing to me from time to time: I will reply in keeping with the tone of your letter. When it is gay, even giddy, I shall avoid all resemblance to Jeremiah. But promise me also, when you feel that malaise, that weariness, that disgust which you cannot fight off, to express it frankly and to tell me the thoughts suggested by that discontent. Establish a correspondence with me and do not break the thread which will in a sense attach you to something more serious than society. That something else is not I, who am worth no more than anyone else, but is the faith in me, not through any merit of my own, but through the grace of God. You think you will never see me again, you say, and I hope you are mistaken. I remember the time when you thought that only a trip to Italy could restore your health. Such a time could return, especially if you have resumed the life that led you to such a sorry state. Perhaps your family and you even deem wise not to wait for the trouble to take hold and think of preventing it. Whatever the case, if you feel unwell again and if a change of air and routine can do you good, remember that in Italy you will find not only sun but also care. I live in a province whose air is marvelous for the chest. If yours threatens you, do not forget the gray sister* you have beyond the Alps.

You wish to know what I am doing and how I am faring? Nothing worth telling. I am surrounded by books and by poor people who are even more downtrodden than miserable. I try to improve myself with the first and to improve the second. I rarely know what day of the week it is since all days are alike for me. This life, which would kill you with boredom, satisfies me. Valentine is with my sister awaiting a husband. Eleuthère is with me and shares the care I give my poor. Little Marie (you remember her?) is growing, prospering, and enlivens our convent. That is all.

Please give my regards to your mother and your sister. Tell me if you accept the bargain and do not doubt my friendship.

Christine de Belgiojoso

Ten days later—record time if one considers that it takes almost that long for a letter from Paris to reach Milan today—Musset again tries to cross the boundaries of friendship that she had just delimited, in his typical way of grabbing her hand when she offered a finger. In a series of admirable ellipses, he warns her that her offer of a correspondence may revive at a distance the sentiments he felt in Paris. He had loved her on sight, and she found him distasteful knowing him little; she might find him no less so if he were to reveal himself as candidly as she suggests. For if he speaks at all he will tell her everything, including what she does not want to hear, namely that he is still in love with her.

. . . Do not compare the embarrassment I feel with what you choose to call timidity on your part. My "dry and peremptory manner" can only inspire repugnance or annoyance in you. My first impression on seeing you was an impulse of irresistible love, the only one of this kind I have ever experienced. . . . You sometimes allowed yourself the pleasure, very permissible and very legitimate, of making fun of that embarrassment. I might have ended by holding it against you if you were not, deep down, kindness itself, and if the good Lord while making me so maladroit, had not at least granted me the faculty of comprehension. . . . I am afraid that what happened to me close up will happen from afar. I was not known to you, I am afraid of being known and of displeasing you. . . . Diderot, whom you do not like, used to say that he knew how to say everything except good morning; I know how to say nothing except everything.

* The Order of Gray Sisters devoted itself to the care of the sick; Musset's bout of pleurisy had left his family fearful of tuberculosis.

When I wrote you once or twice during my convalescence, you immediately stopped replying because of the very frankness you encourage me to have now. The same thing will certainly happen now and will perhaps be more cruel this time. It doesn't matter, you had the thought; so long as your patience holds out I must go along with it and thank you. . . . Give me your advice, lessons, reproaches, consolations, whatever you like, whatever your kindness inspires when you have the courage to write to me, everything will be welcome, even pity, although I don't much like it. If I am responsible for something that offends you and inhibits you, I only ask that you tell me, if possible.

Of Musset's letters to Cristina, contrasted with his letters to Mme Jaubert, one might say what Musset said of his hero in *Les Deux Maîtresses:* "If there were in him two different men, they never intermingled. He found the way to be honest by never being sincere."

Louise Colet, that formidable woman best known for her long affair with Flaubert and her brief violation of Musset's privacy—he later told his family to say he was out of town when she came to see him—left two portraits of Cristina: in a biographical novel on Musset, *Lui,* and *Les Italiens en Italie.* Bitterly envious of Cristina's beauty, of Musset's passion for her, even of her role in Italian politics, Colet gives a very distorted view of Cristina in both works. However, in connection with Musset, she makes an interesting point about Cristina's personality: "She is one of those women who want above all to feel that a man is under their dominion, either because of moral inferiority or physical weakness, or even some disgrace whose secret they have uncovered."[15] This seems indeed to characterize Cristina's relationship with Musset, for though she was only two years older than he, she nursed him when he was sick, chastised him when he was naughty, sermonized him when he was wayward. A womanizer like Musset—only too reminiscent of Emilio—necessarily inspired in her a desire for revenge, unconsciously expressed perhaps by her maternal solicitude, which placed her in a superior and invulnerable position. It was Musset, however, who chose to surround himself with surrogate mothers: his own adoring one; his sister; even his brother, who protected him during and after his life (witness the omissions in his biography); George Sand, as shown in his letters; Caroline Jaubert, whom he forced into an indulgent maternal role by dubbing her "Marraine" and himself "Le Fieux"*; and finally Cristina, whom he hoped to seduce by playing the irrepressible little boy or the invalid, and whose response to nothing but his physical suffering aroused his ire. "Can you imagine this person (decidedly I am unable to name her)," he

* An archaic form meaning "son," and a corruption of *fileul,* "godson."

ranted to Mme Jaubert in one of his many confidences, "who prevents me from drinking undiluted wine for fear it will make me cough, but who applies to my head a poultice of a hundred thousand pin pricks? How refreshing! One has only to get used to it! Who knows? It might be a marvelous diet: currant syrup and torture!"

As allegedly told by Musset,[16] there was one episode in their difficult relationship that reveals a more light-hearted Cristina. The story is amusing enough to be retold, but not plausible enough to be completely believed. On the day he was to report for monthly duty in the National Guard, Musset hastily penned two notes. The one to Cristina read: *"Ma chère princesse,* You are *charmantissime* like no one else, but every day you need to skewer three or four hearts, as my godmother says. Since that amuses you, I shall come to see you tomorrow. Not today, because I stand guard for the safety of the country. Ready, aim . . . fire!" The other was written to a young woman whose boutique numbered the princess among its clients: *"Ma chère Margot,* This has no other purpose than to send you my marching orders: mere National Guard that I am, I take my post at the town hall of the tenth arrondissement. I shall nonetheless dine at Pinson's with Chenavard, unless you fetch me on the way and we go to another cabaret, where you will add your grain of salt to the stew. *Je te présente les armes!"*

Cristina, apparently intrigued by the adventure and by his sudden lapse into "tu," arrived at his house as suggested.

"Why in the world, Princess, have you come here to catch me in this carnival costume?"

"Didn't you write me to fetch you? And heaven knows what an impertinent letter! The devil take it if I understand this riddle!" Showing him the letter, she asked, "Is it not to me that you wrote this?"

Musset was not so nonplussed as to spoil such a rare occasion. Hiding his confusion, he picked up his cue: "Well then, Princess, shall we dine at Pinson's?"

"Lord no, while I'm at it I'd like to go to a real cabaret. *Alea jacta est.* Let's go to Montparnasse. In the winter there isn't a soul around, not even Sainte-Beuve. Furthermore, I'd never be in danger with a man in the uniform of the National Guard."

"I should have had myself made a corporal for the occasion. Which does not prevent me from telling you like a hussar that I love you madly."

And off they went to the *Cabaret du Divorce,* where they were immediately spotted by d'Alton-Shée (Caroline Jaubert's brother) and another friend.

Cristina was so enchanted by the onion soup and mussels marinière that she vowed to fire her chef, who gave himself the airs of a Brillat-

Savarin. Suddenly there was a knock at the door of their private salon. It was Emilio Belgiojoso asking Musset to dine à quatre. D'Alton-Shée must have been convulsed with laughter over the plot he had engineered. Musset tried to put him off by saying he would join him later.

"Open up!" Emilio shouted playfully. But Musset refused to let him enter.

"Is it that serious?" Emilio laughed.

"I am in criminal conversation!" Musset replied.

Cristina, recognizing her husband's voice, insisted on escaping through a window into the garden. Musset helped her into a cab and returned to the cabaret, determined to pay Emilio back. To his surprise, he found the prince with Margot, the addressee of his other note. Pleading boredom with his own companion, Musset sent Emilio to bring her to their *cabinet particulier*. Emilio, of course, found no one.

"So much the better," said Musset, "I shall dine with you à trois since I cannot dine en tête-à-tête."

Musset was satisfied merely to intrude on Emilio's privacy. But a moment later, Cristina returned under the pretext of an urgent message from Apponyi. The Belgiojosos departed together, and the two originally intended to spend the evening together were left alone. Too agitated over his aborted rendezvous with Cristina to enjoy Margot, he decided to finish the evening at the opera in the hope of finding her there. Disappointed, he went to her house where she was receiving other visitors.

"Oh, it's you," she greeted him airily, "I haven't seen you in ages."

BETWEEN 1837 AND 1842 Musset made many declarations that Cristina received with laughter or silence. Aimée d'Alton, Mme Jaubert's lovely young cousin, was prepared to kneel before her beloved poet. But Alfred preferred to weep at Cristina's feet. The chroniclers of the time claim that she led him on, tempting him when he retreated, withdrawing when he ventured too close. It seems more likely that he never took no for an answer. She was interested in a friendship, *"une amitié amoureuse"* perhaps, more in the nature of his intimacy with Mme Jaubert, which he described as *"un sentiment sans nom."* But Musset kept hoping for more and continued to suffer her refusals of love rather than content himself with the friendship she offered. He made a nuisance of himself, and Cristina told him so, as he reported to Mme Jaubert on October 26, 1837:

> I looked at myself and asked myself if, under that stubborn, complaining, impertinent and not very likeable exterior, if underneath, whatever *la belle petite Milanaise* says, there was not initially something passionate and exalted there, in the style of Rousseau. It is possible.

Only once did I try to give myself to friendship. It is a strange, unfamilar feeling for me, an excitation that may be stronger than desire, for this rapture cannot be quelled.

All attempts at friendship ended in the nasty pranks of a spoiled child. Unlike Heine, who loved like a man, understood, forgave, and remained tender, Musset had tantrums over his inability to win her exclusively for himself. He resented her friends' presence when he was a visitor, even going so far as to insist that Mignet be sent away after dinner when they were both her guests. No one assumed such rights with a Trivulzio! Musset was prepared to go to any lengths to attract her attention, even at the risk of angering her.

One evening at her house there was a discussion of Leonardo da Vinci's conviction that the most beautiful face could be caricatured. Cristina insisted that it had never been achieved in her case since her features were too regular. Musset, proud of his graphic talents, sketched a portrait of a heavy-lidded Roman matron with a Latin epigraph beneath: *Pallida, sed quantumquis pallida, pulchra tamen* (she is pale, and yet though pale, is beautiful).

Handing her his little masterpiece, he whispered, "Ah, Princess, how I love you!"

"That is impossible," she retorted icily, "since this is how you see me." Handing him the drawing, she added, "Here, wear this over your heart, for it is all you shall have of me."[17]

Theirs was a strange and strained flirtation, which reached its climax in 1842. In their continuous duel of pride and provocation, both were nicked. In the final reckoning, Musset wounded her twice but saw himself as Saint Sebastian. The caricature was the first wound and resulted in the loss of his opponent for a while. According to her memoirs, Mme Jaubert warned him when he made the sketch that he was burning his bridges. "But I was never more infatuated than while looking at her as I did the drawing," he protested. "Too bad," she replied, "you offended her." The next point was apparently scored by Cristina. The only details* available come from Louise Colet's biographical novel *Lui*; Musset apparently confided his past chagrins during their brief affair. The episode she relates is so true to life that she cannot have changed much more than the names—and at that with little effort, for Cristina is called "la princesse." What makes the story even more believable is that Musset looks genuinely silly, the victim of his own foolishness, whereas Colet's intention was to "villainize" Cristina—perhaps with Musset's blessing—and not to mock her pathetic victim.

---

* Outside of a letter from Musset (on page 292) in which he complains of having been her neglected house guest for eight days.

Musset was invited to Port-Marly (that much is documented; he went there a number of times and invariably returned home hysterically disappointed). As the story goes, his stay began with a poetic interlude in the garden, where he recited his poems to his hostess. From recitation to embraces seemed a logical progression, but the princess sprinted away with the poet in gay pursuit, until he twisted his ankle and lay on the ground screaming with pain, or more probably fury. Prevented from returning to Paris until the swelling subsided, he accepted his detention cheerfully, trusting that his keeper would become his cellmate. Instead, though attentive and affectionate, the princess also devoted her attentions to two other guests, "[Mignet], tall, dignified and cold; [Liszt], the little pianist, charming boy, vivacious, sure of himself, [who] seemed to be the princess's spaniel. Both of them alternately and very assiduously close to her, and I [Musset] the *patito*."[18] One day, when the pianist was accompanying the princess's song, the poet, who had been lying in the next room cursing his solitude and her two guests, dragged himself to the door of the salon and saw the princess kiss the pianist on the cheek. In response to the poet's noisy accusation of catching her *in flagrante delicto,* the princess mockingly retorted that she knew he was spying on her and wanted to make it worth his while. Furious and humiliated, he insisted on being transported to Paris at once and left in a great huff—his usual state before sending off a lachrymose protest to Mme Jaubert over Cristina's inhuman treatment.

Another fiasco at Port-Marly was related by Musset on July 26, 1842, to Mme Jaubert, who had stayed on as a house guest after his departure.

Tell me, *marraine,* can you imagine anything more inhuman than that person? She tells me she is fond of me. I, imbecile, take it on faith. I repeat to her in a half-dozen letters that she is one of the people in the world I love most. She replies: "Come." I arrive by the Left Bank, risking my life, and then for a bad joke made at dinner, a joke you yourself thought insignificant, she picks a fight with me in the middle of a chess game, which naturally I lose. She sees that she is hurting me deeply, and so she starts hitting me over the head with great blows of her charming smile between her two dimples and dirty looks that gave me a headache. No! It is not possible to be more sanguinary! *

He may have said then, as he had two years earlier, "As to HER, now that my mind is made up never to see her again, I can frankly tell you my opinion of her: I love her, I love her, and I love her very much." This ambivalent attitude throws light on his humbled return to Versailles a

---

* This letter and the others cited below were all sent to Port-Marly. Musset must have realized that the two ladies would read them together.

few days later, as advised by his *marraine*. "Your advice was good, *chère marraine*. Coming from you it had to be; but followed by me, I was very much afraid of it." As always, the irresistible humor of his letters to Mme Jaubert attenuates the silliness of his actions and reactions. One can readily understand why his godmother loved him through thick and thin, losing patience only twice during their long relationship, as we shall see.

> This morning, I climbed into a carriage with a pounding heart, but I nonetheless demonstrated the noblest character in descending the hill of Viroflay* on foot; if you knew how much courage it took for me to ring the doorbell, you would give me the Legion of Honor. When the sun rose, half awake, veiled by a few clouds, but absolutely gentle and charming, casting the purest rays around her, I began to feel somewhat joyful again, and thus burned along the way by the sun, I started to play chess by moonlight.
> (This metaphor is a bit romantic.)
> Whatever the case, the fearsome person was . . . God! how stupid words are. As for me, I think I behaved as I should, avoiding any complaint and swallowing four glasses of reddened water. I felt so sheepish that on returning home I had a milk punch. . . . But how is it, *marraine,* that I was much more furious the other day than I am satisfied this evening? How ferocious, I said to myself the other time, how cruel, how horrible! And this evening, riding back . . . I said to myself quietly, how charming, how sweet, how dear! But I repeat, I am not as content as I was angry. Now there is a low sentiment. Why? If I can venture a guess, I would almost say it is because ferociousness left me with nothing to hope for . . . whereas kindness. . . .

The situation was indeed exasperating. Whenever she was well disposed toward him he took it as a provocation, which was not her intention. And so the cycle of recriminations, reconciliation, and disappointed hopes began all over again. The summer of 1842 exhausted Musset's already taxed patience. In September, he put into rhyme all the bile he had accumulated over the years. The poem, entitled "Sur une morte," appeared in the October issue of *La Revue des Deux Mondes*. This time, the all-forgiving *marraine* did not forgive. Cristina was her friend, the poem was in bad taste, and even if written should never have been published. Much more ink flowed from Musset's pen in the aftermath than he had used for the poem, and more tears than he had ever shed before.

> Have we fallen out as well, *marraine*? Have you gone completely over to the enemy? Or is it that touchiness is contagious and you

* The arrondissement of Versailles.

are riled by a joke? I have no intention of telling you that I am right or wrong because you are too Lombard at the moment; I merely want to state a fact. . . . The fact is that I have suffered enormously and that is why I deserve a pardon. . . .

The princess Turandot . . . does not know what harm she has done me, or she would have been less ferocious.

He then lapsed into the conventional role of misunderstood male, telling Mme Jaubert of the many problems that plagued him, which he felt he could not discuss with Cristina and which, along with his uneven nature, made him irascible.

SUR UNE MORTE

Elle était belle, si la Nuit,
Qui dort dans la sombre chapelle
Où Michel-Ange a fait son lit,
Immobile peut-être belle.

She was beautiful, if Night,
Who sleeps in the somber chapel
Where Michelangelo made her bed,
Immobile, can be beautiful.

Elle était bonne, s'il suffit
Qu'en passant la main s'ouvre et donne,
Sans que Dieu n'ait rien vu, rien dit,
Si l'or sans pitié fait l'aumône.

She was good, if it suffices
That in passing, a hand opens and gives,
Without God seeing or saying anything,
If gold without pity is an alm.

Elle pensait, si le vain bruit,
D'une voix douce et cadencée,
Comme le ruisseau qui gémit,
Peut faire croire à la pensée.

She thought, if the empty sound
Of a sweet and cadenced voice,
Like the brook that moans,
Can suggest thought.

Elle priait, si deux beaux yeux,
Tantôt s'attachant à la terre,
Tantôt se levant vers les cieux,
Peuvent s'appeler la prière.

She prayed, if two beautiful eyes,
Now fixed on the ground
Now raised to heaven
Can be called prayer.

Elle aurait souri, si la fleur,
Qui ne s'est point épanouie
Pouvait s'ouvrir à la fraîcheur
Du vent qui passe et qui l'oublie.

She would have smiled, if the flower,
Which has never blossomed,
Could have opened to the freshness
Of the wind that passes and forgets it.

Elle aurait pleuré, si la main,
Sur son coeur froidement posée,
Eut jamais dans l'argile humain
Senti la céleste rosée.

She would have cried, if her hand,
Coldly placed on her heart,
Had ever in its human clay
Felt that celestial dew.

Elle aurait aimé, si l'orgueil,
Pareil à la lampe inutile
Qu'on allume près d'un cercueil,
N'eût veillé sur son coeur stérile.

She would have loved, if pride,
Like the useless lamp
One lights beside a coffin,
Had not watched over her sterile heart.

Elle est morte et n'a point vécu:
Elle faisait semblant de vivre.
De ses mains est tombé le livre
Dans lequel elle n'a rien lu.

She died and has never lived:
She pretended to live.
From her hands has fallen the book
In which she read nothing.

And so, the lovely Turandot took literally all the peevish things I did
but did not take into account the nice things. I spoke to her openly,
foolishly, clumsily if you wish, but candidly. She replied with the
calm gravity of a mandarin. . . . It is surely bizarre that one pities
a man with a stomach ache but pummels him when his heart is broken.

What upset him most of all was that the poem turned out to be a *coup
manqué.* The one reader for whom it was intended claimed not to have
seen it. Malvezzi explains this enigma by pointing out that during the
late summer the princess was unable to read because of eye trouble.
According to one of her letters of that period, she was taking large
amounts of belladonna, an anticonvulsant, which does indeed dilate the
pupils making it impossible to read. It is nonetheless hard to believe that
all of her entourage would have concealed the poem from her. More
reasonable, and to her greater credit, is the supposition that her diplomatic
silence was effected in collusion with Caroline Jaubert, who felt her
godson deserved to be punished, not pardoned. And surely no worse
punishment could have been administered than this total indifference.

So Urania* has not read the *Revue!* You don't believe, I hope, that
I believe you believe that I believe this. This kind of joke is alien to
me, and my lovely little godmother knows too well the heart of her
godson to imagine he goes in for such gags (he who only understands
neuralgia in connection with an infected tooth, something I know and
respect because it hurts like hell†). As to having a brochure under
your nose, *dove di voi si favella* [in which you are talked about], and
not opening it, *No my dear lady, I can't believe it* [in English in the
original].
    You are perhaps (I don't know, but you are capable of it) in good
faith when writing to me of this fine trait of noble pride; for, joking
aside, with all your intelligence . . . you are at least as much a woman
as I, and you do not believe any more than I what you have told me.
In any case, I will never believe it, even though you say so, not at all
and in no way, not even if it's true.
    I have wanted for a long time to write a story entitled "The See-
Saw," which is to say: "I love you if you don't love me, I retreat if
you advance, etc.," embellished with a few authentic details. . . . The
idea pleases me and, if you permit me to tell you something that explodes all my modesty, if SHE does not read it, well, there are others
who will.

---

* Muse of abstract sciences, often applied to Cristina by her friends, first coined for her
by Victor Cousin.
    † Mme Jaubert evidently ascribed Cristina's ignorance of the poem to an attack of
neuralgia, from which, in fact, she often suffered and for which belladonna would reasonably
have been prescribed.

He goes on to say with increasing irony, that he must now give up her charming little dinners, "the macaroni with tomato sauce" that he is obliged to swallow at her table, and the sight of "the little white orange pips set in currant-colored satin that serve as teeth for the person to whom you are, I don't know why, a mother." For clearly, in taking sides with Cristina, his godmother is more maternal to her than to him, who long ago secured exclusive rights. And so to melt her anger, he offers his bleeding heart for her inspection.

> But let me tell you, *marraine,* I have been driven mad. You do not know, *marraine,* you cannot know to what point I have been slaughtered, vilified, undermined, how I was summoned and neglected,* what profound, perverse and malicious coquetry was used on a poor devil who loves with all his heart, who submits like an animal. . . .

The following day, true to psychosomatic form, *"le fieux"* came down with a raging fever. When he writes to his godmother exactly a week later, he has been chastened by weakness.

> While I was stiff as a board under fourteen blankets, sweating like a pig and coughing to break the windows, I thought back to my recent verses and sincerely regretted them, but very sincerely. It is bad, it is absurd, not to have written them, but to have published them. . . . In all honesty, I don't love her any more, at least I don't suffer any more, not one bit, when I think about it . . . but I am not pleased. I wish there were some way to make amends.
>
> And so you find a way for me. Put your chin in your hand, rest your elbow on your garter, and give me some advice. It is certain that no one here thinks those lines were addressed to Urania. Neither my brother nor I heard a living soul apply them to her.
>
> See what you can do, and be assured that I do not want a reconciliation of any kind, or any rapprochement. I have had enough, now that it's over. But I feel I went too far and would like to make up for the impression I left.

To judge by his words—"I don't love her anymore . . . I do not want a reconciliation of any kind"—"Sur une morte" should have produced a cadaver. The very act of writing it and then publishing it was like a public execution. However, "La Morte" was alive and well, and maintaining a healthy silence. And since Musset's sentiments were as inconstant as his moods, the whole obsession over her was only aggravated in his inflamed mind and produced an acute logorrhea throughout the

* This sounds like an echo of the story retold by Colet (described earlier in this chapter).

month of November. It is interesting to note that during the very month
Alfred turned out his vituperative verses, his brother Paul, his long-time
confidant, wrote an unsurpassed encomium of Cristina to Mme Jaubert
on the subject of her recently published *Essai sur la formation du dogme
catholique.* The letter is dated September 6, 1842: "Many people not
knowing who the author is will want to identify the strength and the hand
as those of a man. The princess resolves a rare and intriguing problem
which has always been considered impossible, that of combining masculine intelligence with feminine grace, without ever letting these two so
opposite qualities harm one another. Since one only sees the woman in
her personal relations whereas the masculine side is totally in her writing,
it will remain a mystery for some people but not at all for you and me."
Alfred himself, in the midst of his hysteria, was also reading and admiring
the book, for he quoted a line about Origen from it to Mme Jaubert,
adding, "Isn't that well said and well felt? It's in a very serious work."

Cristina never openly acknowledged the poem but she did react indirectly. Through Mme Jaubert, the perpetual, go-between, she requested
the return of Musset's translations of Leopardi,* which he had been preparing with her help and at her suggestion, for *La Revue des Deux
Mondes.* "Can you tell me, perhaps," Musset replied to Mme Jaubert,
"what she intends to do with those pages? If she thinks of asking someone else to do the article that may be very wise but useless, since the
Revue would not publish it given the fact that I said I would do it. Are
all Italians rabid? In that case they should take garlic, which is very
effective against hydrophobia."

By comic coincidence, an admiring compatriot of the princess, also
named Leopardi (Pier Silvestro) but in no way related, had taken it upon
himself to defend her honor by turning "Sur une morte" into a hymn of
praise, which he commanded Musset to place in the very review that had
published the original. "I thought at first he was making fun of me,"
Musset explained, "but not at all. Decidedly, they [Italians] are all a bit
mad." Failing to get poetic satisfaction, Leopardi chose to see an insult to
himself in a poem Musset published in November, and challenged him
to a duel. The concocted offense was ridiculed by Musset's friends, who
assured him he would never find seconds. Musset then began won-
dering if Cristina was behind it all and asked Mme Jaubert for clarifica-
tion. If Leopardi was acting on his own, he couldn't care less. If,
however, the princess was seeking revenge, then since Leopardi was
neither her lover nor her brother, Musset would send him packing, but
would take the matter more seriously. The latter possibility was rather

---

* Giacomo Leopardi, who had died only five years before at the age of thirty-nine, was
known only to readers of Italian at the time.

appealing for it implied that he had succeeded in wounding her. This momentary palliative to his vanity was enough to stimulate his bravado: "Since it is understood to whom my verses were addressed, it would do no good at all to retract them. It is done, and I would be even more ungracious if I appeared to be turning back the clock without thereby gaining the slightest profit." Noble repentance was clearly not the motive to inspire contrition in him.

At the same time, Musset had a dramatic falling out with Rachel, France's greatest living tragedienne and one of his former mistresses. Rachel was identified by many as "La Morte" and Musset himself reported that he was told "his verses should be engraved on Rachel's tomb." To which he replied, "And so you believe I was thinking of her? . . . The good public is really quite nasty, but I find it even more stupid." The rumor was current enough so that Cristina may indeed have remarked, when questioned about the poem: "It seems that this Morte is Mlle Rachel, who would have us believe she is alive while playing the dead; it is only a passing shadow."

The combined effect of all these events drove Musset to thoughts of suicide. It was he and not his subject who was disturbed by the poem. He did not even know whether to be penitent or satisfied, since his indulgent godmother finally granted it was "a portrait of circumstance," in her attempt to end the whole affair. But Musset would be neither placated nor punished. He wanted to be justified, if not in the eyes of the princess, at least in those of Mme Jaubert. He persisted in believing that no one had recognized the subject of the poem, but also persisted in telling Mme Jaubert how Cristina deserved his ire. He was not the peevish creature whom Mme Jaubert teasingly called Prince Grognon*; he was gentle and forgiving. He never held a grudge against any woman he loved, however madly, for leaving him: "I can even pride myself in such cases on having demonstrated courage and resignation. As to a woman who would have told me quite simply that she did not love me one bit, I would have said nothing, but would not have exposed myself."

Determined to vindicate himself, he launched into a diatribe against Cristina's behavior toward him that does not stand up as an effective indictment: if she was cold and indifferent, then she should fall into the category of women who "did not love him one bit," and should have been spared his ire.

However, I have letters from Urania in which she tells me, "I thought my friendship might have served you in some way"; or she tells me elsewhere, "Near me you would have suffered, but not without some

---

* She had earlier named him Prince Café, because she found him so stimulating; *grognon* is a grouch.

comfort." I held her hand, I kissed it for a long time, and she let me.
I told her a hundred times that I did not hope to make a conquest of
her, that my vanity had nothing to do with it, that I only asked for a
friendly word to be happy all day. She believed it, she saw it, and she
kept me at her house for eight days, seeking at every moment to avoid
every occasion to talk to me, treating me like a stranger. For that she
can only have had three reasons: she did not trust herself, which I
don't believe; she made me suffer out of pleasure, knowing she ran
no risk in calming me; or she acted coldly out of pride and indifference, which I do believe. Now this is malicious and detestable.
I have more than fifteen letters from her in which she speaks of friendship. Does friendship consist of offering one's arm when going in to
dinner? What a joke! And aside from that hand left in mine, there
are a thousand things that can't be said, you know that, because one
can't explain them to others. But, you can be sure of it, she led me on
for sheer amusement, to tease me and make me play the role of
patito. You know how it is. I didn't want to, so she abused me. As for
me, I really believed in that facsimile of a friendship which was no
more than a comedy, a mere pastime, and which ended abruptly as
soon as she saw me come back and give in. That is what offended me!
First of all, she had no right to treat me that way, and second, while
doing so she was mistaken about me in a most offensive way. That is
the truth, and I shall forget it with great difficulty, though in any case
it will leave a nasty memory. Forgive me, *marraine,* this long explanation. Since *you* have some friendship for me (and I believe in that
one), you will have to endure the burden of it. I am still terribly
upset, in spite of it all, and have to chatter when I feel I am talking
to someone who can and wishes to understand me. Let us speak no
more of this.

Musset's compulsive gushing during that November of torrential
tears and words, finally led him to write to the "mandarin" directly. It is
a great pity that we do not have his letter to her and her reply. On the
other hand, his garrulous missives to Mme Jaubert are perhaps more
trustworthy in that they reveal more about Musset's true nature than his
ballroom manners with Cristina, and at the same time inadvertently reveal Cristina's responses. His own admission that friendship was the
keynote of their relationship justifies Cristina's coolness toward his declarations of love. Never having been able to make him understand that
receiving him in her salon was not an invitation to her bedroom, she
evidently made clear once and for all that she would not be numbered
among his *"succès faciles,"* that he was either too childish or too libertine
to value the friendship of a woman like her. Upon which Musset dived
into a pool of tears, coming up for breath long enough to tell his godmother about it.

Marraine!

Le fieux is undone!
Do you know what this poor soul did?
He wrote, opening his heart like a basket, hiding nothing, prettify-
ing nothing, without mollifying, without mincing, without anything
at all.
He had it thrown back at him.
He received a reply, oh *marraine*!! An UNPRINTABLE reply.
Yes, Madame. Y-E-S, that reply could and should perhaps be set
into type. It contains the most noble pride at a temperature of 80°
below zero and the most perfect tranquillity at 120° above, which
represents a force of 200 horsepower, or close to it.
And do you know what this poor beast did on receiving that immortal reply, or worthy of so being?
He (that is, I) began crying like a lamb for a half hour.
Yes, *marraine,* hot tears, as in the old days, my head in my hands,
my two elbows on my bed, my two feet on my tie, my knees on my
new suit, sobbing like a child being scrubbed, with the further ad-
advantage of suffering like a dog being stitched up (a hunting
metaphor).

He then became so vexed he "swam in the ocean of bitterness" that
flooded his room and was subsequently enraged for two hours, during
which time he thanked God for having broken nothing.

I then began to feel tired and started to cry again, only a little, to
refresh myself. Then I ate four eggs. Fried. . . . I suffered so much
I could not stand any more, which is why I am telling you all this
nonsense. . . . To hell with games of love! They are even worse
then games of chance. . . . I shall refrain in the future from any
correspondence or contact whatever with her Serene Highness, under
any pretext whatever. I will not play any more.

And yet, as before, there is hardly an interval before another missive
reveals a change of mood. "One thing that seems singularly bizarre to me
is that the beautiful mandarin disguised as a princess bamboozles you
with her great big cruel eyes to the point of injecting in you a taste for
sermons. It is certain that I am terribly in love, but I don't know with
whom, perhaps with you, and I don't know how to address this. If I
wrote, for example, To Mme la princesse Jaubert de Bel/rue Taitgiojoso
bout*/do you think it would reach Saint Germain?"

* Mme Jaubert lived on the rue Taitbout in the elegant bourgeois quarter on the
Right Bank; Saint Germain, on the Left Bank, was the traditional quarter of aristocracy from
the end of the eighteenth century.

Having wept and cursed and fumed enough, he decided on a departure, anywhere to be distracted, and left for the country to avoid any
danger of reckless thoughts or actions: "Some misfortune could have
befallen me, and will not unless the devil intervenes." It was from this
safe retreat, where he spent his days hunting, that he composed the
summation of his brief. Despite its petulant self-justification and evident
distortions—as when he says "what kind of behavior is it to treat a man
younger than herself . . ." when she was only two years older, or suggests he would have accepted a platonic relationship, or portrays himself
as the victim of perverse women who delight in torturing him—this final
letter on "the Belgiojoso Affair" turns out to be an eloquent plea in
defense of the princess! His analysis of his relations with women, and his
quotation of Cristina's remarks to him, offer a clearer insight into their
tumultuous relationship than any objective commentary. One has only to
read objectively rather than suffer with Musset, as his biographers have
done. It is commendable to side with a victim, but in Musset's case he
was his own hangman; George Sand and Cristina Belgiojoso were merely
the objective correlative of his compulsive suffering.

But *marraine,* but Madame, listen, happiness could have been mine;
let us understand each other, for I am not a fool. There could have
been between that person and me a bond, an affection which, with
time and habit, could have become a very nice thing, even without
actually sleeping together, but merely living under the same roof.
Now, however, I speak very seriously knowing myself very well as
I am: everything is absolutely broken off, finished. It will be a second
edition of my story with Rachel, whom I ditched for no good reason,
upon which said Rachel got mad, wanted it known that she ditched
me first, upon which said myself got roaring mad, exchange of letters,
commotion. . . .
There you have more or less what happened all over again on the
subject of that beautiful southern lady. I am crying over spilt milk,
you told me the other day. *It is exactly true* [In English in the original.
All italics are Musset's]. No one is weaker, more irresolute and more
scared than your incorrigible* godson, but once across the bridge,
goodbye river. C[ristina] is now as though dead for me. Comparison:
imagine an egg that one balances on one's head, fragile, delicate, but
always ready to be cooked if not broken. However, once it falls to the
ground and breaks, there is no spoon, there is nothing that can put
the yolk back inside and make it become an egg again. Such is the state
of my gentle heart.
And so, dear godmother, I take the liberty of saying—and I have
the right or the devil take me—that those women who pretend to be

---

* *Indécrottable* is more colorful, denoting uncleanable mud or manure (*crotte*).

prudes, who mistreat me, misunderstand me, make me suffer for their pleasure, and ultimately make me hate them, are fools of the first order: it is not out of interest or instinct, it is only for the fun of it, which does not fool me. What else can I assume when *Marco** writes me from the altitude of her great eyes that "the only benefit of conquests that are *too easy* is to prevent one from pursuing impossible ones."

What does she mean by easy conquests? Certainly, nothing was less *easy* than certain *conquests* (horrible word) I can think of, and nothing less *possible* than SHE. What kind of behavior is it to treat a man younger than herself like a little boy or a jaded libertine, a man who, in the final analysis, is certainly as worthy as she. What, you may ask, should she have done, give in? Should she give in at the risk of incurring the august wrath of *Monsieur*?

Musset in his final jibe regarding "Monsieur" was clearly alluding to Mignet, since the prince's infidelities were too notorious for Musset to imagine an outraged husband, whereas "august wrath" would fit Mignet's stiff-necked jealousy, well known to Mme Jaubert. Whatever Mignet's status at the time—lover or platonic intimate—he was always around and enjoyed special privileges. Since Musset found him dull, he evidently could not understand why Cristina would not yield to a younger, gayer, more seductive man than the pedantic *secrétaire perpetuel*.

WERE IT NOT for the lasting image Musset managed to stamp on Cristina's reputation, this story of their relationship might have been abbreviated. But since it left its imprint on the minds of their contemporaries, and made its way into all the biographies that followed, it has been reconstructed here in their own words for a direct confrontation with that image. The name of the princess Belgiojoso became invariably associated with stereotyped traits, much like Homeric epithets—*la princesse allumeuse*† (itself a pun on her other epithet, *la princesse malheureuse*), coquette, femme fatale, devourer of hearts—all of them faces of *la belle dame sans merci*. There is no doubt that her phantasmal beauty and indifference to passion identified her with this archetype, in common currency for centuries from the medieval romance through the poetry of Keats. It is also likely that she was not displeased to see hearts strewn at her feet. According to Mme Jaubert, "In the eyes of the princess, men

---

* Marco, an Italian ballerina, is a briefly seen but striking figure in *La Confession d'un Enfant du siècle*, discussed on page 301.

† An *allumeuse*, a dirty word in masculine parlance, is a woman who sexually arouses men she has no intention of gratifying.

formed a single and vast category divided into three amorous series: he is
in love, he was, or he must be. 'I cannot imagine,' she used to say, 'what
interest life holds for us when eyes no longer look at us with love.' "
Emilio had not loved her, but others had. Those of Emilio's stamp, like
Musset, doubtless offered her compensation and revenge for her husband's
neglect, whereas Mignet, like Lafayette, fulfilled her need to look up to
a man who could guide and protect her.

Her reputation for cruelty rests largely on the fragile stilts of Musset's resentment and on the chroniclers' taste for sensationalism. A typical example of the vignettes in Musset biographies is the one in Maurice
Donnay's *Vie amoureuse*:[19] "*La femme qu'il a sans doute le plus aimée
après George Sand c'est cette Christine qui a de la race, de l'allure, de la
ligne, de la tige et de la branche, mais allumeuse supérieure, et qui ne
s'est pas donnée*" (The woman he doubtless loved the most after George
Sand was that Cristina, who had class, style, lineage, pedigree, but was a
consummate tease, who did not give in). As though Musset's passion
obliged her to accept him as her lover! Cristina amply disproved the
argument in *Così fan tutte*—unlike the opera's heroines, she felt it was
not enough that a man desired her for her to succumb—thus making
herself doubly obnoxious to generations of Don Alfonsos by going
against the nature they determined for her.

A far more scabrous imputation than that of *allumeuse,* and far more
intriguing, is to be found in Houssaye's chapter on her in his *Confessions.* In his earlier chapter on Musset, in which she also appears, he
repeated a story allegedly told him by Musset, who stormed into Cristina's house one evening, comparing her to Mme de Montespan, who
refused Lauzun, the man she loved (read Musset), but gave herself to
Louis XIV, whom she did not (read Mignet). She burst out laughing
and led him to her bedroom. Instead of throwing herself into his arms,
she offered him to his former mistress (Sand). However incongruous,
Sand's presence in Cristina's bedroom sets the scene for a later episode
that begins: "In those days, Sappho came back to life in Paris, not knowing whether she loved Phaon or Erinna." In barely veiled terms, he
recounts Sand's affair with Marie Dorval, the blond actress who was then
Vigny's mistress.

> Every evening at midnight, when the actress had ignited every heart
> . . . at the Comédie-Française, she found on returning home . . .
> that strange woman who awaited her quarry smoking cigarettes.
> The brunette undid the blond locks. The blond undid the dark locks.
> And those locks interwove in kisses and bites. . . . But that sweet
> dream did not last; a day came when *la femme d'un quasi-ambas-
> sadeur* took *la femme éloquente* from the actress. . . . The quasi-

ambassadress held open house so that the great minds of the day could scatter their grain of salt on this passion, already so violent. . . . It was the game of hell with a door open on paradise lost. This time, there were no more blond locks. She and She were brunettes. . . . Since the quasi-ambassadress was subjected to the authority of a husband, it was quite a Spanish jealousy. . . . One would be hard put to imagine what burning epistles came and went like flames; it was the eloquence of Sappho, of Mary Magdalen. . . . Alas, all that was burned and burns still. When the quasi-ambassadress died for her sins—one must, after all, die for something—the quasi-ambassador, who did not forgive, even to the grave, condemned all this eloquence to be burned alive. The two women most loved by Alfred de Musset were thus ideally suited to laugh about his persistent passions and to comment as initiates on the maddening raptures of Sappho.[20]

The only gloss needed for this passage is to recall Mignet's mission to Madrid in 1833, when he was sent with ambassadorial status to represent France in the matter of the Spanish succession. Even without this biographical detail, which clearly identifies the authoritarian Mignet and his quasi-marital *"jalousie tout espagnole,"* Cristina is transparent behind the allusions to her salon and *"les deux femmes les plus aimées d'Alfred de Musset"*—a line Houssaye used when naming Cristina and George in his chapter on Musset. The innuendoes may have been lost to most of his readers of 1885, the year his *Confessions* were published. Mignet had died the year before at the age of eighty-eight. Houssaye, though much younger, was himself seventy by then. Few, if any, of their contemporaries were alive to contest or appreciate the libel, if they recognized the ladies, so that his revelations appear to be more gratuitous than sensational. Sand's biographers and even the writers most inimical to Cristina seem to have overlooked her identity in this passage, a rather choice tidbit after all.

Houssaye's assertion of an intimacy between Cristina and George must have stemmed from gossip of the 1830's. For in the next chapter, describing a visit with Cristina years after the Musset episode, he said, "I wanted to penetrate the mystery of her burning friendship with Lélia, but we were too far removed from those first flames of joy." However, his mention of Cristina's death suggests that he heard more after 1871. Like most gossip, Houssaye's story doubtless had some starting point in fact. Travestied or true, what does emerge is the near certainty that the two women were more than casual salon acquaintances. They may never have been lovers, but they had too many common friends and interests to have known each other only formally. Charles Didier, for example, was in Paris during the first years of Cristina's residence there. He could have provided a natural link with George, to whom he would surely have spoken about Cristina in connection with Italy. Having lived in Italy for some years himself, he was asked by George in 1833 to provide letters of introduction for Jules Sandeau, recently dismissed as her lover. Following Sandeau's attempted suicide, a subscription was raised among their friends to send him to Italy for a change of scene. It seems hard to believe that Cristina would not have been approached, if not by George herself, then by Didier or by Balzac, who knew her well by that time and was Sandeau's partisan in his rupture with George. And since all of Paris had heard about this extravagant princess, it is unthinkable that George Sand was unaware of her. They were related by a long chain of mutual friendships—Heine, Liszt, Balzac, Cristina's own brother-in-law, Charles d'Aragon, not to mention Musset. And yet, their own relationship remains an insoluble mystery.

The very absence of documentation is suspicious. It seems more than likely that written evidence was willfully obliterated, for both George and Cristina kept enough of their correspondence with everyone else, including insignificant notes, to fill volumes. Since nothing has turned up in George's papers—and she was apparently unconcerned for herself about expurgating them (she did not destroy her unrestrained correspondence with Marie Dorval on the latter's death in 1849, or with Michel de Bourges, a small-town lawyer with a family to protect from scandal)— Houssaye might be right: perhaps there was something to hide in her relationship with Cristina. Whatever it was, it was hidden with great care.

Had a single letter remained in Cristina's papers, Malvezzi would surely have cited it as testimony to a friendship between these two remarkable women, said, by Houssaye and others, to have admired each other. Malvezzi mentioned George repeatedly, but never in direct connection with Cristina—and he too had read Houssaye, quoting or referring to all passages involving Cristina but this sensational one. However, in trying to exculpate Cristina of unspecified charges, he inadvertently suggests something dubious about her relationship with George and confirms the general view of her immoral conduct. Regarding George's sojourn at the Hôtel de France with Liszt and Marie d'Agoult in 1836, he said:

> Even if la Belgiojoso did not personally participate, as a fourth, in the trio of the Hotel de France, she did have much in common with them . . . and precisely, a friendship with those who, by showing that they were as pleased to be together at the Hotel de France as in the salon of the rue d'Anjou, could lead people to believe that they found the same pleasures in either place. To be with people whose moral reputation was not unimpeachable, and not be confused with

them, was indeed on the part of la Belgiojoso an intrepid undertaking and one that necessarily had to fail.[21]

When Musset died, Cristina's letters to him were returned to her by his family. It may be that on Cristina's death, five years before her own, George received, or asked for, her letters and destroyed both parts of their correspondence, possibly at Mignet's request. It would surely have been in keeping with his puritanical character to want to protect Cristina's reputation, perhaps even more for Marie's sake than for Cristina's. It was bad enough that he had had to endure Musset's invasive presence over the years, and that Cristina had tolerated the attentions of that *débauché*. What a loss, if there ever was such a correspondence! To think that one might have been able to hear those two fascinating women talk openly about their many shared concerns—love, marriage, the role of women in society, and, not least, Musset.

To understand Cristina's view of Musset when he was less a celebrated poet than a social-climbing poetaster, one might take another look at him through her eyes. A few admired the daring and freshness of his first poems; far fewer shared Heine's opinion that he was France's greatest lyric poet. By 1840 his lyric genius had exhausted itself. Musset's great champion, Henriot, wrote: "Had he died at thirty-five, like Watteau, Raphael and Mozart . . . we would not be missing anything (except *Carmosine*). His major works were finished."[22] Whether Cristina came to appreciate his poetry or not—she did enjoy his plays, whose wit was more to her taste than his versified melancholy—is unimportant. For apart from his literary stature, there was too much in Musset the man that could not appeal to a woman who sought the wisdom and moral guidance of sober men, whose intellectual tastes netted her the reputation of pedant and bluestocking, and who distrusted philanderers. Musset, from his aristocratic posturing to his publicized amours, was virtually the antithesis of her inclinations. What may have appealed to her, in addition to the irresistible charm he was capable of at times and his persistent infatuation (for even if not reciprocated, such attentions from an attractive man are nonetheless pleasing), was the noble purpose he offered her: to change a rake into a paterfamilias, an alcoholic troubadour into a serious writer, a would-be seducer into a trusted friend—the pipe dreams of an unimpassioned woman. Like her other personal and patriotic causes, Musset might have provided one more outlet for her compulsion to devote herself to someone or something needful of her energy, her counsel, her protection—a compensation for her own physical weakness and inability to construct her private happiness.

For such reasons, it is difficult to accept the notion of a vampiric female luring a gifted youth for the sheer pleasure of torturing him.

When Musset quoted Casanova to explain Cristina's behavior to Mme
Jaubert—

> I am forced to believe that you make a cruel point of tormenting me,
> and excellent physician that you are, you have learned in the most
> accursed of schools that the true means for rendering impossible a
> young man's recovery from a love affair is to irritate him cease-
> lessly—

later readers accepted this as a sound analysis of her motives. Such an
explanation is not implausible, and it satisfies the craving for a culprit.
To posterity, the princess Belgiojoso's reputation was more expendable
than Alfred de Musset's. A beautiful woman, an Italian, eccentric, enigmatic, she was the ideal scapegoat for Musset's broken spirit. No one
thought to blame his own tormented imagination or to recognize the echo
of Petrarch's complaint:

> Oh lovely face created for my despair
> By whom I have suffered without ever being happy
> Oh sweet illusion, oh deceptive love
> Give me some joy after so many chagrins.
>
> (SONNET CCLIII)

Certainly Musset fits the Petrarchan mold far better than Cristina does
that of the femme fatale. But since Musset had to see himself as her
victim in order to justify his cruel poem, and since public attention became more focused on him than on her, this view perpetuated itself.
She was a cannibal of poets' hearts: Musset dixit.

Yet his own letters make perfectly clear that she was as consistent in
her rejection of his amorous advances as in her offers of affection and
concern. His maladies, his anxieties aroused her compassion, but she
never promised more than she was willing to give. With all his humor
and elegance, Musset remained faithful to his model of *"l'enfant du
siècle"*—self-centered, peevish, demanding, irresponsible, but utterly
charming when pampered. Had Cristina left a companion piece to
George Sand's *Elle et Lui,* her self-portrait might have exonerated her of
his accusations. Instead, she was at the mercy of Musset's lachrymose
fabrications, of the gossip resulting from his confidences, and of the
memoirs that repeated and embellished them fifty and more years later.

IT IS CURIOUS that Musset's poetic portraits of her were not examined
with similar interest. They are surely to his greater credit, and more

faithful to her. The *chagrins d'amour* that run throughout his writing have less to do with George Sand, or any of the women he once possessed and who briefly returned his love, than with his insatiable desire for love. And no woman could have sustained that desire, except one: the one he desperately wanted and could not have. Cristina was that one woman who remained a constant provocation, a reminder of his will to suffer and his yearning for purification. Torn between debauchery and idealized love, he wanted to be punished. Only a love that denied him pleasure, and even better, one that was not returned, could expiate his guilt. More than once he told her that his unsatisfied longing for her "kept me alive, brought me to my senses, corrected me, made me better. . . . with my love and your friendship God might have done something but he does not want to."

The work he is presumed to have consecrated to George Sand, *La Confession d'un Enfant du siècle*,[23] presents this aspect of Cristina in two portraits that have never been identified before, although Musset himself gives one of them away in his letter to Mme Jaubert (quoted on page 295): that of the Italian dancer Marco, with whom the hero, Octave, waltzes at a carnival ball. Her willowy body bends in his arms like a jungle vine, her languid poses overwhelm him with desire: "To excite such palpitations of the heart, evoke such fantasies, with nothing more than her beauty, . . . certain movements, the contours of a beautiful arm; and all that without a word, without a thought, without her even seeming aware of it" (p. 110).* Intrigued, he asks his host and mentor in debauchery, Desgenais, about her: "Marco is not any ordinary *fille*;† she is kept by and almost married to M. de——, the ambassador to Milan" (p. 111). The allusion to Mignet is transparent—his post at the Ministry of Foreign Affairs and his recent mission to Madrid endowed him with ambassadorial status—as is the evocation of Cristina's native city.

This nine-page episode bears striking similarities to Balzac's *La Peau de chagrin*. Foedora and Marco resemble each other so closely that they can only have had a common model. Marco, like Foedora, is described as a pale statue, "livid as a cadaver," with a "forest of black hair woven into braids." The deathly pallor and plaited black hair shared by these two figures cannot have been just a commonplace fashion of the time since those traits were precisely what Parisian society found so stunning about Cristina. As enigmatic as her Balzacian avatar, Marco so bewilders Octave that he asks her: "Are you good or wicked? Sad or gay? Have you loved? Do you wish to be loved? What do you like, money,

---

* Page numbers in parentheses refer to the 1947 Garnier edition of the novel.

† A prostitute, though in this sense more like today's "call girls"; the corps de ballet of opera houses traditionally provided young mistresses for the well-to-do.

pleasure, horses, champagne, balls? What delights you, what do you dream about?" And to all his questions, the same smile plays on her face, "a smile without joy or pain, that seemed to say 'Does it matter?' and nothing more. 'Marco,' I told her, 'woe to him who loves you!' " (p. 114).

Equally reminiscent of Balzac's novel are: Musset's hero, who, like Raphael, is obsessed with debauchery as an alternative to the impossible love; his exchange with Desgenais, who arranges for him to meet Marco, as Rastignac arranged Raphael's meeting with Foedora; the scene in Marco's apartment in which she sleeps while he watches her, with the difference that Raphael concealed himself (at once suggesting his inability to possess her), whereas Octave is rendered manifestly impotent by her impassiveness—"Strange! The more I admired her and more beautiful I found her, the more the desires she aroused in me vanished." For Octave and Raphael—and their creators—this black-haired sphinx was unforgettable. Although each appears briefly, Foedora in fact marks Raphael for the rest of his fictional life, just as Marco continues to haunt Octave in the traits of his great love, Brigitte.

The heroine of Musset's novel—always identified as George Sand—is Brigitte Pierson, a young widow of means who lives withdrawn in the country, occasionally spending time in Paris. Her great charity toward the local peasants earned her the sobriquet of "Brigitte la Rose," *la rosière* signifying the virtuous maiden who was traditionally awarded a crown of roses. "Despite the simplicity of everything surrounding her—her furniture, her clothes—one could see its up-to-date elegance; she neither cared about it nor tried for it but it was there all the same" (p. 142). Highly educated, she is also an accomplished musician; she sings and plays the piano admirably, and even composes music. Though capable of discussing any subject with ease, she is unpretentious: "At the same time that one found her naïve, one felt the depth and richness in her" (p. 142).

Were it merely a question of Brigitte's intellectual acuity, one could perhaps accept George Sand as the model. However, Brigitte's musical gifts—and to convince the reader of their significance, she is often seen at the piano playing and singing—immediately dissociate her from George, who was not known for such talents, whereas Cristina was distinguished for hers. And when it comes to a physical description of Brigitte—"pale and rather thin" with "large black eyes" (p. 135)—there is no way of recognizing Musset's former mistress. "With her pallor and her huge black eyes, I am unable to say how one was struck by them . . . it was clear that she had suffered and that life had marked her. Something in her told you that the sweet serenity of her forehead had not come from this world, but that she had received it from God. . . ." (p. 142). Nor do any of the metaphors of grace and delicacy used for

Brigitte, such as a flower or a swallow, fit George, who was short, rather stocky, and olive-skinned besides. Maurice Allem, in his introduction to the novel, comments quite rightly, "In this Brigitte Pierson it is not possible, on first sight, to recognize George Sand." It is even less possible on second sight, although Allem and everyone else have nonetheless accepted Brigitte as Musset's impersonation of Sand.

As the story progresses, Octave falls desperately in love with Brigitte but does not dare tell her, though seeing her almost daily.

> Although my love, which began the very first day, had grown beyond bounds, the respect I had for Madame Pierson closed my lips. If she had taken me less readily into her intimacy, I might have been more daring, for she made such a violent impression on me that I never left her without raptures of love. But there was in her very frankness and in the confidence she showed me something that stopped me (p. 148).

It will be remembered that George Sand and Musset became lovers a month after their first meeting, which had taken place in an atmosphere of professional camaraderie. As new contributors to *La Revue des Deux Mondes,* they had been seated side by side at a dinner given by its publisher, Buloz. And even after they ceased being lovers, they continued to write *tu* to each other, testifying to the uninhibited familiarity that marked their beginning. In contrast, the tone of Octave's thoughts and remarks about Brigitte, the character of his sentiments—so reminiscent of Musset's with regard to Cristina—are always formal, always reticent until the end of Part III. It was here, with the exchange of their first embrace, that Musset had wanted to end the novel. His brother Paul quotes him as having said: "My hero will be more fortunate than I, since I have led him to the moment of his consolation. Let us not go farther; the future would be too painful.[24] Paul, however, convinced him that a happy ending would make the novel less substantial. Had Musset stopped at the point he originally intended, the novel, as Allem recognizes, "would have revealed nothing of the love affair between Musset and George Sand." For what Part III depicts is an idyllic love that serves to redeem the hero from his dissipated past. "You are the only human being," Octave tells Brigitte, "who can make me love God." Surely this bears no resemblance to Musset's spontaneous affair with George Sand, which began with mutual desire and ended with mutual bitterness. It does however ring very true to Musset's tortured relations with Cristina, which continued for years under a halo of virtuous reform and divine guidance.

When Octave tells Brigitte "God sent you like an angel of light to pull me out of my abyss," warning her that without her beneficent influence he might fall back into his old ways; when he muses that his tranquil existence in her presence may be endangered if he broaches love—"Why more? Is this not enough? Who knows, God may have done no greater thing for me"—one hears the theme elaborated in all his correspondence concerning Cristina: the noble love that was to keep him on the narrow path of virtue. Brigitte's rejection of any mention of love, her firm response to his choked declaration and subsequent refusal to see him again, hardly evoke George's quickly won embraces. "Every time I happened to touch on that subject in passing, Madame Pierson barely replied and changed the subject." But how like Cristina when Brigitte says, after Octave has fallen to his knees, mute with emotion, and grasped her hand: "I understand, but if it is to that degree, Octave, you must leave. You have been here every day, have you not been welcomed? Is that not enough? . . . You have won my friendship; I would have wished you had the strength to keep me yours much longer" (p. 151). Nor does Brigitte's request that he space his visits, to avoid village gossip, recall the immediate openness of the Sand-Musset liaison. Nothing, in fact, suggests George, but everything evokes Cristina, just as Octave's ambivalent emotions portray Musset's feelings for her: Brigitte's tantalizing presence exalts his yearning for purity, yet her unwillingness to respond to him exasperates his patience. Octave's mystified questioning of Brigitte's behavior echoes Musset's incomprehension of Cristina's: "If she is moved . . . why such reserve? If she is merely a coquette why such candor?" (p. 167). Even the mention of Stradella and Baroque church music, frequently performed in Cristina's salon, lays Part III at her feet.

As if all this were not enough to establish Brigitte's true identity, Musset adds a humorous touch to complete her portrait. He transforms Mignet into the urbane priest Mercanson, nephew of the village curate, who has just come from Paris, where he frequents high society. The only name Mercanson drops is that of "Madame de B———, who was an angel; in her salon [Mercanson] gave sermons which were listened to on bended knee." To which Octave, the first-person narrator of the novel, adds, "The worst thing about it is that it was true" (p. 144). Mercanson has "the slow and cadenced diction that bespoke a pedant. His very carriage, which was neither young nor forthright, shocked me." So much for Mignet! Inexplicably close to Brigitte, it is Mercanson who, "in excuses as tedious as he was himself," informs Octave, no longer able to contain his passion, that Brigitte is sick and cannot receive him. There is a draft of a letter on record, dated October 18, 1834, written in Mignet's hand with Cristina's corrections in parentheses, that was destined for Musset under similar circumstances.[25] Although the final copy was doubtless in Cristina's hand, Musset may have recognized Mignet's style:

> I have received your letter and thank you for the high price you seem to set on my esteem and my friendship. I cannot say that I approve of your recent boldness, but I refrain from judging it since I do not know its motives. . . . It is up to you to prove by your conduct in the future that your motives were commendable (if they are; or at least that they were less reprehensible than one might guess). It is your actions that will justify you (or at least excuse you) and I will be the first to rejoice sincerely because of the amicable interest I have always taken in you and your situation: which tells you amply that this interest (my friendship) is not extinguished and only asks to be legitimized by your conduct.
>
> C. de Belgiojoso

There is not a detail in the whole of Part III that does not evoke Cristina or declare Musset's unrelenting love for her, from the "old tapestries" and "antique furniture" of her sitting room, to "her exalted devoutness," and "soul as pious as ardent." Even the language of the text recalls the language of his letters: Brigitte's "disdain," her "cruelty"; her irritable refusal to see him one day, then, moved by "her instinct of sister of charity," relenting the next at the sight of his pitiful sadness; the suddenness of his infatuation: ". . . to meet a woman, look at her, say one word, and never again forget her." One even hears Cristina's words when Brigitte writes: "It is three months that I have been seeing you, and one month since I became aware that you feel for me what at your age one calls love. . . . What you consider love is no more than desire. . . . I am older than you by a few years, and ask you not to see me again. It would be useless for you to try and forget a moment of weakness; what passed between us can neither occur a second time nor be completely forgotten."

The novel that Musset asked George Sand's permission to write in April 1834—"it would cure me and elevate my heart; I would like to raise an altar to you"—was not the one he began writing in August 1835. Their misadventure was merely the impetus for setting down on paper the outlines of his broken heart. "What does it matter to God," Octave asks near the end of the novel, "what livery my sorrow wears? Suffering lives within my skull; it belongs to me." The contours of that suffering were filled in with the traits of Cristina's face and character, Musset's thwarted longing for her, the impossible relationship between them that could be neither love nor friendship. Had the novel been a recapitulation of Musset's affair with Sand, there would have been no impediment to

the fulfillment of Octave's love. However, it is not until Part IV, documented as an afterthought, that Octave and Brigitte become lovers.
Sainte-Beuve, sensing the incongruity of the added parts,* regretted that
the novel had not ended with the next to last chapter of Part III, the
exchange of their first kiss. The exalted love that Musset felt compelled
to portray in Part III was an altar raised not to George but to the woman
whose love he continued to seek for the next seven years.

Cristina very probably recognized her portraits. According to Mme
Jaubert's memoirs, "The princess ended up by indulgently accepting an
unusual and poetic expression of amorous desperation." She apparently
accepted along with the others the bitter caricature in "Sur une morte,"
for on the opening of Musset's play *Louison* in February 1849, she wrote
to congratulate him.

> I cannot resist the need to tell you that you have just produced a little ·
> masterpiece. Your *Louison* is adorable in its grace and veracity, its
> finesse and sensitivity. You feel and think like Shakespeare, and speak
> like Marivaux; this is a strange amalgam whose effect is highly cap-
> tivating. You may no longer remember that I exist; no matter. You
> have found an excellent way of perpetuating your memory, even in
> the minds of the most forgetful. I thank you for the few more than
> pleasant moments I owe you.
>
> Christine Trivulce de Belgiojoso

* "The new Mme Pierson . . . is no longer the same as the first; the one who wears
the blue shirt [and trousers, mentioned earlier] is no longer the one who, somewhat pious
and very charitable, always went about in a white veil. A subtle substitution has taken place
which enters into the lack of continuity I spoke of above.[26]

10

ℒa 𝒫rincesse ℬellejoyeuse

AMONG BALZAC'S HOST of characters Foedora, *"la femme sans coeur,"* would seem to be the one that has most fascinated his critics. This Russian countess, of mysterious background but calculated wealth, appears in only one episode of *La Peau de chagrin.* Yet she emerges as a haunting figure, ultimately standing in the novel's closing lines as its central symbol: "Foedora is, if you like, society." For Raphael de Valentin, the impoverished young nobleman of undisclosed talents, she encompasses everything he desires: prestige, wealth, beauty, the spark for his untried ambition. Begging her to accept his love, he vows he will become anything she wants him to be: "Accept me as a husband only when I am a minister, a peer of France, a duke. . . ." But she does not love him, or any other man. Some dreadful experience has made her prefer life alone to misery with a husband or a lover. "Why were you not satisfied with my friendship?" she asks Raphael. "I would like to be able to console the pain I caused you . . . but love alone can repay your devotion . . . and I do not love you" (p. 169).* Raphael, recognizing that he must forget her and return to his "studious solitude" destroys himself in the process.

Raphael has not yet heard of Foedora when Rastignac announces her as *"la femme à la mode,"* the loveliest woman in Paris, with an income of 80,000 *livres.* Rastignac offers to introduce him; Raphael is at once spellbound: "How to explain the fascination of a name? Foedora. That name, that woman, were they not the symbol of my desires, the theme of my life?" (p. 113).

Careful examination of the first edition of the novel and of Balzac's correspondence amply suggests that Foedora's model was Cristina. Surely the name Belgiojoso, meaning beautiful and joyous, is more consonant

---

* Page numbers in parentheses refer to the 1959 Garnier edition of the novel.[1]

with the theme of Balzac's own life than the name of his fictional character. Foedora first appears in an early fragment, the plot outline of a poem Balzac projected in 1823. But only the heroine's name and nationality were retained for the character in *La Peau de chagrin,* who, Balzac later told Mme Hanska, was patterned after two women he had known, though not intimately. He made no mystery of Raphael's model; it was Balzac himself. The manuscript of a later work, *Les Martyrs ignorés,* in which Raphael reappears shows that Balzac first named him "MOI."[2] Raphael has the virtues of grace, early youth, and nobility that Balzac did not have, but the sensibility and talent that were Balzac's own. Raphael's dreams are Balzac's: "The conquest of power or of a great literary reputation seemed to me a triumph less difficult than success with a woman of high rank, young, intelligent, graceful. . . . I would have given my life for a single night" (p. 92).

In 1831, when he began writing *La Peau de chagrin,* Balzac was thirty-two and had not yet met the grand ladies who were to inflame his imagination and gratify his senses: the duchesse de Castries, Countess Visconti-Guidoboni, Baroness Hanska. His only successes had been with Laure de Berny, twenty-two years his senior, herself a commoner but married to a petty nobleman, and briefly with the duchesse d'Abrantès, whose title was freshly minted under Napoleon. Nor had he achieved the fame and fortune he aspired to, although his first novels were beginning to be known and he was in demand as a journalist. In *La Peau de chagrin* he could still write with genuine despair that like Raphael, whose monologues seem to echo Balzac, he was "devoured by excessive ambition." Despite Raphael's self-assurance when he compared "the new works admired by the public to those that flitted through [his] mind," he was as insecure as a child and saw himself as ugly and clumsy (p. 91). This sudden reference in Raphael's narrative to physical unattractiveness (never confirmed elsewhere in the novel) and to literary ambitions (the ruined son of a nobleman, Raphael had been trained, like Balzac, in law and was to become a statesman) further suggests the authenticity of Balzac's voice behind Raphael's words. Raphael's desperate resolve to seduce Foedora—"The heart of that woman was my last lottery ticket to fortune" (p. 121)—is utterly incongruous in a young man who has not yet lived, but perfectly congruous in a man of thirty who has not yet found love or fame.

It is curious that Balzac scholars, who rarely take at face value Balzac's letters to Mme Hanska, should have accepted as gospel the date he assigned to his first meeting with Cristina, and ignored all the contradictory clues in the novel and in his other correspondence. As late as 1838, he registered surprise in a letter to Mme Hanska[3] that "there are still people who persist in seeing a *novel* [Balzac's italics] in *La Peau de chagrin"*—which seems to imply something more personal than a moral portrait of Parisian society. In the same letter he wrote to her about Cristina for the first time:

> You have heard people speak of la Belgiojoso and of Mignet, the princess is a woman very unlike other women, not very attractive, twenty-nine, pale, black hair, chalk white, skinny and playing the vampire, she has the good fortune to displease me, though she is intelligent, but she tries too hard for effect. *I had seen her five years ago at Gérard's, she had just arrived from Switzerland* where she sought refuge, but has since regained her fortune through the influence of Foreign Affairs and holds a salon, a gathering place of wits; I went there one Saturday and that will be all. [Italics added.]

The letter is a typical example of Balzacian duplicity; he reveals the truth while trying to hide it. The verb tenses—*"je l'avais vue . . . elle arrivait"*—indicate the contemporaneity of their meeting with her arrival, which was not in 1833, as his arithmetic suggests, but at the end of March 1831. Despite his feigned distaste for her, he continued to accept her invitations for the next ten years, wrote about them to Mme Hanska, and prided himself on his *"grandes et petites entrées chez elle."* As to her unattractiveness, when Balzac ecstatically wrote his sister after he met Eveline Hanska for the first time, his only measure of beauty was Cristina: ". . . a masterpiece of beauty which I can only compare to la princesse Bellejoyeuse."[4] This was a considerable misrepresentation, for Mme Hanska, though not without charms, was a thick-necked, overweight matron of thirty-three (she only admitted to twenty-seven). Small eyes and seven pregnancies did not enhance her beauty, but her titles of countess and baroness, her vast estates in Russia, and her interest in Balzac made her very appealing to him. It will be remembered that he received an anonymous fan letter in February 1832 signed "L'Etrangère," which began the famous correspondence that made her his mistress for a few weeks in 1834, and his wife for five months before his death in 1850. The letter to his sister, dated October 12, 1833, clearly indicates that she had long since heard of Cristina, for how else would she have identified "la princesse Bellejoyeuse" as a criterion of beauty?

By mid-April 1831, two weeks after her arrival, Cristina had already achieved considerable celebrity in Paris. A contemporary writing about her some years later affirms that "Princess Belgiojoso always had the privilege of engrossing Parisian curiosity."[5] Balzac's statement that he met her at the house of the court painter Baron François Gérard is one of the few accuracies about her in his letters to Mme Hanska. He had been a faithful at Gérard's Wednesday receptions since 1829; a letter to Sophie Gay of May 1831 confirms his attendance that month. Mme Ancelot, whom Balzac is known to have frequented in 1831, also places Cristina at Gérard's in the same period: "The revolutions brought to Gérard's a host of illustrious refugees. There was first the beautiful Princess Belgiojoso, as remarkable for her wit as for her beauty, which had something particular about it that was strangely striking."[6] The word "first" refers to Cristina's arrival in Paris before the other distinguished Italians who are named later on. The paragraph furthermore speaks only of Italian refugees, thereby identifying "the revolutions" as the insurrections of March and April 1831. Mme Ancelot was also a friend of the duchesse d'Abrantès (with whom Balzac remained close after she ceased being his mistress), at whose salon she often saw Balzac and where Cristina was received as well. In a letter to her mother in April, Cristina mentions the names of dignitaries she met at her first important reception; all of them frequented all the major salons of the time, of which Gérard's was one. Mme Ancelot's account of those salons clarifies the nature of the institution: "Balzac . . . used to go to the same houses as I and came to my soirées; there was thus a certain number of people who saw each other every evening in houses where, as at Gérard's and mine, one received all through the year. . . . We had then [she is speaking of the 1830's] a true society, diverse and unified at the same time, which brought together everyone who had some celebrity in our day."[7]

Cristina recounted in her memoirs that Mme Récamier was the first *lionne de Paris* to receive her. This is extremely likely, given Mme Récamier's irrepressible ambitions for her salon at L'Abbaye-des-Bois; Parisian hostesses were notoriously jealous of their "firsts" to receive a celebrity, and Cristina was then very much the talk of Paris. Count Apponyi, the Austrian ambassador and himself a major social figure, must have been as besieged by Parisian curiosity regarding Cristina as he was by dispatches about her from Vienna and Milan during that spring of 1831. Journalists, with whom Balzac had close contacts, were intrigued by this remarkable creature whose vital statistics, marital status, and estimated revenues had swept through le Tout-Paris, and French statesmen were vociferous in her behalf. This new society of Louis-Philippe was composed of Bonapartist survivors like Mme Récamier; political neutrals like Gérard, who had served the Empire and the Restoration; anti-Restoration noblemen, who now flocked to the Tuileries; along with the jurists, politicians, writers, and artists who enlivened their salons. Only legitimist aristocracy, entrenched on the Left Bank, shunned Cristina because of her Orleanist and "republican" acquaintances, but the antiquity of her titles was more than a match for their Bourbon snobbery, and for Balzac's own.

In his introduction to *La Peau de chagrin*, Maurice Allem states:

"the character who has most intrigued [critics] and spurred investigations is Foedora." A letter from Balzac to Mme Hanska of January 1833 only serves to complicate the intrigue:

> You wish to know if I met Foedora, if she is true? A lady from frigid Russia, Countess Bagration, passes in Paris as the model. I am at my seventy-second woman who has had the impertinence to recognize herself. They are all of a ripe age. Mme Récamier herself wanted to *foedoriser* herself. None of that is true. I made Foedora out of two women whom I knew without having entered into intimacy with them. Observation was enough for me, in addition to some confidences. There are also kind souls who would have it that I courted the loveliest of all courtesans in Paris and that I hid behind her curtains. These are calumnies. I met a Foedora but that one I will not portray; and by then *La Peau de chagrin* had appeared long before.

The Foedora Balzac says he will not portray, identified as Mme de Castries, was in fact portrayed in *La Duchesse de Langeais* before the year was out. However, Mme de Castries could not have been the model for Foedora, since she was unknown to Balzac until her anonymous letter of February 1832. *La Peau de chagrin* had already appeared a good six months before they could possibly have met. As to Olympe Pélissier, "the loveliest of all courtesans," who became Rossini's wife and is commonly accepted as the model for Foedora, her favors were too easily obtained to inspire the figure of an unyielding woman. It may well have been prudence that prompted Balzac to speak of two models. The question "who?" is inevitable if there is only one, while two imply an amalgam no longer separable.

Far more important than the mere identification of the model is the impact of the model on the artist, and the artist's image of that model. For most of the Romantic generation—which notably includes Stendhal who, though older, was publishing in the 1830's—*l'italienne* represented whatever was unusual, vivacious, impulsive, passionate. She was raven-haired and marble-skinned with noble features and mysterious dark eyes that sparkled with wit. Descended from Renaissance figures in art and history, she had the sublime beauty of the Virgin, the remoteness of an angel, the compassion of a saint. She could also be as ruthless as Lucrezia Borgia, as heartless as Beatrice Cenci, as cunning as Catherine dei Medici. In short, a myth.

Into this stereotype of the Italian heroine stepped Cristina, a flesh-and-blood Milanese aristocrat, looking exactly as they had imagined her, and with a life story that was the stuff of fiction. Is it any wonder that Musset and Heine swooned at her feet, and that Balzac spent the next fifteen years clumsily concealing from Mme Hanska his fascination with her? For Balzac, as for the two poets, she was unobtainable, thus unforgettable. When Raphael complains, "That woman is killing me, I can neither despise her nor forget her," Rastignac shrewdly replies, "She is like all the women we cannot have" (p. 171). Mérimée, totally prosaic, was affected differently. Writing to Stendhal on May 24, 1832 (which proves that Stendhal must have known a good deal about Cristina before he wrote *La Chartreuse de Parme*), Mérimée tells him: "There is here a Princess Belgiojoso, a singular woman. Some people find her pretty, she's not bad but she does not please me because of her blue airs. When one woos her and asks permission to mount her, she is scandalized by such smuttiness and says she could never love a man with such low tastes. If one insists, she consents and then closes her door to you forever." The interest of this letter is its indication that within a year of her arrival in Paris, Cristina's reputation as *"une femme sans coeur"* was firmly established, even among such men as Mérimée, who hardly knew her.

Painfully aware of his squat figure and common stock, Balzac nevertheless hoped to move Cristina with his genius and sensitivity. Like Raphael, and for better reason, he could lament that "women are accustomed by I don't know what bent of mind to see in a man of talent only his defects, and in a fop only his qualities. . . . the superior man does not offer them enough delights to compensate for his imperfections" (p. 96). Lacking the beauty, youth, or station that he offered his heroes, Balzac became an intuitive analyst of the women who rejected him. Raphael, though endowed with all the requisites but wealth, has Balzac's innocent candor and recognizes that women do not wish their love to be begged, but won. Cristina never responded to the men who courted her with entreaties and bleeding hearts; her experience with her husband taught her that a seducer's heart pumps only lust. With uncanny insight, Balzac, speaking of Foedora, prophesied the only man ever to win Cristina: "She might have been dominated by a dry and frigid man"—a fitting description of Mignet.

TO RETRACE THE FACTS that place Balzac's meeting with Cristina *before* he outlined the character of Foedora, his correspondence reveals that he was in Paris in April and early May of 1831. Although in March he had announced to his publisher, Gosselin, that he was finishing the first part of *La Peau de chagrin* while staying with the Carrauds in Saint-Cyr, a letter to Zulma Carraud in early May says, "My days and my nights have been employed in extraordinary labors [*travaux extraordinaires*], and I will have told you all by confiding that I have not written a line of *La Peau de chagrin* since the few pages I wrote at St-Cyr."[8] The confession is all the more striking when compared with the novel, for the period in question—a few weeks in April—has been devoted to the same kind of activity, as intense as it was unproductive. In the novel, Raphael, after his unsuccessful suit of Foedora, locks himself in his attic room determined "to recover from my folly . . . or die. I therefore imposed on myself exorbitant labors [*travaux exorbitants*], I wanted to complete my work. For two weeks, I did not leave my attic, and spent all my nights in exhausting studies. Despite my courage and the inspiration of my despair, I worked with difficulty and in spurts. The muse had fled" (p. 170).

Driven to fantasies of suicide, Raphael accepts Rastignac's proposal of debauchery as a superior form of self-destruction. "I have found nothing better," says Rastignac, "than to wear away existence through pleasure. Dive deep into dissolution, you or your passion will perish in it. Intemperance, dear friend, is the queen of all deaths" (p. 172). This discussion—to open a parenthesis—establishes a major theme, developed throughout Balzac's *Etudes philosophiques,* of suicide through excess: the excessive cult of an ideal, be it love, patriotism, science, any form of artistic genius, or for that matter, even lust or greed. Gambara, Frenhofer, Raphael, and all the characters in *Massimilla Doni* (the diptych to *La Peau de chagrin*), are every one of them mutilated in some aspect of their being by what Max Milner terms *"l'exaltation dispensatrice de jouissances aigües"* (the exaltation that provides intense pleasure).[9] In *La Peau de chagrin* this theme is formulated for the first time: "Generals, ministers, artists are all more or less drawn to debauchery. . . . War is the debauchery of blood, as politics is the debauchery of interests. All excesses are brothers" (p. 178). Here, it is Raphael's obsession with his failure to arouse Foedora's love that drives him to seek relief from one excess in another, ultimately mutilating his will to live or to respond to another woman's love. Here too is the first statement of a corollary theme of impotence, which receives fuller treatment in *Massimilla Doni;* it emerges as a major metaphor for the artist perpetually afraid of not producing, for ambition powerless against society, for society itself rendered impotent by castrating interests.

By the twentieth of May, after two weeks of unrelenting work in Nemours, away from the distractions of Paris, Balzac informed Gosselin that he was sending him twenty-six of the promised forty sheets, "almost enough to complete the first volume, which will end on the thirtieth sheet."[10] The Foedora episode does not appear until the end of volume one in the first edition of 1831. Balzac thus had ample time to write Cristina into the novel, assuming that they met in April or early May. In fact, the novel was not completed until the end of June. It appeared at the beginning of August with a great deal of advance publicity prepared by Balzac himself, which included a reading in Mme Récamier's salon some time in July. One cannot resist imagining Balzac's vindictive pleasure if Cristina happened to be among the audience, as is not unlikely.

The text itself is the richest source of clues pointing to Cristina, particularly the first edition (the novel underwent numerous changes after the third edition of 1833, by which time Mme Hanska had become a jealous, inquisitive reader). One of the more surprising revelations regarding Foedora is that this Russian countess has not a single Slavic trait. Wherever a national adjective is used, she is given characteristically Italian attributes: her "beautiful brilliant" eyes are "veined like the stone of Florence";* her "Italian eyelids" evoke love; her "polished" skin is always likened to marble: "of a stark whiteness," "her marble forehead." Even her smile is that of "a marble statue." In the first edition her hair is black,† like Cristina's; it was later changed to brown. Another detail is "the imperceptible down that adorns her smooth and delicate skin," changed in 1835 to "*gilds* her skin," which completely alters the notion of startling pallor emphasized in the first edition. Mme Hanska was a brunette with "*la peau suave des brunes,*" as he wrote his sister. This may account for some of the later changes.

Even more pertinent to Cristina are Foedora's "thick eyebrows that seemed to meet"—a trait often noticed by Cristina's contemporaries and in itself hardly an adjunct to beauty. Mme Ancelot, to take one example, described Cristina as "very pale, with very big eyes, thick eyebrows and luxuriant black hair; her physiognomy was serious and imposing; she was very beautiful."[11] As though to underline the singularity of this trait, which cannot have been attributed to Foedora gratuitously, Balzac commented that "a rival might have criticized her thick eyebrows that seemed to meet as being severe. . . . I found passion in everything. Love was written on the Italian eyelids of this woman. . . ." (p. 119). Lehmann's strongly Ingresque portrait of Cristina shows eyebrows so pronounced and so little arched that one can indeed imagine a meeting point. This portrait, which caused no small furor in reviews of the 1844 Salon, was mentioned on April 7 to Mme Hanska with Balzac's usual duplicity: "The anti-Ingrists call it *the danger of onanism!* If you could see that white and hollowed face, those eyes that bulge out of their orbits with a fixed stare that borders on madness, you would die laughing." In April of 1844, he felt obliged to mollify his distant mistress because

---

* Balzac's notion of Florentine stone was purely fanciful, since he had not yet been to Italy at the time.

† A variant overlooked by Allem; this appears on p. 308 of the August 1831 edition.

all of Paris thought, and wrote, that *Modeste Mignon* had been dedicated to the princess, as well it may have been.*

Sainte-Beuve, in fact, was scandalized that "a person whom one may consider serious, since she wrote four or six volumes on the formation of Catholic dogma, authorizes such effusive tributes."[12] His opening comments† announced that "Balzac's novel is dedicated to *a Foreign Lady* [*à une Etrangère*] who is none other, it is affirmed, than the princess Belgiojoso." The novel itself, not one of Balzac's masterworks, is in many respects less noteworthy than the dedication. As one reviewer pointed out, "the dedication, in any case, is what first attracts attention. . . . this dedication even more incredible than mysterious." However, the novel abounds in references to Cristina: Modeste is twenty, as "svelte as one of those sirens invented by English etchers for their *livres de beauté";* her face has "the oval so often used by Raphael for his madonnas"; she is capricious and independent, scorns convention, and dreams of heroic action. There is even a reference to one of Balzac's earlier novels (whose heroine, Massimilla Doni, was yet another portrait of Cristina, see note, page 323) in his description of Modeste, scrutinized by her mother's friends: ". . . that young girl, studied by these people with the profound attention of a painter in the presence of Margherita Doni" (painted by Raphael). The dedication itself evokes Cristina at the age of twenty, when Balzac first knew her: "you who are still Beauty" (*toi qui es encore la Beauté*).

In a planned afterthought to a letter of April 9, Balzac assured Mme Hanska that the book edition of *Modeste Mignon* would settle the matter of the dedication, but embarrassed laughter betrays a guilty author: "Ah yes, I have heard that all of Paris thought *Modeste Mignon* was dedicated to the princess Belgiojoso! How's that for a joke! Shall we laugh together? I will tell the nationality in *La Comédie humaine!*"

* Originally addressed *"A une Etrangère"* in the serialized newspaper edition of 1844, the dedication reads: "Daughter of an enslaved land, angel in love, demon in fantasy, child in faith, venerable in experience, man in mind, woman in heart, giant in hope, mother in pain, and poet in your dreams: to you who are still Beauty, this work in which your love and your fantasy, your faith, your experience, your pain, your hope and your dreams are like the warp that holds a woof less ingenious than the poetry hidden in your heart, and whose expression when it animates your face is, for one who admires you, what for scholars are the characters of a lost language." The dedication was subsequently changed to read: *"A une Polonaise."* It will be remembered that Mme Hanska signed her first anonymous letter "L'Etrangère." Had Balzac really had her in mind for *Modeste Mignon* he would more reasonably have dedicated it "A L'Etrangère," thus avoiding any equivocation. His choice of the indefinite article appears to be typical Balzacian subtlety and a definite signpost *away* from Mme Hanska. Furthermore, the characteristics of the dedicatee have so little to do with Mme Hanska that it is hardly surprising Cristina was recognized by all of Paris.

† In a letter to Juste Olivier, editor of *La Revue Suisse,* who incorporated Sainte-Beuve's remarks in his review mentioned below.

Nothing prevents an author from using the same dedication twice, especially if each "Etrangère" is a "daughter of an enslaved land." Balzac
delighted in such connivings and took rather considerable pride in this
one. Two weeks after his first pacifying words, he wrote Mme Hanska,
"You will never imagine how much talk there is about the dedication. It
has caused more of a stir than the book."

Still another detail in *La Peau de chagrin* that is strikingly personal
to Cristina is the sum and currency of Foedora's income. Throughout the
novel, money is quoted in francs, except for the 80,000 *livres* of Foedora's
income. Cristina's total net revenues in 1831 were 80,236.68 Austrian
lire,[13] translated into French as *livres autrichiennes*. To make Foedora
rich, Balzac could just as well have chosen the round figure of 100,000
livres, as he did on page 49, the only other mention of this currency,
when speaking of a munificent income. Foedora is presented as a young
woman "about twenty-two, dressed in white." Cristina's age in the spring
of 1831 was twenty-two. She wore white gowns so often that portraits of
her, verbal or painted, always make note of it. Théophile Gautier, in his
caricature of her as "that bluestocking known as *la marquise romantique,"** says that "she would be merely pale, if instead of white she wore
red."

Cristina's striking appearance commanded attention wherever she
went. Even women—like Mme d'Agoult, who was no admirer of hers, or
Mme Ancelot, who was—recorded that when she came into a room all
eyes turned to her. "I often met the princess in many houses and her
appearance always struck me; I could not tear my eyes from her. . . .
She did not attract me, she stunned me. One evening she appeared
while Nourrit [a famous singer] was holding the public under the spell
of his contagious melancholy, dressed in a white silk gown trimmed with
jet. Her extraordinary pallor, her gown, her huge eyes black and bright,
her tall slim figure, everything combined to give her the aspect of an
apparition. . . . The sight was captivating."[14] Foedora is described,
more succinctly, at the opera as "a spectacle within a spectacle." Foedora's movements, in contradiction to her langorous beauty, are lacking
in "anything soft or amorous. . . . there was something abrupt and eccentric about them." Rodolphe Apponyi, who as a proper Austrian official was more scandalized than captivated by his emperor's contumacious
subject, commented that Cristina's "walk and her every movement are in
harmony with the role she plays: sad and bizarre state of a woman whose
mentality has gone awry."[15]

As though to make the identity unmistakable, at least for his own
secret pleasure, Balzac inserted an inconsistency that can only have been

---

* Cristina had in fact been dubbed "La Muse Romantique."

deliberate. Just as Raphael is about to be introduced to Foedora, whose title of "countess" has already been mentioned and remains constant throughout, Rastignac warns him: "Do not appear to be too over-whelmed by the princess." Although a blatant discrepancy, this was not changed despite all the corrections Balzac made in the next six editions. Earlier, Raphael has said, speaking of Pauline, a poor girl who loves him, "To have the manners of a princess, one must be rich. In the light of my romantic fantasies, what indeed was Pauline?" Elsewhere in the novel when a title is used figuratively, it is that of queen. Here, "prin-cess" marks the difference between Pauline and Foedora—both inspired by real women, one of whom *was* a princess. Pauline's reality was con-firmed by Balzac in a letter to Mme de Castries: "Pauline exists and very much so." Her spiritual model was Laure de Berny, then fifty-three, Balzac's no longer desirable but still devoted former mistress. Her love was a comfort and her means adequate for a petty title in the provinces, but hardly commensurate with Balzac's "romantic fantasies," whereas Princess Belgiojoso's 80,000 *livres* could well provide "the manners of a princess."

Foedora is characterized as an "enigma"—the substantive most repetitively applied to Cristina by all who ever wrote about her. Foe-dora's past is never revealed, but after Raphael's first brief meeting with her, he speculates that perhaps "the memory of her early marriage gave her a horror of love" (p. 120). All we ever know is that she is "rich, without a lover, and resistant to Parisian seductions," and has arrived in Paris not long before we meet her: "Since my return to France my for-tune has tempted some young men," she says. Raphael is at once in-flamed: "Was this not the incarnation of my hopes, my visions? I created for myself a woman, I sketched her in my mind, I dreamed her."

In comparing the first and later editions of *La Peau de chagrin,* perhaps more significant than the altered physical details is the change in Raphael's optic. In 1831 he sees Foedora with the long-distance lens of a complete stranger. By 1835 his imagination no longer "sketches" the lines; he has seen her close up and knows the finer points. All of Raphael's judgments in 1831 are speculative: "There was surely a novel in that woman." In 1835 this became "This was more than a woman, this was a novel," just as "the promises made to love that I read into this structure" later became "the promises that this rich structure made to love." As Balzac came to know Cristina more familiarly, Raphael's early conjectures changed to certainties. Already in 1831, however, Raphael recognized that "one needed an observation as sagacious as mine to dis-cover in this nature the signs that marked her for sensuality," implying that her sensuality lay only within the realm of his wishful thinking. Like the countless stalwarts who went out to daunt the Sphinx, each of Cristina's suitors thought he could awaken her. Balzac evidently shared their dream.

Raphael saw two conflicting women in Foedora: one was cold while the other, at least behind her brilliant eyes, was passionate: "the head alone seemed to be amorous" (p. 119). In their first private conversation, his lover's observation galvanizes his analytical mind—"that alliance of veritable idolatry and scientific love." He proposes to seek with her "that psychological anomaly" (p. 128) which caused her disinterest in love. She has told him that her pride might have been satisfied by the many declarations she received, but that she has "never seen again the persons who were ill-inspired enough to have spoken of love" to her. (How curiously reminiscent of Mérimée's remarks to Stendhal.) However, her affection for Raphael is sincere enough to give him this warning which, she explains, "stems more from friendship than pride." She hopes he will "appreciate the solidity of the affection I offer my friends. . . . I would give them my life, but you would despise me if I tolerated a love I did not share."

These are the very words Cristina used to similarly bewitched suitors, such as Heine and Musset. In fact, the similarity of sentiment and expression, recorded in Cristina's letters or paraphrased in letters to her, seems too great to be coincidental. Balzac must have heard these same arguments from her own lips. They are certainly not the arguments ordinarily used to ward off undesired attention, and particularly not by a Foedora, whose consummate coquetry is established at the outset by Rastignac. Foedora's incongruities can only be explained by the hasty grafting of real traits and words onto a sketchy fictional character. When Balzac wrote *Massimilla Doni,* he included a critique that covers this very problem in *La Peau de chagrin*: "When the artist has the misfortune to be filled with the passion he wishes to express, he will not be able to paint it. Art proceeds from the brain and not the heart. When your subject dominates you, you are its slave and not the master."[16] The two works, seemingly unrelated, were clearly connected in his mind, as revealed in a letter to Mme Hanska: "If I can realize all my ideas . . . it [*Massimilla Doni*] will be as overwhelming a book as *La Peau de chagrin,* better written, more poetic perhaps."[17]

In 1831 Balzac was too close to his experience; the Foedora episode appears to have been written at full speed immediately after his encounter with Cristina. But Massimilla Doni, for whom Cristina once again served as model, was conceived without passionate involvement, for by 1837 Balzac had recovered from his infatuation and could manipulate his fascination with artistry. There are traces of Cristina in many other characters as well, but only Foedora and Massimilla, because of their verisimilitude, their thematic significance, and their kinship warrant analysis here.,

Foedora's confessions to Raphael are strikingly evocative of Cristina. Foedora's candor only exasperates him: "To be tortured by a woman who does not think she makes you suffer, is that not an atrocious torture?" (This was Musset's complaint in 1840.) Yet he continues his clinical approach. She is "the only woman with whom [he] can discuss philosophically a resolution so contrary to the laws of nature." He asks if she was "mistreated by love the first time. . . . Do you have imperfections that make you virtuous in spite of yourself? . . . Nature, who has made people blind at birth, can surely create women who are deaf, dumb, and blind in love. Truly, you are a precious subject for medical observation!" (p. 128). Balzac was indeed a gifted diagnostician, for not until the late 1950's was the relationship between epilepsy and hyposexuality determined, and then in much the same way that Balzac had stated it: the absence of a faculty, sexual inappetence in this case being no different from the lack of vision or hearing. When one adds to these remarks Raphael's description of Foedora's glance, "as though something mysterious happened inside her, one might say a convulsion"—convulsion being the last simile imaginable for the eyes of a beautiful woman—and Balzac's sympathetic letter about Cristina to Mme Hanska, "she has had maladies. . . . one must render her this justice that she had them from the prince,"* it becomes apparent that Balzac knew very early the secrets of this "feminine mystery" that he named Foedora.

Foedora completes Cristina's portrait by replying, "Better to be dead than unhappy," when Raphael asks if she ever considered that a desperate man might kill the woman he loves. "A man that passionate," she answers, "must one day abandon his wife and leave her impoverished after having devoured her fortune." Raphael understandably comments, "This arithmetic baffled me" (p. 129). As it does the reader as well! For Raphael has been speaking of assassinating the mistress who scorns him, whereas Foedora speaks of a wife and a dissipated fortune. In 1831 close to half of Cristina's revenues went to pay off Emilio's debts, an arrangement to which she had agreed in 1828 as a condition of her freedom after discovering that he had infected her with syphilis. Only someone who knew the circumstances of Cristina's situation; had learned about the maladies that were quite rightly the cause of her "virtue"; had been as captivated as Raphael—"it was no longer an admiration, a desire, but a spell"—only such a person could have inserted details so inapposite to

---

* Letter of March 2, 1844, to which he added: "that alone would make me flee a thousand leagues the provocations of a woman; but she is loved, at the moment, by many."

the Russian countess first announced, or for that matter dialogues so uncharacteristic of any courtship. Foedora is so like Cristina, physically and morally, that it is difficult to understand why this identification was not made earlier, even without the certain knowledge that they could have met in April 1831. Far wilder guesses fill the pages of literary history. Balzac, evidently familiar with literary transformations, thought he recognized Cristina in Stendhal's Sanseverina, whom she resembles far less than his own creations. Stendhal cryptically assured Balzac that he had never seen her ("*Je ne l'ai jamais vue*"), which is not to say that he had never heard of her, or that hearsay alone might not have affected his thinking when conceiving the character. Balzac, still unconvinced, sent Cristina a copy of *La Chartreuse de Parme* in the hope that she might confirm his guess. Her reply was disappointing: "I return *La Chartreuse,* Monsieur, with all my thanks. I have read it with infinite pleasure while allowing myself not to recognize the accuracy of certain portraits. There are no *Italiennes* as active as the duchess, nor *Italiens* as immobile as the count. Movement and repose follow each other *chez nous* at shorter intervals. One is fatigued by the one; one is bored by the other; one perseveres in nothing."

From our very first glimpse of Foedora, Balzac seems to establish deliberate similarities between Foedora and Cristina, Raphael and himself. She is "frail and graceful," she leans coquettishly against the door frame "like a woman about to fall or flee," which instantly evokes Cristina's fragile figure and one of her characteristic poses. Raphael says that Foedora has a "heart of bronze" and Rastignac that "she is imperious like all women who have pleasure only in their head." What is surprising is that Balzac should have seen so quickly the traits that would define Cristina for the rest of her life, and long after. Balzac himself repeated this judgment of Cristina in a letter to Mme Hanska thirteen years after creating Foedora: "She is . . . very *impératrice,* with no thought of the past [a rancorous allusion to their intimate conversations of 1831?], neither granting nor permitting any right while giving, or lending if you wish, herself. She is a courtesan . . . but horribly bluestocking."[18] This same unreconcilable contradiction between the imperious bluestocking and the courtesan exists in Foedora. Though unresponsive to love and capable only of mental pleasures, she leads the artificial life of a coquette, perpetually surrounded by admiring men, bereft of any private existence. Raphael remarks on the "artists, diplomats, and men of power" who always hover around her; "she gave herself to no one so as to keep them all. A woman is coquettish so long as she loves no one" (p. 120). Had Musset identified Foedora by the time he accused Cristina of the very same behavior, or was Foedora, already in 1831, a life mask of Cristina as she would be seen by her admirers for the next decade? Had

Cristina donned the mask Balzac laid at her feet, or was she its existential model? To judge from her most authentic image, her letters, it is hard to believe that her true components were bronze and marble. But for a Musset, or for Balzac in 1831, how much easier to explain her away as a coquette than accuse themselves of being inadequate to her deeper needs as a woman?

As to the hero's likeness to the author, although Raphael has no professional activity besides ghost-writing some obscure memoirs based on his aunt's years at court, he nonetheless adds himself to Foedora's "menagerie of scholars" when explaining her initial interest in him: "Foedora saw in me some future celebrity." This was true of Balzac in 1831, but stridently absurd with regard to Raphael, whose future is as ill-defined as his past. What Raphael saw in Foedora is what Balzac thought he saw in Cristina, for he was at least in a position to do some speculating, having gained a foothold in some of the salons that Cristina frequented. Raphael, on the other hand, is a provincial nobody whose only contact in society is Rastignac. Foedora, while the object of prestigious adulation, is said to be "that lonely woman without family, without friends, an atheist in love." How, unless Balzac was thinking of Cristina, who had just arrived in Paris alone, had made a few acquaintances among "men of power," as Balzac calls Foedora's admirers, but had neither friends nor lovers, could Foedora, "the toast of Paris," be so pitifully alone? Even Cristina's celebrated wit and fresh triumphs in diplomatic parrying are evoked by Foedora's "cruel memory; her quick wit would drive a diplomat to despair." Moreover, Foedora is received by "the whole Bonapartist coterie, the most distinguished ladies"—the very society that welcomed Cristina during the spring of 1831, beginning with Mme Récamier and Lafayette.

A noteworthy detail, omitted after 1835, is the date of May 2 given to Raphael's first prolonged tête-à-tête with Foedora. Elsewhere in the novel, as in the opening line ("Toward the end of October"), dates are indeterminate, whereas May 2 was evidently charged with significance; it was later changed to "last May." Balzac did not leave Paris until May 6 for Nemours, where he hoped to finish "that miserable work that doesn't end," as he told Zulma Carraud. It is thus not impossible that on May 2 he had a private conversation with Cristina, during which he declared his sentiments with Raphael's futile urgency: "My tone was that of a dying man's final prayers on a battlefield" (p. 167). For an hour or so Raphael and Foedora chat familiarly. The discussion gradually becomes impassioned as he tells her that unlike other men, who can only see the female in a woman, he wished "to live heart to heart with you . . . who have no heart." Foedora consoles him by promising that she will belong to no one. "I am doubtless very criminal not to love you. Is it my fault . . . ? I am happy to be alone, why change my life, egotistical if you like, for the caprices of a master? Marriage is a sacrament through which all we manage to communicate is our chagrins." (Foedora is first presented as *"une femme à marier,"* a marriageable woman with an income of 80,000 *livres;* here she clearly speaks as a woman who has had a bitter marital experience, again suggesting Cristina.) In Raphael's frantic plea that follows, one can hear the style of Balzac's love letters, wishing he could prove his love "with all of his blood." "All men tell us these classic words," Foedora teases, exactly as Cristina did, "for I meet such corpses everywhere." Raphael now asks that she merely let herself be loved by him: "Tell my pen to speak, tell my voice to ring, only for you; be the secret motive of my life." Infuriated by her smiling indifference, he explodes: "You have the present and I the future. . . . Time is heavy with my vengeance: it will bring you ugliness and a lonely death; and glory to me!" (p. 170).

Raphael returns to his room filled with hate, determined to forget his madness. "Soon, I was obliged to bring the manuscript of my memoirs to my agent. Occupied with my passion I did not know how I had managed to live without money." This coincides precisely with Balzac's overdue deadline for *La Peau de chagrin.* The two weeks Raphael spent closeted in his attic to finish his manuscript fit perfectly the seventeen days Balzac spent in Nemours to finish his novel. The "extraordinary labors" mentioned in Balzac's allusive remark to Zulma Carraud could also refer to a few days of debauchery intended to stifle his unrequited passion, which were then epically amplified into the novel's orgies. In the context outlined here, Balzac's curious remark that the work was still seen as a *novel* in 1838 would seem to imply that at least some portions were more personal than fictional, and perhaps even that *a particular person* had not yet recognized the truth behind the fictional façade.

Into this work Balzac poured all the bile of his frustrated love and his unfulfilled ambitions. The muse had not fled, as Raphael complained. Quite the contrary. After May 2 Balzac seems to have had a focal point for the project that had been languishing since March. It was then that Cristina, thinly disguised as Foedora, "that female mystery . . . aroused in [his] heart all the human sentiments, pride, ambition, love, curiosity" (p. 150). This woman, "all woman, yet not a woman," became the symbol of all that society had to offer—fame, wealth, love—but cruelly withheld because such things cannot be solicited, only conquered. "I loved her as a lover, as an artist, while it would have been necessary not to love her in order to win her." Raphael, one of the first of Balzac's long progeniture of *obsédés,* was unfit to wage this war. Rastignac's battle cry *"A nous deux!"* was born of Raphael's wasted ambitions—symbolized by the shrinking parchment of the title—as perhaps Balzac's prodigious energy was first ignited by his desire to avenge Cristina's rebuff.

BY 1837, BALZAC had long since forgiven her and enjoyed her friendship —often very helpful to him—all the while lying to Mme Hanska out of both sides of his letters. *Massimilla Doni* is a gift of reparation for that vengeful portrait of a frigid woman who destroyed an ardent youth. It is not, as he announced to Mme Hanska, "as stunning as *La Peau de chagrin*," but, as a portrait, it *is* "better written and more poetic." The relationship in his mind between Cristina and the two novels, and the thematic evolution of the first into the second, is subtly revealed in his letter of January 22, 1838. The letter begins by announcing a new edition of *La Peau de chagrin*. He then mentions his recent hostesses, among them the princess, whom he describes to Hanska for the first time. In the very next paragraph he informs her that the following day, he will begin the final revision of *Massimilla Doni,* adding:

> You cannot imagine with what resignation I envisage the nasty idiocies that this work, *Massimilla Doni,* will bring down on me. . . . But I have long become accustomed to these disparagements, there are still people who persist in seeing a *novel* in *La Peau de chagrin.* . . . In five years *Massimilla Doni* will be understood as a beautiful explanation of *the most intimate workings* of art. In the eyes of first readers, it will be what it appears to be, a lover who cannot possess the woman he adores but does possess a miserable wench. Make them deduce from that the engendering of art works! [Balzac's italics.]

On the most superficial level the two novels are thus clearly related: neither hero is able to possess his love. But Balzac's italicized remark suggests a more important relationship: the transformation of a life model into an artistic theme, the limitless ability of art to transcend not only life but even itself. *Massimilla Doni* is therefore a corrective counterpart of *La Peau de chagrin*—as well as Balzac's supreme homage to Cristina.

The title at once suggests the kind of punning Balzac delighted in: *doni* in Italian means gifts as well as talents, and *massimo* the greatest.* Massimilla, by the way, was first baptized Giovannina Fieschi, and she was Genoese, not Florentine. But by the end of his manuscript, Balzac's

---

* The name Doni was apparently inspired by Raphael's portrait of Margherita Doni, which he saw in Florence that year, but the multiple allusions were surely not unintentional.

final thought (the change of name occurs on the last page) was evidently to ennoble the character even more through Florentine art and aristocracy, thereby "maximizing" her and his offering. "Massimilla, beloved daughter of the Donis, in whom the beauty of the Italian has congenitally perpetuated itself, you who do not belie the portrait of Margherita, one of the rare canvasses entirely painted by Raphael, to his greater glory!" says inwardly the man who adores her but is unable to possess her. "Would I be worthy of you if I profaned a heart of which you are sole mistress? No, I will not fall into the vulgar trap my rebellious senses have laid for me."

In *La Peau de chagrin* he had already enunciated the theme of *Massimilla Doni*—and of all the other *Etudes philosophiques*—in the antiquarian's homily to Raphael when he sells him the ass-skin talisman: "Man exhausts himself through two instinctively accomplished acts that dry up all the well springs of his existence. Two verbs express all the forms that are taken by these two causes of death: *vouloir et pouvoir*" (p. 37). Balzac as an artist, a creator, is in a privileged god-like state: within the framework of his creation he can desire and he can fulfill that desire.

In 1831 Balzac was not yet ready for the *voie oblique,* the indirect interventions that Stendhal used to gratify his authorial or private impulses. He was still under the empire of his failure. But in 1837, secure in his success as a man and a writer, he could generously attribute to Massimilla what Foedora had lacked—the capacity for love—all the while preserving Raphael's inadequacy, now made symbolic, in Emilio Memmi, her inhibited lover. He had also the greater amplitude of a firsthand knowledge of Italy and could place Cristina in her natural habitat, thereby avoiding the incongruities of the Italianized Russian Foedora had been. He had just returned from his first real contact with Italy, a trip of two and a half months to Venice, Milan, Florence, and Genoa.* He spent over a month in Milan, where the most inaccessible of patrician doors were opened to him thanks to Cristina's recommendations to her relatives, the Viscontis, Trivulzios, and Archintos among others. For an understanding of Italy, introduction to such families was far more meaningful than contact with the Austrian governor of Lombardy, Count Hartig, arranged by Austria's ambassador in Paris, Count Apponyi. Max Milner, in his excellent introduction to *Massimilla Doni,* stresses the importance of Balzac's sojourn in Milan, "where his Italian initiation was assuredly the most complete." Balzac spent only six days in Venice

---

* In 1836 he spent a few weeks in Turin representing Count Visconti-Guidoboni in a heritage suit, as he did again in Venice a year later. But Turin was not the real Italy for him. In *Gambara* a character says, "The Piedmontese, the Savoyards have left, but the . . . real Italians have stayed on."

and made few acquaintances there. That he chose to set *Massimilla Doni* in Venice rather than in Milan would seem to be a choice born of delicacy. Cristina is recognizable enough without mention of her native city. Balzac's purpose, thematic and personal, is served equally well by Venice, which like Milan, but unlike any other major city except Milan, was in an Austrian province subjected to the same humiliation of occupation —a mutilating force that renders the will to act as impotent as do the obsessions of the novella's characters.

Here again, the original manuscript* furnishes the details that were in Balzac's first creative impulse. Added to the definitive version, the two texts unmistakably identify Cristina/Foedora as his model. Like Foedora, Massimilla is twenty-two, but this time we learn that "she was married at sixteen to Cataneo, with whom she remained no more than a year" and that "her great wealth was used for charity" (p. 204). Cristina was exactly sixteen at the time of her marriage to Emilio, with whom she officially lived for four years, but the marriage had in fact collapsed before the second year. As to Cristina's philanthropy, it was so outstandingly generous that two Paris newspapers published inventories of her charitable works.†

Balzac's low opinion of Cristina's husband appears more than once in letters to Mme Hanska. In one, quoted earlier, he refers to the "maladies" Cristina contracted from him. In another, he writes of a shiftless Polish baron who makes his wife unhappy: ". . . he lives in the manner of Prince Belgiojoso, does nothing, or rather many of those things that have made Poles lose our friendship. Their inconstancy is atrocious. They are all gamblers." The comparison is so mutually unflattering one hardly knows which of the two is the greater scoundrel. Cataneo is not just a sketch of the prince, but a Dorian Gray portrait in its last stages. The background facts are true to life: "Cataneo, who only wanted a duchess, found it perfectly ridiculous to be a husband; when Massimilla complained about his behavior, he placidly told her to look for a *primo cavaliere servente* and offered his services to bring her a few to choose from. . . . The duchess wept, the duke left her . . . she found no one . . . and began to travel" (p. 90). This is a precise account of Cristina's life in 1828, when Emilio offered her the same freedom he was then enjoying with Paola Ruga among others, and she began the two-year peregrinations that finally took her to Paris. Balzac then goes beyond the facts to paint a vengeful caricature of Emilio Belgiojoso for having com-

---

* Printed in Max Milner's edition of the novella, to which all page numbers in parentheses refer.

† "Rich and generous, the princess Belgiojoso flung her wealth, and continues to do so daily, into philanthropic creations. . . . *Le Moniteur* and *Le Journal de l'Instruction publique* have published a long and indiscreet list of the charitable and educational institutions she founded."[19]

municated syphilis to Cristina, while he himself remained healthy until paresis caught up with him in 1858. Cataneo is made to bear all the physical ravages of the disease.

> His complexion, suspected of containing numerous metals* infused by the prescription of some Hippocrates, had gone near black. His pointed forehead . . . crowned his mask of a face with reddish bumps. . . . For anyone with a stomach strong enough to observe him, his past was written . . . on this noble clay turned to mud. You might have divined the great lord who, rich since youth, had sold his body to Debauchery to obtain from it excessive pleasures. . . . Thousands of bottles had passed under the purpled arches of that grotesque nose. . . . His eyes had paled under the lights of gaming tables. His blood had filled with the impurities that altered his nervous system [p. 100].

The only thing of beauty still remaining in this human detritus is his expert musicianship—still another trait of Belgiojoso, whose magnificent tenor voice was legendary. (Cataneo's instrument is the violin, borrowed perhaps from another Emilio, Count Visconti-Guidoboni, who shares with Cataneo one more similarity: they were both cuckolded by Balzac, the first in life, the second in fiction. Sarah Visconti-Guidoboni became Balzac's mistress in 1835. There the resemblance ends, for Count Emilio was a gentle husband devoted to chamber music and pharmacology. His final contribution to the novella may have been his sister's name, Massimilla. He was, by the way, Cristina's cousin, as Balzac well knew.) Emilio Belgiojoso's Christian name and title, in another transfer from life, are given to the impoverished, noble-hearted hero, Emilio Memmi, Massimilla's would-be lover, who is more deserving of the title of prince than the debauched rogue of a Belgiojoso, now demoted to the rank of Neapolitan duke.

Cristina, on the other hand, is glorified almost in direct proportion to the defamation of her husband. Contrasting perhaps too sharply with the debased prince Emilio, Cristina's new avatar is presented as a Florentine aristocrat—far nobler than Cataneo's Neapolitan lineage. "The duchess is the most accomplished woman in Italy," says Vendramin, the Venetian patriot who opiates his humiliation as an Austrian subject. "To me, who see things here below through the vaporous inebriation of opium, she appears to be as the highest expression of art, for nature truly produced in her . . . a Raphael portrait" (p. 120). In this second metamorphosis, she still has the black hair and striking white skin that Foedora had, but

---

* The allusion is to mercury, the classic therapy for syphilis at the time.

here the hairstyle is unmistakably Cristina's: "beautiful black hair . . . in shining plaits on either side of a luminous forehead" (p. 90).

In the Lehmann portrait of 1843, Cristina's hair is parted in the middle, with a braid, like a diadem, encircling the two bands of gleaming hair that frame her prominent brow. This same hairdo is even more visible in a profile bas-relief of 1835, proving that she wore her hair that way long before Lehmann painted her. Balzac's detailed description of Massimilla is so evocative of Lehmann's portrait as to seem a photographic likeness—the same hairstyle, the same serene expression of her perfect oval face, the ambiguous Leonardo da Vinci mouth that might conceal a smile, the velvety doe's eyes. Moreover, throughout the story, Balzac makes constant associations between Massimilla's singular beauty and paintings, specifically Renaissance paintings. Except for the lighter hair of those idealized figures, Cristina shared most of their characteristic traits—their otherworldly glance, their dimpled chins, their high, rounded foreheads, their pale oval faces. Heine was right when he said that Cristina had taken her face from Leonardo's pupil, Luini; his lovely Madonna del Roseto could easily have been Cristina's forebear. Lehmann's portrait, though admittedly suggestive of Ingres, is also strongly reminiscent of those sublime quattrocento Madonnas. Here is the portrait of Massimilla:

> The Florentine attracted attention because of her voluminous snow-white forehead, crowned with her braid of black hair that gave her a truly royal air; the calm delicacy of her traits which recalled the tender nobility of Andrea del Sarto's heads; the cut of her face and the framing of her eyes, those eyes of velvet that communicated the rapture of a woman dreaming of happiness, still pure in love, yet at the same time majestic and pretty [p. 118].

Lehmann, however, painted Cristina six years after *Massimilla Doni* was written! It may thus have been Balzac or Heine who influenced Lehmann. In any case, as Balzac insisted with regard to la Sanseverina, *"le personage existe"*; the model surely existed as these artists saw her since their figures resemble each other—a simple Euclidean proposition. What is fascinating is the kind of mirror play that occurs between the Renaissance prototype, the living figure, and the resulting art work. In such an interplay Cristina emerges as a living work of art, a mythopoeic figure: "Massimilla, though young, had that majesty which mythological tradition attributes to Juno, sole goddess to whom mythology did not grant a lover" (p. 92). This subtle allusion surely points to Cristina, whose lover-less existence mystified society; Mignet was never taken seriously as a lover, being neither young nor passionate.

Like Cristina, Massimilla knows nothing of passion though she has at least discovered the emotion of love, for she fully returns Emilio's. But he, overwhelmed by her physical and spiritual beauty, is stricken with "that noble malady which only attacks very young and very old men" (p. 92). The exaltation of his love has rendered him incapable of the act of love. Massimilla thus finds herself "between a husband who knew he was so far from the mark he no longer cared, and a lover who overshot it so rapidly . . . he could no longer return." This seems to allude, rather wittily, to Belgiojoso's cavalier indifference to his wife's humiliation, and to Mignet's rumored inadequacy, a rumor possibly spread by Balzac's own malicious tongue. More important than the innuendo, Emilio Memmi's problem—one of hyperexuberance rather than impotence—reflects the theme that pervades the work: the inability of the individual possessed by an ideal to cope with his personal life, a theme as applicable to Cristina as to any character in the novel. Emilio, like all of Balzac's unheroic heroes, is lucid. That is the very crux of his and their misfortune; they are all too cerebral. Emilio's life is like a Canaletto street scene, representative but immobile. "He saw the present as it was: a palace without a soul, a soul without action on the body, a principality without money, an empty body and a full heart" (p. 96). How evocative of Cristina these paradoxes are. The ideal of patriotism is as undermining to Vendramin as is the ideal of pleasure to Cataneo, of esthetics to Capraja, or love to Emilio. Only the artist is saved by his creation, if he remains detached from it; otherwise it destroys him. The novella's celebrated singer Genovese, an artist of sorts, loses control of his voice and suffers a fiasco on stage once he falls in love with his partner, the diva Tinti. (She, a Sicilian, is described as "primitive," thus uncerebral, and naturally competent in art and life.) When Genovese watches la Tinti adoringly, so spellbound he does not hear his own braying, he is rendered as "impotent" as Emilio is with Massimilla. But when Emilio finds himself in the arms of la Tinti, whom he does not love or idealize, his performance is above reproach.

In a speculative generalization that seems also to refer to his own willful idealization of Mme Hanska, Balzac rationalizes his figurative impotence with Cristina: "If in solitude, a woman of mediocre beauty, ceaselessly studied, becomes sublime and imposing, perhaps a woman as magnificently beautiful as the duchess succeeded in stupefying a young man in whom exaltation was constantly revived . . ." (p. 90). An even more satisfying rationalization appears in his theory that desire is preferable to fulfillment, something Raphael/Balzac was unable to appreciate in 1831. Now in his fourth decade and no longer neglected by love or fortune, Balzac could indulge in the poetry of frustration. Emilio was anguished over his inadequacy, while Massimilla was genuinely satisfied with their unconsummated love, for she "took pleasure in desire without imagining its culmination." The idea, Balzac insists, is more important than the act, "otherwise desire would be less beautiful than pleasure"; desire is thus more "potent" since it "engenders" pleasure, he concludes (p. 113). To prove his point, he constructed a dénouement so grotesque it seems to defy artistic validity. A visiting French doctor, learning of Emilio's affliction and near suicidal distress, offers a stratagem to cure it though he derides Emilio's foolishness:

> He can see his mistress perpetually sublime and pure . . . perpetually under the fire of those two eyes that offer him the warm golden atmosphere that Titian placed around his Virgin . . . and that Raphael was the first to invent . . . and man only aspires to sully such poetry! Oh feminine forms outlined by a pure and luminous oval . . . divine feet that cannot walk, slender figures that will never conceive, virgins glimpsed by us on leaving childhood, admired in secret, adored without hope . . . what swine of an Epicure ever wanted to plunge you into the mud of this earth [p. 172]!

THIS POETIC OUTBURST—Balzac's highest vindication of Cristina's anaphrodisia, his most lyric statement of the image she represented—enshrines her forever as the Romantic Ideal. She had already been beatified by Heine in his *Florentinische Nächte* of 1836, and sanctified by Musset, who saw her as a Beatrice, a Laura. Liszt worshipped her, calling his feeling for her, like Heine, a cult: "My cult remains the same," he wrote her in 1840, "I will not relinquish it to the catacombs until the day I know for certain it bothers you. . . . Believe in my intense adoration and total devotion." All this, read, seen, or guessed by Balzac, must have annoyed him no end. His letters to Mme Hanska, written long after the facts, still carry the rancor he felt at the sight of those fawning Apollos, handsomer than he, more seductive, more graceful, who could drape themselves across Cristina's sofas in sinuous poses, while his little tub of a body looked ridiculous drawn to its full five feet two inches. In May 1843, inventing with greater fantasy than in his fiction, he informed Mme Hanska: "She took Listz [*sic*] from la d'Agoult, as she took Lord Normanby from his wife, Mignet from Mme Aubernon and Musset from George Sand, etc., etc. As to Prince Belgiojoso, he has just carried off a Lebrun, comtesse de Plaisance. . . . You wanted news, here you have it!" Only the last was true, and was in fact the choicest scandal in Paris . . . the year before. Could this portrait of Cristina/Massimilla have been written in a spirit of competition? Balzac could not compete with Liszt, true, but when it came to words, he was a giant compared to the others. His works were being read from the cliffs of Dover to the Urals.

He could produce something that made their prose poems and sonnets about Cristina look puny. He could create the *entire* figure so that she would be seen and heard forever. This was the maximum tribute.

As armature for this monument to an elusive divinity, Balzac reinforced the doctor's panegyric—after all, a French doctor was not exactly an authority on esthetic matters—by adding to it the insight of Capraja, that infallible critic who "divines everything through the power of his mind." At the end of the doctor's encomium, Capraja exclaims, "Not bad for a French doctor, you have just explained what Europe understands least about Dante, his *Bice!* Yes, Beatrice, that ideal figure, queen of poetic fantasies, consecrated by tears, deified by memory, ceaselessly rejuvenated by unfulfilled desires!" (p. 173). This is precisely the poetic demiurge Cristina was for Musset and for Heine. Unlike Musset, who wanted the world to know he had been mistreated and then was too ashamed to ask her pardon, Heine and Liszt, mature men, understood the meaning of their "cult" and never ceased writing or talking about her with love. Balzac clearly understood as well, and he too remained devoted to Cristina until his untimely death.

There are ample documents to prove this, but since malice makes better reading, only his derogatory remarks about Cristina have ever been quoted, and at that, without comment. As everyone knows, his judgments of women to Mme Hanska are not trustworthy since he was trying to forestall her jealousy. Nonetheless, his lies and misrepresentations are also revealing, certainly in Cristina's case. He pretended to see her little and care even less, yet she crops up in his correspondence all the time, and in ways that demonstrate how familiar they were: "As the Princess B says, it's the monster volume," he wrote Hanska about volume eight of *La Comédie humaine.* Why mention Princess Belgiojoso rather than Sainte-Beuve or any other known critic, unless "Princess B's" opinion really matters to him? The frequency of her name in his letters, and ironically it appears most often in his correspondence with Mme Hanska, becomes more significant than the remark itself taken literally.

In August 1844, after a decade of slander ("Rest assured, *ma chère adorée,* that Princess Cristina does not compare with you; she is excessively thin, a *Harpy,* and I found her dreadfully ugly the other evening"); of indifference ("I went there one Saturday and it will be all"); of indictments ("Liszt is at the princess Belgiojoso's and *so openly* that . . . Christine is no longer worthy of respect"); of mockery ("She thinks she knows it all. She receives a bunch of *criticons* who can no longer write")—he was still dashing out to Port-Marly whenever she invited him. And on occasion he was even honest about her: "With regard to the reprinting of *Splendeurs et misères,* Cristina Trivulzio graciously rendered me many services." In the most bungled deception ever to reach Mme Hanska, he reported a visit to Port-Marly (the second in two months!) ostensibly for help, since "Cristina has an in with journalists":

> I went to Saint-Germain to the house of Princess Belgiojoso who can do me a little favor. I was so sick I couldn't dine there. I returned dying of fatigue and related aches. All that, my dear, was almost cured by the sight of your letter, which I have put off reading until tomorrow, since I came home at ten o'clock and nature demands I go to bed.

If he was really so sick, how is it he came home at ten? And if he stayed there that late, what was he doing while the others were having dinner? At that time, dinner was always served by five o'clock, and Cristina's invitations to Port-Marly were made early enough for guests to return to Paris, a good hour's drive. And if dear Eveline's letter was such a panacea, how is it he was too tired to read it but not too tired to write to her? Somehow, he could not resist the temptation to speak of Cristina, if but to Mme Hanska, thousands of miles away, who had never laid eyes on her. There were many other women he mentioned with greater ease, kindly or not, but when it came to Cristina, he always got entangled in his subterfuges. If Mme Hanska was fooled, others were not. A letter to Cristina from Liszt in 1840, during her prolonged stay in Italy, divulges Balzac's interest.

> Heine comes up to me daily, asks for news of you, as always, and winds up with the most colossal, the most enthusiastic and most fitting panegyric of the beautiful princess. He does not accustom himself at all to your absence and bewails you more from day to day. . . . A few steps farther, there is Balzac, same questions, same regret, only a trifle more tempered.

Cristina's own letters to Balzac, of which few, alas, remain, bear witness to the old familiarity of their relationship. They also reveal meetings that were never mentioned to Mme Hanska, such as one that took place *sixteen years* after their first encounters.

29 August 1847

Mon cher Monsieur,

> I did not dare ask you the other day to lend me the *Vautrin* as well, which was in your study. I nonetheless want so much to do so, that like the ostrich, I hide my head under a sheet of paper and pre-

sent you with my request. I read *Le Cousin Pons* without stopping. In exchange for that good man, send me Vautrin, and tomorrow evening it will be he whom I replace in your paternal hands. Be a good chap and do not refuse me.

Mille compliments et amitiés
Christine Trivulce de Belgiojoso

Apart from the fact that she evidently read with astonishing speed, the tone of the letter and her presence in his house testify to a more informal relationship than might be assumed from his presence at her parties. Another point is that Cristina only invited friends to her summer house, reserving more formal entertainment for her house in Paris. Balzac's repeated presence at Port-Marly indicates that she received him *dans l'intimité*, informally, which would justify his boast that he had *"mes grandes et mes petites entrées chez elle."* Cristina never took any man from any woman, no matter what Balzac wrote to Mme Hanska, for she gave herself to no one. Like Foedora, she merely kept them all . . . spellbound.

UNTIL THE FINAL PAGES of the novella, Emilio Memmi is a platonic lover, a *primo cavaliere servente* (as Mignet was assumed to be). But Emilio's desperate state has driven Massimilla to accept the doctor's stratagem. In a substitution scene out of classical comedy, she receives the unsuspecting half-drunk Emilio in la Tinti's bed, while la Tinti (who out of fondness for Emilio has generously agreed to the ruse) similarly restores Genovese. But the happy ending is soon reduced to mockery: "How to tell the dénouement of this adventure, for it is horribly bourgeois. One word will suffice for worshipers of the *ideal*. The duchess was pregnant." And to make sure the reader does not overlook the significance of this news, Balzac fills the last paragraph with a long list of feminine divinities, all of whom "rushed to Massimilla's bed and wept!"

At first glance, these final words of the story seem to be a breach of taste, ascribable to Balzac's not infrequent coarseness. But however gross the ending seems, it is perfectly consistent with his artistic purpose. Massimilla, like the other characters, is possessed by a dream, and because of it she too must in some way be mutilated. She has now sacrificed her divinity for her idealized lover and has become the *"femelle"* he wanted, proving once again that nothing survives those ethereal heights but the artist's creation. Balzac must have been staggered by his own powers of prophecy when he learned that seven months after he wrote *Massimilla*

Doni Cristina gave birth to a daughter.* He had already predicted a man like Mignet in *La Peau de chagrin*—*"un homme sec et glacé"*—as the only one who could win a Cristina/Foedora. Now "this slender figure that will never conceive," this exalted Cristina/Massimilla, had also become a mother, a woman like any other.

Two major subjects linking Cristina with the novella are Italy and music. *Gambara,* another *Étude philosophique,* written contemporaneously and completed a month after the first draft of *Massimilla Doni,* is a companion piece whose theme and techniques interweave with its twin even to interior references. Gambara is an obsessed composer, living in Paris among other Italian exiles, whose hermetic music reduces him to playing on the street for his daily bread. His pathetic situation "comes from having listened to the concerts of angels and having believed that men could understand them. The same thing happens to women when love assumes divine forms for them." This grave warning is given by Gambara to his unexpected benefactress, "une belle Italienne, la *principessa* Massimilla di Varese"† in the presence of her husband "prince Emilio" on the last page of the novella. There can be no doubt that Cristina was intimately associated with the theme of the danger of idealization. And this direct address to Cristina (the italics are Balzac's) is doubly astute for it also points to *Massimilla Doni,* as does the subject of opera, with which the two novellas are filled. In *Massimilla Doni,* as in *Gambara,* Balzac dabbles in musicology (with professional help in both cases), this time inserting a lengthy analysis of Rossini's *Moses,* where in the other, Gambara discourses volubly on Meyerbeer's *Robert le Diable* and his own opera *Mahomet.* Here it is Massimilla, and not a professional musician, who initiates the French reader—through the person of the French doctor—into the mysteries of Rossini's music and its expression of Italian patriotism. Balzac, himself a recent tourist, appears to have cast himself in the role of the doctor, but his own initiation doubtless took place long before in Cristina's salon with her old friend Rossini as co-sponsor.

The doctor tells Massimilla that on entering the Fenice, Venice's beautiful lyric theater, he noticed her at once: "Were it granted to a woman to represent her country, you are that woman; I seemed to per-

---

* If Balzac had any suspicions that the child was Mignet's he kept them to himself, which is surprising for such news would have made choice gossip for Mme Hanska. His only cryptic judgment—"She is, with regard to the Liszts and the Mignets and all her caprices, of the period of Louis XV"—does not imply that kind of scandal.

† This is the same title given to Emilio Memmi, who becomes prince of Varese at the beginning of the novella. Varese, a lakeside town near Milan, is the site of a villa Cristina inherited from her father and where he died. She spent quite a lot of time there over the years as proved by the many letters she wrote from there.

ceive in you the genius of Italy" (p. 123). Surely no other woman among Balzac's Italian acquaintances could have occasioned such a remark, for Cristina and Italy had become synonymous in Paris. By 1837 her commitment to Italy's liberation was public knowledge. One has only to hear Juliette Adam, a younger contemporary, speak of Cristina: "Princess Belgiojoso has remained one of my greatest admirations. She loved Italy ardently, faithfully, until her death, lived for Italy exclusively and devoted to it her beauty, her intelligence, her fortune. . . . Princess Belgiojoso is one of the most beautiful female figures that Europe had in the last century. . . . She was an incomparable heroine."[20]

The subject of the opera scene announces Cristina; the content presents her. It is here that Balzac records her words, her ideas, her wit. The presence of an Austrian general in the box makes Massimilla say outrageous things about Italy that befuddle the doctor: "You condone despotism?" he exclaims. "I thought Italians were more patriotic." When the general leaves, Emilio explains Massimilla's "performance," which had been sheer irony: "Do you think we would be wise," he asks the doctor, "to speak openly before our masters?" In a series of sublimely chauvinistic monologues, Massimilla not only expresses truths about Italy but about France as well, and in words unmistakably Cristina's, for they appear in her letters and her books. Reminding the doctor that Italy was once dominated by France, and that the only difference between the French and the Austrians as masters is that "You counted on keeping Italy, they think they will lose it," she tells him that Italy does not wish to be protected as France's "mistress"—the doctor's formula. "We wish to be free, but the liberty we wish is not your ignoble and bourgeois liberalism that would kill the arts" (p. 126). It will be remembered that from the time of the first expedition to Savoy in 1831, Cristina found no reason to revise her contempt and distrust of Louis-Philippe's "bourgeois liberalism," which had betrayed its promise to stand by Italy. Massimilla proudly informs the doctor that "in this land whose decline is deplored by dull-witted travelers and hypocritical poets"—a jeer from Cristina at French tourists who only saw art works and understood nothing of Italian patriotism, and at Musset, whose bitter experience with George Sand in Venice had made him allergic to Italy—"there is still the artistic genius that will always allow Italy to rule the world." And it is specifically music—France's artistic weakness and Cristina's forte—that symbolizes Italy's greatness.

Cristina had often said, in various forms, that if life were an opera she would prefer the music to the words. This same priority is given to music in the novella, which is curious considering that Balzac's genius, and that of his countrymen, is predominantly verbal. Capraja, described by Massimilla as the only music lover to surpass the duke, authoritatively places music in the required perspective: "Music addresses itself to the heart, while words speak only to the intelligence; music immediately communicates its ideas, in the manner of perfumes." Gambara is now evoked in the novella. Capraja quotes him in a theoretical discussion of sound, which is followed by Massimilla's lengthy analysis of *Moses* (sixteen printed pages), delivered to the doctor during the performance! To have given her (rather than Capraja or Cataneo, the two great connoisseurs in the novella) this noble task appears as another of Balzac's gifts of reparation. For in *La Peau de chagrin* he had Raphael say: "Foedora did not listen to the music. The divine pages of Rossini, Cimarosa . . . translated no poetry in her life; her soul was arid." It also allowed him to repeat, or paraphrase, some of Cristina's anti-French sallies. When the doctor facetiously likens one of the opera's melodies to a country dance, she exclaims *"Français! Toujours Français!* . . . Yes, you are capable of utilizing that sublime élan for one of your folk dances. The loftiest genius has to run the gantlet of your caricature. . . . *Chez vous,* wit kills the soul just as rationalization kills reason there." How evocative of Cristina's oft-repeated indictments of those doctrinaire French—*"les gens de la raison glacée"*—who justified France's inaction by scorning Italy's ability to unite as a nation.

The opera is explained as an oratorio to Italy's enslavement and eventual liberation: "Dear Rossini," Massimilla murmurs, "you did well to throw that bone to the *tedeschi* who denied us the gift of harmony and science!" Turning to the doctor, she adds, "You who accomplished the bloodiest of revolutions, the day this oratorio is performed in your land you will understand this magnificent lament of victims whose God avenges his people. Only an Italian could write that seminal theme. . . . Do you consider it insignificant to dream of vengeance for a moment?" (p. 142). The scene reaches an apotheosis of metonymy as Massimilla exposes Egypt for Austria, the Hebrews for Italians, and music for all the arts, the highest expression of artistic language: "The language of music is infinite, it contains everything, it can express everything."

Balzac could justly pride himself that not even Heine had glorified "la belle princesse" to this extent. *Massimilla Doni* is not just an ode to Cristina's beauty, which for Heine was the incarnation of a pictorial ideal, but to everything about her—her sensitivity, her intelligence, her patriotism, her country. She was compared to a work of art by all who knew her. Balzac did more. He created a work of art around her, richer than any artist could paint, subtler than any poet could versify.

11

The Wanderer's Fantasy

MUCH HAS BEEN WRITTEN on the women in Liszt's life, but to qualify for such immortality one apparently has to have been his mistress. Even a peccadillo as slight as his few nights with Lola Montez enshrined her in the pages of his biographies. Yet in most such works, the Princess Belgiojoso merely flits through as a once-famous party-giver, despite their remarkable correspondence and long-lasting friendship. Mention of her relationship with Liszt is generally limited, as in Harold Schonberg's *Great Pianists,* to her connection with a composition dedicated to her, *Hexameron.* The story of this work, whose first performance date has long been debated, begins with a grandiloquent article in *Le Journal des Débats* of March 21, 1837, announcing a unique charity event.

Mme la princesse de Belgiojoso, noble witness of the misfortunes of her compatriots detained among us through exile, poverty, or illness, who has already undertaken to console so many miseries, has decided to make an all-powerful appeal to the sympathy of France on behalf of all those unfortunate Italians. This time it is not a question of political pity, it is better than that; it is a matter of philanthropy and Christian charity. Never has an advocate pleaded a finer cause. Thus Mme la princesse de Belgiojoso has encountered the most laudable enthusiasm. Everyone who bears an illustrious name in society or the arts has claimed the honor of participating in this generous enterprise. To accomplish the finest possible end, an auction and a concert have been prepared for the benefit of those unhappy Italians. The concert and auction will take place in Mme la princesse de Belgiojoso's own house, rue d'Anjou-St. Honoré, no. 23.

The auction will last three days and begin the twenty-eighth of this month. This auction would be remarkable even if it did not have the purpose of aiding such terrible miseries. All the great artists of today, Messieurs Delacroix, Schnetz, Delaroche, Granet, Lehmann, Scheffer . . . have sent beautiful works. M. de Sommariva, with rare generosity, has stripped his own museum of an admirable fresco by Luini, that worthy pupil of Leonardo da Vinci; this fresco was removed through a completely new process by means of which the plaster is totally separated from the painting. . . . Meyerbeer has promised an unpublished song, the energetic young sculptor Mercier has given up his beautiful medallions of Liszt and George Sand; Messieurs Liszt, Thalberg, Chopin, Pixis, Czerny, Herz, talents so different and so varied, have united to compose a series of variations on the great duet from *I Puritani.*

An idea of the importance of this event can be gleaned from the fact that *Le Journal des Débats,* the most widely read daily of the time, devoted a quarter of a large format page to this article. The queen, the king's sister, the royal princesses, the most distinguished ladies in society, all offered their patronage and their talents. Tapestries made by royal fingers were sold by duchesses and marquises at the bazaar. The duchesse d'Abrantès offered an unpublished manuscript and her time at the booths, promising in her acceptance note to Cristina that she would contribute in any way desired: "Surely I wept over Poland's misfortunes . . . but Italy! Italy is my homeland! My mother taught me to speak in her tongue . . . and when I said my first prayer, it was in Italian that I addressed God." This statement from a French noblewoman provides an interesting highlight on the pro-Italian sympathy of the time, for many felt like Mme d'Abrantès that Italy was their spiritual homeland. Poland's plight had indeed wrenched many French hearts, but Italy and France shared a common border, a common enemy, and, at that moment, a common culture; the Italian cause was virtually pro domo.

The variations by the six keyboard masters, on a theme proposed by Cristina, were published under the title of *Hexameron:* "Grandes variations de bravoure pour piano sur la marche des *Puritains* de Bellini, composées pour le concert de Mme la princesse Belgiojoso, au bénéfice des pauvres, par M. M. Liszt, Thalberg, Pixis, Henri Herz, Czerny et Chopin. Dédiées à Mme la princesse Christine de Belgiojoso." So reads the title page. The theme is the march figure that appears in the second act duet for baritone and bass to the words "Suoni la tromba intrepida," an admirable battle hymn for Italian patriots. Each pianist composed a variation, to which Liszt added a prelude, interludes, and a finale. For decades, music historians and biographers have refuted one another over the question of *Hexameron'*s first performance. To many it was evident that the work must have been performed at Cristina's house since she had commissioned it for the great charity event. Raymond Lewenthal, in the notes to his fine recording of the work, categorically denies that it was performed by its six composers "chez Belgiojoso or chez anyone else." Since his sources were not indicated, I felt obliged to do my own spade work and uncovered a proof, apparently overlooked before, that his verdict is correct. A letter from Cristina to Liszt dated June 4, 1837, thus two months after the bazaar, resolves the problem once and for all: the work was not yet completed at that time.*

> Here, my dear Liszt, are the variations of M. Herz and the others that you know. No news from M. Chopin and, since I am still proud enough to fear making a nuisance of myself, I do not dare ask him. You do not run the same risk with him as I, which prompts me to ask if you would find out what is happening to his adagio, which is not moving quickly at all. It will be one more kindness on your part, for which I shall be as grateful as for the others. You know, I hope, that this implies a great deal. Try also to work seriously on the overture and finale of the piece, as though it were something that had to be completed at once. You will think no more of it afterward and I will remember it only to thank you and no longer to torment you.[1]

Her eagerness for him to finish had nothing to do with its performance—not scheduled for the bazaar in the first place—but with its publication before general interest subsided, since the proceeds were to go to needy Italian exiles. Once completed, the work often appeared on Liszt's programs, along with another set of variations on themes from the same opera, which he had dedicated to her earlier. Far more exciting to the musical audience at large than *Hexameron* was the concert announced for the fourth day of the bazaar, which did indeed take place. "It will truly be the most memorable afternoon recorded in musical annals," clarioned the reporter. "In this concert, the two greatest pianists of our time, whose names are repeated in all of Europe with a thousand different comparisons, are to meet as though in an arena, in chivalrous combat, namely M.M. Liszt and Thalberg." A month earlier their rivalry had become a public joust separated by one week and two halls. On March 12 Thalberg performed his fantasy on Rossini's *Moses* and his variations on *God Save the King* at the Conservatoire. On March 19 Liszt one-upped him by renting the Opéra, where he played his fantasy on Pacini's *Niobe* and Weber's *Conzertstücke*. It was a resounding success for Liszt, but not decisive, whereas this unique occasion, when both pianists would be heard in the same room, the same afternoon, was bound to produce a sensation, and perhaps a victory as well.

> M.M. Liszt and Thalberg will thus be the two heroes of this festivity; at the same time a number of talents well loved in the salons will also

---

* Mr. Lewenthal later informed me he was not familiar with this letter.

be heard, Mme Merlin, . . . Prince Belgiojoso, M. de Candia [an Italian count known on stage as Mario]. . . . It is said that the concert tickets will cost 25 francs; it is too little for the beneficiaries, too little for the music-lovers, too little for that white hand held out to you with so charming a smile, and from so high.

Sigismund Thalberg, the Swiss-born court pianist of Austria's emperor, who first stunned Paris the year before, was Liszt's major rival. However formidable the other keyboard virtuosos of the day, and there were many, only Thalberg had succeeded in dividing all of Europe's concertgoers into two warring camps, his and Liszt's. He too was a composer of operatic fantasies, some fifty or sixty, which Liszt considered pretentious trash. He too was an astounding performer who, alone with Liszt, represented in Mendelssohn's view "the highest class of pianists today." Where Liszt was an extravagant showman, Thalberg sat motionless and elegant at the keyboard. Yet the very serious Clara Schumann sobbed aloud when she heard Liszt in 1838: "Beside Liszt," she wrote, "other virtuosos appear so small, even Thalberg." Robert Schumann felt that no artist except Paganini possessed "to so high a degree as Liszt, the power of subjugating, exalting . . . an audience." And as early as 1836, the rarely pleased Berlioz, reviewing Liszt's performance of the *Hammerklavier* Sonata, wrote, "Liszt, in thus making comprehensible a work not yet comprehended, has proved he is the pianist of the future."[2] In 1837, however, Thalberg had not yet retired to his Italian vineyards and was still a discomfiting partner to Liszt's laurels of the present.

Cristina, long a declared Lisztian and a friend besides, had been the originator of the sublime idea of a mano a mano. It was a stroke of genius, and not only for the publicity it gave her bazaar. For the audience, though necessarily small compared with that of a concert hall, was composed of cognoscenti whose opinion would be heard and read long after the applause died down. Heine recorded the event for the rest of Europe, Jules Janin for Paris, on April 3, in the *Journal des Débats*.

Princess Belgiojoso has worthily concluded the admirable work she began so well. That charming, almost Italian house, was filled at two in the afternoon with the handsomest crowd. . . . A ticket cost 40 francs, and for the last week there was not one to be had. In that scintillating crowd, mingled together in the same sympathy were M. and Mme Apponyi, M. Thiers, M. Berryer* . . . all the opinions that divide the world and conciliate on the neutral ground of philanthropy. . . . At the appointed hour, the contest between the two

* The presence of Apponyi, the Austrian ambassador, is indeed surprising since those "unfortunate Italians" were Austria's victims. Thiers, a confirmed Orleanist, was a minister in Louis-Philippe's government. Berryer was a legitimist politician and noted lawyer.

heroes began and each was on his guard. Never was Liszt more con-
trolled, more thoughtful, more energetic, more passionate; never has
Thalberg played with greater verve and tenderness.* Each of them
prudently stayed within his harmonic domain, but each used every one
of his resources. It was an admirable joust. The most profound silence
fell over that noble arena. And finally Liszt and Thalberg were both
proclaimed victors by this brilliant and intelligent assembly. It is
clear that such a contest could only take place in the presence of such
an areopagus. Thus two victors and no vanquished; it is fitting to say
with the poet ET AD HUC SUB JUDICE LIS EST.

The decision was in fact rendered by the princess, in a verdict not
"tarnished by repetition," as Mrs. Perényi says, but by misquotation.
What Cristina said was "There is only one Thalberg in Paris, but
there is only one Liszt in the world." The oft-repeated version has her
saying: "Thalberg is the best pianist in the world and Liszt the only
one."

CRISTINA'S COMPETENCE as arbiter was based not on her role of impre-
sario but on her musicianship, highly respected by Liszt. A quarter-
century later, he wrote to a friend: "Mme la princesse Belgiojoso . . .
apart from the eminent qualities of her mind and her lofty philosophical, literary, historical and patriotic merits, is in addition one of the rare
people for whom one enjoys making music, for she has what I would call
an *intuitive ear.* Thus I am grateful for the way she was willing to listen
to me and, if I did not consider myself now a defunct pianist, would
immediately try to gain her approval." Their friendship spanned more
than three decades, probably beginning in 1831, when both were new-
comers to Paris and both frequented the Saint-Simon salon on the rue
Taitbout. Their correspondence offers the only reliable documentation of
that friendship, and it is a fascinating one. Though some of the letters
were published by Malvezzi in 1936, and compiled in 1941 by Daniel
Ollivier, it would seem they were overlooked by Liszt's biographers. For
had they been read with any attention, it would have become evident, as
it did to the present writer, that Cristina was not an occasional friend or
frequent hostess, but one of the most constant figures in the first half of
his long life.

Certainly their relationship was well established by 1835, by which
time Liszt also knew Emilio. When Liszt settled in Geneva with Marie

* Liszt is reputed to have said, "Thalberg is the only man who can play the violin on
the piano."

d'Agoult in the fall of that year, he renewed acquaintance with Emilio, then also a resident of the city, and on October 3 agreed to play at a concert organized by Emilio for Italian émigrés. In May 1836 Liszt returned to Paris to re-establish the reputation Thalberg had encroached on with his debut concert earlier in the season. Thalberg had left by the time Liszt arrived, but his triumphs still rang through the city. Determined to prove not only his pianistic but also his musical superiority, Liszt gave two concerts at the Salle Erard, at which he played the *Hammerklavier* so admired by Berlioz. "Until now," said Berlioz in his review, "this has been the Enigma of the Sphinx for almost every pianist. Liszt, another Oedipus, has solved it in a manner that would have sent quivers of pride through the composer, had he heard it in his grave. Not a note was omitted, not one added (I followed score in hand), no inflection lost, no change of tempo permitted. . . ." This was high praise indeed from the master purist himself, responsible for our modern notion that a composer's notes are to be respected by the performer as scrupulously as a playwright's lines. No one would have dreamed of adding a few hexameters to Racine, but few musicians denied themselves the pleasure of tinkering on stage. Cadenzas were improvised at will, tempos and even whole passages were altered to suit the mood of the artist. Writing after the concerts, on May 22, to Mme d'Agoult, who had remained in Geneva, Liszt beamed: "I saw Principessa. She is always charming to me, comparing me to no one else at all and deriding the Thalbourgeois. Principessa, who has definitely constituted herself my admiring defender, wants me for dinner with l'abbé Coeur." Cristina's pun on Thalberg's admirers must have doubly pleased Liszt, who was a simple bourgeois himself, whereas Thalberg was the natural son of a count and a baroness and had been raised as an aristocrat.

Marie d'Agoult and Cristina had not yet met, but Marie was prepared to dislike her, especially for Liszt's appreciation of her musical judgment. Music was not one of the passions shared by the two lovers and Marie, though she had been seduced by his very quality of public idol, despised the performing part of his life. Now that she lived with him, bore his children, she was embarrassed by what she felt was "the depravity of the being who amuses for money."[3] Cristina suffered no such discomfort; she was too grand a *grande dame* to be such a snob. Marie, descended from a German-Jewish banking family on her mother's side, was more aggressive about her aristocracy; she preferred not to associate with "riffraff" who worked for their money. To sacrifice all for an idol, yes, but then the idol must no longer descend into the arena. Cristina, on the other hand, delighted in Liszt's playing, whether in her salon or in a public hall, and understood, far better than Marie, his financial and egotistical need for audiences. "I have no need to tell you," she wrote to him in 1839, when

Lisztomania had become a mass psychosis, "that I would even become a habituée of the Tuileries if you played there. This year, however, I shall listen to you with the masses (if you don't mind) and shall be consoled for not hearing you alone by seeing the effect you always produce on everyone. This, for me, is truly a pleasure." More democratic than Marie, Cristina preferred to hear Liszt in a public concert hall, amid swooning ladies and shouting men, than in the royal salon of the king she despised.

Daniel Ollivier* claims that the two ladies met at the end of 1836, when Liszt and Marie resided at the Hôtel de France. (In that case, Cristina would necessarily have become acquainted with George Sand—if she had not already known her—since George rented an adjoining apartment in a spirit of "Piffoëllian"† friendship.) Cristina's *Souvenirs dans l'exil* seems to confirm this date, for in her account of a visit to Marie in 1840, she says that she was afraid "Nélida's** pride might suffer to appear before me in a situation so different from the one in which I had seen her a few years before." The salon of the Hotel de France, jointly shared by George Sand and the Liszt ménage, was the delight of their friends and the despair of the management. Elegant perfumes mingled with heavy cigar smoke in an atmosphere of bohemian jollity. Such commotion, such incongruities, had never been witnessed there before. Over the next few years the ladies had few occasions to meet again. Liszt did not return to Paris until 1840, after an extended stay in Italy and a European tour that took him back to his native Hungary, where he had become a national hero. By May of that year, when he left Marie in Paris to start a tour in England, her antipathy for Cristina had reached new heights and provoked a serious rift in the couple's already faulted union.

Liszt's brief reunion with Cristina that spring had been eagerly awaited by both of them. Their letters from 1837 to 1839 are long and affectionate, brimming over with recollections and anecdotes of common friends and events that predated Liszt's formalized liaison with Marie. It was a friendship solidly based on one of those nameless feelings shared by a man and a woman who are attracted to one another but never become lovers, whose untapped attraction spills over into a relationship more exciting than a platonic friendship and less ephemeral than a love affair. The favors they did one another were prompted by pleasure rather than duty. They were never intimate enough to become disillusioned, nor together long enough to lose interest. The spicy scent of the possible still

* Editor of Liszt's correspondence and a descendant through Blandine Liszt's marriage to Emile Ollivier. Marie had three children with Liszt: Blandine, Cosima (first married to Hans von Bülow, whom she left for Wagner), and Daniel.

† George Sand had given herself the name of Piffoël during her travels with Liszt and Marie in Switzerland earlier that year.

** Nélida is the heroine of Marie's autobiographical novel.

exudes its aroma from their correspondence. Cristina tactfully refrained from any criticism of "la resplendissante comtesse," as she called Marie. (Marie, less gracious, referred to Cristina as "la Comédienne," the actress, when writing to Liszt.) When he reminded Cristina of his past misdemeanors, she responded with her own mea culpas.

Liszt, from Italy, October 1839:

Recalling our past relations, I discovered in myself so many breaches and wrongs (in form at least) that I am infinitely grateful to you for not giving up on me. Do you still remember that ill-fated dinner to which I did not come when you had the kindness to invite in my honor Meyerbeer, Chopin, Herz, and others? Do you also remember my ridiculous exclusions toward Mme J[aubert] and that fateful box at the Opera? In fact, the more I think of those details (which come back to me after three years for no rhyme or reason) the more I remain astounded. What a scatterbrained and incorrigible boor I was then! And how right the illustrious author of *La Révolution française* [Mignet] to say about me "There is a great confusion in the head of that young man." Happily, you were willing to forget and forgive (*Tout comprendre c'est tout pardonner . . .*) and consider only the sincere and delicate affection you have inspired in me since the first days. . . . [Liszt's ellipses.]

Cristina's reply, from England, October 14, 1839:

. . . You remind me of very old wrongs which are even older given their distance. On my side, I also remember your patience à propos those poor Italians [the benefit concert], all the annoyance you endured without a murmur, and certain evenings when you played at Mme J's. Would it be presumptuous of me to suspect you did it just a bit for my sake? And furthermore, even if you had done nothing for the Italians and Mme J, I would still bear you no grudge for, let it be said in passing, it is not your virtues that move me; and now that I see and feel myself old enough not to fear being misunderstood, I will tell you it is quite simply *un non so che*.

According to Cristina's *Souvenirs dans l'exil,* Liszt asked her to visit Marie when he left for England in the hope of encouraging a friendship between the two. He had by then had his fill of Marie but felt guilty toward her. It was also the first time she was in Paris alone since their elopement, and Liszt doubtless wanted to be sure she would not be ostracized by the society she hoped to reconquer, for Marie had decided to build a new life of her own in Paris. She would spend the summer months with Liszt at the close of the concert season, and the remaining nine months would hold a salon in Paris and begin writing. As Cristina tells it, Liszt was distraught at leaving her "sick and alone in that vast egotistical city peopled with bitter memories." Although assured that his male friends would not neglect her—and Sainte-Beuve was only too impatient to substitute for him—Liszt nonetheless felt that Marie needed the sympathetic companionship of another woman, and specifically, a woman like Cristina, influential in society and devoted to him. (George Sand was not a member of Parisian society and in any event, Marie had managed to alienate her the year before.) Out of discretion, or perhaps ignorance, Cristina does not mention that the great romance was all but over.* On the contrary, she speaks of their separation as "a sacrifice made perhaps on the puritan altar of Britannic society," which would not have tolerated such flagrant adultery in its Victorian midst. Or perhaps money was the cause for leaving Marie behind; taking her on tour with him would surely have diminished his profits as well as his respectability. Cristina, never one to pretend that money was a subject undignified for a lady and a princess, writes very entertainingly about it.

> Liszt, as of his earliest years, made enormous sums of money which he spent with as much ease as he earned it, so that his fortune was always in the making. He covered the capitals of Europe, collected a few hundred thousand francs and armfuls of laurels; after which he returned to Paris to lead for a few weeks the life of a Russian prince, a Monte-Cristo, flinging gold all around, looking for people kind enough to borrow his money with the same zeal others use in seeking lenders; contributing to victims of famine, flame, and flood, trying to diminish through his donations all public calamities. Then the faithful Belloni [his factotum] would come before his lord and master, ears hanging, crestfallen, to say, "Monsieur Liszt, our purse is empty, we must leave!" Without inquiring how the deficit occurred, Liszt would pack his bags and fly off again in search of glory, which for him was the cloud that held the rain of gold.

Cristina dreaded the idea of visiting Marie, having no assurance that such a visit was desired by anyone but the departing lover. Marie might think it was Cristina's own initiative. What was she to do at Nélida's except appear in a tearful role, and worse still, a rehearsed one? If she did not weep with her, she would seem heartless. On the other hand, would Nélida not be offended by a stranger's consolations? Liszt had depicted her to Cristina in a deplorable state of mind and body, sick and abandoned. Financial difficulties doubtless added to her other misfortunes, otherwise Liszt would not have left her alone in Paris. "I took

---

* *Souvenirs dans l'exil,* it will be remembered, was compiled from letters written to Mme Jaubert.

stock of my position. Where am I going? To an unhappy person. Why am
I going? Because the alter ego of that suffering individual begged me to.
Should I not feel some pride at having been chosen to lighten the burden
that weighs on a lonely soul?" Once inside the door, opened by a liveried
servant, Cristina realized that money was not the problem. Satins, velvets,
gilded woods, paintings, bespoke luxury and taste. As Marie swept into
the room in a gown of black velvet, looking like Mary Stuart, Cristina
began to feel ridiculous.

> I tried to remember quickly all the hidden torments with which Liszt
> had so movingly aroused my compassion. From my entrance into the
> hallway, I crossed off poverty. Nélida's first words evaporated any sup-
> position of a woman whose heart was rent. There still remained the
> chapter of physical suffering. I seized this chance and hastened to ask
> about her health, to which she flippantly replied, "My legs bother
> me," and went on with the conversation. I participated little, listened
> distractedly. Nélida doubtless noticed, for interrupting herself, she
> asked, in the hope of unsealing my lips, that abrupt question, "And
> what are you doing now, Madame?" I consider this impertinent, for
> it implies that you are stupid or sullen. It is an attempt to find out if
> there is some subject you can talk about. . . . When this question is
> addressed to me I take it badly and never reply. I thus let the silence
> that accompanied it continue. . . . Nélida, totally despairing of get-
> ting anything out of me, answered herself. "As for me, I am interested
> at the moment in *The Loves of Minerals*."
> For a moment I thought I had misheard her and asked her to repeat
> her remark. . . . A German poet had guided her in this new study.
> . . . She wandered through it with the same ease as I through my
> garden; she explained why gold was not well tempered, why copper
> and tin sought each other out . . . what degree of passion was re-
> quired to give birth to a diamond. . . . In short, all very pretty, but
> I would have given the earth to be back in my own house. I was
> disoriented by a reality that was absolutely contrary to the picture
> painted by Liszt. . . . After vainly waiting for an opportunity to
> sneak away (other visitors had arrived in the meantime), I finally took
> my leave abruptly, received Nélida's compliments on the pleasure my
> visit had given her, etc.
> Ouf! I exclaimed once outside. What idiocy, what credulousness
> on my part! That Liszt does not question the despair his absence causes
> is all very fine. But what have I to do with it? . . . Nélida is as-
> suredly a person of true distinction; in other circumstances, I might
> have enjoyed her wit, her conversation, or originality, and even the
> loves of minerals might not have found me indifferent. But how to
> enjoy the charm of people . . . when one is placed on the sinking
> sands of ridicule? This unfortunate beginning resulted in my not see-

ing Nélida again; my memory of her is mixed with an unfavorable impression, while on her side, she surely conceived an unflattering opinion of me.

Cristina was perfectly right, and Marie communicated her opinion to Liszt at once, whereas Cristina waited eight years before writing about it, and then not to Liszt. Marie constructed her account very dramatically, first setting herself up as Cristina's defender against the reproaches of Mme de Montault, who "spoke at length to me about la Comédienne in relation to you. I trust you would have been pleased with my replies. She told me, with more energy than I have dared with you, what is ignoble and scandalous about her . . . and I took la Comédienne's side; which proves I haven't a trace of jealousy." She then recounted Cristina's visit with a catty vengeance that is markedly different from Cristina's view of her. And to make it doubly pungent, Marie added as epilogue the outrage of "sensitive souls" over Liszt's "manner of a lady's man." (Alphonse Karr's poison-penned monthly *Les Guêpes,* rightly titled *The Wasps,* had reported on May 1 that "Liszt's concert yesterday was remarkable. M. Liszt, as always, offered the spectacle of a great talent that often gets lost in exaggeration. It serves to influence certain women. . . . A princess, faithful to pianists in general, did not want to sit down, out of enthusiasm; she stood the whole time, leaning against a column." Marie made sure to point it out to him in another letter.)

> La Comédienne has just left, and I hasten to tell you my impression without any reticence or diplomacy. I found her face utterly ravaged, almost ugly, her body skinny and sickly, not at all grande dame, much less witty than I thought. She stayed an hour and said not a word; a rolling of the eyes, very affected and unpleasant, and on top of that an ineffable impression of falseness and nastiness. I thought I was very natural and in any case wittier than she. . . . I did not at all feel in her presence that discomfort, that inner anxiety, that sinking of the heart that I have so keenly experienced with other women I knew who pleased you. I found her a hundred thousand leagues removed from what used to be Piffoël's attractiveness. At first she was very constrained, then more and more at ease; in short, I can only be completely satisfied with her civilities, but I have the most detestable opinion of her (did you know she communes?). . . . The great grievance of sensitive souls is your manner of a lady's man.
> . . . the duchesse de Rauzan, speaking to Rouchaud at Lamartine's, said, "That poor Mme d'Agoult. I was truly sorry for her at the concert seeing the Princess Belgiojoso and Liszt together; this is not to speak ill of her or even less of him, but it was curious to say the least."[4]

Liszt minced no words in his reply. It had been a two-sided attack that required a double-barreled retort.

You are very harsh toward the princess; she has always seemed to me honest and kind, rather than false and nasty. . . . I thought she might suit you as a friend and perhaps please you as a person. I have found her more appealing than George (talent aside), and her manner of being *herself* pleases me. As to the scandal over the concert, as you call it, I found nothing scandalous about it. Let Mesdames M., R., and others talk as they like. The grievances of sensitive souls have little effect on me. Had I listened to them, we would probably not be writing to each other now.

Properly chastened, she informed him that she had paid a return call on the princess: "I found her much more at ease than the first time, more beautiful, and more charming in conversation, but my basic opinion remains the same, which does not mean that she is not an extremely interesting relation that I thank you for having made on my behalf." Cristina's miraculous recovery of beauty and wit in the space of a few days is impressive. It was not Cristina who regained her attributes but Marie her senses, although the letter reeks of hypocrisy. For Liszt's tone was most unconciliatory, and if they were fated to quarrel, Marie's pride could not allow that it be over Cristina! The amusing dénouement of this episode is that Marie did not see Cristina on May 13; she was still in bed, the servants told Marie. On May 14, in a note of confused apology, Cristina wrote: "Madame, It just occurs to me that it was you who were announced as la comtesse d'Argout and I never dreamed it might not be she. I have just now seen her. You cannot imagine how distressed I am, Madame, at the thought of this error. I shall come myself at three o'clock to ask your pardon. But I did not want to leave you until then in the belief that my response yesterday was intended for you. Until shortly, Madame, if you permit."

The same day Marie wrote to Liszt that she would continue her *histoire Comédienne* "because I am certain it amuses you," and informed him of her aborted visit. "This morning, a note arrived from her telling me that she thinks it may perhaps be I and not Mme d'Argout who came yesterday, and announcing herself for three o'clock. She came and made a thousand excuses saying that she had lied in order to escape Mme d'Argout. . . ." Liszt, less amused than she had hoped, again rushed to Cristina's defense by adroitly slipping into his account of people met in London the name of General Alava. "It seems he made the same mistake as la Comédienne when he was in Paris. He would have been very happy and eager to see Mme d'Agoult but not Mme d'Argout. He returned three times to this subject and was very insistent about it." When it came to Cristina, Liszt would not let Marie get away with any of her jibes, including her sobriquet for the princess which he repeated in evident irritation.

Liszt was not the only subject of rivalry between them. When Marie returned to Paris in 1840 she was determined to outdo every salon in town. She had the good fortune of finding a childhood friend, Delphine Gay, now Girardin, in a position of power and, like her, fallen from grace with Saint-Germain aristocracy: thus, a perfect ally. Marie, of whom Lamennais said, "I have never encountered in any woman a will of such resistance," was also endowed with no small opinion of herself. Her letters bubble over with self-praise: "Sainte-Beuve! He comes two or three times a week. That is quite a success. . . . People are very enthusiastic about me. When I start giving dinners, I will arouse fanatacism!" Even granting her some humor and the need to show Liszt she could manage without him, it is difficult to be amused by such exclamations as: "Viardot has just left. I was charming." Or "I too have my great success. Society is infinitely interested in me." Or "Koreff told me the other day that I shall soon have a circle such as there is no longer in Paris." Marie was a parvenue in everything: passion, motherhood, society, literature, even Italian nationalism, into which she fashionably threw herself in 1848. Instead of reacting negatively to this upstart who was invading a field legitimately hers, Cristina graciously acknowledged Marie's contribution. "Madame, Allow me to thank you in my name and in that of my unfortunate country, for the words of encouragement and consolation that you addressed to us in the press. We have great need of generous and intelligent friends. Fate is thus not entirely against us if it accords us such noble and enlightened ones. Continue your support, Madame. You will acquire the gratitude of a proscribed nation. . . ." Milan had capitulated to Austria, the future looked bleak. France sat by, as she had since 1831, watching Italy suffocate. Once again, Marie wrote in defense of Italy, and once again Cristina wrote in gratitude: "A thousand thanks, Madame, both for the noble words you addressed to my country and for the kind thought of sending them to me in my hermitage. I begin to think that France will only regain her rank in Europe when she has confided the care of her honor to the sex that until now has inspired little confidence. If that is so, we who wait for France to regain the sentiment of her own dignity in order to live, will have, I fear, to wait a long time. . . ."

Cristina was a lady, and a generous one. Which was why, long before and long after Marie entered his life, Liszt was devoted to her. She was a genuine person and a genuine friend, despite the affectations some chose to see in her. In 1837, when Liszt sent her an overdue letter from Bellagio, on the lake of Como, where Marie was awaiting her second child, Cosima, Cristina demurely answered: "I am enchanted by your reproaches. I wrote you this summer. . . . I concluded that you enjoyed receiving letters as little as you enjoyed answering them and kept my silence." Liszt quickly replied: "I really don't know, Belle Princesse, how I could have written a letter so silly as to suggest such a conclusion. As a general thesis, I doubtless prefer not to receive letters so as not to be bothered answering them. But what have these general theses to do with you, you who were born an exception and whatever you do . . . will die an exception. Let us speak no more of this and let it be understood once and for all that you will write me when and how you can, were it no more than to tell me how unbearable, detestable, etc., I am. . . ."

FROM 1837 ON, their exchange was more frequent and more animated, Liszt supplying news of musical life in Milan and his own contribution to it. "Last Sunday I gave my concert at La Scala. The evening was very elegant; I pocketed a large number of *zwanziger,* and the assemblage seemed more than satisfied with my circus dog tricks. The next time I shall play your piece from *I Puritani* . . . and also *Hexameron,* the definitive title of the monsterwork. . . ." Cristina in turn told him about Paris, as he requested, and supplied an interesting detail about the "monsterwork." She had it printed at her expense in Paris, and Hermann Cohen, Liszt's gifted pupil who later entered holy orders, was to send him the proofs. A missing letter from him apparently informed her that he had arranged for its publication in foreign capitals, for she thanked him in her reply of January 19, 1838.

> Your Milanese successes delight me and do not surprise me at all. It is not for your sake that I say this, but for my compatriots'. It is not for nothing that the Milanese and I are compatriots. . . .
>
> You want me to give you news of Paris. First, I can tell you that we too have our serious music; Tuesdays we barricade ourselves in and let no one enter but a violin, a cello, a bass, a viola, a flute, and a clarinette; Hermann [Cohen], my sister and I; sometimes my husband; sometimes also a lady who sings very well; and we make very substantial music, Beethoven, Weber, Schubert, Hummel too. You do not imagine that my sister and I can play more than a scale, you intimidate us so. You might ask Hermann, but you suspect him of partiality in my favor; so then, trust what I tell you and be certain that I am very capable. . . . I have hardly seen M. de Musset, who claims he is working. I am willing to believe it, judging by the charming stories that appear from time to time in *La Revue des*

Deux Mondes. On the other hand, I see Heine more often, who, he says, has regained his freedom. You know I have always maintained that the satanic Heine was really a good devil. I continue to, and am grateful to him for having always remained the same toward me. . . .

A continuous give and take of teasing reproaches adds to the charm of their extremely long letters. She accuses him of writing to everyone in Paris, which she does not mind so long as he continues to write to her. He defensively asks if she considers "everyone" her husband, whom in fact he had thanked for some letters of recommendation:

> I don't know why this reproach, against which I would not dream of vindicating myself if it were a reproach, hurt me. Yes, be informed, dear, beautiful and ideal Princess, I still claim, though alas it matters little to you, that I go only to your house and write only to you; and my quixotic manner is sincere in this respect. . . . Two things that gave me extreme pleasure: 1. Your gown (Venetian bodice, I think) at the Court Ball which I absolutely must see when I return; 2. The sort of little "furor" caused in Milan, Venice, and Vienna by that old piece I dedicated to you while awaiting better, or less bad.

By May 1838 she had already gone into seclusion in Versailles. Writing on the second to congratulate him on his success in Vienna, her tone is charming as always but a note of depression has crept in. Replying to his request for confirmation of the rumor that she is expected in Milan—she had not returned since 1828—she tells him that her trip is postponed, asks that he tell no one, and explains that she was warned about trouble getting out of Milan. She does not tell him the real reason, which is her pregnancy. But she does speak of Victoria's coronation, planned for the following summer, at which time she hopes to see him. Though only three years older than he, she frequently makes the difference sound much greater. Teasing him about his "abandonment" of Milan, she asks if it is the absence of newspapers and Parisian wit that made him leave. "What, do you feel the need for the wit of others? It is because you are still very young; I, who no longer have that failing, would ask to have near me no more than a loving smile and an intelligent expression, and around me only books and silence. If life were an opera, I would prefer the music to the words. You will say that if my desires are so modest it should be easy to satisfy them. Alas, no. Do you think quiet, gentle people are easy to find, above all in la belle France?" A year later, writing from England, she closed her letter with the melancholy remark that she was as impatient to see him as to hear him again, and all the more so because he was entering the world just as she was about to leave it: "I am thirty-one, and as soon as I have married off my youngest sister I shall live for myself, that is, outside the world. I have little hope that you will come looking for me there, and have little time left to meet you."

A letter from Liszt written from Italy in early June 1839 indicates that she had stopped writing to him during the preceding year; her letter from England quoted above was in reply to this one. Mystified by her silence and not a little hurt, he attempts a formal overture. "It would be presumptuous of me, Princess, to complain of your silence. Your letters have always been for me a privilege, a delight. Which is not to say that I have the slightest right to them. However, since you no longer answer me, I hope you will allow me at least to tell you how sensitive I am to the least sign of your good will, and what value I attach to your memory." He then makes a valiant effort to revive her interest by telling her of his innovation—a landmark in musical history: that of giving solo recitals—which he modestly contrasts with the concerts given that spring in her salon.

> . . . A few issues of the *Gazette Musicale* that happened to fall into my hands informed me that you pitted church against church and made magnificent harmonies resound in your charming salon. I confess that is perhaps the only regret of my winter. I would so deeply have wished to be there, to admire you, applaud you. Many people who had the good fortune to be present at those select soirées told me about them with enchantment.
>
> What a contrast with those boring "musical soliloquies" (I know no other name to apply to this invention of mine) which I thought might please the Romans, and which I am capable of importing to Paris, so boundless has my impertinence grown! Can you imagine that, having given up all hope of composing a program that made any sense, I dared give a series of concerts all alone, smacking of Louis XIV, and declaring cavalierly to the public *"Le Concert c'est Moi."* As a mere curiosity, I transcribe here for you one of the programs of these soliloquies:
>
> 1. Overture to *William Tell,* performed by M. Liszt.
> 2. *Réminiscences des Puritans,* Fantasy composed and performed by the same mentioned above.
> 3. Etudes and Fragments, by the same again.
> 4. Improvisations on given themes still by the same.
>
> And that is all. . . .
>
> Barring changes, I still plan to spend the end of next winter (March and April) in Paris. Will you allow me to make up for all the spaces in my correspondence at the rue d'Anjou? I still count on your friendly and indulgent kindness. But will you carry it so far as to give me some sign of life before the end of my stay in Italy?

To mark his resentment over her silence, he closes with the most formal of salutations: *"Veuillez bien agréer, Madame la Princesse, l'expression de mes sentiments les plus respectueux et les plus dévoués,"* still used today for business letters. Her reply two weeks later does not reveal the whole truth but, by way of apology, recognizes that she did not answer him the previous summer because she was "so dreadfully ill" she could think of nothing else. Their correspondence is resumed with one lengthy missive after another, and to his implication of a musical polemic on her part against contemporary music she answers:

I pitted church against church? Which church? The resplendent countess? The roulades and bravura arias? No such thing, dear Liszt. I merely had performed old and serious music because I like it, and asked all my socialite acquaintances not to honor me with their presence. I think that is what attracted them. Those namby-pambies must have ached to yawn at Mozart's *Requiem.* However, they betrayed nothing. But when you are in Paris, which I desire greatly, if you do not neglect the rue d'Anjou too much, as I hope, Mozart, Haydn, Handel, et al., may well be wronged, for I will doubtless wrongly prefer what you choose to call your soliloquies to all their masterpieces. . . .

Their reunion in Paris in April 1840, though brief, restoked the affection that had smoldered during the three intervening years. Marie's crisis of jealousy and his own distaste for the whole tiresome liaison may have served to heighten his admiration for Cristina. For beginning that summer their letters are more personal, less bantering. Yet nothing in them, and some are even quite direct, suggests that there was any physical intimacy between them, any act, word, or gesture that crossed over from affection into passion. In fact, an exquisite letter from Liszt dated October 1841 corroborates this.

You tell me, "Try to convince yourself that writing to me relaxes you." I would have no difficulty convincing myself of many things which you would never guess I am convinced about regarding you. This ideal cult (and do not mistake this for a platitude) that I have always had for you has not made my relations with you easy, as you claim. I was always above or below the mark, and even now, I invoke what is indefinite and unexpressed between us far more than what we have managed to say or write. My life is filled with obstacles, irritations, miserable trifles. From time to time and from very far away, a ray of light fell on me, a shaft of fortitude reached my heart. You were full of sweet indulgence and noble kindness at a time when others had little indulgence, little kindness. I shall never forget the first year I had the honor of knowing you. Since then, you have been something else, let me tell you, something more for me.

The delicacy of his sentiments and words is all the more striking coming from a man of his artistic and physical febrility. Cristina had once told him, and he quoted it with pride to Marie, that he lived as though he were immortal. The enormous expense of energy and emotion that went into his artistic life, the constant availability of women for a day, a night, or for life—they were literally falling at his feet all over Europe; they kept his gloves, his handkerchiefs, his cigar butts like religious relics—make his relations with Cristina quite unique. Here was a woman who was anything but available, and who made herself even less so after the birth of her child. Never mentioned in her letters to Liszt until November 1841, the event is referred to so casually—"I have my books, my research, many letters to write, my little Marie who interrupts me a hundred times an hour . . ."—that she must have told him about it when they met the year before. Their letters were often separated by months, their meetings by years, and rendered even more difficult by her seclusion in Locate. In the interim, Liszt lived in a vortex of concert tours and turmoil with Marie. Still, he found the time to think of Cristina and to write her astonishingly long letters at fairly regular intervals. Was she perhaps the antidote to his poisoned existence? Until the advent of Carolyne Sayn-Wittgenstein, it was as though he had fixed his sights on Cristina as his guiding star. He knew he could count on her affection, knew she understood him, perhaps even believed that one day . . .

> Will we ever talk freely, abundantly? Let me hope it will be next fall in Venice. Oh! do not view that project of Venice as a castle in Spain. I need to go back there, I want to go back. The external determining motive for that return will be my *Corsair* (I confide this to you alone and beg you not to speak of it to anyone at all). Although my reputation as a virtuoso has grown since we left each other and, at the moment—forgive me one more arrogance—I am on the point of being the only one of my breed, I nonetheless do not wish to grow old in this career. In three years, positively, I will close my piano. It will be in Vienna and in Pest, where I began my career, that I will end it. Before that, as of winter '43, I want to do an opera (*The Corsair*, after Lord Byron) and it is in Venice that I want to produce it. . . .

He never composed the opera, nor did he retire from the concert stage until 1847, but in October 1841, when he wrote the letter, it was a comforting illusion to a man who had been in perpetual motion for the past fourteen months, often playing two concerts a day. "In two weeks I will be in Berlin," he wrote in closing. "Be very kind and write me a few lines care of general delivery. And above all, do not ask me to keep 'a memory of my friends'! You know very well that I am devoted to you heart and soul, and that I wish to keep my little 'cult' and not a memory." Six years later his "cult" was still very much alive, and important enough for him to want Marie to know what Cristina thought of him. His motive could not have been perfidious, for his life with Marie was over. They continued to correspond, as would any divorced couple who had had children together, but they lived separate existences. It was thus not to hurt her that in a letter to Marie of January 29, 1846, he included a long quotation from Cristina's latest letter to him.

> After all, what it is that you need? A disposition favorable to composi-
> tion, and perhaps any kind of fever is that disposition. You are not
> one of those natures that delight (because they take pride) in the
> tortures they impose on others through the force of their own will.
> Be of those who believe they have conquered all because they have re-
> jected all combat (this smacks a bit of the mother of the Church,
> doesn't it?). You need fever? And do you believe that any effort is
> accomplished without some auxilliary fever? But you like fevers that
> come and go at will. So be it. Have the fever that suits you. Set fire
> to your houses, but take care to insure them beforehand.

What a testimonial, and what an astute analysis of his temperament! No, Liszt was not one to inflict tortures or even petty vengeances on others. In fact, among his contemporaries, he stands out as a grand sei-gneur: generous with his time, his money, his interest; always willing to help, be it an aspiring musician or a desperate cause. Contrasted with Chopin the man—aloof, distrusting, jealous of his privacy—or with Chopin the correspondent—expansive about business details and com-plaints, but otherwise grudging of his pen, humorless, and uninspiring—Liszt's ebullient and generous nature becomes even more striking. Cho-pin was the undisputed poet laureate of piano composition, yet he was touchy enough to quip: "Liszt rides to Olympus on another man's Pega-sus." And when Ernest Legouvé informed him that Liszt had asked to review Chopin's concert of April 26, 1841, Chopin was anything but pleased, preferring that Legouvé write the review. When Legouvé as-sured him that Liszt's admiration would provide him with "a magnificent kingdom," Chopin retorted, "Yes, in his empire." Not so, however, for the article which appeared in the *Gazette Musicale* of May 2 is a long and glowing tribute to Chopin's art as a composer and performer. No-where is there the slightest hint of rivalry; one would not even guess another pianist-composer had written it, were it not signed. If anything, there is a hint of self-criticism in Liszt's subtle comparison: "He had no need to astound or capture his audience; he sought delicate sympathies rather than noisy enthusiasm."

Cristina left other appraisals of Liszt's character, one in the form of a remonstrance, recalling her then-recent meeting with him in April 1840. Writing in September, at the beginning of her long seclusion in Locate, she found the courage to tell him what had been on her mind for some time.

> . . . You know that I have always had for you not only admiration, but affection as well. This last sentiment prompts me to speak of observations I could not help making for quite a while, but fear of displeasing you held me back. Admiration runs no risk, and in truth neither does affection; but there is something intermediary called sympathy which was inspired in me by a man whose heart was filled with trust, selflessness, benevolence, attraction to all noble things and respect for sacred things. Is that man disappearing and yielding to a mocking, blasé, sceptical person, disgusted with his own kindness? Do not let that happen, I beg you, if you do not wish to cause me real pain. . . .

Liszt, gracious and lucid, did not try to argue with her: he immediately conceded she was right. He merely tried to draw her attention to the reasons for his "blasé" manner, and to assure her he was not really like that underneath. At the same time, he captured the pungent flavor of Parisian mores in a passage that this writer has never seen quoted before. Passing through Paris on his return from London, he met Heine and Balzac on the street, both of whom asked about her, and a host of other luminaries on the same boulevards, including Chopin and Berlioz.

> . . . At last, amazed, overwhelmed, charmed, enchanted by so much wit, genius, transcendence of every kind, I left for Fontainebleau. Along the way, someone asked me what impression Paris had made on me: "That of an old coat which is not worn enough to throw away but which one only puts on with disgust and displeasure."
>
> A propos, I would like to reply to the reproaches you so delicately make. And first of all, I concede the case. Appearances surely make you right. But is it so underneath? I do not think so. The local influence of Paris is largely responsible for my scepticism and mockery (which do not go very far, by the way). It is so certain that your neighbor will mock you at the first occasion, and often straightaway, that you are obliged to take the offensive so as not to be too disadvantaged. . . . One howls with the wolves, one wallows in dirty streams with the derelicts, however little taste one may have for howling or mud. Perhaps I am deluding myself, but it seems to me I am a better

person elsewhere, and I would so much like to see you again in Italy* so as to show myself in a better light.

In 1841 he gave three concerts in Paris between March 15 and May 5. Cristina was still in Locate. Writing from London, Liszt told her how many times during those six weeks he had passed the rue d'Anjou with feelings of heavy melancholy. He had finally gone to see Bianchi to ask him "to put me at your feet, epistolarily at least." This time, he felt he had conquered Paris. "Thank heaven, I have finally settled my score of vanity with the city of Paris. It was about time. My three concerts have definitively set me apart and established me in a suitable manner. I do not hide from you that this gave me just a little bit of pleasure. And had you been there, I imagine you would have been sympathetic enough to my weakness to be amused by it too. . . ." Cristina was more than sympathetic. Six months later, with half a dozen letters in between, she was able to contribute to his vanity after having heard Thalberg play his *Moses* variations again in Milan.

> I have often been told that I was unjust toward Thalberg and that my admiration for you muddled my judgment. I do not admire you any less than before, but it is a long time since my admiration has been refreshed. Furthermore, peace between you and Thalberg having been signed, I believe, nothing prevented me any longer from opening my eyes to his blinding light. Alas! they remained hermetically closed, and throughout the entire concert, the shadows could not have been deeper. The variations reminded me of the Italian poet who claimed to have adapted *Gerusalemme liberata* in *versi sdruccioli*† . . . and who did nothing more than add a "lo" to each verse, for example "Canto l'arme pietose e 'l capitano lo/Che 'l gran sepolcro liberò di Cristo lo," and so on to the end of the poem.
>
> The enthusiasm was pretty thin for Milanese enthusiasm. On the spur of the moment, the listeners admitted their disappointment; but today, they have gone back on their deception and deny their honesty: the Thalberg who made such a splash in Paris, London, Vienna, all the way to St. Petersburg, must be a genius, and so they go off swooning. . . .

IF ONE WERE TO JUDGE from the sequence of their letters in the published correspondence, one might conclude that after 1838 their only

---

* *Vous retrouver encore en Italie* implies that they had met there before—in Venice? This would seem to be confirmed by his letter of October 1841 (quoted on p. 353).

† An Italian verse form in which each line ends with a *sdrucciola* (a word whose accent falls on the antepenultimate syllable), thereby adding another syllable to the standard eleven-syllable line.

contact was epistolary. Fortunately, other writers who had personal griefs to air have filled in the gaps. In the summer of 1842, when Cristina returned to Paris after her two-year reclusion, she received friends in the house near Versailles, Port-Marly, that Mignet had rented for her. We know from Musset, then at the height of his desperate infatuation, and from Louise Colet's account in *Lui,* that Liszt was noticeably present. And from Balzac's frequent mention of Liszt in connection with Cristina, when writing to Mme Hanska, we have all manner of chronological and psychological indications.

On May 15, 1843, referring to Liszt's tournée in Poland, Balzac furnishes a never-quoted detail regarding *Béatrix,* his novel built around George Sand, Marie d'Agoult, and Liszt, long assumed to be the model for the singer Conti: "You saw Liszt and I am happy to have procured this little pleasure for you. Alas, I have never dared tell him that Conti is Sandeau qua musician, just as Lousteau [another character in the novel] is also Sandeau.* Marie d'Agoult is a frightful desert animal. . . . Liszt is happy to be rid of her." The next day, he writes: "It is la Belgiojoso who took Liszt from Mme d'Agoult. . . . As to la Belgiojoso, who at the last concert did honor to Liszt by sitting at the feet of his piano, she no longer gives him a hoot! She has just finished four volumes on The Establishment of Catholic Doctrine. . . ." Balzac is a source to be used with discretion. His news is presumably fresh for he would not be sending Hanska out-dated stories since she had other Parisian contacts. On the other hand, his analyses are often unreliable since they are intended to amuse her and keep her distracted from his own activities. However questionable, these bits of 1843 gossip demonstrate that in Balzac's mind Liszt and Cristina were linked, and that he saw them together. In 1844 his letters ascertain that Liszt was very much at home in Port-Marly for the better part of June, since Balzac saw him there on two spaced occasions. His overreaction to Liszt's informal manners as Cristina's house guest betrays his own envy. And when irked, Balzac could be as unreliable in his appraisals of men as of women. Liszt is hardly recognizable in Balzac's exclamations: "He has the conceit of an actor and the rancor of a public prosecutor." Balzac had just returned from a visit to Port-Marly on the tenth of June, outraged that "Liszt is absolutely like the master in Cristina's house . . . ordering the carriage harnessed in front of her to take me to the train." On the 23rd, having met Liszt at a dinner in Paris, he was still complaining that "Liszt is at the princess Belgiojoso's and *so openly,* that he goes back there at 11:30 P.M.! Cristina is no longer worthy of respect!"

* Jules Sandeau was George's former lover and Balzac's former colleague; both were bitterly disappointed by him.

One might deduce from this that Cristina and Liszt had become declared lovers. It would be a lovely tale to spin, were there enough
threads. How pleasant to think that she had finally succumbed to a man
so attractive in every way. Liszt, direct, handsome, wholesome, was by far
the most appealing among her illustrious admirers. Heine, though en-
dearing, could inspire compassion rather than passion in her. Musset,
forever petulant and playing for pathos, could be an enchanting child but
not a man, and his dissolute fraternity with Emilio did little to enhance
him in Cristina's eyes. Mignet, with his ramrod correctness, was a moral
rock and the perfect antidote to Emilio's toxic effects on her, but was
hardly titillating. Liszt was not a man like any other; he was a force of
nature, magnetic, irresistible. His overwhelming sexuality caused women
in his audience to faint, to sigh, to scream, in some cases even to fight
over a memento. Lisztomania, rapidly diagnosed as sexual hysteria by
Heine, swept through Europe like a fever. Cristina tells of a "great
English lady" who had her magnificent piano sealed forever after Liszt
played on it "so that no other mortal would ever again place his fingers
on that sacred instrument." Cristina herself was apparently not insensitive to Liszt's charisma; she confirms his effect on audiences in her
own letters, and with undisguised pleasure. It is thus not impossible that
a grain of truth lay behind Balzac's fantasies. Granted, they were constructed largely to protect himself from Mme Hanska's possessive curiosity. And the more he fantasized on Cristina's relations with Liszt, the less
he could be suspected of any hanky-panky with her, since Liszt was
a virtual chaperone for his visits to Port-Marly. Whatever transpired in
June 1844 will, and perhaps should, remain a mystery. As Liszt once told
her, when looking for the right adjective to apply to her, "There are
occasions when I hate the precision of terms. Should there not always be
a bit of *sous-entendu* in relationships that have a certain charm?"

    In 1845, after more than a decade of youthful friendship with Cris-
tina—always confidential, occasionally flirtatious—Liszt saw himself as a
mature man, *nel mezzo del cammino,* faced with a lonely future. Cristina
had long since renounced her own youth and any claim to happiness as a
woman: "I am thirty-one," she had written six years earlier, "and as soon
as I have married off my youngest sister, will live for myself, outside the
world." As can happen to old flirtations, a sudden spark—ignited by melancholy, a rush of memories, a fleeting desire—bursts into flame, casting
a new light on a familiar face. Was it the summer of 1844, the final
separation with Marie, the draining routine of anonymous crowds, empty
honors, temporary addresses? Whatever the reason, his life could be
summed up as "care of general delivery." The year 1843 had come and
gone and he was still a wandering minstrel, his ambitions dangling like
the strings of his devastated pianos. Suddenly the lonely wanderer had a

fantasy. Could not this cult he had been celebrating like an errant monk find a permanent altar? Cristina, herself a displaced person in her private and political life, had replanted roots in Locate since 1840 to provide an estate and a name for her daughter. In 1845 she added second roots in Paris by buying the Montparnasse property. To Liszt, her life seemed secure and enviable. She had had the courage to do what she wanted. Sometime in the late summer or early fall of 1845—his letter is missing—Liszt announced his intention of spending a fortnight with her in Paris or Port-Marly. Their month together in June 1844 had certainly placed their relationship in a different register, for there is a hint of intimacy, the right of possession, in her reply of September 1845 to his promised visit:

> I find you very cowardly not to show your golden face. However, you promise to come in a month and I will hold you to it. I am philosophical enough to believe that even waiting is good. But be prompt, my dear Liszt; tell yourself that nothing is more common than inexactitude and place yourself on the side of virtue. My little Marie's cough of last winter still rings too painfully in my ears for me to delay my passage across the Alps later than the first days of November. So if you plan on giving me a fortnight, arrive on the fifteenth of October at the latest. I will say more and better: see to it that your laziness and my entreaties prevail, and if you wish to give me fifteen days, take the necessary measures to be able to give me twenty or thirty.

She signed the letter with *"Adieu, mille amitiés,"* a considerable change from the *"Votre amie dévouée"* of all her letters through 1841.

During that visit they evidently discussed a number of major projects. One was Liszt's interest in buying a lot on her property in Montparnasse and building a house near the ones she planned for herself and Thierry. Another was his plan to write an opera entitled *Sardanapale,* once again based on a Byron text, for which he wanted her help with the scenario. Still another was her new publishing enterprise. The only project realized was his association with *La Gazzetta Italiana.* Until she took over this bankrupt newspaper, its first director, Falconi, had been unable to find money or contributors for the paper since no one took him or it seriously. As soon as it was known that Cristina had assumed direction, with Falconi as editor, the left and the right began to attack it. Mazzini and Metternich both saw the *Gazzetta* as a potential weapon in Cristina's hands and neither liked it, each being opposed to the peaceful revolution she was propagating which foresaw neither a republican future nor an imperial status quo. Deciding to run the newspaper like a business, she floated stock. Liszt at once bought an interest by transferring twenty-five shares of his railroad stock to the *Gazzetta.* Outside of Cristina, he was the only significant investor. She was understandably grateful, and he touchingly gracious in his reply to her thanks.

> . . . Let me tell you that you must have a tremendous imagination to believe that I am doing you a favor! I, do you a favor? And in what, if you please. . . . It is true I remember having found for you one day a broken down hansom at the railroad station. The rest is of the same nature and will, alas, always be of the same magnitude. . . . Know me once and for all to be gentleman or plebeian enough, as you like, to appreciate certain nuances, however distraught and distracted I may be.

Anything but distracted, he took advantage of this favorable situation to speak more openly than ever before of their personal relations. Cristina's letter, to which this was an answer, is missing. But Liszt's opening lines suggest enough to whet the curiosity. "For today, let me reply to only half of your *excellentissime* letter; as to the other half (the better), it is wiser to postpone it for another two months and it will be in Locate that we talk about it. Yes, Princess, my trip to Locate is absolutely decided for the end of March.* Not only because you offer me a kind of challenge with charming good grace, which deeply moves me, but even more so because it would give me pleasure to see you again and see you happy in your way, according to your tastes." The reference here is to her preference for a contemplative existence in Locate rather than the more brilliant life of Paris. Three paragraphs later, after telling her about his arrangements to have the stock certificates delivered to her Parisian attorney and offering more—"If by chance that is not enough I expect a little windfall at the beginning of January, which I would be honored to place at your disposal"—he touches on a very personal subject.

> I do not know if it is an illusion, but it seems to me that my way of loving you is not completely unworthy of you; in any event, I hope it will never be unseemly to you, and that the years, by bringing us closer together, will give you more complete assurance of what is absolute in my nature which, thanks to I don't know what chance or sympathy, has not struck you as absolutely unbearable until now at least!

The smiling complacency of his exclamation mark, and the exaggerated understatement of the whole paragraph seem to imply more than has ever been suspected, except by Balzac. No biographer has thought to include Cristina in the catalogue of Liszt's amours, yet for duration alone, she is surpassed only by his other princess, Carolyne Sayn-Wittgen-

* His arithmetic is slightly off since the letter is dated December 15, 1845.

stein. The ambiguities raised by this letter are further enhanced by his closing paragraph, which seems to refer back to an expression she used in her missing letter. If this is so, then she evidently questioned him—and in a manner that pleased him since he speaks of her *"excellentissime"* letter, whose "better" part would be discussed in Locate—about his *"embrasement subit,"* which he put between quotes. In the context, this "sudden conflagration" can only imply a genuine infatuation. After all the years of affectionate teasing, of conserving his "cult," he has now fallen in love with her. It may have been the rekindling of old embers, stirred up by their meeting in October. For it was evidently then that the "paroxysm" began, as he makes pointedly clear in his dating of the event: "for the last five weeks. . . ." In view of her fear of personal involvements—not even her liaison with Mignet had proved a happy one—and her distrust of passionate men, it is probable that she teased him about the suddenness of his infatuation and the certainty of its equally sudden passing. This would seem to explain his equivocal remarks.

> How can I talk to you about my "sudden conflagration" without flaming up in ridicule and stupidity? And yet I want to talk to you about it one day, if you permit, when it will have passed. . . . Soon, perhaps! For the moment, and for the last five weeks, there is a status quo of paroxysm difficult to explain and for which I do not wish to seek the reason. . . . Entirely at your feet.

In January the visit to Locate still seems possible and he is "while waiting, still at your feet." But by April, driven by the need to continue his killing schedule before the season ends—fifteen concerts in six weeks between Vienna and Pest—Locate becomes unrealizable.

> The summer approaches in rapid strides; the fable of the grasshopper comes to mind and I feel little gifted for Terpsichore. The little house in Montparnasse tempts me enormously, but to realize that charming dream, I must not sing too long during the summer for fear of having to dance when winter winds arrive. Oh! money! money! what a dreadful corrosive!

He is serious enough about the house to enter into concrete figures: he will have 40,000 francs available by the end of 1847, but if the cost of land and building exceeds 50,000 he is afraid of running short. "The idea of marriage that you delicately slipped into your last letter is far removed from my thinking. In any case, if there ever were such a possibility, it would certainly simplify the settling of my accounts, for very certainly, I would never marry a woman who had only a cottage and her heart to offer in exchange for my long hair, which is beginning to gray, and for my extracted teeth." The crudeness of his candor cannot have been gratuitous; he seems to be telling her that marriage, which he cannot have with her, has no place in his life except as a convenience; his sentiments are committed elsewhere and she knows where.

As to *Sardanapale*, Cristina had a completed libretto ready to show him in May 1846 and asked him to pay the poet, recently released from prison, who wrote it. "My dear Liszt, You may be the most famous of mortals, but it is impossible to find out where you are. This saddens me since I have in my desk the most beautiful *Sardanapale* in the world, fruit of the labors or slavery of the same poet whom I first contacted and who sent you a 'scenario' through me. . . . The place from which my poor friend emerged was not Peru, and he came out far poorer than when he went in, which was not easy to do." She then closes with a remark about her political concerns—"I do not speak to you about our affairs because I remember that your sympathies are not with us"—which rightly arouses his anger. This is an inexplicable lapse, for only the year before he had contributed so generously to the *Gazzetta*. She seems to have confused him with Mignet and her other Parisian friends *"de la raison glacée."* Liszt replies:

> I am entirely at your feet, Madame, and kiss your hands—but it is impossible not to quarrel with you, and seriously, over the last lines of your letter! Through what distraction, may I ask, can you have written to me: "I do not speak to you of our affairs because *I remember* that your sympathies are not with us." Frankly, if you told me that I had never done anything but hit wrong notes on the piano, that my vocation was to be a grocer, such an opinion, to my mind, would have a greater degree of probability. Evidently, in my dual quality of bourgeois and musician, I am not even in a position to vindicate myself of your unfair charge.
>
> Otherwise, your letter was a great joy; first of all coming from you, then announcing the realization of a desire, an idea, the postponement of which I had, willy-nilly, become resigned to but had not abandoned.

Delighted over her participation in *Sardanapale,* he asks her to make any criticisms directly to the poet. "The notes and comments you added in the margin of Rotondi's [earlier] libretto attest to such a mastery of this genre that one could not do more wisely than rely in total confidence on your decision." He also adds an intriguing remark that relates to their collaboration on the opera, but evidently goes beyond it. "Next spring *Sardanapale* will be ready, and at the same time I will perhaps have something else to tell you, which will be worth my talking to you about." Despite his enthusiasm, he was still smarting over her remark by the time he reached the end of the letter. His sarcasms indicate the degree to which her belief in his solidarity mattered to him, for by doubting his sympathy for her cause, she was excluding him from something as important to her as music for him.

> Be kind enough to reply to these lines, but please, spare me the insults, and do me the honor of believing, without reserve or restriction, in the sincere rectitude of my *sympathies* and my frank and firm intention to translate them into acts or works, according to the circumstances, and within my powers.
> *Bien à vous d'admiration et d'amitié.*

He was truly piqued, as his closing proves—no longer at her feet, merely admiring and friendly. Yet, his final paragraph carries an allusion far more personal than political. His underlined *sympathies,* made collective because she used the term, clearly harks back to his letter of December 15, 1845, and to his *"embrasement subit"* of the preceding fall. His reiterated determination "to translate them into acts or works" suggests her unwillingness to trust his infatuation or his ambitions for the future —*acts* evidently related to her, *works* to the opera and the house in Paris. A few weeks later, on May 24, he is ready to make the first downpayment on that future, but an intervening letter from her, which is missing, has made him apprehensive. Still, he refuses to give up hope. With her assurance that construction costs will not exceed 25,000 francs and her offer of long-term credit for the land, he says, "I no longer hesitate and consider our affair settled. In a week I will return from Vienna and will immediately send you a draft for 12,000 francs to put the masons to work. So then, it is understood that we will build and construct, and I will honor all my commitments. *Amen!"*

This closing sentence reads like a last-stand hope that, despite her pessimistic prognosis for any joint future, *Sardanapale* and Montparnasse will keep them together. This would have been his first opera and his first home—the "desire" and the "idea" that he had postponed but not abandoned. He is determined to go ahead with the opera—*"Sardanapale* will go on next season in Vienna"—but the statement sounds flat. He is equally determined to build the house, but sounds defensive. And he has returned to the formality of addressing her by her title, where in 1845 he had omitted any address whatever to circumvent the problem. He has grudgingly modulated into a minor key of friendship, apparently imposed by the resoluteness of her transition. The clue lies in his opening innuendoes, all of which refer to her and to his disappointment. "I may have forgotten how to hold a pen since I no longer write to anyone, but I have not forgotten to remember the infinitely small number of people who have been more than kind to me." The double-entendre is very deft:

she has forgotten his help—the times he played only because she asked him, the material expression of his attachment to her the year before—but he remembers hers.

> Let me then, Madame la Princesse, thank you for that and for what you are kind enough to remain for me: a friend as intelligent as indulgent, full of those foresights and precautions that only exceptionally superior beings can invent. Having said that, let us get on, not with our castles in Spain, but with our house in Paris, whose roof and foundation will both be provided by your kindness toward me.

The irony is cutting, and made doubly trenchant by his use of the masculine for *friend: "un ami aussi intelligent qu'indulgent."* As in the past, with Heine and Musset, she has once again retreated as soon as an advance threatened her privacy. Platonic love? Ad infinitum. Intimate involvement? Nunquam. She is willing to be a friend, and may herself have written *"un ami"* to distinguish unequivocally from *"une amie,"* which can connote "a mistress." But let him have no illusions about the future, or build "castles in Spain" around the house in Paris. He throws back her "precautions" as the excessive distrust of an unnatural creature (*"qu'il n'est donné qu'à des êtres exceptionnellement supérieurs d'inventer"*), at the same time trying to embarrass her by his enforced consciousness of their class, or moral, differences. Here was a man countless women would have sold their souls to possess for a night, and he was proposing a lifetime. However charming and even modest he appears in his letters, his pride could not have remained unaffected by this kind of cold shower. His entire letter points to the denigrations hers must have stated or implied. His promise to honor his commitments, his resignation to her unflattering view of him (*"Aussi bien ne pourrai-je jamais vous paraître que passablement . . . et faible!"*),* suggest some real spade-calling on her part. Although proud of his unique talents and appreciative of his generous nature, she evidently could not envisage a life with an itinerant pianist in whom, much as she loved him as a friend, she found too many signs of irresponsibility to trust as a life companion. The flame in him was snuffed out, leaving him depressed and apologetic. By way of excuse for reneging on his promise to come to Locate, he tells her that her "two rivals, as you call them, Athens and Constantinople, will also be postponed *aux calendes grecques*," a time that may never come, like his anticipated stay with her in Locate.

> For I feel completely emptied of any enthusiasm for travel . . . or for anything else. These last three months have left at the bottom of my

---

* Liszt's ellipses and syntax suggest a vulgar term of derogation, commonly translated as "jerk."

thoughts a strange unpleasant sediment of sadness and inappetence. My Hungarian popularity has consolidated and doubled in a way, my little successes (if I may speak of them) grow, my youthful follies are becoming reasonable. . . . All that, instead of raising me to the heights of my naïve adolescence, bows me down and wrinkles my brow with painful furrows. But why do I speak to you this way? I will evidently never appear to you as anything more than pretty much of a . . . and weak! Try to remain kind to me, even if I only live up to half what you would like me to be.

One is chagrined to see a Liszt so unlike the cock of Cristina's description to Mme Jaubert: ". . . the proud air with which he stood on his spurs while pressing the keys of the piano." In all fairness to Cristina, it should be noted that in 1846, had Liszt been twice the man she wanted him to be, she would probably have remained unreceptive. For Marie's sake, let alone her own, she could not jeopardize her hard-won reputation for sobriety, scholarship, and self-denial with a figure as public as Liszt. She was furthermore committed over her head to people and projects— her child, Thierry, the houses to be built in Paris, innovations in Locate, the *Gazzetta,* preparation of a new book, and even Mignet, who remained an important if inadequate part of her life.

Mignet's negative role is not without significance in Cristina's attitude toward Liszt at that point. Had her relationship with Mignet been an ordinary love affair that waned with time and habit, she might conceivably have gone on to other lovers, perhaps eventually yielding to Liszt. Instead, what she had with Mignet was more like a routine marriage, with its ups and its downs, staid, formal, and binding. The year 1845 had marked the lowest point in their long intimacy. As she told Thierry, she would never again bind herself to any such *vie à deux* that promised happiness: "There are other associations that one forms for better and more serious purposes than pleasure." Her feelings toward Liszt had been understandably warm in 1845. His generous contribution to the *Gazzetta* had established a meaningful association between them, and their collaboration on *Sardanapale* had strengthened it. But by May 1846 she apparently realized that she had gone too far in her enthusiasm and gratitude. Perhaps for a moment she too shared the wanderer's fantasy. It seems more likely that Liszt's hopes were shattered by her own disillusionment and bad conscience than by his failings.

IT IS QUITE POSSIBLE that the collapse of his fantasy over Cristina made him especially receptive to that other recluse-princess, Carolyne Sayn-Wittgenstein. Most lives are affected by coincidences—the conjuncture of the right people or events at the right time. Princess Carolyne appeared at just such a propitious moment in Liszt's life. His future was then marred with graying hair and decaying teeth. He had just had what he thought to be the last of his *"folies de jeunesse."* Carolyne was anything but captivating—to call her plain is to flatter her—and anything but the kind of woman to inspire a cult, which Liszt bitterly realized he had been celebrating to a hollow idol. To fall in love with a woman like Carolyne, within a few days in February 1847, suggests that what he loved in her was being loved by her—just what he needed then—and being loved for what he was. What may also have contributed to his receptivity are analogies between Carolyne and Cristina. Both women were emotional castaways, marooned by empty marriages with men far beneath them in every way but rank. Both of them had only their daughters to love—by amusing coincidence both named Marie, both in the care of British governesses (one Scottish, the other English). Both filled the emptiness of their hearts with lofty pursuits of the mind. They also shared the same title, as Liszt alluded in a letter to Mme d'Agoult: "Princess Wittgenstein (who is my new discovery in princesses . . . with the difference that we have no thought of falling in love)."[6] Both ladies had retired to their estates deep in the country, where they studied theology; Carolyne, however, was a fanatic, whereas Cristina was merely a historian. And both were wealthy enough to live independently of husband and convention.

The similarities were certainly numerous enough to account for a sense of recognition on Liszt's part. Heine's homeopathic cure has been a known remedy since heartbreak entered literature. The "rebound" is a powerful force and often explains the most unlikely attachments. Carolyne, viewed outside the context of Liszt's état d'âme in 1846, would seem to be a most unlikely choice of consort for a bon viveur like him. She had none of the personal elegance of her title, none of the intelligence of her scholarly pursuits; she was not, as Mrs. Perényi has described her, "the ugly duckling [who] had succeeded where the swans had failed"[5]—she was a silly goose. But she was exactly what Liszt needed at the time: similar enough to the woman who had rejected him to play on his sensibilities, different in precisely those ways that could attract him. Where Cristina's sharp mind and erudition may have made Liszt—a self-taught man of limited scope—somewhat uncomfortable, Carolyne's cultural gluttony and muddled thinking must have made him feel like an intellectual giant. At the same time, a woman without Carolyne's philosophical pretensions would not have satisfied his own. Where Cristina spoke to him of friendship and pointed out his defects, Carolyne told him he was perfect, adorable, lovable "to death and madness." A castle in the Ukraine was doubtless less enchanting than a castle in Paris, but at least it wasn't made of sand. Given Carolyne's girth and gaucherie, her selfless devotion—unlike Marie d'Agoult's public martyrdom or Cristina's patronizing affection—was something Liszt could enjoy in total comfort. Carolyne would never reproach him for what he was not.

Cristina's last known letter to him is a pitiful portrait of the woman, and a perfect example of her didactic manner—so different from Carolyne's. Cristina's "severity" is born of her "sincerity"—qualities, especially when coupled, that most men would willingly be spared. She probes Liszt's patriotism all the way to its soft-bellied vanity, which no one but Heine had ever dared do.* And to top it off, she then points out the emptiness of his uncommitted existence.

Paris, 15 January 1849

Finally, my dear Liszt, you remember that I exist and I thank *La Revue des Deux Mondes*† for it. You found me severe and it is possible that I appear that way for I am sincere. But if I seemed to you severe with regard to the people, be it Lombard or Italian, in general, it is that my words betrayed my thoughts. I did not say to what point royalty and the nobility behaved ignominiously in our recent affairs; I did not say to what point I despise and condemn them, for in truth, the sight of a free man makes my gorge rise. However, as to the Italian people, I cannot praise them enough. They were devoted, honest, courageous, to a degree it would have been unreasonable to expect after such a prolonged slavery. We succumbed, it is true, but we will get even, and this lesson will not be wasted on us; it will teach us not to place our faith in anyone except those whose good faith is known to us. Alas, yes! Your country, at this moment, has succumbed and, like mine, was betrayed, for the Hungarian people know how to fight and this time yielded without inflicting a blow. There must be some dreadful mystery underneath, which history may never reveal. But how is it, my dear Liszt, that you did not take part in the struggle? Is Hungary not your homeland in matter of fact and choice? Did you not declare yourself Hungarian? . . . I know you do not take politics too much to heart; and yet, what is there that deserves attention, if not the establishment of the rights of all, peoples and individuals? We are, it is true, a fleeting race that lives only one day, and it is mad to attach oneself to the goods we leave behind; but if we leave those goods to those for whom we conquered them, it is not mad to chase after them. It is the personal pleasures that do not warrant the trouble we take to acquire them.

* "The piano resounds. There is Liszt returning, the Chevalier Franz Liszt; he lives, he is not stretched out bleeding on a field of battle in Hungary; neither a Russian nor a Croat killed him. Franz Liszt will live a long time, and as a venerable old man will relate to his grandchildren the great facts and events of the Hungarian war. This, he will say like Sir John Falstaff, is how I made the thrust and held my saber."[7]

† Liszt had evidently read her articles on the Five Days in Milan.

Even on the subject of his rumored marriage to Carolyne, she has a little lesson to offer. "I thought you were married, more than married! I hope the delay will not be long. I know that your fiancée, since she is not yet your wife, is young, beautiful, rich, and very much in love with you. Reciprocate it and never take back from her what you have once given. Your old Béatrix* is very changed, I hear. Her hair is almost white and she wears a monk-like costume." About her own life, she offers a picture that lacks any trace of gaiety. Her participation in the Italian revolution has once more cut off her revenues and journalism has become her sole means of support.

> Shall I tell you about myself? Maternal misfortunes† have helped me endure the others. Work has become a necessity for me since Radetzky** is established in my country. *La Revue des Deux Mondes* has offered me, as you saw, its hospitality; other periodicals as well. A number of German newspapers have accepted me as a correspondent, and all that now constitutes my only revenue. The only pleasant thought I now have is the awareness of being self-sufficient. My daughter grows and develops in a way that people find extraordinary, and that is for me the source of constant happiness. Outside of work and her, the world is all shadows for me. The spectacle one has before one's eyes here is disgusting. Cowardice and egotism are in competition.

Sardanapale, despite everything, remained an active project as late as this last letter, in which she amusingly discusses the orgy scene that Liszt wants purified. "I will write your poet," she replies to his request, "telling him to prepare the scene as you want it, but I don't know how he will manage an orgy in which there are no *wines,* no *games,* no *women* [underlined in her letter, presumably quoted from his]. Have you perhaps invented something new? In that case, be so kind as to reveal it to your poet, for I strongly doubt that a poor devil who has gone from prison to war, and from war to exile, has the wit needed to divine such mysteries. As for myself, I would propose a ruse-orgy, that is, great preparations for festivities that end in a moonlight walk and a philosophical dialogue. Sardanapalus might not have disdained such a thing."

When Liszt abandoned this four-year project, which had evidently made serious progress, is not known. But *why* he did, and why he undertook it in the first place, is worth consideration. Sardanapalus, it will be remembered from Byron's tragedy and Delacroix's famous painting, was an Assyrian king devoted to pleasure, but at the same time, courageous,

---

* Balzac modeled his title character on Marie d'Agoult.
† An allusion to the problem of legitimizing Marie.
** Military commander of Austrian forces and governor of Lombardy.

likeable, and cynical. When the Medes began a revolt against him, he was roused from his opulent indolence by his Greek favorite, Myrha, who incited him to action. Defeated after a two-year siege, he set fire to his palace, immolating himself, Myrha, and his entire court. Of the innumerable subjects Liszt might have selected for what he had called his "dramatic debut," his choice of Sardanapalus—a character reminiscent of himself, especially during his legendary *Glanzperiode*—cannot have been sheer accident. Cristina had long before warned him against becoming cynical and losing sight of "noble things" when his successes began projecting him into a world of artificial values and emotions—a grave problem for all performers. That he furthermore selected Cristina as his sole confidante and collaborator appears to be closely related to his choice of subject matter.

Like Sardanapalus, Liszt was a pampered monarch, women were at his feet, gold at his fingertips (that it slipped through is of no importance). Despite his promise to close his piano in 1843, he was still breaking heartstrings and piano strings in 1845. His ambition for a more dignified future than that of keyboard acrobat was still alive, but the bravos were too gratifying, the riches too plentiful, the honors too fabulous to relinquish without a good reason. A woman with whom to share that desired future would have been a reason, especially a woman of noble aspirations. Cristina understood the Lisztian mentality and even assumed responsibility for some of it. Writing to Mme Jaubert from Athens, some ten months after her letter to Liszt, she explained: "What Liszt needed was tempestuous pleasures in which spirituality, vanity, the love of noise, notoriety, even scandal, had their share. . . . Liszt is a child spoiled by the world. Each one of us has contributed to his conceit and we must look with indulgence at some failings that we brought about. No prince, no king, has been exposed as much as he to the flattery, the adulation, the adoration of the public." At thirty-four, old enough to be past his *"folies de jeunesse"* but young enough to romanticize the future, Liszt seems to have seen Cristina as the ideal companion. Their artistic collaboration and joint real estate venture point to Liszt's dream of building a future around her. *Sardanapale* was the collateral against that future. Sardanapalus, encouraged by his valiant Myrha to "noble things" was surely not an unconscious metaphor for Liszt's desire for "spirituality" under Cristina's guidance. He might not achieve it but, like Sardanapalus, he would die trying.

It was an admirable attempt, to which Cristina was not insensitive. So long as it remained a collaboration and not a liaison she was willing to cooperate. She found him the librettist, read and corrected the text, proposed changes, all of which he found so much to his liking that in 1846 he wrote, "I strongly doubt there is any Italian poet capable of hewing

such an intelligent one [scenario] and singularly suspect Your Highness
of having participated in it. Permit me therefore to place my entire musical destiny in your beautiful hands." Those are big words, which could
be attributed to sheer hyperbole were they not written while he was still
under the aura of his *"embrasement subit."* The fire was soon quenched,
but the glow lingered on. He was still hoping she could be persuaded,
and he counted on his creative luck to convince her. He felt so *"en
veine,"* as he told her, that he was certain of completing the score by the
following April, and announced May 1847 as the date for the opening in
Vienna. "In about six weeks," he wrote on April 2, 1846, "I will know
more precisely the date of the staging and the principal singers." In
October he talked about speeding up the incendiary ending, "Sardanapalus burning not only with Myrha but with the obligatory companionship
of his entire harem, setting fire everywhere in his palace; I will try to set
one myself in my orchestra, my chorus, my entire audience!"

Although they still wrote about the opera, the spark was gone; there
would never be a conflagration, musical or otherwise. Cristina left for
Athens, where he never performed, and discovered to her horror that he
was unknown there. Relating her astonishment to Mme Jaubert, she tells
how a Greek, when she asked him to compare his own favorite pianist to
Liszt, exclaimed, "Liszt! What is that?" She was dumbfounded. Was she
emerging from the sleep of Sleeping Beauty, she wondered. But even
that would explain nothing, for "a century would be no more than a
grain of sand on Liszt's reknown, and many centuries would not succeed
in tarnishing it." And yet, in Greece nothing about him was known,
nothing about "that artistic trinity of the virtuoso Liszt, his faithful
squire Belloni, and the fantastic Erard piano which passed under the
master's fingers from death to life, and life to death, sometimes with
terrible convulsions, sometimes exhaling divine songs." Finding herself
in a place where the name of Liszt had never been heard proved to her
the "unharmonic social state of Greece," and to us her unflinching admiration for him.

Six years later, after a long silence, Thierry served as go-between,
sending Cristina's regards when writing to tell Liszt that her sequester
had finally been lifted. And Liszt in 1863, writing to a friend about
Cristina, said, "I am afraid that I have fallen into disgrace with her. It
may be in part my fault, but I am not sure and would not like to think
so." He had not forgotten her, but time and distance take their toll. Still,
in 1866, he asked his son-in-law, Hans von Bülow, to see her during his
trip to Italy: "I hope to profit from your intermediary to remind her of
me." Only ashes remained, but warm ones to the end.

12

A Last Glance

To HAVE BEEN LOVED by some of the great men of her time ought to assure any woman a place in history. To have participated in the great events of her day should further perpetuate her name. And to have been admired, and reviled, in print certainly establishes her credentials as an unforgettable figure. Cristina has yet another claim to lasting celebrity: not least among her achievements is her unique place in the history of the Romantic *Zeitgeist*. Mario Praz, in his noted work *La Carne, la morte e il diavolo nella letteratura romantica,* inadvertently confirms this. Except for Princess Belgiojoso, all his examples of the archetypal femme fatale—Lilith, Medusa, *la belle dame sans merci*—are drawn from literature. Even more remarkable, Lehmann's portrait of Cristina is the only illustration Praz chose that is not of an ancient, mythological, or imaginary subject. "The Princess," Praz writes, "incarnated to perfection the type of bewitching beauty dear to the Romantics, and her presence in Paris left an indelible impression on its artists."[1] One of the first texts Praz cites to support his statement is Marie d'Agoult's fanciful description of Cristina, which sets her among her more colorful compatriots. "She willingly accredited certain rumors that placed in her hand the goblet or dagger of Italian treachery at the court of the Borgias."[2] Cristina surely had no thought of associating herself with Italian treachery, but for those Romantics who had been carried away by Cellini's escape, her Renaissance energy—at a time of Romantic indolence—recaptured that period of Italian bravura.

In 1840, a writer for a popular review reported: "Princess Belgiojoso, so noble and lovely in her corpse-like pallor, often looks like an apparition from a tomb. . . . One admires her with a kind of sacred terror. Someone said on seeing her, 'It is Eurydice returned from Hades to seek her Orpheus in this low world.' "[3] Seventy-three years later, in his preface to a biography of Chopin, Camille Saint-Saëns wrote: "Chopin was

tubercular at a time when good health was not chic. . . . It was fashionable to be pale and drained; Princess Belgiojoso strolled along the boulevards . . . pallid as death in person."[4] Cristina's enigmatic beauty
haunted the Romantic imagination, perhaps because of her identification
with an earlier enigma, Leonardo's Gioconda (not to mention the sphinx
Musset saw in her). Houssaye described Cristina as "a pure masterpiece
of an unsatisfied Gioconda." And other writers who used her as a model
copied the image of her "smile à la Mona Lisa." Walter Pater's 1873
study of Leonardo's mysterious lady summarizes the traits that the Romantics saw in Cristina, that beauty "into which the soul with all its
maladies had passed . . . the reverie of the Middle Ages with its spiritual ambition and imaginative loves . . . the sins of the Borgias. She is
older than the rocks among which she sits; like the vampire, she had
been dead many times, and learned the secrets of the grave. . . . Certainly Lady Lisa might stand as the embodiment of the old fancy, the
symbol of the modern idea."[5]

Cristina appealed to more than the esthetic of the day; she evoked the
deeper preoccupations of the "Romantic agony." Thrust at birth into a
world ruled by the rigid laws of church, court, and atrophied society, she
rebelled. Her stubborn pursuit of an individual destiny acted out the
disoriented restlessness of her artistic contemporaries. Her intense nature,
her reclusiveness, her burning idealism, exemplified the very soul of
Romanticism. Deeper still, she reflected the fears and yearnings that
inhabited the dark recesses of Romantic fantasy; she became synonymous
with the Romantic mystique of death. Fragile and wan, victim of Metternich's persecutions, subject of an emperor whose dungeons menaced
every patriot, threatened with confinement and confiscation, she was a
constant reminder of the prison-nightmare that pervades the literature of
the period.

A recent study of the prison theme and literary imagination examines
the transformation of dread into desire as the prison becomes the symbol
of poetic creation, which in turn becomes the instrument of spiritual
freedom. "Man had always dreamed of prison, but never as intensely as
in the nineteenth century." The history and politics of the time, aided by
"Metternich's detentions throughout Europe, the shadow of the Spielberg,
where Silvio Pellico and other victims languished, the repressions of
popular movements" made this period virtually "incapable of separating
moral indignation from poetic vision."[6] Against this background, Cristina's "poetization," her Romantic persona, emerges more sharply. Her
struggle for national freedom while she remained shackled to solitude,
her view of love as a platonic ideal, her resistance to an intimacy no
dreamer succeeded in conquering—all came to represent what is perhaps
most typical of the Romantic spirit: the yearning to be possessed by an

other-worldly passion, to be bound to a quest, sworn to a cult. When Heine spoke of her as "a prison so beautiful that everyone stops . . . as though under a spell," he was echoing his own Tannhäuser, prisoner of a divine love but condemned to the perpetual punishment of gross mortality. For Musset, lost in the labyrinth of her dark eyes, as for Heine, who served her cult like a monk his devotions, this beautiful "prison" was the very essence of poetry—the living metaphor of the art that "imprisoned" them but allowed them to scale the walls of their human condition. For Balzac as well, Cristina symbolized the unrelenting jailer of society who beckons and does not yield, thus condemning the artist to the forced labor of his art and his unquenchable ambition.

For all who ever wrote or painted her into their works, Cristina was the thread of myth. In her face, her life, her strange personality, were the strands of all the figures who had ever captivated the imagination—demon or demi-urge, goddess or saint, consoling angel or vengeful fury. And yet, in all this there was a woman. She may have hidden behind her compelling eyes, but when she spoke her words were direct. She was a woman who wanted to love, and in her own way she did. Letters to her daughter, her brother, her sister-in-law, her close friends, are filled with the deep and hungry affection of one who has known deprivation. She would never take for granted the attention she received, nor accustom herself to its absence. Her need to "skewer hearts," in Caroline Jaubert's teasing words, had less to do with vanity than with her desire to hold on to the affection she had once gained. On March 1, 1848, a national heroine, surrounded by public adulation, she complained: "I must nonetheless realize that my friends are capable of neglecting me, since I do not wish to call into question the friendship of M. Mignet, who is certainly alive but has not replied to my last letter. It seems that the hour of coldness has struck for some people, but since it has not tolled for me, I feel uneasy with them. Will my heart and my mind ever feel indifference? I doubt it."

Admittedly, it was difficult to understand such a woman. It was easier to make fun of her. Fragmented and multifaceted, she could not be encompassed by the more conventional vision of her day, which saw her as grotesque and laughable. What male political figure, worthy of a full-scale biography, has ever been dismissed by his biographer as she was by Augustin-Thierry: "If Mme de Belgiojoso did not lack literary judgment, she was and always remained totally bereft of political foresight." And what bungling male patriot has ever been called in print a "scocciatore"?* For Ferdinand of Naples, the not-so-bungling Cristina was most certainly a "scocciatrice," a headache, but should that not have entitled

---

* From the Neapolitan dialect for "head," *coccia,* thus a "headbreaker."

her to the respect of her countrymen? Ferdinand was the enemy. To repeat this term of derision, as Montanelli did, without commentary, is to apply it again more than a century later.

Cristina was an original woman at a time when only fictional heroines had the right to be so. Her great error was not so much that she "poached on men's preserves," but that she cheated them; she did not fulfill the destiny of a fictional heroine. Had she been as energetic in her loves as in her causes she might have been forgiven her originality, instead of being mocked. She evidently understood the price she would have to pay. Speaking of another woman who had been ridiculed for being unconventional, she said: "If someone has traced her portrait for you, I fear it was a caricature. This is how the world treats women whose character has not been effaced by their education, while in men, on the contrary, originality is considered a merit."

NOTES
BIBLIOGRAPHY
INDEX

Notes

INTRODUCTION

1. Alessandro Luzio, *Garibaldi, Cavour, Verdi* (Turin: Rocca, 1924), p. 432.
2. Ibid., p. 434.
3. Ibid., p. 446.
4. Heine, "Briefe über Deutschland," *Werke und Briefe* (Berlin: Afbau-Verlag, 1961), vol. 7, p. 302.
5. Hector Talvart and Joseph Place, *La Bibliographie des auteurs modernes de langue française* (Paris: Horizons de France, 1930), vol. 2, item 10A under Boulenger.
6. Charles Neilson Gattey, *A Bird of Curious Plumage* (London: Constable, 1971), pp. 5–6.

CHAPTER 1

1. Caroline Jaubert, *Souvenirs* (Paris: Hetzel, 1881), p. 181.
2. Edmond d'Alton-Shée, *Mes Mémoires, 1826–1848* (Paris: Lacroix, 1869), p. 88.
3. Ibid.
4. From the archives of Duke Giuseppe Crivelli-Serbelloni.
5. Aldobrandino Malvezzi, *La Principessa Cristina di Belgiojoso* (Milan: Treves, 1936), vol. 1, p. 75.
6. Gilbert H. Glaser, "Visceral manifestations of epilepsy," *Yale Journal of Biology and Medicine*, vol. 30, no. 3, 1957, pp. 167–86.
7. Malvezzi, vol. 2, p. 414.
8. Ezio Flori, "Cristina di Belgiojoso e Paolo Maspero," *Rendiconti del Reale Istituto Lombardo di Scienze e Lettere*, vol. 74, 1941, pp. 99–147.
9. H. Gastaut and H. Collomb, "Comportement sexuel chez les épileptiques," *Annales médico-psychologiques*, vol. 112, 1954, pp. 657–95.
10. *Brain's Diseases of the Nervous System*, 7th edition, revised by Lord Brain and John N. Walton (London: Oxford University Press, 1969), pp. 161, 808.
11. In Malvezzi, vol. 1, p. 79.
12. Benjamin Crémieux, *Une Conspiratrice en 1830, ou le souper sans la Belgiojoso* (Paris: Lafitte, 1928), p. 92.

CHAPTER 2

1. Stendhal, *La Chartreuse de Parme* (Paris: Garnier, 1973), p. 1.
2. Cristina Belgiojoso, *Etude sur l'histoire de la Lombardie dans les trente dernières années, ou les causes du défaut d'énergie chez les Lombards* (Paris: Jules Laisné, 1846), p. 56.

3. Belgiojoso, *Osservazioni sullo stato attuale dell'Italia e sul suo avvenire* (Milan: Vallardi, 1868), p. 12.

4. Belgiojoso, *Histoire de la Lombardie,* p. 147.

5. Belgiojoso, *Osservazoni sullo stato attuale,* p. 50.

6. Ibid. (all quotations in the paragraph).

7. Belgiojoso, *Histoire de la maison de Savoie* (Paris: Lévy, 1860), p. 508.

8. Quoted from a letter to Ambrogio Garavaglia, son of her mother's overseer at Affori, in Malvezzi, vol. 1, p. 92.

9. Ibid., p. 93.

10. Ibid., p. 106.

11. Ibid., p. 126.

12. d'Alton-Shée, *Mémoires,* p. 87.

13. Charles-Augustin Sainte-Beuve, *Nouveaux Lundis* (Paris: Pléiade, 1951), vol. 13, p. 476.

14. From Austrian Secret Archives, in Malvezzi, vol. 1, p. 150.

15. Ibid., p. 157.

16. Augustin Thierry, *Histoire de la conquête d'Angleterre par les Normands* (Paris: Tessier, 1836), vol. 6, p. 95.

17. *Le National,* verbatim report, April 13, 1831.

CHAPTER 3

1. d'Alton-Shée, *Mémoires,* p. 57.

2. Virginie Ancelot, *Un Salon de Paris, 1824–1864* (Paris: Dentu, 1866), p. 90.

3. Ibid., p. 148.

4. d'Alton-Shée, p. 78.

5. Richard Bolster, *Stendhal, Balzac et le feminisme romantique* (Paris: Minard, 1970), p. 86.

6. Balzac, *Physiologie du mariage* (Paris: Charpentier, 1838), p. 863.

7. Balzac, *Correspondance* (Paris: Garnier, 1960–64), vol. 3, p. 89.

8. *Journal* (Paris: Le Divan, 1936), vol. 3, p. 1319.

9. Bolster, p. 21.

10. *Fonds secrets, archives secrètes du dernier gouvernement, 1830–1848* (Paris: Paulin, 1848), p. 37.

11. Terenzio Mamiani, "Parigi or fa cinquant'anni," *Nuova Antologia,* vol. 21, pp. 38–60.

12. Rodolphe Apponyi, *Vingt-cinq ans à Paris* (Paris: Plon, 1914), vol. 1, p. 373.

13. Ibid., vol. 3, p. 261.

14. Ibid., vol. 4, p. 264.

15. Marie d'Agoult, *Mes Souvenirs* (Paris: Lévy, 1877), p. 356.

16. Delphine de Girardin, Théophile Gautier, Jules Sandeau, and Méry, *La Croix de Berny* (Paris: Lévy, 1871), pp. 31–32.

17. "Les Académies de femmes en France," par Une Vieille Saint-Simonienne, *Revue des Revues,* December 15, 1899, pp. 557–74.

18. Belgiojoso, *Souvenirs dans l'exil* (Paris: Le National, 1850), p. 34.

19. Manuscripts, Bibliothèque Nationale de Paris, n.a.f. 14099, ff. 308.

20. Quoted from Léon Séché, *Alfred de Musset* (Paris: Mercure de France, 1907), vol. 2, p. 39.

CHAPTER 4

1. Decree cited in full in Malvezzi, vol. 1, p. 254.
2. Marie-Louise Pailleron, "Une ennemie de l'Autriche," *Revue des Deux Mondes,* August 15, 1915.
3. Jules Cloquet, *Souvenirs sur la vie privée du Général Lafayette* (Paris: Galignani, 1836), pp. 290, 296.
4. Comte Hübner, *Une Année de ma vie* (Paris: Hachette, 1891), p. 38.
5. Belgiojoso, *Essai sur la formation du dogme catholique* (Paris: Renouard, 1842), vol. 2, pp. 379–80.
6. J. Lerminier, "Des femmes philosophes," *Revue des Deux Mondes,* June 1, 1843, pp. 673–91.
7. J. Lemoine, *Journal des Débats,* March 8, 1843.
8. Belgiojoso, *Essai,* vol. 1, p. 179.
9. Sainte-Beuve, *Correspondance Générale* (Paris: Stock, 1942–47), vol. 4, p. 315.
10. Juliette Adam, *Mes premières armes littéraires et politiques* (Paris: Lemerre, 1904), p. 157.

CHAPTER 5

1. Yvonne Knibiehler, *Naissance des sciences humaines: Mignet et l'histoire philosophique au XIXe siècle* (Paris: Flammarion, 1973), p. 61.
2. Etienne Délécluse, *Journal 1824–1828* (Paris: Grasset, 1948), p. 308.
3. Sainte-Beuve, *Portraits contemporains* (Paris: Lévy, 1874), vol. 2, pp. 225–56; Heine, *Lutèce* (Paris: Lévy, 1866), pp. 202–03.
4. *Le Figaro, Supplément littéraire,* March 29, 1884.
5. Knibiehler, *Naissance des sciences humaines,* p. 216.
6. This letter and the preceding one appear in Séché, vol. 1, pp. 164–68.
7. Henri d'Ideville, *Journal d'un diplomate en Italie* (Paris: Hachette, 1872), p. 145.

CHAPTER 6

1. Albert Augustin-Thierry, *Augustin Thierry d'après sa correspondance* (Paris: Plon, 1922), p. 191.
2. Ibid., p. 192.
3. Ibid.
4. Charles Monselet, *Statues et statuettes contemporaines* (Paris: Giraud et Dagneau, 1852), p. 5.
5. All letters in this chapter, unless otherwise indicated, are quoted from *Augustin Thierry d'après sa correspondance.*
6. Gabriel Hanotaux, *Henri Martin: sa vie, ses oeuvres, son temps* (Paris: Cerf, 1885), pp. 86–87.
7. Clément de Metternich, *Mémoires, documents, et écrits divers, 1800–1884* (Paris: Plon, 1884), vol. 7, p. 408.
8. Gilbert H. Glaser, "The Convulsive Disorders," chap. 4, vol. X, in *Tice's Practice of Medicine* (New York: Harper and Row, 1970), p. 14; J. H. Jackson,

Epilepsy and Epileptiform Convulsions, in Wood's Medical Monographs (New York, 1890), vol. 1.

9. Metternich, p. 435.

10. Ibid., p. 443.

11. Malvezzi, vol. 3, pp. 132–33: "Did you see the article in *La Patria* about la Belgiojoso? How shameful! . . . She has worked and works for the national cause and is respected. Even worse is when one thinks that all this poison comes from old unlucky or disappointed loves. And indeed, let me say, I am scandalized by your Massari!" (Marco Minghetti to Antonio Montanari, April 12, 1848).

12. See *Revue des Deux Mondes,* vol. 23, September 15, 1848, pp. 785–813; vol. 24, October 15, 1848, pp. 139–65, from which all quotations below are taken.

13. Henry James, *William Wetmore Story and His Friends* (London: Blackwood, 1903), pp. 155, 157.

14. Henry James, *The Princess Casamassima* (New York: Macmillan, 1948), vol. 1, pp. 270–72; vol. 2, p. 234.

15. James, *Story,* pp. 161–63.

16. Indro Montanelli, *L'Italia del Risorgimento* (Milan: Rizzoli, 1972), pp. 345–56.

17. Ibid., p. 349.

18. Colonello Pagani, *Uomini e cose in Milano dal marzo all'agosto 1848* (Milan: Treves, 1907), p. 329.

19. Malvezzi, vol. 3, pp. 301–03.

CHAPTER 7

1. Belgiojoso, *Souvenirs dans l'exil,* p. 3.

2. Ibid., p. 10.

3. Ibid., p. 17.

4. Ibid.

5. Ibid., p. 22.

6. Ibid., p. 26.

7. Malvezzi, vol. 3, p. 289.

8. Belgiojoso, *Souvenirs dans l'exil,* p. 35.

9. Ibid., p. 34.

10. Malvezzi, vol. 3, p. 310.

11. Augustin-Thierry, *Augustin Thierry d'après sa correspondance,* p. 213.

12. Malvezzi, vol. 3, pp. 313–16.

13. Belgiojoso, *Asie mineure et Syrie, souvenirs de voyage* (Paris: Michel Lévy, 1858). All quotations on pp. 206–07 are taken from this work.

14. Augustin-Thierry, *Augustin Thierry d'après sa correspondance,* p. 206.

15. Malvezzi, vol. 3, pp. 323–33; details and quotations on pp. 210–11 are taken from this letter.

16. George Sand, *Journal intime* (Paris: Calmann-Lévy, 1926), p. 2.

17. This and following quotations (pp. 215–16) are from Victor Cousin's *Correspondance générale,* vol. 3, Bibliothèque Victor Cousin, Paris, folios 397–413.

18. Malvezzi, vol. 3, pp. 352, 366.

19. The entire article appears in Malvezzi, vol. 3, Appendix 4, pp. 427–32.

20. Emilio Guicciardi, *Cristina di Belgiojoso Trivulzio cento anni dopo* (Milan: La Martinella, 1973), p. 84.

21. Belgiojoso, "Della presente condizione delle donne e del loro avvenire," *Nuova Antologia*, vol. 1, no. 1, January 31, 1866, pp. 96–113; all quotations on pp. 226–32 are taken from this work.

22. Milan: Vallardi, 1868; all quotations on pp. 233–34 are from this work.

CHAPTER 8

1. Henri Heine, *Mémoires* (Paris: Calmann-Lévy, 1884), p. 92.

2. Jean-Paul Richter, high priest of German Romanticism, stated this long before in his *Forschule der Aesthetik:* "The one and only Mary ennobles every woman; hence, while Venus can only be beautiful, a Madonna can be romantic beauty in the infinite."

3. Heine, *Reisebilder*, "Die Reise von München nach Genoa," chapter 15.

4. Ibid., chapter 17.

5. Ibid., chapter 19.

6. Heine, *Mémoires*, p. 101.

7. Ancelot, *Un Salon de Paris*, p. 257.

8. Joseph Dresch, *Heine à Paris, 1831–1856* (Paris: Marcel Didier, 1956), p. 63.

9. Jules Legras, *Henri Heine poète* (Paris: Calmann-Lévy, 1897), p. 4.

10. Ibid.

11. In Jaubert, p. 37.

12. Ibid.

13. Arsène Houssaye, *Les Confessions, souvenirs d'un demi-siècle* (Paris: Dentu, 1885), vol. 1, p. 263.

14. Heine, *Französische Szene*, chapter 10.

15. Houssaye, vol. 1, p. 264.

16. Kurt Weinberg, *Henri Heine, romantique défroqué* (Paris: Presses Universitaires de France, 1954), p. 197.

17. Heine, *Atta Troll*, chapter 19.

18. Théophile Gautier, *Portraits et Souvenirs* (Paris: Michel Lévy, 1875), p. 106.

19. Jaubert, p. 99.

20. Legras, p. 180.

21. By, among others, Antonina Vallentin, *Henri Heine* (Paris: Gallimard, 1934), p. 169; Dresch, p. 66.

22. In Heinrich Houben, *Heine par ses contemporains* (Paris: Payot, 1929), p. 129.

23. Heine, *Mémoires*, p. 139.

24. Houben, p. 162.

25. Ibid., p. 200.

26. Ibid.

27. Jaubert, p. 295.

28. Friedrich Hirth, *Heine und seine Französischen Freunde* (Mainz: Florian Kupferberg, 1949), p. 195.

29. First discussed by Hirth, pp. 87–90.

30. Legras, p. 365.

31. Belgiojoso, *Souvenirs dans l'exil*, p. 8.

32. Houben, p. 740.

CHAPTER 9

1. Houssaye, vol. 2, p. 2.
2. Sand, journal entry for November 28, 1834.
3. Houben, p. 197.
4. Emile Henriot, *L'Enfant du siècle* (Paris: Amiot-Dumont, 1953), p. 84.
5. Houssaye, vol. 1, p. 265.
6. Ibid., p. 254.
7. Fernand Brisset, *Laure et Pétrarque* (Paris: Perrin, 1931), p. 166.
8. Henriot, p. 93.
9. Sainte-Beuve, *Causeries du lundi* (Paris: Garnier, 3rd ed., n.d.), vol. 13, pp. 364–65.
10. In Jean Pommier, *Variétés sur Alfred de Musset et son théâtre* (Paris: Nizet, 1966), Appendix, p. 206.
11. Maurice Donnay, *La vie amoureuse d'Alfred de Musset* (Paris: Flammarion, 1926), p. 158.
12. André Villiers, *La vie privée d'Alfred de Musset* (Paris: Hachette, 1939), p. 178.
13. Cited in Henriot, p. 121.
14. Paul de Musset, *Biographie d'Alfred de Musset* (Paris: Calmann-Lévy, 1877), p. 259.
15. Louise Colet, *Lui* (Paris: Librairie Nouvelle, 1860), p. 79.
16. As purportedly related to Houssaye, vol. 2, p. 7 ff.
17. Jaubert, p. 179.
18. Colet, p. 79 ff.
19. Donnay, p. 171.
20. Houssaye, vol. 2, pp. 13–15.
21. Malvezzi, vol. 2, p. 198.
22. Henriot, p. 94.
23. Alfred de Musset, *La Confession d'un Enfant du siècle* (Paris: Garnier, 1947), with notes, variants, and introduction by Maurice Allem.
24. Paul de Musset, pp. 152–53.
25. Malvezzi, vol. 2, p. 436.
26. Sainte-Beuve, *Portraits contemporains* (Paris: Lévy, 1870), vol. 2, pp. 210–11.

CHAPTER 10

1. Honoré de Balzac, *La Peau de chagrin* (Paris: Garnier, 1959), with notes, variants, and introduction by Maurice Allem.
2. Charles de Spoelberch de Lovenjoul, "Les 'Etudes philosophiques' d'Honoré de Balzac," *Revue d'histoire littéraire de la France,* July-September 1907, p. 428.
3. January 22, 1838; all letters to Mme Hanska are quoted from *Lettres à Madame Hanska,* edited by Roger Pierrot (Paris: Bibliophiles de l'Originale, 1967–71).
4. Balzac, *Correspondance* (Paris: Garnier, 1960–64), vol. 2, p. 390.
5. Monselet, p. 3.

6. Ancelot, *Les Salons de Paris* (Paris: Tardieu, 1858), p. 76; the date is also confirmed in her other book, *Un Salon de Paris,* p. 256.

7. Ancelot, *Les Salons,* pp. 95, 117.

8. Balzac, *Correspondance,* vol. 1, p. 520.

9. Introduction to Balzac, *Massimilla Doni* (Paris: José Corti, 1964), p. 81.

10. Balzac, *Correspondance,* vol. 1, p. 529.

11. Ancelot, *Un Salon,* p. 257.

12. Sainte-Beuve, *Correspondance générale* (Paris: Stock, 1947), vol. 5, pp. 527–28.

13. From official records published in Malvezzi, vol. 2, p. 403. This doubtless became common knowledge after the proclamation of Cristina's civil death.

14. Ancelot, *Un Salon,* p. 258.

15. Apponyi, vol. 3, p. 265.

16. Balzac, *Massimilla Doni,* p. 171.

17. May 24, 1837; he had just completed the first draft of *Massimilla Doni.*

18. August 7, 1844.

19. Monselet, p. 7.

20. Adam, p. 157.

CHAPTER 11

1. All letters, unless otherwise indicated, are from Daniel Ollivier, *Autour de Madame d'Agoult et de Liszt* (Paris: Grasset, 1941), pp. 135–207. Liszt's letters to Cristina were first published by Malvezzi in his biography.

2. Quoted from Harold C. Schonberg, *The Great Pianists* (New York: Simon & Schuster, 1963), p. 160.

3. Jacques Vier, *La Comtesse d'Agoult et son temps* (Paris: Colin, 1955), vol. 1, p. 393, note 3.

4. Daniel Ollivier, *Correspondance de Liszt et de Madame d'Agoult* (Paris: Grasset, 1933), vol. I, p. 424 ff.

5. Eleanor Perényi, *Liszt: The Artist as Romantic Hero* (Boston: Little, Brown, 1974), p. 256.

6. Ollivier, *Correspondance,* vol. II, p. 383.

7. Heine, *De l'Allemagne* (Paris: Lévy, 1855), p. 272.

CHAPTER 12

1. Mario Praz, *La Carne, la morte e il diavolo nella letteratura romantica* (Turin: Einaudi, 1942), p. 125.

2. Marie d'Agoult, *Mes Souvenirs,* p. 357.

3. *Les Papillons noirs,* April 18, 1840, p. 86.

4. Edouard Ganche, *Frédéric Chopin, sa vie et ses oeuvres* (Paris: Mercure de France, 1913), preface by Camille Saint-Saëns, p. 1.

5. Walter Pater, *The Renaissance* (New York: Mentor Books, 1959), p. 90.

6. Victor Brombert, *La Prison romantique* (Paris: José Corti, 1975), p. 13.

Bibliography

This is a selected bibliography of works cited and those of major relevance. It does not include numerous other works consulted on figures and history of the period, which would needlessly have burdened these pages.

"Les Académies de femmes en France," par Une Vieille Saint-Simonienne. *Revue des Revues*, 1899, pp. 557–74.

Adam, Juliette. *Mes premières armes littéraires et politiques.* Paris, 1904.

d'Agoult, Marie [Daniel Stern]. *Mes Souvenirs.* Paris, 1877.

d'Alton-Shée, Edmond. *Mes Mémoires, 1826–1848.* Paris, 1869.

Ancelot, Virginie. *Les Salons de Paris.* Paris, 1858.

———. *Un Salon de Paris, 1824–1864.* Paris, 1866.

Apponyi, Rodolphe. *Vingt-cinq ans à Paris.* 4 vols. Paris, 1914.

Augustin-Thierry, Albert. *Augustin Thierry d'après sa correspondance et ses papiers de famille.* Paris, 1922.

———. *La Princesse Belgiojoso.* Paris, 1926.

Balzac, Honoré. *Correspondance.* 5 vols. Edited by Roger Pierrot. Paris, 1960–64.

———. *La Comédie humaine.* 11 vols. Paris, 1935–59.

———. *La Peau de chagrin.* Paris, 1831A; 1959.

———. *Lettres à Mme Hanska.* 4 vols. Edited by Roger Pierrot. Paris, 1967–71.

———. *Massimilla Doni.* Paris, 1964.

Barbiera, Rafaello. *La Principessa Belgiojoso, i suoi amici e nemici, il suo tempo.* Milan, 1902, 1922, 1930.

———. *Passioni del Risorgimento.* Milan, 1903.

———. *Voci e volti del passato.* Milan, 1920.

Bassanville, Anaïs de. *Les Salons d'autrefois.* Paris, 1863.

Beaumont-Vassy, Vicomte de. *Les Salons de Paris et la société parisienne sous Louis-Philippe.* Paris, 1866.

Belgiojoso, Cristina. *Essai sur la formation du dogme catholique.* 4 vols. Paris, 1842–43.

———. *La Science nouvelle de Vico.* Translated with an introduction, "Vico et ses oeuvres." Paris, 1844.

———. *Etude sur l'histoire de la Lombardie dans les trente dernières années, ou les causes du défaut d'énergie chez les Lombards.* Paris, 1846.

———. *L'Italie et la révolution italienne de 1848.* In *Revue des Deux Mondes:* "L'Insurrection milanaise," September 15, 1848; "La guerre de Lombardie," October 1, 1848; "La révolution et la république de Venise," December 1, 1848; "La guerre dans le Tyrol italien," January 15, 1849. (Translated and reprinted in Italy in 1849, 1904, 1950.)

———. *Premières notions d'histoire à l'usage de l'enfance: Histoire romaine.* Paris, 1850.

———. *Souvenirs dans l'exil.* In *Le National,* September 5 and October 12, 1850. (Reprinted separately later the same year.)

————. *La vie intime et la vie nomade en Orient*. In *Revue des Deux Mondes:* "Angora et Césarée, les harems, les patriarches et les derviches," February 1, 1855; "Les montagnes du Giaour, le harem de Mustuk-Bey et les femmes turques," March 1, 1855; "Le touriste européen dans l'Orient arabe," April 1, 1855; "Les Européens à Jerusalem, la Turquie et le Koran," Sept. 15, 1855.

————. *Asie mineure et Syrie, souvenirs de voyage*. Paris, 1858.

————. *Récits turques*. In *Revue des Deux Mondes:* "Emina," February 1 and 15, 1856; "Un prince kurde," March 15 and April 1, 1856; "Les deux femmes d'Ismaïl Bey," July 1 and 15, 1856; "Le Pacha de l'ancien régime," a play, September 15, 1856; "Un paysan turque," November 1 and 15, 1857; "Zo-beïdeh," April 1 and 15, 1858.

————. *Emina*. Paris and Leipzig, 1856.

————. *Scènes de la vie turque*. Paris, 1858.

————. *Rachel* [a novella]. In *Revue des Deux Mondes,* May 15 and June 1, 1859.

————. *Histoire de la Maison de Savoie*. Paris, 1860.

————. "Della presente condizione delle donne e del loro avvenire." In *Nuova Antologia,* vol. 1, no. 1, 1866.

————. *Osservazioni sullo stato attuale dell'Italia e sul suo avvenire*. Milan, 1868. (Translated into French and published in Paris the following year.)

————. *Sulla moderna politica internazionale*. Milan, 1869.

For the newspapers and reviews Princess Belgiojoso founded, directed, and contributed to, listed below, I am indebted to Luigi Severgnini's painstaking research:

Gazzetta Italiana, published 93 issues from February to December 1845, replaced by *Rivista Italiana,* published in Paris in 1846, which in turn became *L'Ausunio,* published in Paris from March 1846 to February 1848.

Il Nazionale, published in Naples in March 1848 but abandoned when Milan rebelled and Cristina returned to her native city.

Il Crociato, political supplement to *L'Ausunio,* published in Milan from April to July 1848.

L'Italie, published in Milan from October 1860 to February 1861, later in Turin, Florence, and Rome.

(Cristina also wrote pieces for *La Démocratie pacifique,* the New York *Tribune, La Perseveranza,* and many German newspapers, but these articles cannot be traced, since many were unsigned.)

Bolster, Richard. *Stendhal, Balzac et le feminisme romantique*. Paris, 1970.

Bordeaux, Henri. *Portraits de femmes et d'enfants*. Paris, 1913.

Boulenger, Marcel. *Souvenirs du marquis de Floranges*. Paris, 1906.

Bouteron, Marcel. *Les Muses Romantiques*. Paris, 1926.

Brain, Walter Russell. *Brain's Diseases of the Nervous System*. Rev. ed. London, 1969.

Brisset, Fernand. *Laure et Pétrarque*. Paris, 1931.

Brombert, Victor. *La Prison romantique*. Paris, 1975.

Cate, Curtis. *George Sand*. New York, 1975.

Cloquet, Jules. *Souvenirs sur la vie privée du Général Lafayette*. Paris, 1836.

Colet, Louise. *Lui*. Paris, 1860.

Cousin, Victor. *Correspondance générale*. Manuscript folios, Bibliothèque Victor Cousin, Paris.

Crémieux, Benjamin. *Une Conspiratrice en 1830, ou le souper sans la Belgiojoso.* Paris, 1928.

Délécluse, Etienne. *Journal 1824–1828.* Paris, 1948.
Donnay, Maurice. *La vie amoureuse d'Alfred de Musset.* Paris, 1926.
Dresch, Joseph. *Heine à Paris, 1831–1856.* Paris, 1956.

Ferrari, G. "Des Idées de l'école de Fourier depuis 1830," *Revue des Deux Mondes,* vol. 11, 1845.
Flori, Ezio. "Cristina di Belgiojoso e Paolo Maspero," *Rendiconti del Reale Instituto Lombardo di Scienze e Lettere,* vol. 74, 1941.
Fuller-Ossoli, Margaret. *Memoirs.* 2 vols. Boston, 1852.

Ganche, Edouard. *Frédéric Chopin, sa vie et ses oeuvres.* Paris, 1913.
Gastaut, H., and H. Collomb. "Comportement sexuel chez les épileptiques," *Annales médico-psychologiques,* vol. 112, 1954.
Gattey, Charles Neilson. *A Bird of Curious Plumage.* London, 1971.
Gautier, Théophile. *Portraits et souvenirs.* Paris, 1875.
Glaser, Gilbert H. "The Convulsive Disorders." In *Tice's Practice of Medicine.* New York, 1970.
———. "Limbic Epilepsy in Childhood," *Journal of Nervous and Mental Disease,* vol. 144, 1967.
———. "Visceral Manifestations of Epilepsy," *Yale Journal of Biology and Medicine,* vol. 30, 1957.
Guicciardi, Emilio. "La Principessa Cristina di Belgiojoso a cento anni della scomparsa," first printed in three issues of *Il Risorgimento,* vol. 24, 1972; subsequently published under the title *Cristina di Belgiojoso Trivulzio cento anni dopo,* Milan, 1973.

Hanotaux, Gabriel. *Henri Martin: sa vie, ses oeuvres, son temps.* Paris, 1885.
Hastier, Louis. *Piquantes aventures de grandes dames.* Paris, 1959.
Heine, Henri. *De l'Allemagne.* Paris, 1855.
———. *Lutèce.* Paris, 1866.
———. *Mémoires.* Paris, 1884.
———. *Werke und Briefe.* 10 vols. Berlin, 1961.
Henriot, Emile. *L'Enfant du siècle.* Paris, 1953.
Herriot, Edouard. *Mme Récamier et ses amis.* Paris, 1904.
Heyman, Albert. "Spirochetal Diseases." In *Harrison's Principles of Internal Medicine.* New York, 1966.
Hirth, Friedrich. *Heine und seine Französischen Freunde.* Mainz, 1949.
Houben, Heinrich. *Heine par ses contemporains.* Paris, 1929.
Houssaye, Arsène. *Les Confessions, souvenirs d'un demi-siècle.* 6 vols. Paris, 1885.
Hübner, Comte. *Une Année de ma vie.* Paris, 1891.

d'Ideville, Henri. *Journal d'un diplomate en Italie.* Paris, 1872.

James, Henry. *Princess Casamassima.* New York, 1948.
———. *William Wetmore Story and His Friends.* London, 1903.
Janzé, Alice de. *Etudes et récits sur Alfred de Musset.* Paris, 1891.
Jarblum, Irène. *Balzac et la femme étrangère.* Paris, 1930.
Jaubert, Caroline. *Souvenirs.* Paris, 1881.

Knibiehler, Yvonne. "Du nouveaux sur la Princesse Belgiojoso," *Rassegna Storica del Risorgimento*. Rome, 1971.

———. "Mignet, historien libéral." Doctoral dissertation, Université de Lille, 1971.

———. *Naissance des sciences humaines: Mignet et l'histoire philosophique au XIXᵉ siècle*. Paris, 1973.

Legras, Jules. *Henri Heine poète*. Paris, 1897.

Lemoine, J. "L'essai sur la formation du dogme catholique," *Journal des Débats*, March 8, 1843.

Leonhardt, Rudolf Walter. "Die Leiche im Schrank," *ZEIT magazin*, March 1975.

Lerminier, J. "Des femmes philosophes," *Revue des Deux Mondes*, June 1, 1843.

Luzio, Alessandro. *Garibaldi, Cavour, Verdi*. Turin, 1924.

Malmsbury, Earl of, *Memoirs of an Ex-Minister*. London, 1884.

Malvezzi, Aldobrandino. *La Principessa Cristina di Belgiojoso*. 3 vols. Milan, 1936.

Mamiani, Terenzio. "Parigi or fa cinquant'anni," *Nuova Antologia*, vols. 21–22, 1881–82.

———. *Lettere dall'esilio*. Rome, 1899.

Martini, Magda. *Gli amanti della Pliniana*. Como, 1971.

Masuyer, Valérie. "La Reine Hortense et le Prince Louis," *Revue des Deux Mondes*, vol. 22, 1914.

Maurois, André. *Prométhée ou la vie de Balzac*. Paris, 1965.

Metternich, Clément de. *Mémoires, documents, et écrits divers, 1800–1884*. 8 vols. Paris, 1884.

Monselet, Charles. *Statues et statuettes contemporaines*. Paris, 1852.

Montanelli, Indro. *L'Italia del Risorgimento*. Milan, 1972.

———, and Marco Nozzo. *Garibaldi*. Milan, 1962.

Musset, Alfred de. *La Confession d'un Enfant du siècle*. Paris, 1947.

———. *Correspondance*. Edited by Léon Séché. Paris, 1907.

Musset, Paul de. *Biographie d'Alfred de Musset*. Paris, 1877.

Ollivier, Daniel. *Autour de Madame d'Agoult et de Liszt*. Paris, 1941.

———. *Correspondance de Liszt et de Madame d'Agoult*. 2 vols. Paris, 1933–34.

O'Meara, K. *Un salon de Paris*. Paris, 1866.

Pagani, Colonello. *Uomini e cose in Milano dal marzo all'agosto 1848*. Milan, 1907.

Pailleron, Marie-Louise. *François Buloz et ses amis; La Vie littéraire sous Louis-Philippe*. Paris, 1919.

———. "Une ennemie de l'Autriche," *Revue des Deux Mondes*, vol. 26, 1915.

Pater, Walter. *The Renaissance*. New York, 1959.

Perényi, Eleanor. *Liszt: The Artist as Romantic Hero*. Boston, 1974.

Petit, Edouard. *François Mignet*. Paris, 1889.

Poli, Annarosa. *L'Italie dans la vie et dans l'oeuvre de George Sand*. Paris, 1960.

Pommier, Jean. *Variétés sur Alfred de Musset et son théâtre*. Paris, 1966.

Praz, Mario. *La Carne, la morte e il diavolo nella letteratura romantica*. Turin, 1942.

Reybaud, Louis. "Fourier," *Revue des Deux Mondes*, vol. 12, 1837.

Sainte-Beuve, Charles Augustin. *Causeries du lundi*. 15 vols. Paris, n.d.

———. *Correspondance générale*. 17 vols. Paris, 1942–47.

————. *Nouveaux lundis.* Paris, 1951.

————. *Portraits contemporains.* 5 vols. Paris, 1870.

Sand, George. *Journal intime.* Paris, 1926.

Schonberg, Harold. *The Great Pianists.* New York, 1963.

Séché, Léon. *Alfred de Musset.* 2 vols. Paris, 1907.

Severgnini, Luigi. *La Principessa di Belgiojoso.* Milan, 1972.

Smith, Dennis Mack. *Victor Emanuel, Cavour and the Risorgimento.* London, 1971.

Stendhal. *La Chartreuse de Parme.* Paris, 1973.

————. *Journal.* Paris, 1937.

————. *Rome, Naples et Florence.* Paris, 1956.

Talvart, Hector, and Place, Joseph. *La Bibliographie des auteurs modernes de langue française.* Paris, 1928–52.

Thierry, Augustin. *Histoire de la conquête d'Angleterre par les Normands.* Paris, 1836.

Vallentin, Antonina. *Henri Heine.* Paris, 1934.

Vier, Jacques. *La comtesse d'Agoult et son temps.* 6 vols. Paris, 1955.

Visconti-Venosta, Giovanni. *Ricordi di gioventù.* Milan, 1926.

Weinberg, Kurt. *Henri Heine, romantique défroqué.* Paris, 1954.

Weinstock, Herbert. *Bellini.* New York, 1971.

————. *Rossini.* New York, 1968.

Whitehouse, H. Remson. *A Revolutionary Princess.* London, 1906; French translation, Lausanne, 1907.

Index